Ask Me Anything, Lord

Opening Our Lives to God's Questions

HEATHER C. KING

DISCOVERY HOUSE
PUBLISHERS®

Feeding the Soul with the Word of God

Ask Me Anything, Lord: Opening Our Lives to God's Questions

© 2013 by Heather C. King

All rights reserved.

Discovery House is affiliated with RBC Ministries, Grand Rapids, Michigan.

Requests for permission to quote from this book should be directed to: Permissions Department, Discovery House Publishers, P.O. Box 3566, Grand Rapids, MI 49501, or contact us by e-mail at permissionsdept@dhp.org

Interior design by Melissa Elenbaas

ISBN 978-1-57293-789-5

Printed in the United States of America

Second printing in 2014

To my husband, who always encourages me to obey God, even when it seems as "crazy" as writing a book, and who always prays for me and supports me in ministry; I love you so. And to a group of faithful, praying women who continually lifted me up to God during this writing journey—my heartfelt thanks.

.

Contents

What is your name?

What is that in your hand?

What are you doing here?

How many loaves do you have?

Do you love me?

One

When God Asks the Questions

It was as simple as school supply shopping.

There I stood, my first time out as a mom buying school supplies for her kids. The school had posted a class supply list in Wal-Mart, which had inspired me to begin buying the crayons, markers, and notebooks that would turn my children into academic wonders.

The markers were easy. I tossed them into the cart and checked them off my list. Crayons? No problem.

I was feeling accomplished.

Then I came to the glue. My paper clearly said, "Do not buy no-run or glitter glue." Undaunted, I scanned the glue varieties on the shelves.

Every single bottle was marked "no-run."

Well, what does that mean anyway? You would think a teacher would want her five-year-old student to use no-run glue! Would it really matter if I bought what was on the shelf?

I decided to leave that item until later and buy the rest of the supplies, like the scissors that were next on the list. Blunt child scissors. That's what I needed.

Only there were some scissors with tips that looked more rounded than others. Did I need to get the really rounded ones or just the slightly rounded, more pointy ones? One of my daughters was left-handed. Did she need special scissors?

I decided to leave the scissors for later also. Surely, though, I could figure out the folders. I needed one half-inch binder. After walking down three aisles of school supplies, I discovered that the store didn't have a single binder in the correct size. Staring at the supply list, I began to wonder, *Did the teacher mean one half-inch notebook or one-and-a-half inch notebook?* It was hard to tell.

Thoroughly befuddled by what was probably an easy task for every other mom in the universe, I went home in defeat. I had to ask expert moms what to buy. All because I couldn't tame my incessant need to ask questions. Lots and lots of clarifying questions.

That's what you need to know about me, really, that in any room at any time, I am usually the one asking the most questions.

So it's not surprising that over the years, I've collected questions to ask God. Questions about the mysteries in Scripture. Questions about His love for me. Questions rooted in painful experiences. Perhaps you have a list of questions to ask God, too—things you've wondered over the years. Maybe, like me, you aren't even waiting until heaven to ask God. Instead, your questions have become prayers.

Have you ever asked God: Do you think I'm beautiful? Am I pleasing in your sight? Why did that little girl die from horrible cancer? Do you see that I'm afraid?

We're not the only ones asking God questions.

When one of Jesus' closest friends fell ill, his sisters sent word to Jesus: "Lord, the one you love is sick" (John 11:3). Surprisingly, Jesus didn't rush to their home to heal their brother, Lazarus. In fact, by the time Jesus arrived, Martha greeted him along the path with "If you had been here, my brother would not have died" (v. 21). Then Mary went out, fell at His feet and said exactly the same thing, "Lord, if you had been here, my brother would not have died" (v. 32). Some of the bystanders even bluntly asked, "Could not he who opened the eyes of the blind man have kept this man from dying?" (v. 37).

God is big enough to handle the difficult questions from us. He invites us to be honest with Him and allows us to lay at His feet the things we simply don't understand. This God, who knows all things already, knows the hurt in our hearts anyway. It won't shock Him to discover we're struggling with doubt or bitterness. He won't be surprised by our feelings of insecurity and insufficiency.

That's what Jesus shows Mary and Martha when, instead of punishing them and the crowd for questioning Him, He answered their questions with action. He called Lazarus out of the tomb and displayed His power over life and death. Then He asked a question in return, "Did I not tell you that if you believe, you will see the glory of God?" (v. 40). That was the goal all along, the answer to the "Why?" the crowd and the sisters had boldly asked Jesus. He wanted to show clearly for all to see that He was not bound by death, and in so doing, God was glorified.

Did you see how Jesus responded to these sisters, once hurting, now jubilant with the resurrection of their brother? He asked a question in return.

Jesus didn't ask them this question because He didn't know the answer. Nor was his query designed to put Mary and Martha on the spot or to shame them in front of onlookers. No, it was a way for Jesus to establish intimacy and vulnerability with Mary and Martha. He used a question to stir up their faith and root out lingering doubts about His power over all things. He asked a question so that *they* would know the answer.

Did they believe? Did they know that in all things God would be glorified?

Then I wondered, *Do I believe? Do I expect to see God's glory?*

Recently God's been using questions like these to stir up things in my inquisitive heart. I've been so focused on my own questions for God, my own need for understanding, my own attempts to know God more fully and place Him in a suitable box that I've been monopolizing the conversation. I've neglected His questions for me.

As I began this year, I felt God whispering a question into my heart. It was there in my quiet times when I prayed. It was in my mind as I drove, showered, and exercised. It became my constant thought companion.

This wasn't a question designed just for me. Rather, Jesus asked James and John this same question in Mark 10:36, only to discover they wanted personal glory and to sit next to His throne. He asked it again of blind Bartimaeus in Mark 10:51 and learned that Bartimaeus simply wanted to see.

This year, He asked it of me. "What do you want me to do for you?" Now, before you start thinking of a wish list with a bigger house, no debt, a husband, a baby, or a car, that's not what this was about. God isn't a deified Santa Claus who sits us on His lap and promises whatever longed-for toy we would like. This question was not about material possessions, prosperity, physical needs, or earthly gain.

Instead, it was a way for Him to search my heart. Psalm 37:4 says, "Take delight in the LORD, and he will give you the desires of your heart." That's what this question sought out—the desires of my heart. What did I really desire? Did I want glory for myself like James and John? Did I want to see God more clearly like Bartimaeus? My answer to His question revealed more about my heart's focus than any of the questions I've been asking Him all these years.

From then on, as I read the Bible I discovered more and more questions that God had asked His people. Always questions to which He knew the answer. Always questions He asked not for His benefit, but for theirs—to plumb the depths of their hearts and bring them closer to Him.

When Adam and Eve sinned in the garden, He restored His relationship with them by asking a question—"Where are you?" This question searched out not just their physical location in the garden, but how far they had strayed from God's side and what it would take for Him to redeem them.

When He shared with Abraham promises of a son and Sarah laughed in her tent, He asked, "Why did Sarah laugh? . . . Is anything too hard for the LORD?" God already knew what was in her heart and what motivated her quiet giggle. He used this question to highlight her disbelief in God's ability to do the impossible and bring her a child from a barren, postmenopausal womb.

When Jesus commissioned Peter as a leader in the New Testament church, He asked, "Do you love me?" not once, but three times. It was a way of searching out Peter's shame for denying Jesus, and then restoring Peter to a place of ministry and forgiveness.

Sometimes, as with Peter, the questions are God's way of blessing us. He longs to heal, forgive, and restore.

But God can also use questions to search us, know our hearts, and test what they contain. David asked God to do this in Psalm 139:23–24. He prayed what I consider a dangerous prayer: "Search me, God, and know my heart; test me and know my anxious thoughts. See if there is any offensive way in me, and lead me in the way everlasting."

Honestly, that prayer frightens me sometimes. I *say* I want to know God deeply and walk in relationship with Him, but there are parts of my heart, dark and hidden away, that I would rather not admit exist. What will happen if God searches my heart and finds sin there (as He surely will)? What will He require me to give up and change? It's a radical prayer of intimacy, humility, vulnerability, and submission.

When God started asking me these questions, a part of me wanted to ignore them and hide away, just like Adam and Eve in the garden, camouflaging themselves in leaves and standing breathlessly still, hoping that God would give up on His search for them. I was hiding in my own way, too.

It's the way I deal with mess in my life sometimes. Can I be honest with you? Often I shove stuff into closets rather than cleaning and organizing and purging. The towels in my linen closet aren't all perfectly folded and neatly stacked. I'm just thankful I had time to put the clean linens in the closet rather than leave them all jumbled up on my sofa. Surely I'm not the only one who hopes guests won't open closet doors!

For a time, my system (or lack of a system) works just fine. Visitors to my home see an external facade of cleanliness and order. Yet, behind the closet doors lurk messes. Eventually the mess overwhelms the closet and spills out into my home.

So it is with the secret sins that are hidden in our hearts. Generally, I'm pretty "clean" looking. I'm a church girl, born and raised. I read my Bible. I sit in the front pew. I lead ministries. By God's tremendous grace, I'm not struggling with the big, public, noticeable sins.

It's in the closets of my heart that you can find the hidden sins, all jumbled together and in disorder from lack of purging. These are the deep-down sins like jealousy, pride, anger, coveting, impatience, and impure motives. These sins I tried to keep private—just between God and me—so that I didn't need to deal with them. I could pretend they didn't exist and act as if my heart was as clean as the exterior of me looked.

In Matthew 23:25–28, Jesus addressed a group of people who worried more about outside appearances than the condition of their hearts. He calls these Pharisees "hypocrites" because they "clean the outside of the cup and dish, but inside they are full of greed and self-indulgence." They are "like whitewashed tombs, which look beautiful on the outside but on the inside are full of the bones of the dead and everything unclean. In the same way, on the outside you appear to people as righteous but on the inside you are full of hypocrisy and wickedness."

Wanting God to shove my sins and misplaced motives into closets instead of allowing Him to ask the hard questions that reveal sin deprives me of true freedom, of authenticity, of pureness of heart, and of greater intimacy with Him. It makes me an unusable cup and a whitewashed tomb, no better than a Pharisee.

It's a harsh comparison, but sometimes we need to get a little tough with ourselves. Otherwise we'll never change. We'll remain superficial, comfortable, safe, hidden—and distant from a God who loves us and wants us to draw closer to Him. Instead of sitting by Christ's side, we choose instead to trail behind Him, just like Peter, who "followed at a distance" (Luke 22:54).

God desires more than a superficial relationship with us, so He's forever asking us questions that delve beneath the safe exterior we've created. Surely God knows that even when we look good on the outside, the interiors of our hearts are cluttered and clogged with sin too long left hidden. Before He even asks us what is going on in our lives, He already knows the answer.

King David told his son Solomon that "the LORD searches every heart and understands every desire and every thought" (1 Chronicles 28:9). Moses wrote, "You have set our iniquities before you, our secret sins in the light of your presence" (Psalm 90:8). In Hebrews, we read that "Nothing in all creation is hidden from God's sight. Everything is uncovered and laid bare before the eyes of him to whom we must give account" (4:13). God always knows our motivations and the condition of our heart.

It wasn't for His sake that He started asking me questions. It was for mine. Through His questions, He offered me blessing and His affection. But He also used these questions to search and test my heart—to discover whether my motivations were off and to see if my desires aligned with His will.

Truthfully, I was embarrassed and ashamed to show Him the ugliest parts of my soul, but I didn't need to be. An amazing thing about God is that He sees us fully and loves us completely. No matter what His questions reveal about our hearts, God loves us. That never changes. Chris Tomlin sings about this in "Indescribable": "You see the depths of my heart and you love me the same." To me, that's just as miraculous as His creation of the universe.

Let's be real about this. The process of cleaning out the hidden places of the heart is painful and hard at times. It means allowing Him to interrogate us so that He can bring sin into the open. It demands that we answer questions that identify our weakness. It involves confession and repentance, and not allowing those thoughts and motives to find their way back in again. It requires us to put aside the facade of perfection and deal with the fact that we're sinners.

Sometimes these tough questions are the only way for God to dig past the superficial and the comfortable. It's only when we answer Him that He can actually *do* something about our answers. And isn't that truly our hearts' desire? We don't want Him just to see what's wrong with us; we want Him to be able to do something about it. I want to be more like Jesus so that when people look at me, they see a reason to glorify God. I want to know God more, even when it hurts and even when it's difficult. Don't you?

Do you want to delve deeper in your relationship with God? Do you want to become a vessel fit for His use and designed to bring Him glory? Do you want to stop hiding from Him in shame?

Do you want to clean out the closets of your heart? Do you want to receive the fullness of the blessing He's intended for you?

Then journey with me through the questions that God asked in Scripture. He asked them of people just like you and me. People who were not perfect and sometimes had secret sins they were trying to hide. People He was calling into revolutionary, powerful ministry, but who first needed to know that He could and would equip them for their calling. And now He asks them of us, Christ-followers on a journey to Christlikeness.

Make It PERSONAL

- Have you ever felt like God used a question to search your heart, draw you closer to Him, or challenge your thinking?

- Do you struggle most with visible sins (like stealing, lying, cheating) or with the more easily hidden sins of bad motives or thoughts (like jealousy or anger)?

Make It CONNECT

1. If you were in Mary and Martha's place as they spoke with Jesus after Lazarus's death, what question would you have asked? Have you ever had a reason to ask Jesus that question in your own life?

2. Can you think of other questions God asked in Scripture? Consider both the Old and New Testaments.

3. Read the following Scriptures as a group. Does anything about them frighten or unsettle you?

     a. 1 Chronicles 28:9

     b. Psalm 90:8

     c. Psalm 139:23–24

     d. Hebrews 4:13

4. Read Matthew 23:25–28. The comparison hurts, perhaps, but do you have anything in common with the Pharisees?

Make It REAL

- Luke 22:54 tells us that Peter "followed at a distance." Are you willing to allow God to search your heart and draw you closer to Him—even if the process is difficult—or would you prefer to lag behind where it's "safe"?

- If you're ready to ask God to search your heart, just as David did, pray Psalm 139:23–24 each day this week.

Make It LAST

Memory Verse

Search me, God, and know my heart;
test me and know my anxious thoughts.
See if there is any offensive way in me,
and lead me in the way everlasting.

Psalm 139:23–24

Journal Prompt

If you've decided to let God search your heart, tell Him how you feel about it. Are you excited or frightened? Are there areas of your life that you know in advance God needs to clean out? What do you hope and expect as you pray this prayer and complete this study?

Where are you?

Two

Lost

My baby and I play a game each night. She snuggles close to me and I whisper to her, "Time to get dressed!" She raises up her arms while I maneuver off her shirt, and she lies down for a diaper change. Then, just as I grab the clean diaper, she runs away—all naked and joyful, her one-year-old baby belly poking out. Her giggles become belly laughs and she grins at me with impish pleasure from across the room.

"Come on, Baby," I say. "Pajama time!"

She snickers and inches forward and then runs away again just as my fingers reach out for her tummy.

Back and forth she runs and teases. Finally I scoop her up and fold her into diapers and pajamas. I squeeze her tight in all her footy-pajama warmth and sweetness. "I love you," I whisper, and she puckers up for a kiss.

Hers is a freedom borne from total innocence. No shame in nakedness. She struts around and dodges my grasp and enjoys the game without any concern for hiding in clothes with buttons and zippers.

Innocence and freedom existed in the garden of Eden, too. Adam and Eve walked and talked with God in complete union and connection, "and they were both naked, the man and his wife, and were not ashamed" (Genesis 2:25 NKJV).

Imagine waking in the morning, lifting hands in a yawning stretch, and letting those hands linger in the air, raised in worship to a God who walks with you every day. Adam making small talk with God, "Nice weather, we're having in Paradise! What do you think about the name 'giraffe' for that animal? Does it suit him?"

A relationship with God made intimate by its innocence and trust. No sin and shame to get in the way.

Then came the interruption.

Prior to this moment, Adam and Eve had lived continually grateful for the gift of the garden and their friendship with Creator God. But the cunning serpent planted seeds of dissatisfaction in Eve's mind: "Has God indeed said, 'You shall not eat of every tree of the garden'?" (Genesis 3:1 NKJV). He told her lies—*God's holding out on you. There's something more you don't have.*

Eve eyed her "have-not" and forgot the abundance of what she had. Ungrateful now, she questioned what God had said. She questioned His generosity and His rules, established for her benefit but which now seemed so restrictive. So unwelcome. So unfair. "When the woman saw that the tree was good for food, that it was pleasant to the eyes, and a tree desirable to make one wise, she took of its fruit and ate" (Genesis 3:6 NKJV).

Eve sinned. Adam sinned.

God went for His usual walk in the garden.

God had every reason to enter this moment with the thunder and lightning of anger and condemnation. His precious creation had rejected His love and sovereignty and the abundant gifts to them.

I know if my kids behaved that way, my reaction wouldn't be pretty. I'd probably yell and sputter, interrupting myself and sermonizing about ingratitude and disobedience. How I can't trust them now. How sorry isn't good enough. How they should be thankful for what they have because people in Africa don't have nearly as much. Being loud to emphasize the points. Demanding apology, recompense, change of heart, humility.

Honestly now, we parents have our reactionary moments.

Yet God didn't fall apart and indulge in a righteous ranting session about Adam and Eve's blatant disobedience. He simply walked in the garden, searching for them and requesting communion and relationship, while Adam and Eve hid.

Eating from the tree opened their eyes to their nakedness, now shameful due to innocence lost. They felt their separation from a holy God and hid themselves in the trees, hoping God wouldn't find them among the maples and oaks.

Even though God knew right where they were and all they had done, He asked them questions—not because He needed the answers, but as a tool to draw them back to Him. These questions searched deep into the hearts of His wayward children, who had wandered so far from His side.

He began by asking Adam and Eve, "Where are you?" and continued the dialogue with "Who told you that you were naked? Have you eaten from the tree that I commanded you not to eat from?" and "What is this you have done?" These questions were designed to reveal what was in their hearts. Ultimately, if we allow God to interrogate us, He will shine light on the hidden places of our hearts as well.

Where Are You?

The first in God's series of questions to Adam and Eve serves as a check in our God-human relationship. The question "Where are you?" is central to life because if you don't know where you are, you can't possibly know where you are going.

My favorite place in the world is Washington, DC, with marble monuments, large (and free!) museums, and hushed art galleries with paintings of people I've only ever read about *by* people I've only ever read about. Dotting the sidewalks of Washington, DC, are tourist maps marking out famous landmarks. On each one is a starred location with letters too big to miss—*You Are Here.* I play tourist and stop at every map to see if where I am is any closer to where I want to be. Am I moving in the right direction? Do I need to adjust my course at all?

Sometimes we're going in the right direction, walking close to God. When God asks, "Where are you?" we can answer, "By your side, Lord. I'm here where you are." Perhaps, though, when God asks us where we are we have to check the map to find out. We've wandered away from Him and managed to get lost, or we've felt shame and chosen to run and hide, hoping He won't find us cowering in the leaves like Adam and Eve. In this case, the honest answer to God's question is, "We are lost and broken, and we are hiding from shame."

When We Are Lost

Even though Adam and Eve knew their physical location in the garden, in some ways they were truly lost. When God asked them, "Where are you?" they could have answered, "We just don't know, Lord. We don't know where we've managed to get to or what it will take to return." They had lost intimacy with God, lost their innocence, and lost their future in the garden paradise.

I know what it's like to feel lost, too. Unfortunately, I get lost often, hence my devotion to the tourist maps in Washington, DC. Before I drive off on my own, I carefully write out step-by-step directions with landmarks and mile markers. Google Maps is my best friend. Even if a step seems obvious, I write it down. If I don't, I'll just end up confused and missing a turn on a country road hardly anyone knows about.

Life wanderings sometimes happen by mistake, just as simply as me getting lost on a trip (or in a parking lot). We are distracted and too busy to pay attention to where Jesus is going. Our Savior keeps moving forward and we've failed to stay by His side. It's like being the child lost in the supermarket—the one they describe over the loudspeaker, "Would the parents of a small girl wearing a blue shirt please meet her at the service desk?"

That's me sometimes. I fail to keep up. I get lost.

Other times, we walk away from God, just as Adam and Eve did. We make a bad decision, indulge in ingratitude, or choose to disobey. That's when we stumble and lose sight of the path. Suddenly the way ahead seems uncertain and shrouded in darkness and we feel alone. How lonely it must have been for Adam and Eve as they watched God walk past them while they stooped behind the foliage. This was the God who had so often walked with them hand in hand. Now their intimacy with Him was interrupted by their sin.

From the moment Adam and Eve disobeyed, God initiated a plan for their salvation and redemption. He met them in their lost place and offered them a way home. That's the character of our Savior. He's a seeker of wanderers, a finder of missing sheep, a God who goes walking in the garden to find His wayward children. God's heart is always for reconciliation and restoration.

When We're Broken

Luke 19:10 expresses what I've heard described as the heart of the gospel, declaring that Christ "came to seek and to save the lost." The word *lost* here means "broken beyond repair."

Surely Adam and Eve's relationship with God seemed broken beyond repair as a result of their sin. God could have punished them and left humanity to die, as if they were a failed experiment and not His beloved children. Then they would have been lost from His presence forever.

Sometimes we feel this lost also, like we've been shattered into too many pieces to puzzle back together and glue into place. King David felt this way when he cried out, "My tears have been my food day and night" (Psalm 42:3).

I've been there, too, desperately trying to superglue slivers of brokenness into place, no more expertly than all the king's men piecing Humpty Dumpty back together. Sometimes I can pull myself together temporarily, enough to make me think I'm whole and strong. Enough for me not to sob, blotchy-faced and red-eyed, during every worship song and in the middle of every conversation.

But there's a weak spot left in my heart where cracks and holes remain after my insufficient repair. One day I'm fine. One second I'm okay. Then words and circumstances penetrate the glue and I crash into pieces again. It's because deep down I'm still broken, seemingly beyond repair.

Yet, God walked in the garden the evening that Adam and Eve ate the fruit because He was looking for His lost and broken children even before they had repented and been made whole. In the same way, the Savior who calls our wandering hearts back to Him accepts our offering when all we have to give is our heart in pieces. He accepts us in our brokenness. Like King David, "my sacrifice, O God, is a broken spirit; a broken and contrite heart you, God, will not despise" (Psalm 51:17).

And God does something wonderfully mysterious in our brokenness when we place our shattered hearts at His feet. Jesus was sent:

to bind up the brokenhearted . . . to comfort all who mourn, and provide for those who grieve in Zion—to bestow on them a crown of beauty instead of ashes, the oil of joy instead of mourning, and a garment of praise instead of a spirit of despair. (Isaiah 61:1–3)

Perhaps like Adam and Eve, your brokenness comes from sin that has destroyed your relationship with God and left you hiding in shame. Maybe your brokenness comes from loss—the death of someone close to you or the loss of a dream or ministry that you've poured yourself into. Maybe you are broken because an adult child is making poor choices and you don't know whether to intervene or let him fail. Maybe you've hoped and prayed for children, but every month you stare at another negative pregnancy test.

God binds up the brokenhearted. He compresses our hemorrhaging hearts, applying pressure to stop the uncontrollable bleeding. He brings deep and true healing in miraculous ways to hearts that were broken. Our Savior, with inexplicable love and abundant grace, left heaven and endured the cross to seek and save those of us who wander, and heal and restore those of us who are broken.

Adam and Eve were terribly lost in the garden that night. No matter how they tried, in their own effort they could never piece their hearts back together again or erase their mistakes and return to paradise before sin. But God's question to them, "Where are you?" was the first step in their journey back to relationship and restoration. When He asks us this question, it's because He wants to extend that same grace and draw us close. He doesn't want us to hide or wander any longer.

Three

Hide and Seek

Adam and Eve were lost in the garden after they disobeyed, but they were also purposefully hiding. When God asked them, "Where are you?" some part of them probably wanted to remain silent and continue cowering among the leaves. They had wandered away from God's side, choosing sin over innocence. Then when their eyes were opened, they were so filled with shame that they hid from God.

My daughter feels the same way when she's in trouble. When Momma discovers her disobedience, she's sad. She cries about her punishment and feels remorseful. The ultimate pain for her, though, is if Momma tells Daddy what she did. It's not because Daddy is going to punish her again. She's already received discipline from me. She just so desperately wants to hide her sin from him. She's ashamed of it and knows he will be disappointed.

Shame is so destructive. It builds walls in our relationships, preventing us from experiencing the freedom of vulnerability and intimacy. Adam and Eve were so burdened by shame that they couldn't stand face-to-face with the God who created them and loved them. Have you ever felt this way about God? God longs for us to reopen our dialogue with Him. He lifts our heads that we've hung in shame so we can see His face so filled with love and grace. His questions search out whatever in our hearts is holding us back from Him because He wants to overcome it and stand face-to-face with us again.

When We're Ashamed

It is His grace that counteracts shame in our lives. I discovered this recently after a trip to the zoo with my daughters. With the zoo finished, we flopped into our seats in the minivan, tired, content, hot, and thirsty. We stopped at McDonald's on the way home for a cold drink for everyone and a special treat—hot fudge sundaes.

As I handed each girl her ice cream, I looked directly into her eyes and imparted great words of wisdom with heavy emphasis so she would know I was serious. "Don't . . . spill . . . this . . . on . . . your . . . clothes."

Moments later, my older daughter had finished her treat. She was neat and tidy. No one would suspect she had licked every drop of chocolate out of her ice cream cup.

And then I dared to peek at her younger sister—not a full look, just a slow corner-of-the-eye glance. The horror! She had turned into a monster of chocolate. It covered every inch of her visible skin and she had not one, not two, but five (five!) massive splotches of chocolate on her clothes. I whined. I liked that outfit. It was a hand-me-down that had survived all last year with her older sister and now, after just one ice cream sundae, it was bound for the trash can.

I stripped her down as soon as we got home an hour later, sprayed on my laundry stain remover for set-in stains, and put the washing machine to work. It hummed, whizzed, rinsed, spun, and stopped. Without much hope, I pulled the clothes out and un-crumpled the "ruined" outfit.

The clothes were spotless.

I did a happy dance in the laundry room. I thanked God for all-powerful stain removers.

I paused. I stood quiet. *I thanked God for all-powerful grace.*

This is a grace that Adam and Eve had not yet experienced as they stood among the foliage in the garden, hiding their faces in shame. There had been no sin in that paradise and therefore no need for grace. They didn't know that while there are consequences for sin, there is also forgiveness available.

It's a grace I sometimes struggle to comprehend and feel, even though I've seen and experienced a life overflowing with God's grace. I fall easily into works-based living, expecting perfection and achieving failure. I see the stains of sin on my heart and even when they are washed away, I still feel dirty, unusable, and bound for the trash can. I trap myself in a prison of self-condemnation. Long after I've repented and sought forgiveness, I feel the heaviness of guilt and shame. It's a prison of thoughts—"You're unworthy. God can't use you. You fail, all the time you fail, same sins all the time."

Shame imprisons us and hides us away from God. We feel unworthy of His attention and beyond salvation. That's why Adam and Eve covered themselves in leaves and stood still with hushed breaths as God came walking in the garden. They were paralyzed by the shame of what they had done. It probably seemed as if there was no hope of restoration.

That is what we *feel* sometimes, too, but this is what we can *know*:

- "If we confess our sins, He is faithful and just to forgive us our sins and to cleanse us from all unrighteousness" (1 John 1:9 NKJV).
- "Cleanse me with hyssop, and I will be clean; wash me, and I will be whiter than snow" (Psalm 51:7).

- "He has not dealt with us according to our sins, nor punished us according to our iniquities. For as the heavens are high above the earth, so great is His mercy toward those who fear Him; as far as the east is from the west, so far has He removed our transgressions from us" (Psalm 103:10–12 NKJV).
- "There is therefore now no condemnation to those who are in Christ Jesus, who do not walk according to the flesh, but according to the Spirit" (Romans 8:1 NKJV).

Because of Adam and Eve's sin, God purposed to send His Son, Jesus, to die for all our sins so that we could be cleansed, thoroughly washed clean, all sin stains removed. Why? So that our relationship with Him—the relationship broken by that initial sin in the garden of Eden and then re-broken over and over again in our disobedient lives—could be restored. He "reconciled us to Himself through Jesus Christ, and has given us the ministry of reconciliation" (2 Corinthians 5:18 NKJV).

That was a plan enacted by God in response to Adam and Eve's sin. They and all their descendants were not beyond His reach, even with sin so ugly and shame so heavy that it interrupted their relationships with Him.

God's grace produces reconciliation. Satan's accusations—even long after we've repented—bow us low to the ground with shame. We become burdened with sins already forgiven and are unable to look up into God's face any longer. We can't walk in relationship with our Savior when we are too ashamed to match His gaze. So, like Adam and Eve, sometimes we hide from God rather than respond to His call.

Yet, God whispers the searching question to our shame-filled hearts, "Where are you?" He wants us to return to His side and resume our intimate walks with Him through life, to converse, to share, to listen and respond, but first He must meet us where we are and heal the heart paralyzed by shame.

During His travels, Jesus met a woman that physically embodied what shame does to our spirits. This woman "had a spirit of infirmity eighteen years, and was bent over and could in no way raise herself up. But when Jesus saw her, He called her to Him and said to her, 'Woman, you are loosed from your infirmity.' And He laid His hands on her, and immediately she was made straight, and glorified God" (Luke 13:10–13 NKJV).

God's goal with Adam and Eve was to draw them out of hiding and initiate a plan that would ultimately save them. He never wanted them to stay hidden and cut off from His presence. Similarly, Christ never intends for us to stare at the dirt and shuffle around crippled by accusations and the burdens of guilt. Like the crippled woman, in our own strength, we can in no way raise ourselves up. Yet, He is "the One who lifts up my head" (Psalm 3:3 NKJV). He reaches down a holy hand, extending grace, lifting our heads so we can see forgiveness in His eyes and feel the reconciliation He offers.

So many of those Jesus healed cried out to Him, asking for His help and His mercy. But this woman didn't yell for Jesus' attention. He "saw her, He called her to him." A woman bent low. A woman whose face was forever hidden. A woman with no voice. And when He had healed her, she lifted up her head, released her newfound voice, and gave Him praise.

Jesus calls us to His grace, calls us out of shame and Satan's accusations of past sin. He provides the healing our hearts need so that we're no longer bending low. We are straightened up through His strength, and then, with a testimony of thanks, we glorify God.

Don't you love that God never convicts us of sin only to leave us crippled under its weight? He always offers grace and restoration, just as He did for Adam and Eve.

He did it for Peter also, the disciple who betrayed Jesus three times on the night He was arrested. Peter, who had sworn that even if he had to die, he would never deny Christ, was now the betrayer.

How Peter's heart must have been weighed down by shame and guilt. And like Adam and Eve, Peter ran and hid.

Yet just as God walked in the garden to meet Adam and Eve, Jesus likewise extended grace to Peter.

Three women traveled to Jesus' tomb early in the morning on the first day of the week. They had remembered the spices, but had forgotten something else. Along the way, they realized they had no way to move the massive stone that covered the tomb so they could get in.

They arrived at the tomb to find the door open, the stone rolled away. The tomb stood empty. They stared in shock and confusion. Then an angel announced, "Do not be alarmed. You seek Jesus of Nazareth, who was crucified. He is risen! He is not here. See the place where they laid Him. But go, tell His disciples—and Peter— that He is going before you into Galilee; there you will see Him, as He said to you" (Mark 16:6–7 NKJV).

"Go, tell His disciples—*and Peter.*"

Jesus's message to them was, in essence, "Don't forget Peter. Don't let his shame prevent his relationship with me and impede his future ministry. I have forgiven him. I've restored him. I've called him and I want him specifically to know that he is invited."

This grace, this mysterious, incomprehensible grace, means we are fully forgiven and washed clean. Once God explained the consequences of their sin to Adam and Eve, there is no further record of Him mentioning their sin to them. It was dealt with and no longer a cause for punishment.

Neither does Christ shame us with past mistakes. He doesn't say, "Remember that time when you lost your temper? Remember that time you were jealous?" Instead, He says, "Come walk with me in the garden, Adam and Eve." "Heather, come meet with me in this place." "Don't forget Peter." "Don't forget my forgiven ones." We've been redeemed and made new, and while we might want to hide our heads in shame like Adam and Eve in Eden, He is the lifter of our heads and the healer of our hearts.

Finding Our Way

If our answer to the question, "Where are you?" is anything other than, "Here by your side, Lord," we may have a journey ahead of us. Through repentance and life change, we need to seek a restored relationship with God.

This journey to Christlikeness is ongoing for all of us Christians. Not one of us has attained perfection or perfect communion with God. As long as we are alive on this planet, we are imperfect creatures in need of an ever-closer intimacy with our Savior.

It's a journey that Adam and Eve began as they left the garden of Eden as a consequence for their sin. From then on, they had to live in the world, no longer in a sinless paradise. In this new environment, they had choices, all-the-time choices. They were fruitful and multiplied. With more people came more opportunities to be influenced, to sin, to be jealous, to react in anger, to hate, to murder.

They had to discipline themselves to move closer to God, which always requires moving away from something else. It's a necessity of the road. In order to go forward, we must leave something, perhaps many things, behind—a bad relationship, a habit, an addiction, or a poor use of our time.

Sometimes what we're leaving behind isn't "bad" at all, certainly not sin, and not something others will feel called to abandon. Yet, in order to spend more time with God, we might need to spend less time watching television or playing on the computer, or investing in relationships that lead us in the wrong direction.

Eugene Peterson writes, "Repentance, the first word in Christian immigration, sets us on the way to traveling in the light. It is a rejection that is also an acceptance, a leaving that develops into an arriving, a no to the world that is a yes to God."[1]

That was true for Adam and Eve as they brought up their children to reject the temptation and trickery of Satan. It was true for the nation of Israel, as well. God called them to Canaan when He beckoned Abraham (once called Abram before God renamed him) out of Mesopotamia and its many gods and idols. Later God called them back to Canaan, or the Promised Land, when He led them out of Egypt and out of slavery.

They walked toward promise, but it involved rejection—rejecting the old definition of "normal." It was "normal" for those in Abraham's hometown to pray to statues and worship bits of stone and wood. It was "normal" in Egypt for male babies to be slaughtered simply for population control.

It's "normal" for us to be too busy for God, to lose it with our kids, to be selfish, to feel jealousy, to cheat, to lie, to overindulge, to worry, to rebel, to gossip . . . Sometimes we excuse these sins as acceptable because they are normal—everyone does them and no one can be perfect.

God calls us out of "normal" and into radical. He doesn't ask us the hard questions to shame us or humiliate us. He does it to draw us close to Him so that we are "being transformed . . . from glory to glory" (2 Corinthians 3:18 NKJV). With each step we take closer to Christ, we must consciously move away from entangling sin and bad habits that destroy our progress.

Then, the next time God whispers into our hearts, "Where are you?" we will know we are journeying to Christlikeness, in His will and in His presence. We have returned from our wanderings, been found in our lost places, exchanged our brokenness for His beauty, and replaced shame with forgiveness. When God looks at the map of our hearts, we won't be the only ones standing at the tourist marker showing *You Are Here*. God will be there also.

Where are you?

Adam and Eve

Make It PERSONAL

- If you had to draw a map depicting where God is and where you are, how would it look?

Make It CONNECT

1. If Adam and Eve were your kids, how would you have reacted to them eating the forbidden fruit? What was God's reaction? (See Genesis 3.)

2. Read Luke 19:10. What was Jesus' purpose for coming to earth in human flesh? Why is this significant?

3. Have you ever felt broken beyond repair? Are there parts of your life that still feel irreparable? What can we learn about brokenness from Psalm 51:17?

4. What does Isaiah 61:1–3 say that Christ can do for us when we're broken? Can you share a testimony of a time when these verses became real for you?

5. How does shame impact our relationship with others and with God? Is it possible for God to use guilt or shame to draw us closer to Him? In what ways does Satan use shame to try to defeat us?

6. Read the following verses as a group. Which promise is most precious and meaningful to you? Are any of these verses hard to accept or make real in your own life?

> a. Psalm 51:7
>
> b. Psalm 103:10–12
>
> c. Isaiah 54:4
>
> d. Micah 7:19
>
> e. Romans 8:1
>
> f. 1 John 1:9

Make It REAL

- In chapter 3 we learned that "with each step we take closer to Christ, we must consciously move away from entangling sin and bad habits that destroy our progress." Ask God to reveal one specific area of your life that should be left behind as you step toward Jesus.

- Over the next week, what can you do to see change in that area? Be specific. For example, limit television to one hour a day. Take a break from social media for a week. Refuse to participate in office gossip. Pray when you're frustrated with your kids. Read the Bible for fifteen minutes each day or memorize one Scripture verse a week. You'll need God's help to be successful, so be prayerful during the week. If you feel comfortable doing so, plan to share your experience with the group next week!

Make It LAST

Memory Verse

Come near to God and he will come near to you.
Wash your hands, you sinners,
and purify your hearts, you double-minded.

James 4:8

Journal Prompt

Wherever we are in our relationship with God, our goal should be to move closer to Him. How would you answer God's question, "Where are you?" Do you think God is searching for you right now? Are you hiding or lost? Confess your struggles with shame and guilt to God. Thank Him for His forgiveness. Ask Him to help you step closer to Him.

Where is
your brother?

Four

We're All in This Together, Part 1

Mom, I was playing with this baby doll first!" "Mom, she put her feet on me." "Mom, she ate more Doritos than me!" "Mom, tell her to be quiet because I'm trying to read and she's ruining everything!" "Mom, I want her to play with me and she says no and now I don't have anyone to play with me."

That was today. In my home. All day. The kids and me cooped up in a tiny house left me a very tired momma longing for chocolate.

It's the drama of it all, the constant bickering and jealousy and bossing each other around. The manipulating and hurt feelings and violation of personal space. It all just frustrates, saddens, and exhausts me.

Most families have moments of loud infighting and high-strung emotions, but we probably never come close to the sibling rivalry in Adam and Eve's home.

Imagine the first months of life for their oldest son, Cain, when he acted like the only child of the universe because he *was* the only child in the universe. He didn't have to share food, toys, or attention with any other human creature. He was the first baby born in the history of humankind. Adam and Eve must have been amazed by his very existence and every move he made. They were first-time parents on steroids.

Then came the day when they held up their second son, Abel, for Cain to see and everything changed. No more marveling over Cain's baby talk or toddling. Now his parents knew that all babies would do that. Suddenly Cain had to share the attention of the only two parents in the world with a baby brother.

That's a recipe for disaster.

So, is there any wonder that as adults Cain and Abel weren't exactly best friends? By the time God rejected Cain's farm-goods sacrifice and praised Abel's offering of the firstborn of his flock, Cain's stocked-up resentment and anger spurred him on to commit the first fratricide, the first murder of any kind.

Murder may seem so extreme, so beyond the quarrels and bitterness that destroy many of our relationships. Most people can navigate human friendships without committing murder. However, destruction is still present. Disagreements and petty jealousies escalate into irreconcilable differences sending couples to divorce court and parents to attorneys to cut their kids out of their wills. Churches split over minor, hidden, time bomb grievances that finally detonate at church business meetings.

God could have enacted vengeance on Cain the moment that he began to wipe Abel's blood from his hands. Death for death. But He didn't. Even before Jesus died on the cross, there was grace. Grace is an essential part of God's character. Instead of destroying Cain on the spot, He disciplined him, confronted the character issue, and established the principles of community living all with one question, "Where is your brother Abel?" (Genesis 4:9).

It's a question Cain tried to shrug off with a flippant response: "'I don't know,' he replied. 'Am I my brother's keeper?'"

God didn't accept Cain's shoulder shrug. He punished Cain, sending him away from his family—from his community—and making him a wanderer in the land. Yes, there was discipline, but there was also mercy. God protected Cain from the revenge of others "so that no one who found him would kill him" (v. 15).

How often do we allow atomic bombs of different opinions and personalities to lay waste to our relationships? How often do we shrug our shoulders when God asks us about the devastation and announce that we aren't our brother's (or sister's) keeper? We declare that we aren't responsible for where they are, how they've been hurt, or what they're doing.

Nevertheless, God designed us to live in community. He created the family unit and used the disciples and apostles to organize the early church and establish principles for navigating conflict. And yet, living in community is hard. We get on each other's nerves. We step on each other's toes. We feel jealous of those around us. We get hurt and we hurt others. We disagree.

That's because we're human.

Sure, it would be easier at times to go-it-alone and give up on relationships and fellowship with others. But God's instruction is clear: "Let us consider how we may spur one another on toward love and good deeds, not giving up meeting together, as some are in the habit of doing, but encouraging one another—and all the more as you see the Day approaching" (Hebrews 10:24–25).

So how do we do it? How do we live in community? How do we become the keepers of our brothers and sisters? When we feel the pent-up resentment, jealousy, and rage over perceived injustice and favoritism that Cain felt, what do we do about it?

We can choose to follow eight Cs of community living:

1. Care about other people.
2. Check your own heart.
3. Cheer for others.
4. Continue in your own calling.
5. Change your perspective.
6. Control your tongue.
7. Choose to believe the best.
8. Confront in love when necessary.

Care about Other People

It's likely that Cain and Abel had a long history of brotherly problems. Probably some name-calling. Likely some fights. Maybe some mean-spirited pranks. In His grace, God even warned Cain about his growing bitterness, using questions even then to search his heart. Scripture says, "So Cain was very angry, and his face was downcast. Then the LORD said to Cain, 'Why are you angry? Why is your face downcast? If you do what is right, will you not be accepted? But if you do not do what is right, sin is crouching at your door; it desires to have you, but you must rule over it'" (Genesis 4:5–7). Yet Cain ignored the questions, ignored the opportunity to respond, repent, and transform. He allowed the anger and jealousy to fester until he finally rose up against Abel and murdered his brother. That's when God spoke up again.

The majority of us will never act violently toward another person out of anger, jealousy, and a desire for attention. So it's pretty easy to judge Cain, to condemn him, and to write him off as a "bad guy." He was the bad brother. He was the first murderer. He didn't give the sacrifice that God wanted. A villain through and through. We judge him quickly and move on, trusting that we don't have anything in common with him.

But aren't there times when we forget to be people-focused? Times when we lose God's perspective on the value of human life and relationships?

When God asked Cain, "Where is your brother Abel?" He revealed an essential part of His nature—He loves people. We matter to Him. Each life is valuable, precious, and uniquely beloved.

I was reminded of this a few months ago when visiting a funeral home. Family and friends gathered around a casket that should be too small to exist. A slide show displayed pictures of the sweetest little girl enjoying her first birthday and meeting Chuck E. Cheese. She looked no bigger than my youngest daughter—and a few feet away sat this baby girl's casket.

A moment like that is a shock to all of us, and it certainly was for me. I'm a to-do list maker, a get-things-done kind of person. I'm too often task-focused and not people-focused. When you attend a child's funeral, though, you see the unmistakable reminder that people are ever so much more important than any deadline or production goal.

From God's perspective, people are always top priority. His goal from the creation of the world was to build relationships with us. When Adam and Eve's sin caused a breach in that precious communion with God, He immediately began planning a way to reunite us, ultimately sacrificing His Son all because of His great, enduring, and passionate love for us. Relationship with us was always part of His plan.

If God loves people that much, then we should reflect His heart by loving people also. In his book *A Long Obedience in the Same Direction*, Eugene Peterson writes:

> People are at the center of the Christian work. In the way of pilgrimage we do not drive cumbersome Conestoga wagons loaded down with baggage over endless prairies. We travel

light. The character of our work is shaped not by accomplishments or possessions but in the birth of relationships.

In our efforts to love people, we must be careful not to fall into the trap of "ministering" to people and "serving" in the church but never really loving anybody. Even ministry—the programmed and scheduled kind of ministry—can get in the way of actually ministering to people. Are we too busy attending meetings to take dinner to a sick friend? Are we on so many committees we no longer have time to meet another woman for lunch to encourage her?

Then there are times when we neglect to love and serve the people who deserve most of our attention. We're "showing God's love" to the neighbor, to the single mom at church, to the child in our Sunday school class. Yet our families get little time or the worst part of us. We can be gentle with anyone but our kids. We can be encouraging to everyone except our husbands.

Paul wrote in Colossians 3:23–24: "Whatever you do, work heartily, as for the Lord and not for men, knowing that from the Lord you will receive the inheritance as your reward. You are serving the Lord Christ" (ESV).

It's easy to read that verse as a call to work hard at your job, give your best effort in ministry, and just generally *do* stuff for God. Is there any greater work or ministry, though, than serving and loving those closest to us? Our husbands and our children? Our friends and extended family? These relationships should be our primary focus and top priority.

That means being patient with our kids as they learn to tie shoelaces, or taking a break from the to-do list to play a board game. It means fixing your husband's favorite dinner instead of saving it for the luncheon at church next week. It means writing your husband a note of encouragement, calling a friend just to see how she's doing, or making a meal for the woman at church who just had surgery.

We do all of these things "as for the Lord and not for men" because we are "serving the Lord Christ." We will get no earthly recognition, plaque, award, or bonus from loving people. In fact, if we love as we're supposed to—humbly, quietly, and sacrificially— no one may ever know it's happening. Nevertheless, God always sees our actions and heart when we, like Him, make people our priority and He will give us "the inheritance as [our] reward."

Check Your Own Heart

When God "looked with favor on Abel and his offering, but on Cain and his offering he did not look with favor," Cain wasn't just a little disappointed or mildly annoyed. He was "very angry, and his face was downcast" (Genesis 4:4–5). Maybe it seemed unfair. Maybe it seemed like heavenly favoritism. Maybe he felt like he couldn't do anything right. Maybe it was something else.

The bottom line is, he was mad. God, however, immediately directed Cain's focus inward. He prompted Cain to think about why he was angry and told him, "If you do what is right, will you not be accepted?" (v. 7). Later, John tells us what was at the root of Cain's anger: "Do not be like Cain, who belonged to the evil one and murdered his brother. And why did he murder him? Because his own actions were evil and his brother's were righteous" (1 John 3:12).

God told Cain exactly what to do—to check his own heart, to rule over sin, to worry about himself. We can be so focused on what God is doing in the lives of others or so upset and hurt that we fail to let God search our own hearts. We need to ask ourselves, Are we to blame? Have we done anything wrong to create conflict in a relationship? Is there a log in our eye that we must remove before addressing the speck in the eye of another, as Jesus says in Matthew 7:3?

Similarly Paul told us to "examine yourselves to see whether you are in the faith; test yourselves" (2 Corinthians 13:5).

This is the kind of self-examination that Cain should have done, the kind of soul-searching that may have led to repentance and reconciliation rather than murder and punishment.

This is also the kind of self-examination that the twelve disciples performed at the Last Supper. They ate, laughed, and sang hymns in worship. Sitting at that table, they were jovial, anticipatory, and looking forward to Christ's triumph in Jerusalem. Then Jesus leaned in and said, "I tell you the truth, one of you will betray me" (Matthew 26:21 NLT).

Suddenly the mood shifted to silence, stillness, seriousness.

If Jesus said this in a church service, many of us would nudge our neighbor or make concerted efforts *not* to stare at the person across the room. "It's you, it's you, it's you" we might think, pointing accusatory mental fingers at those around us.

The disciples, though, looked inward, doing what God had urged Cain to do. "Greatly distressed, each one asked in turn, 'Am I the one, Lord?'" (Matthew 26:22 NLT).

Am I the one, Lord?

This seeking is our salvation. We ask the dangerous question and we allow the Holy Spirit to turn over our hearts and reveal our true need. Instead of thinking of how a sermon or Scripture applies to others, we can be still and ask the Lord to reveal fault in us, if there is any. After all, in order to repent, we must first experience conviction.

Years ago a friend of mine prayed that God would "correct her gently and not bruise her spirit." God is gracious enough to do just that, to teach with quiet correction, but only when we are truly listening and asking Him to show us where we are wrong. How much better to have Him speak quietly to our hearts and change us than to need Him to get our attention after we have ignored His voice, continued on our stubborn way, and experienced the consequences!

It's our complacency and satisfaction with our spiritual condition that leads to our downfall. It's when we overlook our own sins and spend all of our time blaming others and assuming they are at fault that relationships break down.

Peter sat at that Passover table and with the others asked the dangerous question, "Am I the one, Lord?" He allowed the searching of his heart and it wasn't him. Eleven of those at the table endured their souls being turned over and could say that they were innocent of this betrayal.

Then they stopped asking. That's our weakness, too. When we stop asking the Holy Spirit to search us, when we become complacent and self-assured, that's when we will betray.

Like Peter. Jesus predicted Peter would deny Him. "Peter answered and said to Him, 'Even if all are made to stumble because of You, I will never be made to stumble.' Jesus said to him, 'Assuredly, I say to you that this night, before the rooster crows, you will deny Me three times.' Peter said to Him, 'Even if I have to die with You, I will not deny You!' And so said all the disciples" (Matthew 26:33–35 NKJV).

But Peter was wrong. Jesus was arrested and taken away in chains, bullied, beaten, spat on, and mocked. Peter in the courtyard answered the questioning accusations of others by the fire. "I never knew the fellow. I wasn't one of His disciples. I didn't follow Him."

He stumbled into betrayal because he was complacent. Peter thought he knew what was in his heart, that he was right with God and strong in his faith. So he stopped asking, "Am I the one, Lord?" and started saying, "Not me."

Before allowing friendships, marriages, and churches to be broken into pieces and cast away as trash, we can follow this powerful principle of checking ourselves first. Are we in the wrong? Is there any sin we need to deal with? Ask and keep on asking to make sure that our hearts remain pure. This is what could have prevented the murderous actions of Cain before God even had to ask him, "Where is your brother Abel?"

Five

We're All in This Together, Part 2

Cain was jealous. Jealous of the attention and approval God gave to Abel when his own sacrifice had been rejected. His jealousy exploded into anger directed at his innocent brother, which brings us to the third "C" of community living.

Cheer for Others

In Hebrews, it says, "Let us consider how we may spur one another on toward love and good deeds, not giving up meeting together, as some are in the habit of doing, but encouraging one another—and all the more as you see the Day approaching" (10:24–25).

Cain could have pushed aside resentment and jealousy and chosen instead to encourage Abel in his faith and obedience. He could have said, "Great job, bro. I'm happy for you and I hope you keep pleasing God with your sacrifices. By the way, could you tell me a little more about that? It seems I have a lot to learn."

That wouldn't have been easy to do. It would have required a whole lot of selflessness and a monumental amount of pride-swallowing. Most of us wouldn't have reacted that maturely to God's clear favoring of Abel's gift, and we know Cain certainly didn't respond well.

It's so easy for us to fall into jealousy and to resent the blessings of others rather than discipline our emotions into becoming a source of encouragement to others. God calls us to "spur one another on toward love and good deeds." When we see someone receive a blessing for obedience, we may be tempted to whine and complain about our own situation. We could have used that promotion. That raise could have been ours. Why won't God give us a bigger house, a newer car, a better wardrobe, a stronger marriage, more successful kids?

It's endless really, the list of good gifts we see around us and want for ourselves. We're like little kids making Christmas wish lists. Then when someone else receives what we desire, let the tantrums begin!

Has someone ever been a cheerleader for you? Maybe that person paid you a compliment, wrote you a note, or simply said "thank you" at just the moment you needed it.

Most of us have received words of affirmation. I hear them every day from my baby girl. I finish putting the clothes in the dryer and she claps her hands excitedly for me. I change her diaper; she shouts, "Yay! Yay!" and applauds with enthusiasm. I drop the last of her toys into the basket and she does a happy dance and showers me with praise. When I slide the last puzzle piece into place with her, she cheers and shouts.

If you spent the tiniest bit of time in my home, you'd think I won an Olympic medal every hour all day long because my "crowd goes wild" just that often. My little crowd of one tiny, joyful cheerleader. We need people to lift us up in just this same way.

We who have received encouragement in turn encourage others through our testimony. This encouraging truly is the *giving of courage*, placing it into the heart of another. Isn't that what cheerleading does? It renews our strength so that we persevere and press on. God asks us to do this for one another, to stand on the sidelines of a race and cheer, shout, and applaud for the runners: "Encourage one another and build each other up, just as in fact you are doing" (1 Thessalonians 5:11).

It's not always easy. It would have taken great emotional discipline for Cain to look Abel in the face and speak words of encouragement rather than bitter jealousy. I know that you might be struggling in a situation that is just as difficult. Maybe you've attended baby showers and watched many couples in your church with their newborns, but never had a baby of your own. Maybe you've faithfully attended each of your friends' weddings and even worn a bridesmaid dress more times than you'd like, but never yourself been the bride. Maybe you're struggling with basic necessities of life and your friend just bought a big new house with a two-car garage and swimming pool.

It's hard. I know it. I'm not trying to make this sound easy. Show yourself grace and stretch yourself, but do so gently. If another baby shower is too much for you, send a card in the mail instead. If you need to excuse yourself from the wedding celebration to take a walk outside, then do so. But don't let jealousy lead you to cut off relationships or destroy the blessing of others like Cain did.

Instead, strive to be like Jonathan, who was a faithful friend, always fighting for David's life and well-being even though he knew that David would supplant him as heir to the throne. Imagine what that must have been like. Jonathan's best friend had been anointed by God to be the next king of Israel even though Jonathan was next in line as the eldest son of King Saul.

Jonathan could have pouted, raged, fought, and, yes, even murdered David. Plenty of others in history have done so when they thought their power was in jeopardy. However, when King Saul threatened David's life, Jonathan told David, "Whatever you want me to do, I'll do for you." He then created a plan that saved David's life. He was a truly faithful friend, who chose to lift David up rather than tear him down. That's what Cain couldn't seem to do, to cheer for blessing in another's life.

Continue in Your Own Calling

Cain and Abel were not called to the same career. "Now Abel kept flocks, and Cain worked the soil" (Genesis 4:2). We don't know the specific reason why God "looked with favor on Abel and his offering, but on Cain and his offering he did not look with favor" (vv. 4–5). Whatever the reason, it doesn't seem to be about their different talents and careers. It seems to be an issue of the motivation behind their giving. Abel brought "fat portions from some of the firstborn of his flock," the very best from among his sheep. Cain, on the other hand, brought "some of the fruits of the soil," not his blue-ribbon pumpkin or his prized squash, but just some of the produce.

God wasn't asking Cain to trade in his farmer's hat and weeding tools for a shepherd's staff. This is important to emphasize because we so often pit calling against calling, assuming that there is one right way of doing things—usually our way. Then we begin to judge and condemn those around us for doing things differently.

Of course, this swings both ways and we often feel judged by others. It's an endless battle of hurt feelings. What's worse is that criticism is often based on opinions and personal choices rather than absolutes and scriptural mandates.

Cain needed to learn two important lessons:

- Do what God called him to do.
- Let Abel do what God called Abel to do.

What if we followed these same two principles in our own relationships? What if we stopped worrying about other people's opinions and simply walked in obedience to God's call in our lives? Paul wrote, "Am I now trying to win the approval of human beings, or of God? Or am I trying to please people? If I were still trying to please people, I would not be a servant of Christ" (Galatians 1:10).

Being a Christ-follower requires that we end our people-pleasing ways and choose to be a God-pleaser instead.

It sounds so simple in theory, but reality is much more difficult. I don't know about you, but I want to make everybody happy so desperately. If I could tiptoe through life with everyone always agreeing with me, that's what I'd do.

But it's impossible. If you go to the grocery store with more than 1.5 children, you'll likely hear the opinions of strangers on your family planning skills. If you stay at home with your kids, you'll probably read how you wasted all of the money spent on your education. If you dress up and head out the door every day for work, you'll probably feel condemned by the moms wearing jeans and flip-flops and toting their kids to the library for story time on a weekday morning.

If you homeschool your kids, moms will hint at the damage you're doing by not socializing your children enough. If you send your children to a public school, you'll be reminded that you aren't protecting your children from worldly indoctrination.

If you remain single, if you choose not to have children, if you wait to have children after you marry . . .

The scenarios are endless. It seems like we are walking opinion-dispensers, assuming that we know best about every life situation.

As a result, many of us become women warriors and mama bears defending our choices against the criticism of others. We spend much of our time engaged in battles, aligning with others on our "side" and slinging weighted insults at the "enemy."

The Internet makes it worse. We sit anonymously behind our computers and hurl our opinions at others. Throwing around scientific evidence, philosophical arguments, medical findings, and, yes, even Scripture, we offer proof of why we are right and others are wrong.

Let's face it. Too much of the time, we women are cruel to other women.

So, what's a girl to do? How do you make the right choices for you and your family and not feel the need to defend yourself every time you sense the critical stares of random shoppers or read an article railing against the choices you have made? How do we navigate explosive relationships where even the most innocent remark or most God-directed decision becomes the atomic bomb in the next World War Women?

For starters, we walk in the assurance of our calling.

Cain could have said, "I'm a farmer. That's what God has called me to do. That's what He has gifted me to do. I'm going to be the best farmer possible and bring God the best offerings from my fields." He would have been working for the glory of God within his own calling. He wouldn't have worried about Abel at all.

Cain needed to have the assurance of his calling like David had. When this teenage shepherd boy stood in front of King Saul, he boldly announced that he would fight the bellowing giant, Goliath, even though the battle-trained fighting men were cowering in their tents. At first, Saul declared it was impossible. A wimpy little kid was no match for the expert warrior with size on his side.

But David prevailed and Saul agreed to let him fight Goliath, with one condition. David had to wear Saul's armor. Saul thought he was helping David.

"Saul dressed David in his own tunic. He put a coat of armor on him and a bronze helmet on his head. David fastened on his sword over the tunic and tried walking around, because he was not used to them" (1 Samuel 17:38–39).

How often do we try to sling our own personal tunics over the shoulders of other women, assuming that all they need is our advice, our method, our choices, our plans? We tell them (or imply) that if they want to be good wives, good moms, good Christian women, then they must do it our way and with the tools we ourselves have found useful. But the call God has given you might be a poor fit for another woman.

In the same way, Saul's armor confined David's movements and made him easy prey for Goliath's attack. "'I cannot go in these,' he said to Saul, 'because I am not used to them.' So he took them off. Then he took his staff in his hand, chose five smooth stones from the stream, put them in the pouch of his shepherd's bag and, with his sling in his hand, approached the Philistine" (vv. 39–40).

David had the assurance of his calling. He knew what God told him to do and how he was supposed to do it. So, he declined to wear the armor of another and stood against Goliath bare-shouldered, hurling a stone in a slingshot over his head and killing the giant as a result. He vanquished the enemy that day because he listened to God and not anyone else, even a well-meaning, older, wiser, and more experienced king.

When you feel yourself undergoing an Incredible Hulk–like transformation, from reasonable woman to She-Mama in defense of your life and family and personal choices, stop, breathe deeply, and ask yourself:

- Am I doing what I know God has called me to do?
- Is it possible that she could also be doing what God has called her to do?
- Can I let her obey God without feeling personally criticized by her every decision and action?
- Do I really need to defend myself against implied (or stated) criticism? Or can I let it go, choosing to walk confidently in my own calling and not worrying about anyone else's opinion?
- If I'm doing what I'm supposed to do and she's doing what she's supposed to do, then is this conflict between us necessary?

Paul wrote, "If it is possible, as far as it depends on you, live at peace with everyone" (Romans 12:18). Peaceful relationships in this world aren't always possible and that's the ugly truth. But we need to do everything we can to cultivate peace even in disputed territories where landmines of personal opinion dot the fields. Sometimes that means we stay-at-home moms need to go out of our way to encourage the working moms we know, pray for them, help them out if they need it, and include them in our activities and friendships.

Sometimes that means letting petty jealousies and too-sensitive feelings fall to the ground by choosing not to be offended. By choosing to put on thick skin. By choosing to let comments pass by unanswered. By choosing to assume we've misunderstood comments or motives.

Sometimes we need to keep some opinions to ourselves. We must put down the protest signs and banners about issues that God doesn't clearly address in Scripture. We need to remember that God continues to call each of us to different roles and gifts each of us in different ways.

What if Cain had determined to be the best farmer he could possibly be for God's glory and let Abel be the best possible shepherd? If God has called you to farm, farm. If He's asked you to shepherd, shepherd. Walk in the assurance of your calling and let others do the same.

Change Your Perspective

To Cain, the incident of his rejected sacrifice was worth murdering his brother over. His hurt feelings overshadowed his judgment and he became hyper-focused on the jealousies of the moment. We may never raise a hand to kill our sisters and brothers, but so often our perspectives in the middle of conflict require adjusting. Disagreements become barriers to healthy relationships.

Sometimes all we need in the midst of strife is to ask ourselves, *What is God's perspective in this situation?* We can pray that He gives us His eyes and His ability to see the bigger picture. Is this really the life-shattering event that we feel it is at this moment? What will this look like ten years from now or tomorrow or perhaps even five minutes from now?

Have you ever had a life event immediately shift your perspective? Perhaps someone you love died or was diagnosed with a terrible sickness. Suddenly the everyday crises that seemed so very important before now barely register your attention.

This happened for me after my dad's death. Suddenly heaven was real—not some hazy and nebulous concept we teach at church, but a real place where my dad now lived. My mom chose this verse for my dad's funeral bulletin:

> Therefore we do not lose heart. Though outwardly we are wasting away, yet inwardly we are being renewed day by day. For our light and momentary troubles are achieving for us an eternal glory that far outweighs them all. So we fix our eyes not on what is seen, but on what is unseen, since what is seen is temporary, but what is unseen is eternal. (2 Corinthians 4:16–18)

Paul is instructing the Corinthian church on how to have an eternal perspective.

I had a friend in college whose mother had a degenerative disease. It was difficult and devastating for her to watch her mother slowly lose function, feel increasing pain, and face death's imminence. As hard as that was for her, I have never in my life met anyone whose eyes were more firmly fixed on heaven than my friend. She saw heaven as the soon-to-be home for her mom—a place where her mom would be healed and whole and hurting no longer. She would talk about heaven in casual conversation. She didn't care about earthly possessions, worldly success, or what other people thought of her. Instead, her eyes were fixed on the unseen and the eternal.

I forget sometimes to keep an eternal perspective, and then God nudges my heart to see the light of His eternal hope.

At times we all get angry about stupid things and forget that petty annoyances mean nothing in the end. We worry and fret about the small details of life and forget that in the grand scheme of things, they really don't matter. Paul wrote:

> Their mind is set on earthly things. But our citizenship is in heaven. And we eagerly await a Savior from there, the Lord Jesus Christ, who, by the power that enables him to bring everything under his control, will transform our lowly bodies so that they will be like his glorious body. (Philippians 3:19–21)

How would your life change if you lived as a citizen of heaven in the here and now of earth?

Would you more boldly share your faith? Invest more time in worship and prayer? Build into your relationships more? Abandon the pursuit of earthly status in order to gain heavenly reward? Spend less time worrying about the things you can't control? Love people more and be willing to overlook more of their faults? Be more thankful? Enjoy the little blessings in life?

Cain lost an eternal perspective, got wrapped up in the emotions of here and now, and made a life-changing decision based on a temporary situation. You have the power to make a different choice. A choice based on an eternal perspective.

The next time you have the urge to snap, take a step back and pray to receive God's perspective on the situation. In the light of eternity, is it worth engaging in conflict? Do you really need to defend yourself or can you let it go? How will we feel about our reactions in these moments when we're in heaven kneeling at Christ's feet?

Six

We're All in This Together, Part 3

Maybe you're still not convinced that we have anything in common with the homicidal Cain. He's just a bad guy who did a horrible thing and we're not at all comparable. The sixth "C" of community living might change your perspective.

Control Your Tongue

I've been an eyewitness to a murder at Wal-Mart and you probably have been, too. Not just one. Many. In the baby section. Among the girls' clothes. Along the aisles of frozen foods. Standing in line. Two of them in the parking lot.

And not just at Wal-Mart. Wherever there are groups of people, there is murder by words. Proverbs 18:21 says, "The tongue has the power of life and death, and those who love it will eat its fruit."

Sure, I lose it with my kids sometimes. Most of us do. But the verbal assassinations I witness aren't expressions of exasperation or frustration. No, the outburst is a mom screaming at her preteen daughter about outfits. It's a father mocking his son in the parking lot, bringing the boy to the point of humiliated tears. It's a wife snidely joking about her husband to a crowd. It's a husband yelling into his cell phone.

Jesus came to bring abundant and overwhelming grace through His sacrificial death on the cross. But He did something else, too. He reset standards. He told people that letter-of-the-law obedience isn't good enough. Do more than avoid adultery, He said. Don't even throw lustful glances at a woman who is not your wife.

Do more than avoid murder. Jesus said, "I tell you that anyone who is angry with a brother or sister will be subject to judgment. Again, anyone who says to a brother or sister, 'Raca' [an Aramaic term of contempt], is answerable to the court. And anyone who says, 'You fool!' will be in danger of the fire of hell" (Matthew 5:21–22).

John echoed this idea later, writing, "Anyone who hates a brother or sister is a murderer, and you know that no murderer has eternal life residing in him" (1 John 3:15). Our tongues are murder weapons.

Still, we do it. We call each other names. We gossip. We slander. We quibble and argue in a public show of disunity and disrespect. We talk about our husbands behind their backs. We make jokes that humiliate. We put others down, and then say, "Just kidding!" As if that makes it better. As if that erases the damage done by our words. Proverbs 26:18–19 says, "Like a maniac shooting flaming arrows of death is one who deceives their neighbor and says, 'I was only joking!'"

Maybe that's not you. Maybe you don't do that.

But do you ever find yourself "sharing opinions" about others, perhaps even about your friends, commenting on their parenting decisions, their career choices, their clothes, their money, their ministry? Do you feel it necessary to share your thoughts about everything? To criticize and judge and judge and criticize?

James wrote, "Everyone should be quick to listen, slow to speak and slow to become angry, because human anger does not produce the righteousness that God desires" (James 1:19–20). How often do we skip right over listening and jump to the speaking part?

God held Ezekiel to the highest standard imaginable when it came to his tongue:

> I will make your tongue stick to the roof of your mouth so that you will be silent and unable to rebuke them, for they are a rebellious people. But when I speak to you, I will open your mouth and you shall say to them, "This is what the Sovereign LORD says." (Ezekiel 3:26–27)

God essentially glued Ezekiel's tongue to the roof of his mouth. The only time Ezekiel could talk was when he was saying what God wanted him to say.

What if that became the standard we used to decide when to talk and when to keep our opinions tucked away in our brains rather than spewing out of our mouths? What if we asked, *Is this something God wants me to say?*

Maybe we could give ourselves a little grace and just ask, *Is this something God would approve of me saying?*

Either way, I know I don't meet that standard 100 percent. I wonder if any of us do.

Paul also laid out a standard for when we should speak and when we should remain silent: "Do not let any unwholesome talk come out of your mouths, but only what is helpful for building others up according to their needs, that it may benefit those who listen" (Ephesians 4:29).

No unwholesome talk. Nothing hurtful. Nothing weighted down with criticism and oozing with judgment. Instead, we ask ourselves, *Is what I am saying right now helpful? Will it encourage someone and build up that person?*

If not, then the words are best left unsaid. Words are powerful. They are life-or-death weaponry in our arsenal. We speak words of hope and people remember them for years, thriving on encouragement and being renewed by praise. We speak words of criticism and people remember them for years, dying a slow death from the poison of language. And we're holding the murder weapon. Just like Cain, we're responsible for the murder of our brother or sister.

Choose to Believe the Best

When Abel chose the best of his flock to offer as a sacrifice to God, was he trying to upstage Cain? Did he intend to monopolize God's favor or was he purposely working to steal God's blessing?

Given the purity of his heart, Abel was most likely motivated by a desire to worship God with his very best. His actions weren't about Cain at all and weren't intentionally hurtful. But Cain didn't see it that way. He chose to believe the worst about Abel, assigning malicious intention where there was none.

It's easy to do. We humans are often so quick to judge one another. Ages ago in my college psychology class, I learned that it's nearly impossible to overcome a first impression. What people think about you in the first three seconds of meeting is likely how they will think of you forever. The trouble with these first impressions is that they leave little room for grace.

We form opinions and label people all the time. We push each other into categories and we assume that we know what is in another person's heart and what motivates their actions. Oswald Chambers wrote in *My Utmost for His Highest*:

The average Christian is the most piercingly critical individual known. . . . Criticism serves to make you harsh, vindictive, and cruel, and leaves you with the soothing and flattering idea that you are somehow superior to others. . . . There is always at least one more fact, which we know nothing about, in every person's situation.

In 1 Chronicles 19, we read about what happens when we make faulty assumptions and judgments about others. "Nahash king of the Ammonites died, and his son succeeded him as king. David thought, 'I will show kindness to Hanun son of Nahash, because his father showed kindness to me.' So David sent a delegation to express his sympathy to Hanun concerning his father" (1 Chronicles 19:1–2).

Off went David's men with a message of comfort to the grieving prince. However, the foreign king's advisers questioned the delegation's true intentions. They asked the king, "Do you think David is honoring your father by sending envoys to you to express sympathy? Haven't his envoys come to you only to explore and spy out the country and overthrow it?" (v. 3). Full of mistrust, the Ammonites humiliated David's men, shaving off their beards and cutting off their clothes so they were naked, and sent them home full of shame.

Even then, King David didn't react in anger. He reclothed his men and made accommodations for them to regrow their beards in privacy. In the meantime, the Ammonites, knowing they had acted badly, preemptively allied themselves with Israel's enemies and traveled out in battle array against Israel. They fought a war, which they lost, all because they didn't believe in the genuine sympathy that David expressed through an act of kindness. They assumed the worst about him and made unfair judgments. They were quick to take offense and suspicious of others.

Jesus' standard, on the other hand, is high. He said, "Do not judge, or you too will be judged. For in the same way you judge others, you will be judged, and with the measure you use, it will be measured to you" (Matthew 7:1–2).

What would happen if we showed others the same grace we desire from them? What would happen if we gave second chances and allowed people to grow rather than assuming that one mistake was a sign of a permanent character flaw? What would happen if we assumed the best about others instead of allowing mistrust and suspicion to inform our perceptions of their actions and words? What would happen if we focused on the positives in others and refused to comment on their faults?

We would give the same grace we've received. We would show abundant love to others just as Christ has shown to us. Paul wrote this about love:

> Love never gives up.
> Love cares more for others than for self.
> Love doesn't want what it doesn't have.
> Love doesn't strut,
> Doesn't have a swelled head,
> Doesn't force itself on others,
> Isn't always "me first,"
> Doesn't fly off the handle,
> Doesn't keep score of the sins of others,
> Doesn't revel when others grovel,
> Takes pleasure in the flowering of truth,
> Puts up with anything,
> Trusts God always,
> Always looks for the best,
> Never looks back,
> But keeps going to the end. (1 Corinthians 13:5–7 MSG)

Pause a moment on each line and truly consider whether you're living out love with those around you, in your home, in your workplace, in your church, and in your community. For the next few days, carry these words with you and let them guide your interactions. Can you look for the best? Can you never give up? Can you avoid putting "me first"? Can you keep from flying off the handle?

Cain couldn't. That's one of the things God's question revealed. When He asked, "Where is your brother Abel?" God focused on the relationship—their brotherhood. Being Abel's brother meant Cain should have believed the best about him and should have shown self-sacrificing love. Instead, he ignored Abel's innocence and killed him in anger over his own poor decisions and feelings of shame.

Confront in Love When Necessary

Abel was the innocent victim in this case. Still, if Cain had an issue with his brother, instead of calling Abel out to the field and killing him, Cain could have solved the problem with gentle and loving confrontation. He could have brought his hurt feelings and anger to Abel and asked for help, seeking understanding.

That's the formula God has given us for handling conflict within the church.

> If your brother or sister sins, go and point out their fault, just between the two of you. If they listen to you, you have won them over. But if they will not listen, take one or two others along, so that "every matter may be established by the testimony of two or three witnesses." If they still refuse to listen, tell it to the church; and if they refuse to listen even to the church, treat them as you would a pagan or a tax collector. (Matthew 18:15–17)

We're not just supposed to sling accusations at people, though. Nor are we to expect people to change whatever they are doing simply because it makes us feel bad or uncomfortable. But if they are truly in sin and we've prayed about it and feel that God desires us to address the issue, then we confront in love. That's what Paul wrote in Ephesians 4:15: "Speaking the truth in love, we will grow to become in every respect the mature body of him who is the head, that is, Christ."

Our hope and desire is for repentance and reconciliation. We confront others because we love them and want them to be right with God. We don't want them to be hurt by the consequences of their sin.

Unfortunately, they won't always receive or accept what we have to say. They may choose to duck behind the aisles at the grocery store rather than talk to you again. They may ignore your phone calls and unfriend you on Facebook.

If you believe God has called you to confront someone in love, go in covered in prayer. Pray that God will guide your words and He will make their heart receptive. Be sure you are indeed motivated by love and concern for their well-being. Knowing that the confrontation may cost you the relationship, be sure to do this cautiously, prayerfully, and only with the true confirmation that it is God's will for you to do so.

Where Is Your Brother or Sister?

As much as I hate when my daughters bicker, there are those moments when they generously share with each other, praise each other's efforts, play together for hours, and work together on projects. I love those moments and I pray so often that my girls will be best friends through life, not growing distant or being pulled apart by competition or jealousy. I pray for them to be the kind of sisters who walk down the aisles in each other's weddings and drop whatever they are doing to visit each other in the hospital when they have babies.

If my heart rejoices when my daughters walk in love with each other, how much more must God rejoice when we choose to love those around us? The Psalms tell us: "How good and pleasant it is when God's people live together in unity! . . . For there the LORD bestows his blessing, even life forevermore" (133:1, 3). God places His blessing on us when we choose unity and grace instead of conflict and infighting.

It's our incredible love for each other, the kind of grace-filled, patient love that the world can't possibly understand, that is supposed to be our living testimony of Christ in us. "By this everyone will know that you are my disciples, if you love one another" (John 13:35).

That's what God was revealing to Cain when he asked, "Where is your brother Abel?" He showed the disparity between God's love and His value for life and Cain's flippant disregard for another human being.

Instead of walking in love, Cain chose to be ruled by his emotions. He didn't allow God to search his heart and reveal his own sin. So, he cast all the blame on Abel and allowed the hurt and jealousy of a moment to overshadow God's perspective on the value of life. Cain believed the worst about Abel's intentions and motivations and plotted his brother's murder, thinking that killing Abel instead of talking things out would make everything better.

It seems so extreme to murder your brother. If God turned to us, though, and asked, "Where is your brother or your sister?" would we know the answer? Would we be able to answer Him with sincerity, saying, "We've had to work through some stuff, but we're still walking together" or "I've chosen to overlook some hurtful words for the sake of our relationship." Maybe we could say, "She hurt my feelings, but I'm choosing to believe the best about her, God."

Hopefully, we'll never have to answer God's question with a confession. "I'm sorry, God, but I just didn't like her; we disagreed;

he annoyed me; she stepped on my toes; I wanted what she had. So I ditched her. I cut him down. I committed murder by words and now our relationship is broken."

I'm praying for you because you might need to put down the weapon you've used against your brother or sister in the Lord, and take those first timid steps toward reconciliation. Is there someone you need to call or write? Someone you need to extend forgiveness to or receive forgiveness from?

Sadly, there are some situations where forgiveness needs, for safety reasons, to take place from a distance. If you've been abused, I pray that you will seek godly counseling and learn how to forgive even if you never again see your abuser face-to-face.

For most of us, though, a phone call or a card may be the first steps we take to the reconciled relationships God desires for us. We may not be able to erase the words we've spoken, but we can begin to recover from them. That is how we answer God's question, "Where is your brother or sister?" We answer it with the pursuit of love for one another.

Where is your brother?

Cain

Make It PERSONAL

- Is there a relationship in your life that needs restoration or where God is asking you, "Where is your brother or sister?" What about a relationship where you need to give or receive forgiveness?

- Have you experienced conflict in your church? How did the situation resolve? Did anyone handle the conflict well?

Make It CONNECT

1. Read Hebrews 10:24–25. Why does God say that being in fellowship with other believers is important? How is it also messy and difficult?

2. Read through the eight "Cs" of community living. Which is easiest for you? Where do you struggle?

   1. Care about other people.

2. Check your own heart.

3. Cheer for others.

4. Continue in your own calling.

5. Change your perspective.

6. Control your tongue.

7. Choose to believe the best.

8. Confront in love when necessary.

3. Is it difficult for you to make people your priority rather than to-do lists, appointments, or maybe your own personal wants and needs? What can you do to remind yourself that people matter to God?

4. Is it easier for you to see the faults in your own life or to be critical of others?

5. What are we told to do in 1 Thessalonians 5:11? What's the best encouragement you've ever received?

6. Has jealousy ever interfered with or even destroyed one of your relationships? What did you learn from the situation?

7. Read 2 Corinthians 4:16–18 and Philippians 3:17–21. In what ways can you develop a more eternal perspective? What would be less important to you? What would hold the most value?

8. Read these verses as a group. When are you most likely to lose control over your tongue? What sets you off? How can you prevent inflicting harm with your words in these situations? What types of things can you say that will give life?

a. Proverbs 18:21

b. Proverbs 26:18-19

c. Matthew 5:21–22

d. 1 John 3:15

Make It REAL

- Paul wrote, "If it is possible, as far as it depends on you, live at peace with everyone" (Romans 12:18). It's not always possible to have peace in every relationship, but you need to do your part. Ask God if there's anything you need to do to restore a broken relationship, and then do it.

- Choose to be a cheerleader for someone this week. Write a note of encouragement to tell them that you're thankful not just for what they *do*, but because of *who they are*.

- Read through Paul's description of love in 1 Corinthians 13. Identify what you get right and what you most often get wrong. Try to improve one particular area this week.

Love never gives up.
Love cares more for others than for self.
Love doesn't want what it doesn't have.
Love doesn't strut,
Doesn't have a swelled head,
Doesn't force itself on others,
Isn't always "me first,"
Doesn't fly off the handle,
Doesn't keep score of the sins of others,
Doesn't revel when others grovel,
Takes pleasure in the flowering of truth,
Puts up with anything,
Trusts God always,
Always looks for the best,
Never looks back,
But keeps going to the end. (1 Corinthians 13:5–7 MSG)

• God didn't allow the prophet Ezekiel to speak unless it was what God wanted him to say. Try speaking less and listening more this week. Before you talk, ask, *Is this something God wants me to say?* Or, *Is this something God would approve of me saying?*

Make It LAST

Memory Verse

How good and pleasant it is
when God's people live together in unity! . . .
For there the LORD bestows his blessing,
even life forevermore.

Psalm 133:1, 3

Journal Prompt

Confess to God anything that you've done to cause a break in your relationships—jealousy, hurtful words, not believing the best about someone, etc. Ask Him to help you love others the way Paul describes love in 1 Corinthians 13. If you feel like God is asking you, "Where is your brother (or sister)?" about a particular relationship, write a prayer of commitment to pursue peace with that person.

Where have you come from, and where are you going?

Seven

The Invisible Woman

I'm a fan of puzzles and mysteries. Crossword puzzles, logic puzzles, Sudoku, word scrambles, word searches, and more—I love them all.

Except I can never guess the answer to the mystery picture puzzles where you stare at a portion of an object and have to figure out the whole photograph from just that tiny close-up. I'm terrible at these. I always feel that if I could just see a little bit more of the object, I'd instantly recognize it. As it is, there's not enough information.

Isn't this how we often live, staring at the close-up of our circumstances and never being able to see the entire picture? Worry robs us of joy because we're dreading what may happen next. The emphasis here is on what *may* happen, because most of the time our fears are never realized. So we are anxious about "what if's" and "maybes." We can't see beyond the close-up of our life in the present. That means we aren't really seeing much of anything at all, certainly not enough of the big picture for us to make decisions with any confidence.

That's where Hagar was in Genesis 16. This maidservant of Sarai (whom God later renamed Sarah) felt uncertain about her future. After Abraham and Sarah had waited for over a decade for God to give them their promised child, Sarah finally decided God needed some help. So, she did what any woman following the customs of that time and culture would do—she gave her maidservant to her husband as a second wife. The problem is that was never God's plan.

When Hagar did get pregnant and started treating her mistress with haughty disrespect as a result, Sarah was humiliated and angry. She told Abraham: "You are responsible for the wrong I am suffering. I put my slave in your arms, and now that she knows she is pregnant, she despises me. May the LORD judge between you and me" (Genesis 16:5).

That's one angry mistress! The Bible says that Abraham allowed Sarah to do whatever she wanted to Hagar ("Do with her whatever you think best"), so in her anger, she "mistreated Hagar" and Hagar ran away (v. 6).

Hagar, pregnant and abused by her mistress, fled through the desert to escape. Without knowledge of God's promises or His plan for her, she was a runaway weighed down by her circumstances. Was there hope for her and for the child she was carrying? Would she survive? Where was she headed and how would she fare there?

In that desert place, God met her. He said, "Hagar, slave of Sarai, where have you come from, and where are you going?" (v. 8).

Trusting His Plan

God's question gave Hagar perspective. If He had asked only, "Where have you come from?" He would have focused solely on her past circumstances. That's more like us than it is like God. Sometimes we become trapped by the past, focusing so much on what has happened to us and on the reasons we've stumbled into this trial that we become hopelessly ensnared and unable to move forward.

Likewise, if He asked only, "Where are you going?" He would have ignored her motivation and focused solely on her destination. Looking only to the future and never to the past or present is just as treacherous as being trapped by our past experiences. We ignore and never address the issues that have brought us to this place, which means we can stumble into them again and again.

Instead, God pieces the questions together, showing His involvement through the whole movement of her life. We can't know what has been, what is, and what will be. We can focus only on the God who sees every part of our life's journey and can direct our steps along the way.

God had a plan, purpose, and even protection for Hagar, but she wasn't aware of it. In that wilderness meeting, God told Hagar to return to her mistress. That probably wasn't what she wanted to hear. But God didn't stop there. He assured her that her future was in His hands and that He would bless her baby. She could have stubbornly clung to her own plan and failed to yield to God's redirection, but she didn't. Hagar submitted to His will because she trusted the God she met by the spring in the wilderness.

We've all likely had some Hagar moments when our present circumstances threaten to overwhelm us and we long to run away. Crying out in desperation, we question why God has allowed this to happen to us. Why are we hurting? What's the point of our suffering? Is there any hope for us, any future? Does God have a plan? Are we alone? Does He see us at all?

Maybe your life has taken a sudden, unexpected turn and you're wondering why. What is the big picture here? Why did you have to lose your job? Why did the ministry you poured yourself into suddenly end? Why this sickness? Why this infertility? Why this singleness?

We can stare at this close-up picture all we want and make guesses as to what God is doing, but we are handicapped. With our limited, finite vision we simply won't always know why God has brought us to this place. So instead of plotting our course alone, blind and uncertain as we are, we must instead place our trust in the infinite God who can see all that has come before, all that is going on, and all that will be.

He sees us in our questioning and confused despair and responds with a question in return: "Where have you come from, and where are you going?" Then, in His grace, He wipes away tears, promises to be with us, and redirects our course.

We can't step back far enough from our lives to see the big picture, so we must trust God's ability to see and care for us. We allow Him to guide our path, even when He asks us to change our own plans to match His, and even if we must wait for His perfect timing. Then we allow Him to open our eyes to His presence and His provision.

Trusting Him to See Us

Have you ever felt invisible? Maybe you rush around at work meeting the demands and needs of others without anyone looking you straight in the eyes and asking the simple question, "What about you? What can I do for you?" Instead, you push through your day, sling your purse onto the passenger seat of your car at night, and commute home in silence, not even wanting to hear the voices of people on the radio. Then, walking through your front door, you are greeted by need, need, and more need. The rush of dinner and homework and activities is followed by the kids finally climbing into bed and you flopping down on your own pillow.

But in all that activity, did anyone really see you? Hear you?

Or perhaps you spend your days washing dishes, making beds, playing cars and trucks, blocks and Barbies. Your world has become an endless preschool and at the end of the day your adult self just wants someone to ask you a grown-up question and truly listen to what you have to say. Maybe you even fear deep down that ministry to others has buried your identity. You've been hidden away a shovelful at a time. No one knows the real you anymore. You're not even sure you know yourself.

Sometimes we feel as if we are invisible to people.

In addition to the day-to-day grind, there are also moments of crisis and seasons when you don't want to open your eyes in the morning for fear of another piece of bad news. Another house repair when you're drowning in debt. One more day of unemployment. The negative pregnancy test you've dreaded for a month. The call from your doctor saying it's cancer.

In the midst of that, we sometimes want to scream at heaven, "Do you see what I'm going through? Am I invisible to you? Don't you see that I've had enough, that this is too much? That I'm dying inside and I need help?"

Sometimes we feel as if we are invisible to God.

Let me lean in to you to say this. I want you to soak in these words: God sees you.

It's not just a theological truth that feels personally unreal. It's not a platitude that I'm bandaging onto the open sore of your life. Don't rush through the significance of this, please.

You are not invisible to God.

When we read the story of Abraham and Sarah, Hagar seems to play a secondary role at best. She was the maidservant instead of the affluent master and his wife. She was Egyptian, not Hebrew, an outsider in both culture and faith.

Yet, when she ran into the desert in Genesis 16, it says, "The angel of the LORD found Hagar near a spring in the desert" (v. 7). This is the first appearance of the angel of the Lord in Scripture. It's a precious moment of compassion, when almighty God gently prods the heart of this hurting girl. Of all the people in Scripture, He chooses to reveal himself to her in all her need.

He says, "Hagar, slave of Sarai, where have you come from, and where are you going?" (v. 8).

God knew her name. He knew her circumstances. He told her about her pregnancy and the child she was carrying: "You are now pregnant and you will give birth to a son. You shall name him Ishmael, for the LORD has heard of your misery" (v. 11). All of the drama and mistreatment, the tension and abuse she had endured were visible to Him. He knew where she had come from and He knew where she was headed. He didn't ask her because He needed information. He asked her because He loved her, because He saw how much she was hurting, and because He had a better plan for her than the one she was pursuing.

So He gave her instructions to return home and promised to bless her descendants. In return, "She gave this name to the LORD who spoke to her: 'You are the God who sees me'" (v. 13).

God has names throughout Scripture that describe His attributes—The Lord our Healer, Peace, Everlasting Father, Our Provider, The Lord Our Banner. But I find it so special that this hurting woman—a woman overlooked and mistreated by other people, a woman who wasn't even a Hebrew but an Egyptian—was allowed to give God the very first "name" in Scripture—*El Roi, The God Who Sees Me.*

Be assured that God sees you also. He knows exactly where you are in the wilderness. He sees all of your effort, your service, your laying down of self, your sacrificial giving, your stepping out in faith, your steady faithfulness, your lack of sleep, your soul emptied out. He sees you at the sick bed and in the doctor's office. He sees you in the unemployment line and in the job interview. He sees you rocking the baby to sleep. He sees you working your hardest day after day.

Not only does this bring us comfort, but it also brings us motivation to keep going. After a while of feeling invisible, even the most determined among us sometimes wants to hand in our resignation. End the ministry. Stop cleaning and declare a "Mom strike." Walk away from the friendship.

The reason Hagar could obey God and return to a tough situation was because she knew God had her in His sights. This is our joy also. We don't give up, because even when we are invisible to everyone else, we know we are not invisible to God. He's the one watching all that we do; He's the one rewarding our effort and perseverance.

For most of the truly important moments in life, we don't get trophies. No woman polishes the brass trophy on her shelf for enduring labor and having a baby. There's no "stayed up all night with vomiting children" trophy. No trophy for "visiting the nursing home without anyone else knowing you did it." No plaque for "spent hours on knees praying for wayward child."

We don't serve for awards that will hang on our wall or adorn our bookshelves. Other than an occasional mug from our kids saying, "World's Best Mom," we go through our everyday acts of ministry without recognition. Here's the challenge. With pure motives and sometimes hidden service, without seeking praise and recognition, we can still serve with all our hearts *as if we would get a trophy.*

We don't seek the prize, but we strive with all our might to be worthy of it because even when we are invisible to everyone else, God sees us.

He sees you. We pick up toys and wash dishes for the "Well done, good and faithful servant!" (Matthew 25:21). We work at our jobs not only so we receive promotions, but so that our "light [will] shine before others, that they may see your good deeds and glorify your Father in heaven" (Matthew 5:16). We walk away from gossip. We take a meal to the family who needs it. We write a note of encouragement. We pray for our friend. We teach the Sunday school class year after year. We rock the baby.

Because God sees and cares.

This is our worship, the offering we place before Him. When we grow weary or frustrated, feel annoyed or walked all over, or exhaust ourselves for the sake of others, we do not give up. Our motivation remains the same—to serve God, to bring Him glory, to give Him praise.

Because even when no one else notices, we know that God sees.

We remember what Paul wrote, "Do you not know that in a race all the runners run, but only one gets the prize? Run in such a way as to get the prize" (1 Corinthians 9:24), and "Let's not allow ourselves to get fatigued doing good. At the right time we will harvest a good crop if we don't give up, or quit. Right now, therefore, every time we get the chance, let us work for the benefit of all, starting with the people closest to us in the community of faith" (Galatians 6:9–10 MSG).

God sees you hurting. God sees you serving. God sees your circumstances. He sees who you are. Just as He was for Hagar, He is the God who sees you. And He has a plan and purpose for you that He will fulfill as you yield to Him. We can trust Him to direct us because we know that we are not invisible to Him. He sees the big picture of our lives.

Eight

Truly Trusting

We see Hagar pack a bag and head for the wilderness two separate times, once in Genesis 16 and again in Genesis 21. The first time, it says that "the angel of the LORD found Hagar near a spring in the desert; it was the spring that is beside the road to Shur" (v. 7). Shur was an area near the northeastern border of Egypt. So it looks like the Egyptian maidservant was hightailing it back to Egypt, her homeland.

It seems like she had a plan. Maybe she figured she could head home and raise her baby with family. Nothing like momma's help!

Now, don't you like a good plan? I know I do! I make plans for my day and plans for my life. Sometimes my plans work out the way I expect, but most of the time God happens and I'm diverted, delayed, or reversed. That's what happened to Hagar. God asked for her plan:

> "Where have you come from, and where are you going?"
> "I'm running away from my mistress Sarai," she answered.

Then the angel of the LORD told her, "Go back to your mistress and submit to her." (vv. 8–9)

In other words, God said to her: "What's your plan? Great. Now here's my plan."

Trusting Him to Direct Us

When something doesn't go according to my expectations, I usually falter and flail. Even a minor redirection, like a canceled doctor's appointment, can throw off my whole day. I was planning on that, counting on it. I had scheduled my day around it. I have a hard time being flexible and finding something else to do with my time.

Then there are those life plans that God has a way of changing, where we pursue what seems to be God's will but are stopped and turned around. That's the kind of journey my family has been on these past few years.

A little over two years ago, my husband and I handed in a packet of papers to become foster parents. Background checks, fingerprinting, proof of car insurance, the deed to our home, proof of rabies vaccinations for our cats, references, copies of our driving record—we had collected every document that described our lives down to the minutest detail.

We did this because we had confirmation after confirmation that this was what God wanted us to do. It wasn't part of our original plan for our family. When we got married thirteen years ago, we thought we'd have four children of our own. But God had stirred our hearts to foster care and we wanted to obey.

Just as we reached the last step of this process, though, everything stopped. Overwhelming workloads at the Department of Social Services, confusion, and people quitting with no one being hired to replace them halted the entire process for us. I called once every week or two and left increasingly pushy messages. Whenever I spoke to an actual person, I was assured that the next month they would call.

But they didn't.

My husband and I agreed that continuing to call was likely to push us right out of God's will. So I prayed, "Dear Lord, if this is your plan, please let them call us."

Nothing.

Fifteen months after the foster care process halted, we were still waiting and still on hold.

That's when my husband and I both spoke the word: "Incomplete." Our family wasn't full, wasn't finished, and there was someone still missing. So we prayed and prayed, trying to discern what that meant for us. Keep waiting on foster care, have a baby, or try to adopt? Had we been wrong to pursue foster care? Had we missed something? Everything seemed so clear when we started the process, but now we didn't know what to do.

We prayed separately. We prayed together. Finally, we sat holding hands and my husband said, "God, we want what you want, but we need you to show us clearly what that is."

A month later, I gave my husband a present for our wedding anniversary—a baby blanket for use in October. God answered our prayers for direction with a positive pregnancy test in less than a month.

When we ask for God's guidance, sometimes we must wait with determined patience for the neon sign. Other times, it seems like He says, "I was hoping you'd ask me that!" and the answer is right there before we've even finished praying.

So, what does that mean? Did my family miss God's will from the very beginning? Was the foster care journey all a mistake? Did I somehow mess it up and ruin God's plan for us?

I can't say that I've sorted through all of this completely. I'm still confused about why God seemed to direct us this way and stopped us in the end, but I can tell you with certainty that an unexpected U-turn was His answer to our prayers for guidance.

I'm starting to think that He's more concerned about the journey than reaching a destination. Maybe His goal was to stir our hearts for future things, to interrupt our family agenda, or to see how far obedience would take us. Like Abraham, maybe laying down our Isaac was the plan all along, and as long as we were willing to obey, that was enough.

In Scripture, we are promised continually that God *will* direct and guide us:

> The LORD directs the steps of the godly.
> He delights in every detail of their lives.
> Though they stumble, they will never fall,
> for the LORD holds them by the hand.
> (Psalm 37:23–24 NLT)

When I worry about messing it all up, Scripture reminds me that God's plan will prevail, over all our insufficiencies, over every obstacle and inconvenience: "Many are the plans in a person's heart, but it is the LORD's purpose that prevails" (Proverbs 19:21).

So, I return to prayer: "Lord, let your will be done in our lives. I may whine about it. It may be difficult. But I *do* desire to walk in your way." Then I trust Him to lead.

Maybe some U-turns are because we misheard Him or zoomed off in our own direction without seeking His opinion. Maybe some U-turns are actually part of His plans for us.

Scripture reminds me that as long as we wholeheartedly seek after Him and are truly willing to obey Him, we are never really lost.

> Trust in the LORD with all your heart;
> do not depend on your own understanding.
> Seek his will in all you do,

and he will show you which path to take.
(Proverbs 3:5–6 NLT)

God gave Hagar a new plan also. He told her news she didn't want to hear—that instead of heading to Egypt, she needed to turn around and go back to her mistress, the same mistress who had mistreated her. It must have been frightening and disheartening, and it must have seemed terribly unfair.

Full of compassion and knowing the fear in her heart, God gave Hagar the assurance of His promise. He said, "I will increase your descendants so much that they will be too numerous to count" (Genesis 16:10). Yes, what He asked her to do was hard. Yes, it may have seemed confusing. But He wasn't asking her to go without promising to protect her, and that assurance was enough for Hagar. She obeyed Him without question.

Sometimes the plans God has for us don't seem to make much sense. They certainly aren't what we would choose. That job loss. That broken relationship. That sickness. That financial crisis. Circumstances beyond our control can leave us feeling lost in the wilderness. But just like Hagar, we walk through life with the assurance of God's promise:

- "Never will I leave you; never will I forsake you" (Hebrews 13:5).
- "Do not fear, for I have redeemed you; I have summoned you by name; you are mine. When you pass through the waters, I will be with you; and when you pass through the rivers, they will not sweep over you. When you walk through the fire, you will not be burned; the flames will not set you ablaze. For I am the Lord your God, the Holy One of Israel, your Savior" (Isaiah 43:1–3).
- As for God, His way is perfect; the Lord's word is flawless; he shields all who take refuge in him (2 Samuel 22:31).

Walking through life with God's promises is a little like trying to see through fog. That's what Hagar experienced. She had to rely on God to direct her next step in the midst of confusion and hurt, trusting Him to see the future when she couldn't.

Not long ago, I had an uneasy experience of driving through fog down unfamiliar, winding roads. My whole body was tense. I was focused on seeing ahead, and I was inevitably frustrated and anxious because I couldn't see much. It was just haze and darkness.

But I learned something that night. Driving became a whole lot easier when I stopped focusing on what I *couldn't* see and redirected my attention to what I *could* see. I slowed down and shifted my gaze to the point right ahead of my car, where my lights shone, and not the distant darkness.

Do you ever feel like your life is a foggy night and you're trying to navigate a winding and unfamiliar path? Many of us prefer to have the whole plan before we undertake something. We want to know answers to most of our questions before we agree to travel a particular road.

Maybe you have more faith than that, but I'm no Abraham who, "when called to go to a place he would later receive as his inheritance, obeyed and went, even though he did not know where he was going" (Hebrews 11:8).

No, I'm more of a "God, I'll go when you tell me where, when, what, how, and why" kind of person. That makes the faith walk hard for me.

God met with Hagar when she was metaphorically driving in the fog. After He spoke to her, she still didn't know exactly what would happen to her son or what circumstances awaited her when she returned to Abraham and Sarah. Yet, He called her to take this one step of obedience and trust Him with the remainder of the journey.

Scripture tells us, "If people can't see what God is doing, they stumble all over themselves; but when they attend to what He reveals, they are most blessed" (Proverbs 29:18 MSG). This makes me think of Paul, who stood before King Agrippa and gave an account of his life and ministry. Paul says, "I was not disobedient to the vision from heaven" (Acts 26:19). When Christ appeared to Paul (at that point still called Saul) on the road to Damascus years earlier, he didn't give Paul a detailed outline of his future life of ministry. God didn't describe the shipwrecks, beatings, and imprisonments Paul would endure, but He also didn't tell him about the rescues, the travels to faraway lands where he would be the first to take the gospel, or the letters of his that would end up in the Bible.

God's initial call was so basic, so simple, and so lacking in details. God told him, "Now get up and go into the city, and you will be told what you must do" (Acts 9:6). When Paul stood up, he was literally and figuratively blind! All he could do was obey the next step, what God had revealed for that moment. Toward the end of his life he could say with confidence that he obeyed "the vision from heaven."

Years from now, will you be able to say that you obeyed God's call? Or will you wait so long for the details and assurances of success that you never step out in faith and obedience? Will you give up on what God has called you to do because you don't see results and reward? Or will you remain obedient to the vision and refuse to give up when the future seems hazy and dark?

What if Hagar had said, "Forget it," and kept hiking to Egypt? What if Paul had refused to go into the city as God told him and instead opted for life with a seeing-eye dog? They would have missed out on God's blessing, as well as His protection and healing.

Hagar's response to God when He spoke with her was an act of worship. She worshiped Him by confessing His name: "El Roi—the God who sees me." She also worshiped through obedience. Instead of stubbornly pursuing her own plans, she yielded control to Him. That's a worship of sacrifice.

If we want God's blessing and the joy of His presence, we need to trust The God Who Sees to direct our steps. Our job is to readjust our focus away from the unknowns of the future. When we fret over uncertainties, we stumble all over ourselves and get lost in the fog. But when we "attend to what He reveals," focusing only on what God has told us to do right now in this moment, we will be "most blessed."

Trusting His Timing

Sometimes it's not so much *what* we have planned that is the problem, it's *when* we plan to do it. God's timing is sometimes different than ours. Well, often different than ours. Sometimes He asks us to wait. Okay, more like lots of times He asks us to wait.

And wait.

And wait.

And wait some more.

Hagar had to wait. She returned home to Abraham and Sarah, and it may have been that for those years in their home, things were better for her. Years later, though, with Sarah finally giving birth to the promised son, Isaac, the tension in that home was unbearable. Sarah couldn't stand sharing space with Hagar and her son, Ishmael, so she demanded that Abraham send them away.

Abraham loaded some bags with provisions and sent them into the wilderness. Hagar was no runaway this time. She was sent away from her home. We're told, "She went on her way and wandered in the Desert of Beersheba" (Genesis 21:14). She wandered without a plan this time. Perhaps she had long since given up on returning to her own family in Egypt. Now she was aimless and without hope, placing her son down when their water ran out and walking away so she wouldn't hear his cries as he died from dehydration.

God met her in the wilderness again, and this time, instead of sending her back to her master and mistress, he promised to bless her in the desert place. His plan for her was different now because the timing was different.

Is God changing your plans? Is He asking you to alter your course and go somewhere unexpected? Is He telling you, "not yet," and asking you to wait a little longer?

If He asks you, "My child, where have you come from, and where are you going?" share with Him all that is in your heart and dare to ask the question, "Father God, where do you want me to go?" Then trust that The God Who Sees knows the best destination for you and the perfect timing. Not only that, He'll walk with you all the way.

Trusting Him to Open Our Eyes

In the Desert of Beersheba, Hagar was a homeless single mother, without friends, caring for her boy in unfamiliar territory and running out of supplies. Her circumstances were desperate. Placing Ishmael under a bush, she walked away so she wouldn't have to watch him die. "And as she sat there, she began to sob" (Genesis 21:16).

It's in the impossible situations where God is often most visible. So it was with Hagar. God visited her once again and asked:

"What is the matter, Hagar? Do not be afraid; God has heard the boy crying as he lies there. Lift the boy up and take him by the hand, for I will make him into a great nation." Then God opened her eyes and she saw a well of water. So she went and filled the skin with water and gave the boy a drink. (Genesis 21:17–19)

Just like His question, "Where have you come from, and where are you going?" this new question, "What's the matter, Hagar?" shows that He was concerned about her. He knew where she was and what her circumstances were. Not only that, but He opened her eyes to see the deliverance He had prepared for her.

Nothing about Hagar's circumstances changed. She was still a homeless single mother, short on provisions and without friends or direction. It's possible that God miraculously placed a new well near where she sat. Scripture simply says, "God opened her eyes and she saw a well of water." It could also be that the only thing that changed was Hagar's vision. Blinded by impossibilities and overwhelmed with despair, Hagar had given up when a well was so close. God revealed to her grace and provision that she simply hadn't seen before.

In the same way, God miraculously gave supernatural sight to the prophet Elisha's servant in 2 Kings 6:15–17. Surrounded by a large enemy army with horses and chariots, the servant cried out in despair, "Oh no, my lord! What shall we do?" In his mind, clearly they were doomed to defeat. Yet Elisha assured his anxious friend:

> "Don't be afraid . . . . Those who are with us are more than those who are with them." And Elisha prayed, "Open his eyes, LORD, so that he may see." Then the LORD opened the servant's eyes, and he looked and saw the hills full of horses and chariots of fire all around Elisha. (2 Kings 6:16–17)

Suddenly their odds of winning didn't seem so bad anymore, yet their reality was unchanged. Those heavenly defenders had been there all along; the servant simply hadn't seen them.

Pray that God will open your eyes to His provision and plan for you. Sometimes we feel that our circumstances are too impossible even for God. We forget that He is the God of creation, who spoke the sun and moon and all of the earth's creatures into existence out of nothing. God hasn't stopped being a creator. He can still create something out of nothing. He can place wells where there had been no water. He can provide a heavenly army to deliver the defenseless. Remember that "with man this is impossible, but not with God; all things are possible with God" (Mark 10:27). You can trust that The God Who Sees will know what you need exactly when you need it.

What's the Big Picture?

In the moments of Hagar's greatest desperation, God rescued her with His presence, His identity, His care for her, His promise for her future, and His provision. He asked her, "Where have you come from, and where are you going?" and with that question came the reassurance that He cared about every circumstance that had led to her wilderness journey and He cared about her future.

When we allow Him to search our hearts with the same question, we trust that no matter what our plan is, His is better. We yield to Him. That's because He is the God who sees the big picture and knows the reason for everything we endure. He sees the provision He has prepared for us, even when we are blind to it.

Then we worship Him as Hagar did, proclaiming the glory of His name and obeying Him with simple trust and faith in The God Who Sees.

Where have you come from, and where are you going?

Hagar

Make It PERSONAL

- Have you ever felt invisible to people or to God?

- In what area of your life is God asking you to follow His plan for you instead of your own?

Make It CONNECT

1. When God met Hagar in the desert, He asked her "Where have you come from, and where are you going?" (Genesis 16:8). How would His emphasis have changed if He had asked her only where she came from? What about if He asked only where she was going? Why are both questions important?

2. Are you more likely to be trapped by circumstances in your past or obsess about the unknowns in your future?

3. How does Hagar's name for God ("The God Who Sees") give you hope when you face difficult circumstances or feel invisible?

4. Of all the names for God in Scripture—The Lord Our Healer, Peace, Everlasting Father, Our Provider, The Lord Our Banner, and others—which is most precious to you right now?

5. How has God changed some of your life plans? How do you react when you experience these unexpected "interruptions"?

6. Why would God's promise to Hagar in Genesis 16:10 make going back to Abraham and Sarah easier for her?

7. Read these verses as a group. Which promise encourages you the most when life is hard? What other promises from Scripture encourage you?

   a. 2 Samuel 22:31

   b. Isaiah 43:1–3

   c. Hebrews 13:5

Make It REAL

- Even though we'll most likely never receive a trophy for the important ministries or jobs we perform, we should serve *as if we would* get a trophy. Make that your motivation this week as you serve others.

- During your regular Bible reading, keep track of the promises God makes in Scripture. When you pray, ask God to make these promises real in your life.

- Choose an attribute or name of God to focus on all week. As you pray, don't just ask God for your needs, thank Him for who He is and focus on that trait specifically.

Make It LAST

Memory Verse

"I will instruct you and teach you in the way you should go; I will counsel you with my loving eye on you."

Psalm 32:8

Journal Prompt

Hagar knew Him as "The God Who Sees." In a similar way, David wrote, "The LORD is my shepherd," giving God a name based on His attributes. Write your own version of Psalm 23 based on your interests and passions. For example, if you love music, you can write about God as your conductor or composer. If you are a sports fan, try "God is my coach" or "God is my personal trainer."

Why did
Sarah laugh?
Is anything
too hard
with God?

Nine

Doubting Sarah

In one of my favorite *Mary Tyler Moore Show* episodes, Mary and the other newsroom staff hear of the tragicomic death of the beloved Chuckles the Clown. Dressed as "Peter Peanut" for a circus parade, Chuckles had been fatally injured by an elephant attempting to "shell" him. The newsroom for the next few days is abuzz with jokes, jokes, and more jokes about Chuckles.

Mary scolds everyone, telling them as they await the start of the funeral service: "This is a funeral. A man has died. We came here to show respect, not to laugh." Everyone promises her—no more jokes.

Then the priest begins the eulogy: "Chuckles the Clown brought pleasure to millions. The characters he created will be remembered by children and adults alike: Peter Peanut, Mr. Fee-Fi-Fo, Billy Banana, and my particular favorite, Aunt Yoo Hoo."

At that point, unmistakable sounds of laughter emerge from Mary's seat. Everyone else sits straight-faced and somber while she unsuccessfully tries to hide and control the guffaws, giggles, and snorts. Finally, the priest concludes by saying, "And what did Chuckles ask in return? Not much. In his own words, 'A little song, a little dance, a little seltzer down your pants.'" Mary can't control it any more. She laughs loudly and unmistakably.

But when the priest asks her to stand up, to laugh for Chuckles's sake because tears would have offended him, Mary immediately begins to cry.

She knew all about the misfortune of inappropriate laughter. Maybe Mary would have felt a little compassion for Sarah, who laughed with disbelief when God promised that she'd give birth to a son.

The problem for Sarah wasn't the laughter but what inspired it. No question about it—deep down it was a giggle of unbelief, a silent chuckle of incredulity at God's ridiculous promise. It was impossible for her, a woman of ninety, long past menopause, to give birth to a son.

It's easy for us to look back at Sarah and shake our heads in disapproval. Sarah didn't trust God enough. Sarah didn't wait long enough. Sarah meddled and manipulated. Tsk, tsk, tsk.

We've never done any of those things . . . right?

Truth be told, I've struggled with unbelief in the midst of long waits and seemingly impossible circumstances. Haven't you?

So when the Lord showed up at Abraham's camp and declared that Sarah was going to give birth to a son in one year, I understand why Sarah's unbelief burst out in a quiet giggle to herself.

And then God searched her heart. He rooted out all the pain she had endured from years of unfulfilled promises, watching other women have babies while she remained barren. He dug all of that bitterness up and spoke grace and blessing directly to her. He did it with a question, "Why did Sarah laugh? . . . Is anything too hard for the LORD?" (Genesis 18:13–14).

Feeling Left Out

If you've ever been the last one picked for a dodgeball team or eaten lunch by yourself while a group of popular girls giggled away at the next table over, you may be able to relate to Sarah. She experienced years in which the people around her received blessings, sometimes the very blessing she desperately desired. Is there any wonder, then, why she was slow to accept a personal promise saying she would finally have the longed-for son?

God asked, "Why did Sarah laugh?" Well, because it was hard for her to believe that she was finally the one receiving the blessing.

Last week I needed to emphasize a life lesson and a character issue with my oldest daughter. Leaning in close to her, nose to nose, I cradled her chin gently in my hand and met her gaze. Her face was reddened by anger, her fists clenched tightly at her side, her body tense. And I began with these whispered words, "I love you."

Behind her, my youngest girl stood watching us intently. When she heard my first words to her older sister, my tiny one began bouncing up and down in excited anticipation. With the limited vocabulary of "Mama, mama, mama!" and her little dance, I knew what she meant. She was saying, "Me next, Mom! My turn! What about me? Do you love me, too? Tell me you love me, too!"

Have you ever been the "other child" jumping up and down before God, trying to attract His attention? Have you listened to a friend testify to the miracle God did for her and cried out, "Me next, God"? Have you sat silently in your small group, listening to others talk about how God spoke to them—how He gave them this verse, how He told them to do something—and wondered exactly what God's voice sounds like? Because you don't know if you've ever heard it. So you sit at your table with your Bible and journal and pen and say, "Okay, God, let's get this you-speaking-to-me thing started!" And you read God's Word. And that's it. No lightning strikes or neon signs for you.

So you ask, What about *me*, God?

I know you "so loved the world," but do you love *me*?

I know you "know the plans" you have for people, but do you have a plan for *me*?

I know you are "The God Who Sees," but do you ever see *me*, one tiny person on this planet of people?

There are times, even for those of us who have walked with God for decades, when we hear silence from heaven and our prayers, heartfelt and constant as they are, seem to go unanswered. We've checked our hearts; it's not sin blocking God from our view. And so we wave our hands at heaven, we dance for Him, we remain on our knees a little longer, we press in a little closer—all so that He will get personal with us. Not general love. Specific love. Not universal plans. Personal plans. Not just words on a page. A message designed for us.

I wonder if Sarah was doing her own jig before God and asking, "What about me?" Walk through this story with me and you'll see what I mean.

In Genesis 15, God came to Abraham and promised him a flesh-and-blood heir and offspring as numerous as the innumerable stars in the sky (vv. 4–5). But God was silent about Sarah. As far as the promise stood, Abraham could have fathered the child of promise through anyone. From Sarah's perspective, Abraham was the chosen and anointed one and she was the barren wife standing in the way.

In Genesis 16, moved by a desire to see God's promise fulfilled, Sarah stepped aside and told Abraham to marry her maidservant Hagar. When Hagar became pregnant while Sarah had spent decades with no results, Hagar started to mock her mistress and Sarah threw her out. Forget this surrogate motherhood thing. Sarah decided no heir was better than an upstart maidservant with a baby on her hip.

There in the wilderness on the way back to Egypt, God appeared to Hagar. He told her to name her son Ishmael and added, "I will increase your descendants so much that they will be too numerous to count" (Genesis 16:10).

Can you imagine what Hagar's homecoming reception must have been like for Sarah? She stood by while Hagar announced that not only was she carrying Abraham's child, but that it would be a son, his name was picked out by God, and he was promised numerous descendants.

It sounds like the answer to the promise to me. It probably sounded that way to Sarah, too. God appeared to Abraham and blessed him. God appeared to Hagar, the Egyptian slave girl, and blessed her.

Sarah stood in the corner, feeling overlooked and pushed aside.

In Genesis 17, God reappeared to Abraham and clarified the promise, "As for Sarai your wife, you are no longer to call her Sarai; her name will be Sarah. I will bless her and will surely give you a son by her. I will bless her so that she will be the mother of nations; kings of peoples will come from her" (vv. 15–16).

How precious are those words: "I will bless her . . . I will bless her." He lavishly poured out blessing on a woman who had waited so long to receive one.

Finally, in Genesis 18, the Lord made this promise even more personal for Sarah. He visited Abraham's camp and asked one important question before making any more statements of promise—"Where is your wife Sarah?" (v. 9). This was no message just for Abraham. This was no promise meant for everyone other than Sarah. No, God called her name to get her attention, to make sure she was listening at the flaps of her tent before He said anything else. Then, once He knew she was poised to hear, He gave the promise, spoken for her benefit: "I will surely return to you about this time next year, and Sarah your wife will have a son" (v. 10).

She laughed! It seemed unbelievable that God could include her in this promise, a promise so outside the realm of physical possibility. After all this time, it must have seemed like God's promises were for everyone but her, that He appeared to others but not to her, and that He had a plan for everyone except her.

And yet God had a plan for Sarah, a blessing for her, a message just for her.

He does for you, as well. Heaven might seem silent at the moment. You may see God at work in the lives of others and feel His absence in your own circumstances. God, however, is a personal God, with a plan, a blessing, a message just for you. "Though it linger, wait for it; it will certainly come and will not delay" (Habakkuk 2:3).

When God Takes a Long Time

Not only did Sarah have to watch others receive blessing in the midst of her barrenness, but she also simply had to wait a long time. Have you ever had to wait for God to fulfill a promise? Sometimes I've waited days, months, even in some cases a few years. But Sarah knew more about waiting on God than I do. She waited decades to have a baby.

God asked, "Why did Sarah laugh?" Well, because she had waited so long for God to give her a baby that now He seemed too late. She no longer believed it was possible. She didn't trust that God could do it.

Do you ever have similar moments of unbelief or lack of trust? I do. I pray for things but make plans and decisions based on God *not* answering my prayers. I lay at His feet my anxiety and concerns about situations but snatch them back up when His answer doesn't come quickly enough for me. I hover over His shoulder and share my opinion on the kind of job He is doing in my life. *I think you could provide better for me if you changed this about my job. Don't you think so, God? Don't you think I've waited long enough?*

I pester and nag and "help" and act like a know-it-all backseat driver. Sarah had her moments of grasping for control just like many of us do. She helped things along, made "suggestions" (demands), and pressed ahead with plans without considering consequences.

To be fair, Sarah had waited years for God to fulfill His promises and trusted that God would give Abraham "a son who is your own flesh and blood" (Genesis 15:4). It may have been thrilling and easy to believe at first. A promise from God, a child, the deepest desire of her heart was assuredly in her future! Surely she headed to the wilderness version of Babies 'R Us and set up a registry just days after Abraham came home and told her what God had promised. Faith is easy when the promises are fresh.

But then, nothing. No pregnancy. No baby. Promises faded. Questions arose. Cultural expectations weighed heavy on her. A decade after the original promise, Sarah's faith finally buckled under the heavy weight of circumstantial evidence mounting up against God. He hadn't done what He had promised. No baby was coming. Sarah's biological clock had ticked and tocked out and she clearly needed to step in and help God.

And so the trouble began. A second wife for Abraham. Conflict and abuse between Sarah and Hagar. A runaway maidservant. Ishmael born, son to Abraham, but not the child God had promised.

Thirteen years after Ishmael's birth and about twenty-four years after the original promise, none of Sarah's ideas or attempts to help (or control) the situation had yielded results.

Yet in all this time, God's plans never changed. His intent from the beginning was to birth an entire nation through Abraham and Sarah, and He was willing to let Sarah reach the point of impossibility, of clear human failure, before fulfilling His promises. She was past menopause, now ninety years old. There was simply no earthly way for Sarah to birth the promised heir.

That's what unbelief would say. That's what lack of trust would claim.

God is so gracious to us in our weakness, though. He certainly was with Sarah. When He visited Abraham again and reiterated the promise, this time He added a clarification: "I will bless her [Sarah] and will surely give you a son by her. I will bless her so that she will be the mother of nations; kings of peoples will come from her. . . . Your wife Sarah will bear you a son, and you will call him Isaac" (Genesis 17:16, 19).

The first time, God said that Abraham would have a son and heir. This time, He clearly said to Abraham, "You know Sarah, as in your wife Sarah? She will have a son by you. Together. Nobody else needs to be involved in this. Just you and her. Got it?"

In this promise God specially noticed Sarah by calling a childless woman in her nineties to be the Mother of Nations. As kids we sang the silly song, "Father Abraham had many sons, and many sons had father Abraham." Why don't we ever sing about Sarah? After all, the poor woman had to give birth to the promised child at ninety years of age with no epidural. I think she deserves her own song!

Abraham and Sarah were nothing without God's miraculous involvement in their lives. "Look to Abraham, your father, and to Sarah, who gave you birth. When I called him he was only one man, and I blessed him and made him many" (Isaiah 51:2). God did what could not have happened otherwise. He is the one who blesses us.

Therefore our testimonies are not that we have accomplished much or attained great things in our own strength and ability. If Sarah had produced the promised heir through surrogate motherhood, fertility treatments, or even naturally while her body was still ripe for childbearing, then there would have been no need for God's personal touch.

As Beth Moore wrote, "If Isaac's birth says anything at all, surely it says that nothing is too difficult for the Lord."[2] That's the question God asked Abraham while Sarah stood laughing in her tent over the promise of pregnancy in her old age. "Is anything too hard for the Lord?" (Genesis 18:14). Isaac's birth proves God's possibilities even in impossible situations.

In Genesis 21:1, it beautifully says, "Now the Lord was gracious to Sarah as he had said, and the Lord did for Sarah what he had promised." And so He will for you. God will do what He has promised. And when He does, when He so graciously delivers you, He will receive all the glory and give you a testimony of miraculous provision so that others may believe and trust in a God for whom nothing is too difficult.

Ten

Do This in Remembrance

Psalm 30:11 says, "You turned my wailing into dancing; you removed my sackcloth and clothed me with joy." That's certainly what God did for Sarah. She had been an onlooker while others were blessed, she had waited (at times impatiently) for God to fulfill His promises, and finally the blessing was hers. The quiet laugh in her tent upon hearing the promise had turned into the laughter of joy when holding her newborn son. "Sarah said, 'God has brought me laughter, and everyone who hears about this will laugh with me'" (Genesis 21:6).

Why did Sarah laugh? At first, because it all seemed so impossible and unbelievable. Yet now, with the promise fulfilled, she laughed with praise at abundant grace. Indeed, "the LORD was gracious to Sarah as He had said, and the LORD did for Sarah what He had promised" (Genesis 21:1).

He did what He had promised. He always does. "The one who calls you is faithful, and he will do it" (1 Thessalonians 5:24).

It was always God's plan for Sarah to be the mother of nations. He had chosen her along with Abraham from the beginning of this faith journey. Yes, she struggled to control things. Yes, she struggled with unbelief. Even so, she had been chosen. Her mistakes didn't negate His promise.

We might *know* that God keeps His promises. When God asks us, "Is anything too hard for me?" we probably give the "good church girl" answers: "God can do anything." "Don't tell God how big your problem is, tell your problem how big your God is." "God keeps His promises."

We say it. We may even believe it. But what about when life is hard? How do we keep from forgetting the promises when trials batter our faith, leaving us bruised, broken, and uncertain? What do we do when, like Sarah, we endure decades of unfulfilled promises?

What do we do then? How do we remember that God always does what He promises—even when it seems unlikely, even impossible?

In the midst of these trials, it's hard to see truth, and it's hard to remember what God has done for us in the past. All we can see are the impossible circumstances we currently face.

But in the seasons of blessing, we can prepare ourselves to combat the lies of the Enemy and our own fickle emotions by setting up physical reminders of His acts of grace. That way we can look back and remember with clarity and with evidential proof that God is indeed faithful to keep His promises. We write prayer journals. We create scrapbooks of family blessings. We write down answered prayers. We carry verses on note cards. All so that when our circumstances tell us God has failed us, that He has left us, that He has let us down and we are drowning, we can look at our reminders and recognize truth. When I feel like God has abandoned me, the truth is: "Never will I leave you; never will I forsake you" (Hebrews 13:5).

When I feel like God can't provide: "My God will meet all your needs according to the riches of his glory in Christ Jesus" (Philippians 4:19).

When I feel heartbroken: "The Spirit of the Sovereign Lord is on me, because the Lord has anointed me to proclaim good news to the poor. He has sent me to bind up the brokenhearted, to proclaim freedom for the captives and release from darkness for the prisoners" (Isaiah 61:1).

God's "word is truth" (John 17:17). Regardless of how our circumstances appear, what our friends say, or what our emotions scream at us, God does what He promises to do. He might not do it the way we expect or at the time we expect (just ask Sarah!), but He will keep His promise to us. It is our job, then, simply to remember and be grateful for what He has already done and trust that He will do it again.

Not long ago, I searched through my journals for a specific entry. I could so clearly remember writing it. I knew exactly where I had sat, what I was reading, and what I ate as I wrote. But when I looked through the shelf, I saw journals lined up for each year with just one missing—the one I wanted.

This might not seem like a crisis to you, but it was a difficult moment for me. I switched into "frantic search mode" and dumped books off the shelf and shuffled others aside. I was stressed. That's because my journals aren't personal diaries of my experiences and feelings. They are records of the verses, quotes, prayers, and thoughts I've had as God interacts with my life. Losing my journal is like losing some of my testimony, the written record I keep of God at work in my life.

In the Bible, many of God's people created monuments or kept mementos of times when God rescued them. It was their way of remembering that God saved them before and He could save them again. My journals record the story of God's faithfulness to me.

Thankfully, I found my missing journal the next day and—amazingly, if not miraculously—it was flipped open to the exact page I wanted.

Samuel the prophet found a different way to remember God's activity: "Samuel took a stone and set it up between Mizpah and Shen. He named it Ebenezer, saying, "Thus far the LORD has helped us" (1 Samuel 7:12). We often sing the hymn "Come Thou Fount of Every Blessing" without realizing that when it says, "Here I raise my Ebenezer," it's referring to this monument Samuel created. Literally, it means "a stone of help."

Samuel's stone reminded Israel of how God delivered them when they repented and returned to Him. After rebelling against God and being punished as a result, "all the people of Israel turned back to the LORD" (1 Samuel 7:2). Following this new beginning, this repentance and restoration, God routed the enemy Philistines in a mighty and miraculous way. All of Israel could see that God was faithful to save them as long as they walked in obedience.

Samuel didn't want the people to forget what God did in that place. We humans are forgetful creatures. God saves us. We praise Him. Things are good for a while. Then a crisis occurs and we fret, we worry, we wonder, *Is God going to let me down this time?*

We need an Ebenezer, a record of what God has done, so when life is hard and we need healing and provision and intervention, we can look at the monuments of the past and say, "Look what God did for me. He saved me here, here, and here—and He'll do it again."

Jennifer Rothschild wrote, "Remembering is a discipline that takes effort and focus."[3]

After all, we can be forgetful creatures. I walk into a room with an agenda and quickly get distracted by toys and books. Mess, mess—always mess. How do we make so much mess? So, I tidy (and busy myself with complaining) and leave the room empty-handed, my original purpose long forgotten. What did I come in here for again?

I trek to the grocery store for one item I really need and walk back out with ten items in my shopping bag, none of them the one vital ingredient for tonight's dinner.

I start sentences and somewhere in the middle lose track of thoughts and words and trail off into silence.

Worrying at night over bills and forgetting past provision. Fretting over children and forgetting His past activity. Stressing over a decision and forgetting how He led me through dark and shadowy places before.

It's an enigma really. Words spoken and things seen that I long to forget replay in my mind with troubling regularity. Yet life necessities and God's promises that I simply must remember I forget with ease and . . . troubling regularity.

Sarah and I aren't the only ones who forget God's faithfulness. Over and over, in broken record style, God told the Israelites to remember what He had done, to recall the miracles of their past, and over and over they forgot. He tells them, "You have forgotten God your Savior; you have not remembered the Rock, your fortress" (Isaiah 17:10).

They tried, really tried. Joshua commanded twelve men from twelve tribes to hoist twelve stones from the dry bed of the Jordan River onto their shoulders, carrying reminders of a miracle as the nation crossed through the river on dry ground. Stone memorials to:

> serve as a sign among you. In the future, when your children ask you, "What do these stones mean?" tell them that the flow of the Jordan was cut off before the ark of the covenant of the LORD. When it crossed the Jordan, the waters of the Jordan were cut off. These stones are to be a memorial to the people of Israel forever. (Joshua 4:5–7)

Just like Samuel and just like the Israelites crossing the Jordan, we set aside physical reminders of a God-intervention, a sign on our life-road saying, "God at Work!"

In the Psalms, David sometimes talked to himself. He bossed his emotions around a bit and told his mind and soul what to do. He said, "Bless the LORD, O my soul; and all that is within me, bless His holy name! Bless the LORD, O my soul, and forget not all His benefits" (103:1–2 NKJV).

There are times when we have to do the same thing. We must command our souls to remember to thank God for what He has already done. In so doing, we also trust and believe that God will keep His promises in the midst of what we face today.

Sometimes it's not just our own Ebenezers that shine light on God's work in the past. We can listen to the testimonies of others, including those in the Bible, and be reminded of God's character in every time and circumstance. Eugene Peterson wrote:

> With a biblical memory, we have two thousand years of experience from which to make the off-the-cuff responses that are required each day in the life of faith. If we are going to live adequately and maturely as the people of God, we need more data to work from than our own experience can give us. [4]

Our lives are short. Our experience with God is just a fraction of His activity here on earth. So when we look at life through the filter of our personal experiences alone, we miss out on thousands of years of people experiencing God. We read the testimonies of people who lived a long time ago and find out they needed God as much as we do and He loved them and cared for them just as He loves and cares for us.

Why did Sarah laugh? Well, because she had forgotten what God had already done over the years. How He had called Abraham out of his homeland and faithfully led them through the wilderness, allowing them to prosper and keeping them safe among alien nations. She forgot how God protected her twice from the amorous advances of foreign kings. She forgot that God had always been good, that He had always been faithful, that He had always provided, that He had always been with them.

Sarah didn't have a method of remembering. So, when God promised her the impossible, a son in her old age, she laughed with the giggle of unbelief.

What happens when you read God's promises? Do you trust Him or do you laugh with discomfort and faltering faith? Do you look on with jealousy as others receive the promised blessing and you do not? Do you believe God's promises at first, but struggle to have faith after years of delay?

Like Sarah, we must choose to "remember the deeds of the LORD; yes, I will remember your miracles of long ago. I will consider all your works and meditate on all your mighty deeds" (Psalm 77:11–12). This is how we battle against doubts and unbelief—with the evidence of God's past faithfulness, the declaration of His character, and the assurance of His future provision.

Why did Sarah laugh?
Is anything too hard with God?

Sarah

Make It PERSONAL

- Have you ever felt left out by others or by God?

- When have you encountered a situation that you thought God could not or would not handle?

Make It CONNECT

1. Review the following list. We may be used to judging Sarah for doubting God, but how many of Sarah's struggles trouble you as well?

   a. Letting God be in complete control of your life.

   b. Waiting patiently for blessing and the fulfillment of promises.

   c. Believing that God can do impossible things.

d. Remembering what God has done in the past when your current circumstances appear bleak.

e. Feeling jealous of others who have what we want.

2. Complete this verse according to Ezekiel 34:26: "I will make them and the places surrounding my hill a blessing. I will send down showers ___ _____; there will be showers of blessing." How does this give you hope during a prolonged time of waiting?

3. Sarah had to wait years for the promised son. What's the longest you've ever waited for God to fulfill a promise or grant you the desire of your heart?

4. In Genesis 18:9, what question did Abraham's visitor ask? How is this a reminder that God is a personal God?

5. God's "word is truth" (John 17:17), which means that we can use the promises of His Word to combat our sometimes unruly emotions—which, believe it or not, are not truth! Read these assurances from God's Word and circle the one that is most meaningful to you right now.

a. When I feel like God has abandoned me: Hebrews 13:5

b. When I feel like God can't provide: Philippians 4:19

c. When I feel heartbroken: Isaiah 61:1

6. The Israelites hefted twelve stones out of the dry Jordan riverbed and Samuel set up Ebenezer as a reminder of God's faithfulness. What do you use to remind you of God's provision and help?

Make It REAL

Choose one of the following ways of remembering what God has done for you, or come up with your own method.

- Start a prayer journal, recording prayer requests and their answers.

- Create a scrapbook of family blessings and choose specific times of the year to update it, such as every Thanksgiving or Christmas.

- Choose to meditate on one verse a week. Write it down on index cards that you place around your home. Pray through it and recite it. Keep a small notebook where you collect the cards when the week is done.

Make It LAST

Memory Verse

I will remember the deeds of the LORD;
yes, I will remember your miracles of long ago.
I will consider all your works
and meditate on all your mighty deeds.

Psalm 77:11–12

Journal Prompt

Put aside the "good Christian girl" answers to the question, "Is anything too hard for the Lord?" It's time to be honest. Are you impatient for God to work in your life? Jealous of the blessings of others? Anxious to be the one to receive the blessing? Uncertain about the direction God is leading you? Overwhelmed by circumstances? Tell Him all about it and ask Him to help you have faith even when it's difficult.

What is your name?

Eleven

Who Am I?

In the movie *Fried Green Tomatoes*, Kathy Bates played overweight, middle-aged, unhappy housewife Evelyn Couch. Even her last name, Couch, makes you think of inaction and a boring life. Same old, same old, every day. Routine. People walking all over her. A passionless marriage.

And then she's introduced to the name "Towanda." It's exotic and exciting. Suddenly Evelyn has newfound enthusiasm for life and the boldness to stand up for herself. She drives to the grocery store and after weaving through the parking lot looking for a space, finally spots someone about to leave. Waiting patiently, blinker on, she is shocked when two young and sassy women zoom their sports car into the space ahead of her. Laughing to themselves, they yell back at her, "Face it, lady, we're younger and faster." At first, Evelyn looks like she's going to drive away and allow herself to be beaten down once again.

But then she remembers that she is trying to transform herself. No more submissive and subservient Evelyn. Enter bold and wild Towanda. Empowered by thoughts of a new identity, Evelyn smashes into their car over and over again. When the parking space thieves come out of the store screaming, she says, "Face it girls, I'm older and I have more insurance."

Now, clearly she went overboard with the "Towanda power." Still, Evelyn changed when she stopped thinking of herself as plain-old Evelyn and started envisioning herself as empowered Towanda.

There's power in a name.

That's why God was personally involved in naming and re-naming so many people in the Bible. Their names often denoted particular character traits or held symbolic meanings. My Bible has most of these names footnoted so that I can understand the significance behind Isaiah naming his son Maher Shalal Hash Baz—because obviously he had to have a reason to pin that moniker on a child! Often biblical names described the role God wanted the person to play or even fulfilled prophecy in Israel's history.

To a much lesser extent, we consider some of these things when we name our children today. Together my husband and I prayed about each of our daughters' names for months, investigating meanings and listening to how names sounded. We had to rule out the names already used by our brothers and sisters for their kids (no easy task when we both come from families with five kids!). It was particularly important to my husband that the initials did not spell anything silly that the girls could be teased about at school. Naming our kids was something we took seriously.

God took names seriously, too. In Genesis, we learn about Jacob, one of the twin sons born to Isaac and Rebekah. Jacob's name means "heel grabber" or "he who supplants." Others say it means "deceiver" and "cheater."

Jacob was both a heel-grabber and a trickster, his name a perfect fit. As Rebekah birthed her twin sons, Esau came out first, with Jacob holding on to his heel. Later, after tricking his brother Esau out of his birthright (the inheritance reserved for the firstborn son) and his father's blessing, Jacob fled from his home in fear that Esau would murder him.

Years later, now with wives, sons, and many possessions, Jacob packed up and left his father-in-law Laban's house to return home and face Esau. The night before meeting Esau face-to-face, Jacob sent everyone and everything ahead of him across a stream and he remained behind. "So Jacob was left alone, and a man wrestled with him till daybreak" (Genesis 32:24).

All through the night, Jacob wrestled with a man, probably the first fair fight he'd ever undertaken. Hour after hour they fought, and Jacob simply refused to give in, not until he received a blessing. This was a unique encounter in Scripture, a way that God specially worked on Jacob's character, curbing Jacob's tendency to trickery and testing his determination for God's blessing. Ultimately the blessing didn't come because Jacob won the wrestling match. Instead, God blessed Jacob simply out of grace and favor and because Jacob didn't give up.

Wrestling is so often our story, too. We find ourselves struggling desperately and incessantly, sometimes against an opponent we can't even identify. Like Jacob, so many of these battles occur in the darkness, either literally at night in our beds when fear grips us or figuratively because our circumstances have left us unable to see God.

Just as there was for Jacob, there is a blessing available to us. It's there! If you are struggling, do not give up. Refuse to give in and stay in the battle until the end. Your fight has a purpose and overcoming brings reward and blessing, but just like with Jacob, sometimes it all begins with a question.

What Is Your Name?

Following this all-night wrestling match, "the man asked him, 'What is your name?'" (Genesis 32:27).

It's such a deceptively simple question. We know our names. It's one of the first words we learn, one of the first words we write with our tiny hands gripped around a thick pencil and guided by our moms and dads. Our name. Who we are wrapped up in a few letters and typed up on our birth certificate and Social Security card.

Sometimes, though, it's not so easy to remember what our name is. A few weeks ago, I was sound asleep but slowly awakened by a sound traveling across the house, into my room, and all the way into my two ears so comfortably resting on my pillow: "Mama, mama, MA-ma, ma-MA, mama, mama, mama . . ."

From the time I put feet to floor and walked the small distance between my room and my baby's room, I had heard "mama" sixty-two times. It was never an upset cry or a yell, just a determined and incessant calling out for me. And in those few moments between my bed and her crib, I longingly recalled the days when my name used to be Heather.

Is that what my name had been? Most days it really isn't anymore. Perhaps you find yourself in this position, too—so defined by roles that your true identity is shrouded in mystery and long since lost. Are there days when you feel like who you are deep down is buried under mounds of roles and expectations? You aren't you anymore, you're "Mom," "Wife," "Daughter," "Employee."

It's as if name tags are no longer needed at events. We meet, we shake hands. The first question is "So, what do you do?" We answer and suddenly that's how they know us, not by who we are but by what we do.

Nicole Johnson, a dramatist with Women of Faith, wrote and performed a skit about a woman who uses a label maker to define and categorize everyone around her, even to the point of hurtfulness when she labels her young daughter "fat." Do you ever feel like your face is obscured by neon-colored labels printed out and stuck all over you by the people you meet every day?

These labels oversimplify who we really are, transforming us from a dynamic person with unique feelings and thoughts into "working mom" or "stay-at-home mom," "churchgoer," "liberal," "conservative." Often people think they know us because of the box they have placed us in. Sometimes even we forget that we aren't defined by labels and roles and categories and boxes. We wake up one morning and feel like somewhere along the way, we've just gotten lost.

God doesn't lose sight of us, though. Even when we forget our name and the essence of ourselves, He remains intimately aware of us, His creation. Part of God's unfathomably deep love for us is that He never overlooks our complexities. Isaiah tells us that God says, "Fear not, for I have redeemed you; I have called you by your name; you are Mine. . . . Since you were precious in My sight, you have been honored, and I have loved you" (Isaiah 43:1, 4 NKJV). Later Isaiah writes:

> Zion said, "The LORD has forsaken me, the Lord has forgotten me." "Can a mother forget the baby at her breast and have no compassion on the child she has borne? Though she may forget, I will not forget you! See, I have engraved you on the palms of my hands." (49:14–16)

God knew Jacob's name. He didn't need to ask. It's the same with us. He knows exactly who we are and what has brought us to this place. Yet He draws us into closer intimacy with Him by asking, "What is your name?" He wants to remind us that individuals matter to Him. He isn't just a Savior who died for all humanity;

He died for you and me and every other person uniquely and specifically.

Individuals matter to God. That's why He framed the Bible the way He did. It tells of God's activity among humanity through the stories of people—broken, messed up, sinning people just like you and me. "In keeping with His character, God told the history of a nation through individuals."[1] As we learn about these people, we ultimately learn about God.

By asking Jacob, "What is your name?" God was saying to Jacob, "You matter to me. I am interested in you personally, not just because you were the son of Isaac, the son of Abraham. And I have a plan to use you regardless of your brokenness." He says the same to us.

Every Name Matters to God

Jacob could easily have assumed that God's promise to give Abraham descendants would be fulfilled through his brother, Esau. Esau was the oldest and therefore the one who was supposed to receive God's blessing. There was no real reason for Jacob to think he mattered in God's plan, or that he would receive any special attention from the Almighty. He wasn't a long-promised son like Isaac had been. He may have felt like nobody special, just a person who would fade into history unremembered.

Sometimes it's easy for us to forget that we are important to God. Do you ever feel insignificant? Maybe it seems that others are more gifted by God, more blessed by God, or have more ministry success and impact. We look around and see God choosing other people and wonder why He's asked us to serve in this small place.

And yet, every one of us is important to God. He uses each of us in unique ways. After all, it was Jacob whom God chose to be part of the genealogy of Christ. It's his name that appears in

Matthew 1:2: "Abraham was the father of Isaac, Isaac the father of Jacob, Jacob the father of Judah and his brothers."

To be honest, Matthew 1 and other biblical genealogies aren't my favorite Scripture passages. I've skimmed over the hardly pronounceable names in biblical genealogies many times to rush on to the "good stuff." (I can't be the only one who has done this, right?) But Eugene Peterson reminds me:

> The biblical fondness for genealogical lists is not dull obscurantism, it is an insistence on the primacy and continuity of people. Each name is a burnished link connecting God's promises to his fulfillments in the chain of people who are the story of God's mercy.[2]

It's certainly true for Jacob, the younger son who ended up receiving the birthright, the blessing, and the place in the Jesus' family tree. God's promises found fulfillment and continuation in him. Because of that, we are reminded that every individual, every name among the list of names, matters to God.

There are other lessons to be found in these often overlooked genealogies. The Gospel accounts include two genealogies for Jesus, one in Matthew and one in Luke. While several theories exist about why Matthew and Luke track Jesus' ancestry in different ways, one possibility is that Matthew follows Joseph's family line and Luke accounts for Mary's. Matthew's genealogy, then, is the adoptive family of Jesus, the earthly father who brought up Jesus as his own son. This list includes some names I readily recognize. Jacob is there along with Abraham, David, and Solomon. These are the flannel board characters that made it into Sunday school curricula. The famous ones with stories we've heard hundreds of times before.

Then there are a few names I remember from my personal reading of Kings and Chronicles. These are the not-quite-so-famous guys. Their stories are in the Bible, but they're not typically covered by preachers or teachers. Names like Asa, Hezekiah, and Josiah.

Finally, there are names on this family tree that I simply don't know anything about. Who are Azor, Zadok, and Achim anyway? How do these men fit into Scripture and into the heritage of Christ? What part do they have to play in the greatest ministry of all—the bringing forth of our Savior and Messiah? Maybe the scholars know and have written commentaries and heavy academic books about these mystery men. To simple me sitting at the kitchen table with my Bible, they are empty names I struggle to pronounce.

But they are not empty names to God. Just as He knew Jacob's name and story, God knew the individual names of every person in the biblical genealogies. And He knows you now and sees your ministry to Him.

Of course, God values the famous ministers that reach thousands of people seated in arenas and the authors who write Christian books that millions of people read. He blesses their service and receives glory through their efforts. They are the well-known ones, who might have ended up on a flannel board had the Bible been written during our lifetimes.

Yet in individual homes and in small churches across the country, there are people just like you and me serving every day. They may never achieve the worldly definition of ministry success. Nevertheless, their every act of self-sacrifice is witnessed by God and is valued by Him.

No ministry is too small for Him to notice. Every name matters to God.

Hidden away in another genealogy in 1 Chronicles 9:31 we read that "a Levite named Mattithiah, the firstborn son of Shallum the Korahite, was entrusted with the responsibility for baking the offering bread." A one-liner in Scripture. His chief job was baking bread to be used as an offering in the temple. Others in this long genealogy were gatekeepers, guards, officials in the house of God, and caretakers of all the holy instruments used in worship. But Mattithiah was a simple baker who was entrusted with a responsibility. And what he did mattered. Without Mattithiah, the offering table would be empty of an element of worship. His ministry, however small, was essential to his faith community.

We can look back now and see the fullness of Jacob's story. We know about his children, like Joseph and Judah, and the roles they played in building Israel and in the genealogy of Christ. Jacob himself didn't have this ability to see the full picture. As far as he was concerned, as he wrestled all night with a stranger, he was a runaway man with a troubled past, a trickster, a cheat, and a liar, who was journeying back home for reconciliation.

Yet God chose Jacob, the younger son and the renegade, and it was God's desire to raise him up and use him to lead the growing Hebrew nation.

You are not just one name among a sea of names to God and neither was Jacob. God loves you—individual, uniquely designed you. He knows your name and He has created you for His purposes. Whether it's to be a link in a chain of a family heritage of faith like Jacob was or to bake bread for the church like Mattithiah, your ministry is important to Him. More than that, *you* are important to Him.

God Uses the Broken

Not only could Jacob have felt like an insignificant younger son, but he also could have felt unusable because of the overwhelming brokenness from his past. How could God use someone who had cheated his older brother out of a birthright and a blessing? Who had deceived his blind and aging father? Who had experienced intense sibling rivalry and the havoc created by parents playing favorites with their twin sons? How could God use someone who was broken from a family that was broken? Why would God care enough about Jacob to establish a uniquely intimate relationship with him by asking, "What is your name?"

Have you felt imprisoned by a broken past? Maybe it's shame from your own missteps and bad choices, or perhaps you are the innocent recipient of a family broken to pieces. Either way it's hard to see how God could use you.

Jacob may have felt that. I've been there as well. In college, I took a class called Family Studies that focused on identifying and resolving family conflicts through counseling. One of our assignments was to create a family tree, but not a typical family tree that confines itself to names, important dates, and marriages. Using different colors and symbols, we had to mark on this family tree all divorces, infidelity, prejudice, abuse, illegitimate children, addictions, and "isms" (alcoholism, workaholism, etc.).

Talk about depressing. My family tree was a colorful display of what I would call "generational sins," or recurring problems hitting generation after generation, tracing back to every branch of my broken and pitiful familial oak. Even the innocent ones, who made decisions to break the hold of these sins on our family, were impacted anyway by the actions of others—wrapped up, entangled, and choked through sins by association.

Can you imagine Jacob's family tree dotted with second wives, rivalries, and people not speaking to one another? He didn't have the picture-perfect family either.

Then I read statistics about these hand-me-down burdens. The numbers were clear. My life should have been marred by abuse, alcoholism, marital infidelity, and divorce. My marriage doomed. My kids hurt.

Yet God's grace has a way of showing up in statistical anomalies.

Have you ever surveyed your past, maybe your own sins or the baggage you carry from the family's closet skeletons? Have you looked back and thought, "God can't use someone like me, not with what I've done or where I've come from?" It's something I wonder if Jacob ever thought about at night instead of sleeping. Did he regret tricking his dad, Isaac, into blessing him instead of Esau?

As Jacob's family grew and as he saw clear evidence of God's blessing on his flock, he must have been amazed at God's grace, to forgive him and prosper him despite brokenness.

Have you been breathlessly in awe of God's blessing before? Have you asked like King David, "Who am I, Sovereign LORD, and what is my family, that you have brought me this far?" (2 Samuel 7:18). That's my whispered prayer sometimes as I thank God for a faithful husband, healthy kids, and life filled to the brink and over-flowing with God's goodness. Who am I and what is my family?

Jacob is a messed up, sinful guy in Jesus' genealogy in Matthew 1. But he's not the only one. Jesus' family tree includes unknowns and broken people. It is no impressive oak, stately, strong and unharmed by conflict and sins. Instead, like mine, his genealogy is the story of redemption poured out one generation after another.

I survey the names and their familiar stories.

- Tamar, who dressed up like a prostitute and tricked her father-in-law into sleeping with her after he failed to fulfill his promise to marry her to his youngest son (Genesis 38).
- Rahab the prostitute (Joshua 2:1).
- King David, himself an adulterer and murderer (2 Samuel 11) and Uriah's wife, Bathsheba, the adulteress.
- Manasseh, son of Hezekiah, who "did evil in the eyes of the LORD, following the detestable practices of the nations the LORD had driven out before the Israelites. . . . He sacrificed his own son in the fire, practiced divination, sought omens,

and consulted mediums and spiritists. He did much evil in the eyes of the LORD, arousing his anger" (2 Kings 21:2, 6).

That's not exactly a family tree to tack up over the mantle with pride. Unless . . .

Unless you're God, who wants to remind us that He has "called you out of darkness into his wonderful light" (1 Peter 2:9).

That "if anyone is in Christ, the new creation has come: The old has gone, the new is here!" (2 Corinthians 5:17).

That it is a "great love the Father has lavished on us, that we should be called children of God!" (1 John 3:1).

God does not define us by statistics or confine us because of our sins or the problems in our families. He is forever making us new, redeeming and restoring what has been broken and destroyed. Through our salvation we are removed from heritages of sin and brought into a new family. Slaves no longer, we have been adopted as sons and daughters into the family of Christ.

Gloriously Redefined

The best part of this story is that when God asked Jacob, "What is your name?" He had every intention of doing something new in Jacob's heart and life. He was offering Jacob a redefinition, a name change, a shedding of the brokenness of the past and putting on of a new identity in Him.

> The man asked him, "What is your name?"
> "Jacob," he answered.
> Then the man said, "Your name will no longer be Jacob, but Israel, because you have struggled with God and with humans and have overcome." (Genesis 32:27–28)

Sometimes I long for a new name just like Jacob received. A new identity! A new freedom! A new vision of how God sees me.

Some women are loathe to abandon their maiden names when they marry. They hyphenate or simply decline to visit the Social Security office for a name change because they do not want to give up their connection to their own family heritage and identity.

I've already told you about my family tree full of divorce, addictions, abuse, and infidelity. When I married, I was eager to take on a new name, to be grafted into a different heritage and allowed to flourish as a new branch on a family tree. It was a fresh start for me, just like the changing of his name was for Jacob.

Spiritually, we are promised a new identity in Christ. Once we turn our lives over to His lordship, He transforms us into something new. What is this new identity? Scripture says that in Christ, we are

- *God's children*: "To all who did receive him, to those who believed in his name, he gave the right to become children of God" (John 1:12).
- *Coheirs with Christ*: "Now if we are children, then we are heirs—heirs of God and co-heirs with Christ, if indeed we share in his sufferings in order that we may also share in his glory" (Romans 8:17).
- *Friends of God*: "I no longer call you servants, because a servant does not know his master's business. Instead, I have called you friends, for everything that I learned from my Father I have made known to you" (John 15:15).
- *Free from condemnation*: "Therefore, there is now no condemnation for those who are in Christ Jesus" (Romans 8:1).
- *Citizens of heaven*: "Our citizenship is in heaven. And we eagerly await a Savior from there, the Lord Jesus Christ" (Philippians 3:20).
- *God's temple*: "Don't you know that you yourselves are God's temple and that God's Spirit dwells in your midst?" (1 Corinthians 3:16).

- *Christ's ambassadors*: "We are therefore Christ's ambassadors, as though God were making his appeal through us. We implore you on Christ's behalf: Be reconciled to God. God made him who had no sin to be sin for us, so that in him we might become the righteousness of God" (2 Corinthians 5:20–21).

- *God's handiwork*: "We are God's handiwork, created in Christ Jesus to do good works, which God prepared in advance for us to do" (Ephesians 2:10).

- *New creations*: "Therefore, if anyone is in Christ, the new creation has come: The old has gone, the new is here!" (2 Corinthians 5:17).

- *God's chosen people*: "Therefore, as God's chosen people, holy and dearly loved, clothe yourselves with compassion, kindness, humility, gentleness and patience" (Colossians 3:12).

- *More than conquerors*: "In all these things we are more than conquerors through him who loved us" (Romans 8:37).

- *The Bride of Christ*: "Let us rejoice and be glad and give him glory! For the wedding of the Lamb has come, and his bride has made herself ready" (Revelation 19:7).

I don't know about you, but I don't always walk in the fullness of this new identity in Christ. Sometimes I don't feel like God's handiwork. Sometimes I focus on the here and now and forget to live as a citizen of heaven. Sometimes I allow Satan to condemn me for past mistakes rather than live in grace and free from condemnation.

Yet God gave His own precious Son so that we could live as a new creation. We need to receive this gift and treasure it by living the life He has called us to live.

Not only does God offer us a new identity when we believe in Him, but He also promises a new name of our own, just like Jacob's name change to Israel. This name is personal to our relationship with God, uniquely our own. After Jacob had wrestled through the night, received a new name and a blessing, reconciled with Esau, and returned home to Canaan, he built an altar and called it El Elohe Israel, or "God, the God of Israel" (Genesis 33:20). Israel as a nation didn't exist yet. This altar wasn't about the faith of an entire people; it was about the newly personal relationship with God and the acceptance of the new identity He had given.

Likewise, God gives us a new name. We are assured in Revelation 2:17, "To him who overcomes, to him I will give . . . a new name" (NASB).

So, we struggle to overcome because that's what brings this transformation. Jacob's faith was made personal, his identity made new only after a struggle. Like Jacob wrestling through the night, we fight against sin, taking a stand for holiness. We battle against Satan's attacks on us and on our families.

Beth Moore writes, "Few things define us more than how we struggle. When we struggle through the crisis with God all the way to the blessing, we are gloriously redefined."[3]

It is our trials and troubles that define us and ultimately allow us to be made new. If you're wrestling and fighting right now, don't stop. Hold on to the very end for the blessing and the transformation, for the inevitable result of knowing God more personally and intimately than ever.

God begins that glorious redefining by first asking us the same question He asked Jacob: "What is your name?" He draws us up into His arms and shows us that He knows us intimately and loves us dearly. He reassures us that we—you, me, and each of us as individuals—matter to Him. No one is overlooked or lost in the shuffle of life. Then, in exchange for all of the brokenness we carry with us now, all of the baggage from our past and the junk passed through our family lines, He offers us a new identity borne out of Christ's victorious struggle against sin and death on the cross. He did that for us.

What is your name?

Jacob

Make It PERSONAL

- How do you feel about your name? Love it? Hate it? Wish it were something different?

- Have you ever wanted to start fresh with a new name, new identity, new everything?

Make It CONNECT

1. Besides Jacob, what other biblical characters had names changed by God? (Hints: Genesis 17:5; 17:15; John 1:42.) Why did their new names matter? Did they earn their new names, or were they a gift?

2. Do you think Jacob's name fit him? What about his new name?

3. Does your own name have a special meaning or fit you in a particular way?

4. What are some of the labels we attach to other peo- ple? (Examples: Christian, non-Christian, fat, thin,

diva, scatterbrained, etc.) What's the danger in trying to fit people into easily defined categories?

5. Have you ever been better known as "John's wife" or "Jane's mom" than as yourself? How did that make you feel?

6. What do Isaiah 43:1 and 49:14–16 tell us about how well God knows us as individuals?

7. Take a look at Jesus' genealogy in Matthew 1. Which names do you recognize? Are some names only vaguely familiar? Can you pick out any names you don't know at all? Why would God include people that we know nothing about? What does this say about how He views individuals?

8. Why do you think God would include people like Rahab, David, and Manasseh in the genealogies listed for our Savior? What does this show us about God's heart and character?

9. At times we may struggle with feeling unknown, but God tells us exactly who we are in Scripture. Which of these verses describes who you are in Christ in a way that is most precious to you?

a. God's child: John 1:12

b. Coheir with Christ: Romans 8:17

c. Friend of God: John 15:15

d. Free from condemnation: Romans 8:1

e. Citizen of heaven: Philippians 3:20

f. God's temple: 1 Corinthians 3:16

g. Christ's ambassador: 2 Corinthians 5:20–21

h. God's handiwork: Ephesians 2:10

i. A new creation: 2 Corinthians 5:17

j. Chosen: Colossians 3:12

k. More than a conqueror: Romans 8:37

l. The Bride of Christ: Revelation 19:7

10. In Genesis 33:20, Jacob returned home to Canaan and built an altar and called it El Elohe Israel, or "God, the God of Israel." Israel as a nation didn't exist yet. What did Jacob mean when he chose this name for his altar?

Make It REAL

- Sketch out your family tree, noting any addictions, psychological conditions, divorces, remarriages, or abuse. This isn't meant to be a big project—just jot down your thoughts on paper. Pray over it and ask God to give you freedom from the sin and pain of the past. Pray that He brings restoration and wholeness wherever there is brokenness and pain.

- Practice personalizing Scripture this week, inserting your name into verses so that you remember that God loves you specifically, personally, and individually.

Make It LAST

Memory Verse

Thus says the LORD . . . , "Fear not, for I have redeemed you; I have called you by name; you are mine."

Isaiah 43:1 (ESV)

Journal Prompt

Tell God if there are any labels, sin, brokenness, or shame that make you feel like an unusable vessel. What is it that you need God to transform or make new in your life? Choose one of the descriptions of who we are in Christ and tell God why you treasure that characteristic. Then tell Him which characteristic is hardest to accept, believe, and live out.

What is that in
your hand?

Twelve

What's in the Utility Belt?

At the moment, the most popular show in my house with three daughters doesn't involve princesses or pink ponies. It's Batman, as in the 1960s Adam West Batman, complete with puns, homemade-looking costumes, and the announcer telling you to stay tuned, "same Bat-time, same Bat-channel!" at the end of each episode. We especially love the moment in each show when Robin exclaims, "Holy popcorn, Batman!" or "Holy snowball, Batman!"

No matter how impossible the situation, Batman escapes the clutches of the enemy and averts disaster, always at the last possible moment. The villain, thinking he or she has gotten the best of the hero, gloats and brags about defeating the "Dynamic Duo" only to learn of Batman's miraculous escape. In the fistfight scene that concludes every encounter with villainy, my daughters and I yell out the words splatted across the screen with each punch—"Pow!!

Orff!! Zonk!!" and then watch as Commissioner Gordon and Officer O'Hara congratulate the Caped Crusader and his Boy Wonder and carry the bad guys off to jail.

The thing about Batman is that he doesn't have x-ray vision and he can't fly. He isn't able to "leap tall buildings in a single bound" or scale skyscrapers like a spider. What makes Batman special is his utility belt full of gadgets and gizmos. With his Batzooka and Batarang, Batrope and Batcuffs, he always manages to defeat evil and save Gotham City.

We may not be cape-wearing superheroes, but God has equipped each of us with a utility belt of our own carrying the tools of our unique passions, training, experience, personalities, and spiritual gifts. He doesn't ask us to serve Him with skills we don't have or abilities He hasn't given us. Nor is God expecting us to achieve worldly standards of success all to appease Him.

Sometimes we feel the pressure anyway to be as good as someone else or to do as much as another. Yet God simply asks that we be who He has made us to be and offer in worship to Him what He has already placed in our hearts and lives.

We can see the way God uses tools He's already given us by looking at the calling of Moses. At the time of his burning bush experience at Mount Horeb, Moses had been away from Egypt for forty years. No longer living in an Egyptian palace, he now lived among shepherds and even became one himself. He had married. He lived a life of monotony and quiet, long days and hard work. It didn't seem like God had prepared him for leadership or intended anything special for this runaway prince of Egypt.

Until God caught his attention. During a plain-old, ordinary day of herding sheep in the wilderness, Moses saw in the corner of his eye a fire in a bush, and when he turned aside to see what was going on, God called to him to the very ministry He had prepared Moses to do. The years in Egypt and the wilderness had been a long and intense season of training, but not one of Moses's life experiences was wasted.

God introduced himself to Moses as the "God of Abraham, the God of Isaac and the God of Jacob" and as "I AM WHO I AM" (Exodus 3:6, 14). And He commissioned Moses to deliver the Hebrew nation from their four hundred year enslavement in Egypt.

If God revealed himself to me that powerfully in the middle of a mundane life moment, I'd be overwhelmed and maybe speechless. I may feel totally insufficient for the task He's called me to, but I can't imagine expressing that inadequacy to Him. I'd probably be tongue-tied and mutely nod my head in agreement to anything He said.

Moses wasn't speechless, though. Initially overcome by awe, Moses had hidden his face. But after a few moments of conversation with God, he spoke candidly. Expressing uncertainty, Moses asked, "What if these people don't believe that you appeared to me?" He declared his inability to do what God was asking him to do. He incited God to anger by declining the job altogether: "But Moses said, 'Pardon your servant, Lord. Please send someone else'" (Exodus 4:13).

Can you imagine telling God, "No thanks, you've got the wrong girl for the job"?

Do you ever look at what's required of you, glance back at yourself, and decide you simply fall short?

Moses felt that same way.

When God appeared to him in the burning bush, Moses pelted Him with questions. Why in the world would you call me, a murderer-turned-fugitive and now a lowly shepherd? Who are you anyway? What if I say God sent me and the people don't believe it?

God responded with a question of His own, "What is that in your hand?" (Exodus 4:2). Obviously, God could see the shepherd staff Moses was holding. He didn't ask the question out of ignorance or blindness. It was a question that showed how God had already prepared Moses for this leadership position. It didn't matter how ill-equipped or insufficient he felt. He simply had to obey God and God himself would perform the miracles and bring success. God was responsible for the results, not Moses.

God often asks us a similar question. "What is that in your hand? What tools do you have in that utility belt I've given you? You don't have to be anything more or less than how I've made you and trained you. Just use what I've already given you in service and I'll take care of the rest."

Moses gripped in his hand a shepherd's staff, a symbol of all those years moving sheep around the wilderness and reminiscent of the quiet nights alone with nothing more than the animals and God for company. It probably didn't seem like much, this crooked stick in his hand. Still, this is what God asked him to throw down onto the ground and Moses did. As the staff hit the dirt, it wriggled into a snake. Moses's first miracle, performed because he obeyed and because God did the rest, involved transforming something ordinary into something extraordinary. That kind of miraculous transformation is what God had been doing in Moses's life all along.

Moses's Utility Belt

When God asked the question, "What is that in your hand?" He knew that Moses had far more tools in his utility belt than just a shepherd's staff. That was simply all Moses could see or recognize at this "low point" in his life story.

God had already preserved Moses's life as a baby. Moses's mother must have cried from the moment she saw her red-faced baby boy because she knew he was not supposed to survive his birth day. In an effort to quell the rising slave population, Pharaoh had ordered that all Hebrew male children be murdered at delivery. The day of his birth should have been the day of Moses's death, but God had other plans for him.

Because of the boldness of the midwives, who refused to obey Pharaoh's harsh command, Moses nursed at his mother's breast and cuddled into her arms. His parents hid him for three months. During that time, they probably prayed over him and blessed him, giving him an early foundation of love and a heritage of faith—the first step in Moses's training for his future ministry.

"Then Pharaoh gave this order to all his people: 'Every Hebrew boy that is born you must throw into the Nile, but let every girl live'" (Exodus 1:22).

So weaving reed and forming a basket, his mother kissed Moses's forehead, brushed aside her tears, and placed him in the tiny boat nestled among the reeds in the river, leaving Moses's sister to watch over the baby and see what happened to him. Ultimately he was discovered by an Egyptian princess and carried into the palace, adopted into a royal family as a prince of Egypt.

But God did not allow Moses to grow up unaware of his identity as a Hebrew or the faith and traditions of the people he would one day lead. Moses's very own mother was chosen as his nursemaid, and he heard the songs of faith she sang as she rocked him to sleep and learned the stories of Abraham, Isaac, and Jacob as he sat on his mother's lap. The history he learned so captivated his heart and mind that he later, under the inspiration of the Holy Spirit, penned the first five books of the Bible, the Pentateuch, the history from creation to the Promised Land.

Knowing the history of his people came from time with his biological, Hebrew family. Yet, the ability to write that history down most likely came through the expertise and training of tutors in the Egyptian palace. God knew that Moses needed to learn faith and his identity at home with his family but learn leadership, literacy, oratory skills, and more from the most skilled educators in the land.

"Moses was educated in all the wisdom of the Egyptians and was powerful in speech and action" (Acts 7:22). This was training that no other Hebrew slave had access to and no one else needed because God had chosen and equipped Moses for the job of deliverer.

Unfortunately, when Moses as a young adult saw an Egyptian beating a fellow Hebrew, he jumped ahead of his calling and killed the slave master. Superhero Moses attempted to save the day and failed. He tried to do it in his own strength. Instead of a deliverer, he became a murderer and a fugitive. He hadn't learned that when we act in our own strength, we reveal our utter weakness and incapability. We fall all over ourselves. We mess it up. We fail.

So, off into the wilderness Moses ran, not knowing that the next forty years spent as a shepherd among foreign peoples would be the final step in God's training school for him. During those years of manual labor and loss of privilege, Moses would grow humble, becoming over time "more humble than anyone else on the face of the earth" (Numbers 12:3).

This humility was necessary. God had to build it into his character. Otherwise, years of leading the people, arbitrating disputes, hearing directly from God, delivering God's commands, and performing miracles would have left Moses too prideful to be of any use to God. The wilderness was necessary for God to mold Moses's character and transform him from well-educated, well-spoken royalty to a gifted-yet-humble servant of the Most High God.

"What is that in your hand?" God had asked. Although Moses held up only a shepherd's staff, God saw so much more.

Our Utility Belt

God used every part of Moses's life to fill his utility belt and fit him for the ministry God had designed for him. Nothing in his life was wasted. No experience was superfluous.

This is true of us as well. It may not seem like it now, but the season you are in, the wilderness journeys you've taken, the jobs and ministries you've been called to, the passions and gifts God has given you are all pieces of God at work in your life. Paul wrote, "For we are God's handiwork, created in Christ Jesus to do good works, which God prepared in advance for us to do" (Ephesians 2:10). Just like Moses, you are God's handiwork. He has created and designed you for a specific purpose—to fulfill the calling He has prepared for you since before your birth.

We don't have the ability to step back far enough from our lives to see the big picture. We can't see how the hurts from our childhood have softened our hearts and fit us for a ministry of compassion to others. We can't see how our college education matters as we wash dishes and change diapers as stay-at-home moms. We may not know how all those years of piano practice at the insistence of our mothers have done anything for us. But God knows how He has equipped us, and He knows His plan for us in the next season of our lives.

He says to us: "Everyone who is called by My name, whom I have created for My glory; I have formed him, yes, I have made him" (Isaiah 43:7 NKJV). We all have a purpose and it's to bring God glory. He's called you, created you, formed you, made you, gifted you. You're a handiwork designed to show off the Master Craftsman.

Moses didn't feel useful to God. As far as he was concerned, he was a failure. He was the son of slaves, and he had murdered an Egyptian in a failed attempt to save his people from their bondage. After fleeing from Egypt to escape punishment, he had spent forty years wandering around with sheep. When God asked Moses, "What is that in your hand?" he might very well have answered, "Not enough to do anything with!"

Here God was telling him that he was chosen to lead his people out of slavery. Hadn't he tried this leadership thing already? Hadn't he stood up to the Egyptian slave master, lost his temper, and killed him? Wasn't he little more than a murderer? He'd spent the past four decades of his life as a fugitive hiding out in shepherding country. A failure at leading people, he'd resorted to leading animals around the wilderness.

That didn't seem like a resume fit for the job of deliverer of a nation or spiritual leader of two million people.

Our shortcomings can similarly paralyze us. Moses saw his inabilities as insurmountable obstacles to God's ability to use him. He thought he had an empty utility belt. He told God, "Please send someone else." I can almost hear the subtext in his heart—"You must be able to find someone better than me, God. I'll only mess this up for you."

When it comes to spiritual matters, I confess I sometimes want to swap out parts of me for what looks better, not out of jealousy or pride, but because I long to give to God the best offering possible. For most of us, our deep-down motives are pure. But sometimes out of a desire to worship and give glory, we glance to our sides at the offerings of others and feel we fall short.

What about you? Have you ever looked around and wished you prayed like her, knew exactly what God called you to do like him, knew Scripture as well as she did, or had the same spiritual gift as a friend?

Paul says about the church,

Just as a body, though one, has many parts, but all its many parts form one body, so it is with Christ. . . . Even so the body is not made up of one part but of many. Now if the foot should say, "Because I am not a hand, I do not belong to the body," it would not for that reason stop being part of the body. And if the ear should say, "Because I am not an eye, I do not belong to the body," it would not for that reason stop being part of the body. If the whole body were an eye, where would the sense of hearing be? If the whole body were an ear, where would the sense of smell be? (1 Corinthians 12:12–17)

Imagine the body of Christ as a Mr. Potato Head—now how silly would we look? We'd be walking on our eyes and hearing with our toes.

Unfortunately, when we spend all our time trying to be something else, we leave the body of Christ missing what it needs to function. "God has placed the parts in the body, every one of them, just as he wanted them to be. If they were all one part, where would the body be? As it is, there are many parts, but one body" (vv. 18–20). Your gifting, your passion, your experiences are all uniquely packaged together by God and useful to Him.

All He asks is that we raise our hands to release what He has already given to us: the fullness of the talents He has bestowed, the passions He has stirred up deep in the fires of our hearts, the issues that make us raise our voices to defend others, the service that we wake in the morning excited to perform, the experiences from our past that soften our hearts and make us tender to those hurting in our midst.

The only thing God needed Moses to do was use the gifts and training he'd been given to minister to God's people. God didn't compare Moses to other job candidates and settle for second best. He had set Moses apart at birth, trained him up, and called him out, insufficiencies and all.

We're the only ones at times looking around to compare the gift we bring to the presents of the other worshipers. God isn't sitting at the gift table, shaking packages and estimating value. It's just us. We watch the offerings and shift our gaze with embarrassment when an attendee brings in a package wrapped in silver paper and topped with a fancy ribbon. Another arrives with gift bag filled to overflowing, tissue paper barely covering the treasures inside, and we want to take our gift back. It's not enough. Not for a King so worthy. Not for a God we adore.

When Jesus stood in the temple with His disciples, He pointed out to them a widow, who knew that true worship simply meant giving all that she had, sacrificially placing her "two very small copper coins, worth only a few cents" as an offering to God (Mark 12:42).

Others had given more, even ostentatiously so. "Many rich people threw in large amounts" (v. 41). She could have watched from a corner of the temple in shame at the earthly value of what others gave and walked away clutching her cent pieces, confident that God would despise a gift so meager.

And yet, she didn't. She gave. Jesus noticed.

He called His disciples over to learn from her. Men who would eventually be asked to give up everything—even their very lives—learned how to give sacrificially from a pauper widow almost lost in a crowd of those richer and more important than her. All because she "put in everything" when she gave to God (v. 44).

What two cents are you laying at the altar? Your spiritual gift, your ministry, your service to your church, your sacrifice for your family, your care for another, your laying aside of personal dreams, your causes, your secret encouragement for a friend? It's being a hand when He made you to be a hand and being an eye when He asked you to be the eye in a body of Christ that is so dependent on every part.

Your two cents is a gift precious to God; He only asks us to give what we ourselves have been given. "What is that in your hand?" That's all He asked Moses. That's all He was looking for in the temple as people put in their coins. That's all He wants from you—whatever He's already placed in your hands.

Thirteen

It's All about Him

Years ago I fell in love with a song called "Jesus, Lover of My Soul (It's All About You)." The song begins with a simple, worshipful declaration that, "It's all about you, Jesus. And all this is for you, for your glory and your fame."

Frequently, I would belt out the first line of this song with an impassioned Freudian slip, crooning, "It's all about *me*, Jesus."

Oops!

I didn't really mean it, of course. There are some lyrics I mix up at times—none of them quite as telling as that mistake. Sadly, but truly, there are so many days and moments when my focus is on me and not on God at all. It's those days and seasons of my life when I wish God would just do things my way and when "surrender" becomes my least favorite word.

There are moments and days when I begin to wonder how I could possibly minister to others when I'm working so hard at basics like keeping calm with misbehaving children and not stressing about my calendar. When I feel so empty, how can I pour out to others?

It's one thing to serve and encourage when we're overflowing; God's goodness sloshes over the tops of our lives and refreshes all who cross our paths. But what about when our cup seems dry? What happens when a thirsty neighbor lifts up needy hands in our direction and we ladle out empty air?

In some ways, that's where Moses was. He felt enthusiastic to the point of foolishness about leading the Israelites decades before when he was still in Egypt. Unfortunately, he was oozing confidence and overflowing with a vision of leading a slave revolt that depended on his own strength. He believed then that if it all depended on him, well, then he was enough.

He murdered an Egyptian in his enthusiasm. His own people rejected him. Pharaoh sought to punish him. That's what happened when he served in his own strength.

At the burning bush, Moses clearly recognized that if this deliverance thing depended on him, well, he simply didn't cut it.

The Bottom Line

When God calls us, it isn't about us at all; it's all about Him. We're the ones looking at our qualifications and feeling mismatched for the job He's assigning us. You want me to parent these children? You want me to stay in this marriage? You want me to lead this ministry? You want me to start this program?

You want me to do what, God?

Moses asked God, "Who am I that I should go to Pharaoh and bring the Israelites out of Egypt?" (Exodus 3:11). It was his way of saying he wasn't qualified for that and "It's all about me and *me* isn't good enough."

God, on the other hand, focused not on Moses, but on himself. He said, "I will be with you. . . . I AM WHO I AM. This is what you are to say to the Israelites: 'I AM has sent me to you.' . . . Say to the Israelites, 'The LORD, the God of your fathers—the God of Abraham, the God of Isaac and the God of Jacob—has sent me to you.' This is my name forever, the name you shall call me from generation to generation" (vv. 12, 14–15).

Moses was worried about what he couldn't do. He considered the assignment, looked only at himself, and decided he would fail. It makes sense. If my friend has a problem and the source of my answer is *me*, then I can't help her. If I sit to write devotionals and the words and thoughts are dependent on *me*—on my ability, my ideas, my inspiration—then I have nothing worth saying.

Think about how you approach your everyday life.

- As you lift that early rising baby out of the crib and she's tired and cranky and doesn't even know why, you can depend on your own strength to be calm, cheerful, and comforting, or you could depend on God.
- When your teenage child sits across the table from you and spills out what he's struggling with, you could depend on your own quick thinking and wisdom to give advice, or you could depend on God.
- When your aging parent faces medical issues that force you into making difficult decisions about his care, you could depend on your own strength and counsel, or you could depend on God.

In *My Utmost for His Highest*, Oswald Chambers wrote, "Jesus was saying, 'Do not worry about being of use to others; simply believe on Me.' In other words, pay attention to the Source, and out of you 'will flow the rivers of living water' (John 7:38)."

Similarly, according to the Psalms, "Then those who sing as well as those who play the flutes shall say, 'All my springs of joy are in you'" (87:7 NASB).

God is the Source, the Spring from which comes all our joy. He's not an immovable Fountain either, located at only one place, or accessible at only certain times of the day. He is our Portion and Provision every moment of every day. When we find ourselves carrying our cups back to Him like Oliver Twist in the orphanage, asking shamefacedly, "Please, Sir, can I have some more?" we're forgetting that we serve a generous God who longs to pour out His grace on us. He isn't stingy and doesn't want us thirsty or starving. The more times a day we lift our cups to Him, the more times He will fill them. If that means we're praying every five minutes all day long, then that's what it takes that day to fill up at the Fountain of God.

I know that when I'm running back to the well every few minutes, it's because I'm a needy and leaky person, with holes punched in my heart from stress and busyness. Yet, it's also because I'm pouring out to others and God is willing, even joyful, to replace what I've spilled over into the cups of my husband, my children, my friends, my Bible study girls, my church members, the grocery store cashier, and the girl who cuts my hair.

The frequency of our visits to the well doesn't reveal our weakness or failure. It reveals our dependency on Him.

So when we peer into an empty cup and think we're too dry to walk this Christian life, too empty to share with another, we're forgetting that *it's all about Him*. That's the mistake Moses made. He assumed the ministry depended on himself. Truthfully, though, no ministry we perform in our homes or outside of them is contingent on our ability, brains, beauty, education, character, or godliness (thank goodness!).

Paul and Barnabas showed this at Iconium where they "spent considerable time . . . speaking boldly for the Lord, who confirmed the message of his grace by enabling them to perform signs and wonders" (Acts 14:3). The ministry they performed was only possible because God enabled them to do it. He empowered them, He directed them, He filled them, and He blessed what they gave. He was willing to enable Paul and Barnabas and Moses and us, as well.

There's one person in Scripture who clearly understood this. John the Baptist "confessed freely, 'I am not the Messiah'" and when the priests and Levites asked him exactly who he was, he quoted from the prophet Isaiah, "I am the voice of one calling in the wilderness" (John 1:20, 23).

He was a voice. Jennifer Rothschild notes: "It's like saying, 'an instrument, a guy, a tool, a woman, a mom, a wife, a daughter, a vessel. His response shows that he was not the center of his thought closet—Christ was."

John knew what Moses did not, that salvation, effective ministry, impact, and success all depend on God. In fact, our inability reveals that the "all-surpassing power is from God and not from us" (2 Corinthians 4:7).

Jesus said, "Apart from me you can do nothing" (John 15:5). On the days when we feel like everything is good, we've got everything under control, and our cups are filled to overflowing, it's hard to tell whether we're depending on God or on ourselves—whether it's all about Him or all about *me*. If Moses had been successful in his first attempt to lead the Israelites, he would have missed out on seeing God's miraculous power to free His people.

Moses learned that God is the only Source. He's what fills us up. He's what provides what we need for our own cup and also for the cups of those around us. It's all about Him, and He promises:

"For I am the LORD your God who takes hold of your right hand and says to you, Do not fear; I will help you" (Isaiah 41:13).

Trust and Obey

Moses almost passed on God's offer of ministry to him. He looked at the staff he had in his hand, considered his past and his present, and actually said, "Pardon your servant, Lord. Please send someone else" (Exodus 4:13). He felt ill-equipped for a job so big. He said he had "never been eloquent" and was "slow of speech and tongue" (Exodus 4:10).

When he obeyed, though, taking the staff in his hand and throwing it to the ground as God said, then the miracle happened. As long as Moses gripped that staff, it was of no use to anyone but him in his shepherding tasks. But by obeying God even when it didn't make sense, that simple staff became a tool God would use to deliver a nation, lead them across the Red Sea, and defeat their enemies in battles where they were outnumbered.

You may think others have more gadgets in their utility belts than you do, you may feel like what you have in your hand is unimpressive, you may feel like this season you are in of changing diapers and driving children around town will last forever. But if God is telling you to lay down your staff, asking you to step out in obedience and use the talents and passions He's given you, then take courage and obey Him.

Don't worry about what will happen after that. It's not your responsibility to achieve worldly success or to bring millions of people to Christ. You simply obey and trust God with the results.

Eventually Moses became a powerful leader for the wayward nation and saw God more intimately than almost any other human ever has. But that weakness of his, that tendency to wonder if God could come through against overwhelming odds, that problem with feeling as though success depended on him and not God, caused trouble for him later on.

When the Israelites arrived at Canaan about two years after taking that first step out of Egypt, God told Moses to "send some men to explore the land of Canaan, which I am giving to the Israelites" (Numbers 13:2). Moses's instructions to these twelve spies were a little more hesitant than God's. He said, "Go up through the Negev and on into the hill country. See what the land is like and whether the people who live there are strong or weak, few or many. What kind of land do they live in? Is it good or bad? What kind of towns do they live in? Are they unwalled or fortified?" (Numbers 13:17–19).

Does it seem like Moses is wondering just how possible the conquest of Canaan would be? Sure enough, ten of the twelve spies came back announcing that there was no way they could take that land, no matter what God had promised.

They were insufficient for the task at hand. Their utility belt was ill-equipped for the battle ahead. They weren't enough. The spies thought they should just give up, all except Joshua and Caleb.

You see, unlike Moses, Joshua believed that if God said it, then it would happen. He placed his confidence in God's ability and not in his own. The first time we read about Joshua in Scripture is in Exodus 17:9–10: "Moses said to Joshua, 'Choose some of our men and go out to fight the Amalekites. Tomorrow I will stand on top of the hill with the staff of God in my hands.' So Joshua fought the Amalekites as Moses had ordered."

Notice that Joshua just obeyed. He didn't argue about the task, tell Moses why he was incapable of performing it, or explain why someone else would be better equipped for the job. And any of those responses would have made sense. As far as we can tell, Joshua had no military or leadership training. One day Moses walked up to him and said, "Make an army and defeat the enemy"—all in one day's time. Talk about impossible expectations! Yet Joshua obeyed.

Maybe that's why after the Israelites spent another thirty-eight years in the wilderness, God chose Joshua to lead the people into the Promised Land. God told Joshua what to do and Joshua did it—without arguing or asking God to send somebody else.

God gave Joshua one consistent message when He called him to be the new leader for the nation. Three times in Joshua 1, God says, "Be strong and courageous" and ultimately tells Joshua, "Have I not commanded you? Be strong and courageous. Do not be afraid; do not be discouraged, for the LORD your God will be with you wherever you go" (v. 9).

And Joshua believed God and obeyed Him—no matter how ill-equipped he felt for the task. He focused on God's powerful ability and faithfulness to His promises. He believed that God equips those He calls.

Priscilla Shirer in *One in a Million* writes,

Is there something in your life right now that God has called you to do, but you just don't have the courage to engage in? What do your excuses reveal about yourself and how you feel about God? For each of Moses's excuses, God had a response. It took time, but He assured Moses that human inability could never override God's divine ability to work through him and to accomplish His purposes. How much different, though, to be a person like Joshua who doesn't need coddling and explanations? Look what God can do through someone who receives His instructions not just personally . . . but fearlessly.[1]

If God has given you a child to care for, He will equip you in your ministry to that child. If God has asked you to teach, He will equip you as a teacher. If God has asked you to be a caregiver, He will equip you with strength and compassion. If God has asked you to be a witness for Christ to an unbelieving family, He will equip you with a testimony of grace and give you courage to be a light in a dark place. If He has given you a vision for a ministry far beyond your ability to produce, He will equip you with the skills and ministry partners you need in every situation.

We simply need to trust in a God whose word is always true. If He said it, we can believe it. No, we're not capable enough to be used or sufficient enough for the circumstances we face. But He is. Therefore, we don't need to be afraid or discouraged because "the LORD your God will be with you wherever you go."

"What is that in your hand?" God asks. Really God's plans for us don't depend so much on what we have in our hand as whether or not we're willing to obey Him.

With the burning bush in his sights, Moses discovered that when we stop focusing on our inabilities and trust God with what we have, God will produce the results. Moses threw a stick onto the ground; it became a snake. God will similarly transform the tools He's given you into miraculous sufficiency for what He's called you to do. You just need to obey and trust Him with the rest.

What is that in your hand?

Moses

- What's in your utility belt? Consider your passions, training, experience, personality, and spiritual gifts.

- Do you struggle with wanting the spiritual gifts or talents of others? What's one skill you wish you had?

Make It CONNECT

1. Put yourself in Moses's shoes. You're a wanted murderer who has lived as a shepherd in the wilderness for forty years. How would you respond to God asking you to lead the Israelites out of four hundred years of Egyptian slavery?

2. Skim through Exodus 3 and 4. What were some of Moses's excuses and arguments?

3. Moses might not have felt equipped for such an important job, but what does Acts 7:22 assure us? In

what other ways do you see Moses's past as preparation for God's plan for him?

4. Numbers 12:3 tells us that Moses was "more humble than anyone else on the face of the earth." Why was this a necessary trait for the man who would lead the nation of Israel? How did Moses's failures prepare his heart for service? Has God ever used failure for your ultimate benefit?

5. Read Exodus 3:12–15. Why do you think God responded this way instead of bolstering Moses's ego?

6. When is it easiest to remember that God is our only Source, the one who enables us and equips us: when times are hard or when we're comfortable and at ease? Explain your answer.

7. How was Joshua's response to his call different than Moses's response at the burning bush? Are you more of a Moses or a Joshua?

Make It REAL

- Begin each day this week with a prayer of dedication and submission. Before you even rise out of bed, ask God to guide your day, to fill you up, and to equip you for everything He wants you to do.

- If you tend to argue with God out of a reluctance to obey Him, make a list of your go-to excuses. Pray over them and write NO EXCUSES on a note card that you post on your fridge or bathroom mirror for the week. Commit to living a life of no excuses where God is concerned.

Make It LAST

Memory Verse

For we are God's handiwork,
created in Christ Jesus to do good works,
which God prepared in advance for us to do.

Ephesians 2:10

Journal Prompt

Moses threw a stick on the ground and it became a snake. What "sticks" do you feel God is asking you to yield to Him? What are you afraid might happen if you obey His call? Ask God to use you as He desires and not according to your own plan or design.

What are you
doing here?

Fourteen

Elijah the Runaway

I've been sad recently.

I'm not usually overly emotional. In fact, it's a "point of pride" for me that I'm a detached and ruled-by-my-head kind of person. But for the past few weeks, I've been hit by waves of sadness. It's not like I'm suffering a life crisis or mourning the loss of someone dear. A series of disappointments and personal hurts have made me feel in need of encouragement, love, and some heavenly direction.

I'm doing all the things I think I'm supposed to do to put myself back together. I'm spending time in the Word, I'm ministering to others, I'm exercising and sleeping and eating right. But I'm still sad. That's the bottom line. And it feels silly to be sad. So I tell myself to "snap out of it," but those unreasonable emotions of mine just refuse to listen.

I've tried faking being okay—being cheerful when people ask me how I'm doing. I thought if I could act happier, I'd feel happier. I've tried talking myself out of sadness, quoting Scripture verses and rationally fixing whatever spiritual problem I think I'm facing. But then I have a day when I cry through my Bible study time, bawl during exercise (not the most effective way to work out), hold back tears when I pick up my kids from school, and cry into my husband's shoulder as he prays for me at night.

I've criticized myself for crying, sermonized to myself about my disappointments, and pep-talked my soul until hoarse.

I'm still sad.

And so, I've begun to ask myself and even God, "What am I doing here in this place?" I don't mean a physical place, a geographical location I can pinpoint with coordinates. What am I doing in this place of sadness? How did I get here? How can I get out of here?

That's what God asked the prophet Elijah. He met Elijah on a mountaintop when the prophet felt so depressed he wanted to die, and God asked him, "What are you doing here, Elijah?" (1 Kings 19:9).

Elijah was fresh from victory. He was a prophet of God at a time of spiritual degradation in Israel's history. King Ahab "did more evil in the eyes of the LORD than any of those before him" (1 Kings 16:30). Not only was the king himself evil, "but he also married Jezebel daughter of Ethbaal king of the Sidonians, and began to serve Baal and worship him" (v. 31).

It was a tough time to be a prophet of God with Ahab and Jezebel ruling. They relentlessly pursued Elijah and threatened him. Other prophets had to be hidden in the hills and were brought food and water so they could survive this wicked reign.

Elijah finally took a stand and engaged in the ultimate match of power, pitting the one true God against the idol Baal. In 1 Kings 18, Elijah challenged the 450 prophets of Baal and the 400 prophets of Asherah not just to a test of their gods' power, but also of their gods' ability to hear them. He declared, "Get two bulls for us. Let Baal's prophets choose one for themselves, and let them cut it into pieces and put it on the wood but not set fire to it. I will prepare the other bull and put it on the wood but not set fire to it. Then you call on the name of your god, and I will call on the name of the LORD. The god who answers by fire—he is God" (1 Kings 18:23–24). And so the prophets of Baal danced and shouted.

At noon Elijah began to taunt them. "Shout louder!" he said. "Surely he is a god! Perhaps he is deep in thought, or busy, or traveling. Maybe he is sleeping and must be awakened." So they shouted louder and slashed themselves with swords and spears, as was their custom, until their blood flowed. Midday passed, and they continued their frantic prophesying until the time for the evening sacrifice. But there was no response, no one answered, no one paid attention. (1 Kings 18:27–29)

Their god was silent. Their god was deaf. Their god was unimpressed by their passion and unresponsive to their cries.

Not our God.

Elijah sloshed water all over his altar and soaking wet sacrifice so that it was running down and gathering in a trench around the altar. He prayed,

"Answer me, LORD, answer me, so these people will know that you, LORD, are God, and that you are turning their hearts back again." Then the fire of the LORD fell and burned up the sacrifice, the wood, the stones and the soil, and also licked up the water in the trench. When all the people saw this, they fell prostrate and cried, "The LORD— he is God! The LORD—he is God!" (1 Kings 18:37–39)

He had the false prophets slaughtered there at the site of their defeat. That same day, Elijah prophesied rain would fall despite a years-long drought and a cloudless sky. And it poured. He tossed the edge of his cloak over his belt and outran the king's chariot to Jezreel.

I'd say he was having a good day as far as prophets go. It was a spiritual high for sure, brought on by the ultimate ministry success.

Yet in the very next chapter, Jezebel threatened Elijah's life and he ran far into the wilderness and hid himself away, wishing God would just end his life. He felt ineffective: "I am no better than my ancestors." He felt alone: "I am the only one left." He felt afraid: "Now they are trying to kill me too" (1 Kings 19:4, 14).

There in the midst of Elijah's sadness and fear, the Lord ministered to his needs and asked him a question: "What are you doing here, Elijah?" (v. 9).

When we allow God to ask us that question in our times of sadness, despair, depression, and fear, then He can rescue us, administering healing and restoring us to the places of faith and service we have abandoned. God "heals the brokenhearted and binds up their wounds" (Psalm 147:3).

Let me speak truth to your heart, my friend. If your depression is long-term, life-threatening, overwhelming, and more than just a spiritual low, please seek the professional help of a Christian counselor, psychiatrist, or psychologist who can help you work through this with every tool available.

So, what was Elijah doing there? Some of the same things still cause us to run into dark caves of sadness even now.

1. He experienced the depression that often follows spiritual success.
2. He was under attack and ran in fear.
3. He abandoned his support system and tried to go it alone.
4. He let his emotions cloud the truth and allowed self-pity to convince him of lies.

Depression after Spiritual Success

Oftentimes it's the moments following victory when we are the most vulnerable to attack and the most apt to feel discouragement, depression, and despair. Maybe we wonder if we'll ever attain that level of success again. Maybe we start expecting that every moment needs to be a spiritual high. Maybe we're just tired from activity or fighting against attacks and we collapse from fatigue. Maybe once we've completed a project, we flounder without having something new to occupy our attention and time.

Whatever the cause, it's a fact of ministry that the moments immediately following a ministry high can be treacherous. Elijah wasn't the only servant of God to feel like giving up.

After leading the Israelites to Sinai, receiving the Ten Commandments from God, and breaking camp after about a year to continue on to the Promised Land, Moses complained to God: "If this is how you are going to treat me, please go ahead and kill me— if I have found favor in your eyes—and do not let me face my own ruin" (Numbers 11:15).

Jonah preached to a pagan nation and incited them to a full national revival. Even the king of Nineveh donned sackcloth and ashes and proclaimed a fast of repentance. It was the greatest evangelistic accomplishment of Jonah's time. He responded by slumping down outside the city and declaring, "Now, LORD, take away my life, for it is better for me to die than to live" (Jonah 4:3).

Paul, in the midst of his ministry to Asia, states that he was "under great pressure, far beyond our ability to endure, so that we despaired of life itself" (2 Corinthians 1:8).

If you're completing a project or ending a ministry, plan for ways to avoid this post-completion despair. Plan a time of rest or retreat. Put something new on your calendar to look forward to— this helps maintain excitement and hope. Ask for prayer support from friends. Put these safeguards into place now, while your efforts are underway, so that you can avoid the season of post-activity depression or at least alleviate it.

Fear of Attack

The Bible tells us, "Elijah was afraid and ran for his life" (1 Kings 19:3). I probably would have run to the wilderness too. An evil, godless queen, known for murdering prophets, said she was going to kill him. Elijah had good reasons to be afraid.

Yet Scripture promises us: "When I am afraid, I put my trust in you. In God, whose word I praise—in God I trust and am not afraid. What can mere mortals do to me?" (Psalm 56:3–4).

Jezebel may have been a mere mortal, but she was a pretty mean and powerful mortal at that. When God asked, "What are you doing here, Elijah?" the prophet could have cried, "Have you not heard Jezebel threaten my life? She may be a more mortal, but she can do a lot to me! She can torture me, banish me, starve me, kill me." Elijah was in that wilderness because he was afraid of attack.

So often in life it seems like our future or success or even relief is in the hands of a mortal. Maybe a boss has to decide whether you receive the promotion or not. Maybe a judge determines who receives custody of your kids in the divorce settlement. Maybe a banker sitting at her desk decides if you get the mortgage.

It seems like people are always controlling our future and making powerful decisions for our good or for our harm. What Elijah forgot in the moment that he fled, though, was that God truly is in control of all things. He directs the hearts and minds of kings and presidents and all those in authority over us. Proverbs 21:1 tells us, "In the LORD's hand the king's heart is a stream of water that he channels toward all who please him."

At the end of the Israelites' long captivity in Babylon, a new ruler came to power, Cyrus the Great, who assumed the Persian throne in 559 BC. He organized the Persians into a powerful army and began conquering the lands around him, eventually taking the capital of Babylon and assuming control of the Babylonian empire.

In 539 BC, he gave the Jews permission to return home and to rebuild the temple. More than that, he restored to them the articles of worship that Nebuchadnezzar had removed from their temple and carried off to Babylon.[1]

Ezra served as the high priest who oversaw the rebuilding of the temple in the Jewish homeland during Cyrus's reign. He wrote:

> In the first year of Cyrus king of Persia, in order to fulfill the word of the LORD spoken by Jeremiah, the LORD moved the heart of Cyrus king of Persia to make a proclamation throughout his realm and also to put it in writing: "This is what Cyrus king of Persia says: 'The LORD, the God of heaven, has given me all the kingdoms of the earth and he has appointed me to build a temple for him at Jerusalem in Judah.'" (Ezra 1:1–2)

"The Lord moved the heart of Cyrus," it says. This pagan king, who did not worship Yahweh, declared that "The LORD . . . has appointed me to build a temple." Even pagan kings are anointed and led by the one true God. They are not outside of His control or apart from His will.

Here's the amazing thing. I hope you are ready for this because God is awesome. About 150 years before Cyrus ruled over the Medo-Persian empire, long before he was even born, the prophet Isaiah wrote these inspired prophetic words:

> who says of Cyrus, "He is my shepherd
>   and will accomplish all that I please;
> he will say of Jerusalem, 'Let it be rebuilt,'
>   and of the temple, 'Let its foundations be laid.'" (Isaiah 44:28)

God declared that Cyrus was his "shepherd" and in Isaiah 45, God further calls Cyrus "his anointed" (v. 1). This is all before

Cyrus's parents ever held him in their arms or picked out his name. God had already declared it.

Elijah forgot that the hearts of kings and queens, even those who don't acknowledge God's sovereignty, are in God's hands. Indeed, what can mortal man do to me? Nothing without God's permission or protection on our behalf.

That doesn't mean things always go our way or that we'll never be attacked or face hardship. The Bible never promises us that. Instead, Jesus honestly told His followers, "I have told you these things, so that in me you may have peace. In this world you will have trouble. But take heart! I have overcome the world" (John 16:33).

Elijah had options. He could have stopped serving as a prophet of God, hidden in the caves with the other prophets, or even more extreme, converted to following Baal, and Jezebel wouldn't have threatened to kill him. We could take the easy way out sometimes, too, and maybe avoid Satan's attacks as he tries to thwart God's plans for us. And sometimes, let's be honest, the easy way out sounds pretty good.

Facing the attack of the enemy is frightening. In my own strength, I know I can't stand up under it. That's why when God calls us forward, we should truly count the cost. Let me tell you, though, it's worth it. Even a costly journey is worth it for the sake of following Christ and obeying His call.

In January of this year, I felt the heavy nudging of the Holy Spirit asking me two questions, one of which was, "Are you ready for where I want to take you next?" The God who loved me passionately was asking me to walk in worship and obedience—holy fear in response to abundant grace.

"That depends," I answered. "Where are we going? How long will it take? What is the expense-to-benefit ratio?" It sounds mercenary, but those are the questions that rumbled around in my head and heart for weeks. Was it safer to stay where I was? Was safer necessarily better?

Have you ever responded to God's call with fear instead of excitement?

It seems so easy when we belt out "I surrender all" in a church service. Then God takes you up on your offer and asks you to surrender your plans for the future, your comfort, your lifestyle, and you wonder how much "all" actually is.

Count the cost and prepare for the attack in advance. Immerse yourself in the Word of God, storing up God's promises to bolster your faith in the days ahead. Gather prayer warriors who will lift you up with their prayers consistently. Then go where God has called you, knowing that He will be with you in the battle and will carry you through to the blessing.

Traveling Solo

On Tuesday nights, I sit at a table with other women, Bibles open. We ask—What's going on in your life? What does the Bible say? Where are you headed? Where have you been? What do you need? How can I pray for you? In my small group, we encourage and challenge one another, grow in faith, show grace, and run after truth. The women that sit with me at that table are my traveling companions.

And this is what we need: community—strength from relationships. Elijah, sitting in that cave filled with dark despair, learned firsthand what happens when you travel solo. When he heard that Jezebel threatened to kill him, he took off running for his life. "When he came to Beersheba in Judah, *he left his servant there*, while he himself went a day's journey into the wilderness" (1 Kings 19:3–4, emphasis added).

Elijah's mistake was traveling alone. He ran to Beersheba— the southernmost portion of the land—left his servant, and ran for another whole day by himself.[2] Alone. No companion to speak truth into his heart. No friend to share his burden and pray with him and point him back to God. No accountability. No encouragement. No truth-speaking. No love.

Others have discovered this powerful truth about community. Just how far would Naomi have made it in her travels if Ruth hadn't insisted on packing a bag for the journey too? Naomi—a hurt woman, weighed by age and life, far from her homeland, had changed her name to Mara, meaning "Bitterness." She trekked back as a childless widow to her people, her nation, and her God.

Without Ruth, Naomi probably would have been buried along the pathway, lost and alone. With Ruth came strength, companionship, blessing. A new home. Food from Ruth's work gleaning in the fields. Redemption by the kinsman-redeemer Boaz through Ruth's marriage. A place in the lineage of King David and Jesus through Ruth and Boaz's son. The blessings accompanied tenacious friendship, shared pain and faith, and the self-sacrifice of one friend for another.

The apostle Paul knew the strength that a good traveling buddy brings. Paul sat with Silas, singing praises in the prison in the night. Paul traveled with Barnabas the Encourager in ministry to the Gentiles. Paul mentored Timothy, building a church and the leadership it needed.

Then there's Titus. In 2 Corinthians 7:5–6, Paul wrote to the church, "For when we came into Macedonia, we had no rest, but we were harassed at every turn—conflicts on the outside, fears within. But God, who comforts the downcast, comforted us by the coming of Titus."

Paul was the apostle who told us all things work for the good, to rejoice always and again rejoice, to be content in all circumstances, and that God can supply all our needs and do abundantly and immeasurably more than our wildest dreams.

Still, Paul was frightened at times too. Just like you and me, he had his moments. God didn't punish Paul for lack of faith or chastise his weakness. Instead, God provided for a need. Paul needed a traveling companion to bring comfort and encouragement in dark days. Titus was God's answer to Paul's fear.

Paul knew this. He usually traveled in partnership. He had written, "Carry each other's burdens, and in this way you will fulfill the law of Christ . . . for each one should carry their own load" (Galatians 6:2, 5).

It seems contradictory at first. Carry each other's burdens. Each one carry their own load. But there's a difference here. Paul says each one of us should do our own daily load of life, the everyday things we can handle. Do it yourself. Don't lay your everyday stuff over the back of someone else and kick back and relax while he or she struggles.

Burdens, though, are meant to be borne in partnership. In community with each other, we lift onto four shoulders what is too heavy for just two. If you don't have a support group, a Sunday school class, a small group, a Bible study, or prayer and accountability partners, please seek them out. They are God-given gifts in a time of sadness and depression. Without them, we so quickly fall into the same sadness and depression that Elijah experienced on that mountain. When God asked Elijah, "What are you doing here?" he could have answered, "I tried to travel alone."

Listening to Emotional Lies

Elijah's actual answer to God's question, "What are you doing here?" was pretty straightforward: "I have been very zealous for the LORD God Almighty. The Israelites have rejected your covenant, torn down your altars, and put your prophets to death with the sword. I am the only one left, and now they are trying to kill me too" (1 Kings 19:10).

Sounds like something I've said to God before. "I'm doing all these great things for you, God, trying to do what is right and obeying your Word. Everybody else is messing up and doing the wrong thing. In fact, I'm the *only* one and I'm going down because you don't have my back. Where's my blessing for making all these sacrifices and standing up for you? It seems pretty unfair that other people are blessed and not obeying, and I'm facing attack because I'm obeying. I can't do this anymore."

It's self-pity. It's the danger of comparing our circumstances with the lives of others. It's the trap of believing that life should be "fair" and whining when it isn't.

Elijah was so overcome by these emotions that he started exaggerating the situation. Not that it wasn't bad. Jezebel was out to get him; that much was true. She had killed other prophets; that was true also. But, "I am the only one left"? Well, that was going a bit far. Elijah let his emotions filter his reality and had dug himself deep into hopelessness.

King David also had moments of feeling overcome by his circumstances. He saw his enemies living well while he was hunted and on the run for his life. It seemed unfair. It seemed unending. It seemed beyond hope.

In Psalm 42:5, he asked a question of his own soul that is very much like God's question for Elijah. He said, "Why, my soul, are you downcast? Why so disturbed within me?" David's answer reminds us of how to respond in the dark places: "Put your hope in God, for I will yet praise him, my Savior and my God. My soul is downcast within me; therefore I will remember you" (vv. 5–6).

David said:

- "Put your hope in God." Cling to hope even when things seem hopeless.
- "I will yet praise Him." Even in sorrow, bring praises to God and believe that you will still have reasons to praise in the days to come.

- "I will remember you." Remember what God has already done. Look at how He has delivered you in the past and trust in His faithful love and His ability to deliver you again.

Elijah allowed his emotions to get the best of him. He had lost hope, felt he was better off dead, and believed he was the only believer left. Fortunately for Elijah, God didn't let him linger any longer in the realm of self-pity.

Fifteen

Coming Down the Mountain

God didn't abandon Elijah in the wilderness or on that mountain of despair, nor will He abandon you in a season of sadness and leave you without hope for a future. God asked Elijah, "What are you doing here?" and hearing the prophet's answer, God ministered to this defeated servant. He didn't lecture or give a divine pep-talk meant to be a spiritual insta-fix for all that ailed Elijah. Instead God:

1. Took care of Elijah's physical needs.
2. Revealed His presence in the small stuff.
3. Renewed Elijah's direction and vision.
4. Spoke truth.
5. Gave him a friend.

Took Care of Physical Needs

Scripture tells us that the first thing God did for the prophet was to give him food, water, and rest.

> [Elijah] looked around, and there by his head was some bread baked over hot coals, and a jar of water. He ate and drank and then lay down again. The angel of the LORD came back a second time and touched him and said, "Get up and eat, for the journey is too much for you." So he got up and ate and drank. Strengthened by that food, he traveled forty days and forty nights until he reached Horeb, the mountain of God. There he went into a cave and spent the night. (1 Kings 19:6–9)

With supernatural rest and miraculous sustenance, Elijah was strengthened enough to make the forty-day journey to the mountain of God.

When you're struggling with sadness, make sure you're taking care of yourself physically. It's easy to be so down that even basics like eating well and sleeping are hard to do. Make the effort. Ask others to hold you accountable. God created us as beings with a spirit, soul, and body. Neglecting the body ultimately damages our spirit and our emotions. Eat healthy, exercise, drink lots of water, and follow a regular sleeping pattern with eight hours of sleep each night. This is the physical ministry that God provided for Elijah that strengthened him for the spiritual and emotional healing yet to come.

Revealed His Presence in the Small Stuff

After such amazing victories against the prophets of Baal, Elijah may have forgotten how to find God in the small things, too.

He didn't remember that God has a plan for our daily lives and that He's present and active in all we do. In one of the most famous passages in Scripture, God revealed himself to Elijah not in a powerful wind, earthquake, or fire, but in a "gentle whisper" (see 1 Kings 19:11–13).

Sometimes we look for God in the amazing, awesome, miraculous moments and we miss the still, small voice that God uses to speak to us throughout our everyday experiences. Washing the dishes, taxiing our kids around town, filing papers, commuting, none of this is beyond God's touch. Zechariah 4:10 says, "Who dares despise the day of small things." In the days ahead, give thanks to God for the small things and learn to see Him in the life you live every day rather than seeking out glorious experiences.

Elijah knew this, but he forgot. When he predicted rain and he stood on the mountain watching for the impending storm, the sky was totally clear. After his servant checked the sky seven times, finally Elijah heard: "A cloud as small as a man's hand is rising from the sea" (1 Kings 18:44). A miniscule cloud was enough for him. He sped back to Jezreel to beat the storm to town. He knew that even great storms begin small. Great blessings begin tiny and great moments with God can happen at your kitchen table.

Renewed Elijah's Direction and Vision

Elijah felt like he was finished. He didn't see a future for himself and thought it'd be much better if God just let him die because he was tired of fighting.

God, on the other hand, still had plans for Elijah. What Elijah needed was renewed vision and a reminder that there was still more to do. God told Elijah to go back where he came from and anoint two new kings and Elisha to succeed him as prophet. He gave Elijah specific directions and clear vision.

If you feel stuck, pray that God will give you a new vision and direction for the next step. Elisabeth Elliott once said, "Just do the next thing." You don't need a complete blueprint of your entire future, but you do need God to show you the next thing. That's what he did for Elijah; He gave him a reason to come down from the mountain and to get busy doing God's work.

Spoke Truth

God spoke truth when Elijah believed lies. The prophet told God, "I am the only one left." God responded, "I reserve seven thousand in Israel—all whose knees have not bowed down to Baal and whose mouths have not kissed him" (1 Kings 19:18). Ouch. Truth hurts sometimes. But it also sets us free from the lies the Enemy uses to ensnare us. As long as Elijah believed the lie, even if it made him feel more important, he would remain trapped in depression. God spoke truth when He essentially said, "You are not alone."

God speaks truth to our hearts, too, and sometimes that truth calls us to account for our behaviors. Sometimes His Word steps on our toes and makes us change our attitudes and choices. Sometimes that truth means we have to stop feeling sorry for ourselves. Sometimes that truth gives us hope, the assurance that we are not alone even when we feel lonely, and the promise that God will not abandon us to any trial.

In John 17:17, Jesus prayed for His disciples, asking that God would "Sanctify them by the truth; your word is truth." Seek out God's truth in every situation, allowing the Bible to combat distorted thinking and ultimately set you free (John 8:32). Ask Him to reveal any false beliefs or assumptions that have led you to despair.

Gave Him a Friend

The next thing God did after sending Elijah out of the cave was give him a friend. "So Elijah went from there and found Elisha son of Shaphat . . . Elijah went up to him and threw his cloak around him." Then Elisha "set out to follow Elijah and became his servant" (1 Kings 19:19–21).

Elijah needed Elisha as his partner, friend, servant, and apprentice. In the same way, if we want to move past seasons of sadness, we need the prayer support and encouragement of Christian friends.

That's the way God designed us—to travel together just like Ruth with Naomi; Paul with Titus, Silas, Barnabas, and Timothy; Elijah with Elisha. We journey to Christlikeness and to abundant life, shifting burdens onto backs along the way and laying them down at the cross together. Alone we will not make it. Together we journey past obstacles, depression, fear, and discouragement, to our hoped-for destination. That's the lesson for Elijah as he sat in sadness. What was he doing in that place? He was traveling solo when he should have been bolstered by the encouragement and ministry of a devoted friend.

When we stray from the group, when we go off on our own and try to live faith solo, we are easy prey for attack. The Israelites learned this on their journey out of Egypt: "Remember what the Amalekites did to you along the way when you came out of Egypt. When you were weary and worn out, they met you on your journey and attacked all who were lagging behind; they had no fear of God" (Deuteronomy 25:17–18).

If your heart is weary and in need of some encouragement today, look to your right and your left for your group. Be sure that you are connected and not lagging behind. The Enemy targets stragglers and solo travelers just as the Amalekites took down Israelites trailing behind the rest of the group. Perhaps your first step needs to be searching for a Christian community that will walk alongside you and encourage you along your faith journey. Christians were designed to live in fellowship and accountability with one another.

What Are We Doing Here?

Even as I write at my kitchen table, I'm praying for those of you who, like Elijah, are in a season of sadness. Not long ago, my kindergartner came home from school talking about something she learned in class. She was excited to learn that there won't be crying in heaven.

I'm excited about not crying in heaven, too! In heaven, we won't be broken people any more. We're promised that in glory, "God will wipe away every tear from their eyes; there shall be no more death, nor sorrow, nor crying. There shall be no more pain, for the former things have passed away" (Revelation 21:4 NKJV).

As exciting as that is, it's not our present reality. In this time and place, sometimes we're broken and it's okay to come to God with sorrow. You don't need to force cheerfulness with Him or hide away the depths of your heart that are being dredged by difficult circumstances. You don't have to pretend to be perfect, always kind, or above sins like jealousy or pride. God is a safe place to go when you're overwhelmed and sorrowful. You can come to Him now, just the way you are, not after you've cleaned yourself up and reapplied your makeup following a good, long cry.

God values your emotions and cares about your tears. David, who certainly knew how to come to God with transparent emotion, wrote, "You number my wanderings; put my tears into Your bottle; are they not in Your book?" (Psalm 56:8 NKJV). David also wrote, "My sacrifice, O God, is a broken spirit; a broken and contrite heart you, God, will not despise" (Psalm 51:17).

Be comforted that God is not tapping His foot impatiently and eyeing His wristwatch with annoyance. He's not giving you a list of the ten things you need to fix to make all this go away. He's not mocking you and laughing at your feelings or scoffing at what you consider worthy of a good cry. Instead the Bible tells us, "He heals the brokenhearted and binds up their wounds" (Psalm 147:3).

It's okay to bring tissues to your quiet time and simply cry out to God with honest sorrow. Don't try to fake your way to happiness, but instead let Him comfort you, just as He did for Elijah. He asked Elijah, "What are you doing here?" and He asks you the same question. What has brought you to this place of sadness? He searches your heart for the hurts and sorrows that resulted in despair and He ministers to your practical and spiritual needs. He speaks truth when we see lies and surrounds us with a support system of fellow believers. He casts a new vision for our future and reveals His presence in the circumstances you face every day.

His ministry to Elijah on Mount Horeb was because He loved that bold prophet who had exhausted himself in service and temporarily lost hope. And He loves you, too—not the lipstick-on, mascara-perfect, happy face you—but the real deep-down you that sometimes needs to cry at His feet.

What are you doing here?

Elijah

Make It PERSONAL

- Have you experienced a season of sadness? When? Can you look back and identify a cause or a solution?

- Do you have a personal experience with depression or anxiety that you can share with others as an encouragement to them?

Make It CONNECT

1. Elijah, Moses, Jonah, and Paul experienced similar letdowns after a season of success. Why do you think this happens?

2. Ahab and Jezebel made life difficult for God's faithful. What human seems to hold power over an area of your life (e.g., boss, parent, spouse, judge, church leader)? Ezra 1:1–2 tells us that the prophecy in Isaiah 44 was fulfilled because God moved in the heart of

a king. In what way can this give you hope in your situation?

3. Who is included in your community of faith?

4. Why is abandoning relationships so tempting and so dangerous when we're struggling with depression, fear, anxiety, and sadness?

5. God tended to Elijah's physical needs first, giving him food, water, and rest (1 Kings 19:6–9). How good are you at taking care of your physical health and well-being, especially during difficult times?

6. God ministered to Elijah in the following ways. Which of them do you need God to do in your life right now? Is there anything you need to do to make this happen?

   a. Took care of Elijah's physical needs.

   b. Revealed His presence in the small stuff.

   c. Renewed Elijah's direction and vision.

   d. Spoke truth.

   e. Gave him a friend.

7. Elijah believed that He was the only prophet of God left. God combatted this lie with truth in 1 Kings 19:18.

Are you holding on to false truths and lies that leave you discouraged and afraid? Write down one of the lies that chips away at your faith and ask God to replace it with truth.

Make It REAL

- Elijah had to learn to see God in everyday experiences, not just the miraculous and amazing moments of victory. Keep your eyes open this week for God's presence in the small things, as you wash dishes, do your job, run errands, hug your children, etc.

- God gave Elijah a friend and ministry companion in Elisha. Reach out to someone this week to begin building that kind of friendship. Seek out a prayer partner or a mentor, or meet up with a friend for coffee or tea.

Make It LAST

Memory Verse

Carry each other's burdens,
and in this way you will fulfill the law of Christ.

Galatians 6:2

Journal Prompt

If God asked you, "What are you doing here?" what would your answer be? Tell God what it's like to be where you are right now in your ministry and faith. Are you excited,

at a high point, and experiencing victory? Or are you struggling with discouragement, failure, and loneliness? Do you
feel like you can't hear God? Describe what it's like to be
in that place and ask God to direct your steps.

How many loaves
do you have?

Sixteen

Lessons from a Lunch

I do it all the time. I pray for things but I don't expect God to answer. Or I'll pray for something and instead of waiting for His answer, I'll brainstorm practical ways to fill that need on my own. By the time the provision comes, I don't need the gift anymore. I've missed out on the miracle and paid too much in the process.

Recently I was on the lookout for bunk beds, the one thing we needed to prepare for foster care. For a few months, every time I drove past the thrift store, I would scan the lot of furniture outside for new bunk bed arrivals. I joined online "yard sale" groups and spent my Saturday mornings shopping in other people's yards in search of what I needed. And I prayed, of course.

So when a set of bunk beds showed up for under a hundred dollars on one of my sources, I bought them that day. The lady dropped them off in her big farm truck and I unloaded faded wooden bunk beds with messages written on them in marker. I thought, "No big deal. They're cheap. I'll paint over them and they'll be fine for what I need."

Then the mattresses came off the truck and let me just say, those things *smelled*! Being outside didn't help them one bit. Neither did all the Febreze spray I had in the house. My husband came home and declared they were not allowed inside and relegated them to the garage until we could haul them to the dump. He wouldn't even put them in our minivan. Better to borrow a truck from someone so the inside of our vehicle wouldn't permanently smell like potty training.

Well, I was disappointed but determined to make the best of it. A little paint. Buy a set of mattresses. It'd all be okay. I guess it was enough.

Then I saw a message the next day from a friend about her daughter no longer wanting the bunk beds in her room. I asked her, would she give them away to me, mattresses and all? Yup, she sure would.

To recap, I bought second-best bunk beds and stinky mattresses from a nice stranger when a friend was willing to give me her nicer bunk beds and unsmelly mattresses for free.

I was so mad at myself, so disappointed with my impatient lack of faith! I had prayed and then quickly set to work finding the solution to my need. Yet, sometimes God asks us to wait for His provision. He may have something better in mind for us that we can't even envision for ourselves, and I needed to reorient my thinking to expect God to meet my need.

Even the disciples struggled with changing the way they thought. Jesus had called them to come follow Him and they'd left fishing nets and tax books to do so. In a brief time, they saw Him teach crowds, heal paralytics and the demon-possessed, calm a violent storm on the sea with the sound of His voice, and even raise a young man back to life as his dead body was being carried to the burial site.

The disciples had front-row seats to the greatest miracle working imaginable. It must have been thrilling! Yet when Jesus pointed to a crowd of hungry people and told the disciples to feed them, they panicked. They searched the crowd for food, any food. Andrew found one little boy whose mom had the foresight to pack him a lunch. (I bet she made him wear clean underwear and sent him with pocket change, too. Just in case.) Still, what the disciples had wasn't enough.

Jesus asked his twelve men, "How many loaves do you have?" It's a question that seems specific to their situation. Does it have any meaning for us?

It does if you've ever felt insufficient. You see, the disciples weren't looking with eyes of faith. They saw only the physical reality of their circumstances. Thousands of people. One tiny lunch. The math was clear. It was insufficient.

How often do we add up our personal resources, our time, money, maybe gifts, maybe patience or energy, and feel we come up short? We've left out the faith factor. We've left out belief in a God who is great at miraculous multiplication. The disciples needed to stretch in some key areas of their faith and sometimes so do we. We need to know the right answer to Jesus' question. When He asks us, "How many loaves do you have?" we should answer "Enough, Lord. In you, I know I will have enough."

Believe He Can Do the Impossible

Circumstances lie. At the very least, they don't tell the whole truth.

The disciples scanned their physical reality and all the truths their circumstances were shouting at them.

- A crowd of five thousand hungry men plus women and children.
- No nearby places to eat.
- No food to give them.

Being practical men and in some cases perhaps successful business men, they developed a plan of attack: Convince Jesus to stop ministering to the crowd so the people could go home and eat (Mark 6:35–36). Has this ever worked for a pastor? Usually it's ineffective to say, "Preach shorter sermons so we can beat the other churches to Wendy's!" It didn't work with Jesus either.

Jesus asked Philip, "Where shall we buy bread for these people to eat?" (John 6:5). And Philip, overwhelmed by the request, did some quick calculations and exclaimed, "It would take more than half a year's wages to buy enough bread for each one to have a bite" (v. 7). That's some elaborate math. Add up all the money a person makes in an entire year, divide that in half. Then add up the number of people in the crowd and the cost of one bite of food for each person.

The mind spins. At least, my math-challenged mind does. I may not know how the calculations worked on paper, but I get the message. Jesus did, too. Philip was saying, "That's impossible."

Philip does what many of us do. He shortchanged God. If Jesus hadn't pressed the issue, Philip may have thrown his hands up and walked away from a situation that seemed impossible. He could have determined, "There's nothing I can do here. I don't have enough to be helpful, so I'll do nothing; I'll give nothing."

Now, it may just be me, but I imagine Jesus grinning a little as He asked Philip how they could feed the crowd. He was asking a difficult question like a professor would of a treasured pupil. He asked and stood back from the chalkboard while the disciple thought through the problem. The Bible specifically tells us that Jesus "asked this only to test him, for he already had in mind what he was going to do" (v. 6). Jesus was pushing the disciple gently into faith. Even after witnessing miracle after amazing miracle, Philip still needed to be reminded that Jesus wasn't confined by what was possible.

This reminds me of the woman at the well in John 4:1–26. There is something about this Samaritan woman's conversation with Jesus that captures my heart and is reminiscent of the disciples' struggle to see past physical circumstances. The Samaritan woman is just so practical.

Jesus said to her, "If you knew the gift of God and who it is that asks you for a drink, you would have asked him and he would have given you living water" (v. 10). This precious woman looked up at Jesus and said, "You have nothing to draw with and the well is deep. Where can you get this living water?" (v. 11). To rephrase: "Mister, I don't know how you think you could give me any 'living water'—you don't even have a bucket!"

That's what Philip was doing to Jesus and it's what I've done to God many times. He's offered to give me provision, healing, comfort, direction, and peace and I've turned to Him and said, "God, what you offer sounds so great, but it's impossible. You don't even have a bucket!"

Oswald Chambers in *My Utmost for His Highest* wrote, "My misgivings arise from the fact that I search within to find how He will do what He says." We think God is confined to what we have to offer and what we are capable of doing in this practical, physical reality of ours. We forget that God is bigger than that. He is almighty and we hinder His ministry and restrict His glory when we treat Him as unable and incapable of doing all things.

There's nothing that God can't handle, but we certainly reach the limits of our abilities often enough. We say all the time as Christians, "God won't give you more than you can handle." Do you know that isn't in Scripture? It's a misquote of 1 Corinthians 10:13: "And God is faithful; he will not let you be tempted beyond what you can bear. But when you are tempted, he will also provide a way out so that you can endure it."

I think God gives us more than we can handle all the time. I know He does for me! Whether it's a big life crisis or just my kids fighting for the twentieth time in one morning, it's too much for me. I can calculate a year's wages and see if it can feed a crowd. I can look around the well for a bucket so I can receive living water. I can focus on the possibilities of my situation. If I do that, though, I'll always come to the same conclusion: It's impossible.

David wrote, "And so, Lord, where do I put my hope? My only hope is in you" (Psalm 39:7 NLT). Don't place your hope in what you have or who you are. Don't look at your circumstances and discount God's ability to care for you in the midst of them. He is God. He doesn't need a bakery to feed a crowd. He doesn't need a bucket to give you living water. Jesus would eventually explain to the disciples, "With man this is impossible, but with God all things are possible" (Matthew 19:26). And on that, we stake our belief.

The book of 2 Chronicles is one of my favorites in the Bible. There is a clear, unmistakable trend in this book. Almost every one of Judah's kings had a life-defining moment when the nation was surrounded by a massive army that was better-equipped and more experienced than they were.

Every time a king fought the enemy in his own strength, either by amassing a defensive force or by making treaties with other nations, he was defeated. Yet when a king turned to God and prayed for His intervention and help, he was miraculously saved. Sometimes the enemy troops would become confused and fight amongst themselves or they would simply run away in terror without ever engaging in battle.

One of my favorite examples is from 2 Chronicles 20. Like many other kings, King Jehoshaphat faced a vast enemy army. The

Bible tells us, "Alarmed, Jehoshaphat resolved to inquire of the LORD, and he proclaimed a fast for all Judah" (v. 3).

He was alarmed. He was emotionally distraught about this seemingly impossible situation. All the circumstances told him that he was about to be defeated and his people slaughtered on the battlefield.

So Jehoshaphat turned his fear of certain defeat over to God. The whole nation fasted, and he prayed with them publicly. In his prayer, he said, "For we have no power to face this vast army that is attacking us. We do not know what to do, but our eyes are on you" (v. 12).

In so many life situations we have no idea what to do. We've worked everything out on paper and still come out short. We've done the mental calculations like Philip and determined that what Jesus is asking is impossible. There is just no physical, tangible way for us to defeat the enemy we are facing.

Instead of struggling to develop effective battle plans or success-ful strategy in this war, Jehoshaphat took his insufficiency straight to God. He told the Lord, "We can't do this. We aren't sufficient. So we're looking to you instead."

That's what Jesus was trying to teach the disciples to do. It's in these moments when we've exhausted all of our own resources and we don't have any other hope that we need to look to God, "fixing our eyes on Jesus, the pioneer and perfecter of faith" (Hebrews 12:2).

God answered Jehoshaphat's prayer, saying, "Do not be afraid or discouraged because of this vast army. For the battle is not yours, but God's" (2 Chronicles 20:15). The next morning, instead of send-ing out his best troops against the enemy, Jehoshaphat "appointed men to sing to the LORD and to praise him for the splendor of his holiness" (v. 21). The Bible says, "As they began to sing and praise, the LORD set ambushes against the men . . . who were invad-ing Judah, and they were defeated" (v. 22). The enemy was totally annihilated without Jehoshaphat's army raising a spear. All they had done was worship God.

Scripture tells us they named that battle site the Valley of Berakah or the Valley of Praise. Ultimately, "the fear of God came on all the surrounding kingdoms when they heard how the LORD had fought against the enemies of Israel. And the kingdom of Jehoshaphat was at peace, for his God had given him rest on every side" (vv. 29–30).

Are you in a valley, surrounded by circumstances that will most certainly defeat you? Are you staring at a crowd full of need and holding only a lunch in your hands? Resolve to fix your eyes on God and transform your valley into a valley of praise. Place your hope in the only One who can do the impossible. That is when God is glorified and we find rest.

Believe He Is Sufficient in Our Insufficiency

Insufficient. Truth be told, it's how I feel many days. I'm insufficient as a mom to manage every detail from getting my kids dressed, fed, teeth brushed, lunch packed, homework done, verses memorized, piano practiced . . . and then train up their character, too! I'm insufficient to balance family, work, and ministry, and easily overwhelmed by things like messy closets or one extra task on my weekly to-do list. I'm insufficient to perform the ministry God has given me and amazed that God allows me to serve anyway.

Just insufficient. That's probably how the disciples felt also as they looked at a hungry crowd and at their own resources. Maybe that's how you feel sometimes too as you face the many demands on your attention and time.

But our hope is in a God who is in the business of taking our meager offerings and multiplying them to be more than enough. He is always sufficient in our insufficiency.

When Jesus told the disciples to feed the crowd, they faced the reality of their insufficiency. Jesus asked them, "How many loaves do you have?" and they searched the crowd for the answer. Andrew discovered one boy among a sea of thousands with a packed lunch. "Here is a boy with five small barley loaves and two small fish, but how far will they go among so many?" (John 6:9). Notice how he emphasizes how small the portions were. Not only was it just five pieces of bread and two fish, they were small pieces at that!

Andrew's question is perfect. How far would that go among so many indeed?! This boy's lunch was utterly insufficient. It probably embarrassed Andrew to even mention it. Have you ever started a project—maybe a ministry event, a Bible study, potty training your toddler, a new program at work—and you just think, "There isn't enough to go around"?

Instead of focusing on how the disciples responded to Jesus' request, consider the little boy. He didn't shrug his shoulders and declare that his lunch wasn't enough for the immense crowd. No, this little guy with a lunch sack willingly and in great faith gave 100 percent of what he had to Jesus. Even though it wasn't nearly enough for the crowd, he trusted that Jesus could use his offering. Similarly we must be willing to offer 100 percent of ourselves, even on those days when we clearly see how we fall short, because we know that He is always sufficient.

Seventeen

Enough Is Enough

Perhaps a little sheepishly, Andrew brought the boy's meager lunch before Jesus. It was the practical and obvious answer to Jesus' question, "How many loaves do you have?" They had a small lunchbox-sized meal to share with a crowd of thousands.

Still, Andrew knew enough to bring that boy's lunch to the Lord and sometimes we do the same. We drag our resources to Christ, knowing they aren't enough and perhaps feeling overwhelmed with the insufficiency. We take it all to Jesus hoping that He has an answer.

Ultimately, Jesus' seemingly simply question to the disciples searched out what they believed about Him, and it checks our heart in the same way. As we come to Him with insufficiency, do we believe He can do the miracle? Do we believe this so strongly that we can give thanks even before the miracle occurs?

Do we believe that He won't give us a meager portion, just enough to fulfill a minimum requirement, or do we truly trust that our generous God can give us enough, more than enough, abundantly enough?

Do we believe that in any circumstance and situation, He can show himself powerful, mighty, and worthy of glory?

Do we believe that the same God who delivered us before and provided for us in the past can and will faithfully continue to care for us here, now, tomorrow, and every day in our future?

The disciples may have thought that they believed. They could have shrugged their shoulders nonchalantly as they assured Jesus that of course they knew He could provide and perform miracles and do wondrous things for them. Yet, when faced with a hungry multitude and a tiny lunch, when they were required to live out that faith and apply a theoretical belief to a practical situation, suddenly they didn't seem so sure.

We're not always so different than that. We may be able to say the right things, quote the right Scriptures, and claim the right Bible promises. But when our provisions seem so clearly insufficient for our need and Jesus asks us how much we have, when He searches our heart in His gentle way, how can we answer? Do we indeed believe our God is always more than enough?

Believe Enough to Give Thanks in Advance

When Andrew placed the boy's tiny lunch into Jesus' hands, the Lord set a powerful precedent for the disciples.

> Taking the five loaves and the two fish and looking up to heaven, he gave thanks and broke the loaves. Then he gave them to the disciples, and the disciples gave them to the people. They all ate and were satisfied. (Matthew 14:19–20)

Did Jesus bewail His plight to God the Father, emphasizing the hugeness of their need and the fact that they were trying to do a good thing here and it would be nice to have some help? Did He complain that God hadn't provided enough? Did He whine about the problem?

Jesus didn't say any of that. Instead He lifted up the bread and fish and gave thanks.

Yup, you read that right. He thanked God for providing what little they had even though it was clearly not enough. It was in the giving thanks that the miracle occurred. As Jesus raised up the lunch, He thanked God for it, and then portioned it out to the entire crowd until everyone had eaten their fill. You may be tempted to withhold thanksgiving until God has already provided, but try something radical. Thank God in advance for His provision. Thank Him in faith for the act that's going to save you. Jesus asked the disciples, "How many loaves do you have?" and that could have been an opportunity for them to complain. They could have said, "You didn't think this ministry through. You brought us out here without food. What are we supposed to do now?"

In Philippians 4:6, Paul says, "Do not be anxious about anything, but in every situation, by prayer and petition, with thanksgiving, present your requests to God." Don't wait until after God provides. Pray with thanksgiving in advance, trusting that God will fill your need, and you will discover peace even while you wait for the answer to your prayers.

Believe He Can Do Abundantly More

One of the greatest moments in this gospel event occurs after everyone had eaten their fill. Matthew says, "They all ate and were satisfied, and the disciples picked up twelve basketfuls of broken pieces that were left over" (14:20). Twelve baskets full of leftovers! They were going to be eating fish sandwiches for a long time! You may glance into your refrigerator and feel dread at the sight of Tupperware containers full of leftovers from the week. But, to the disciples and the crowd, it was a sign of abundance.

God is an abundant God. He is not stingy. He doesn't place arbitrary limits on His grace. He doesn't run out of what you need, and He doesn't deny you requests because you've tapped out your quota of grace for the year.

In his letter to the Ephesians, Paul included a doxology—a hymn of praise to God.

> Now to him who is able to do immeasurably more than all we ask or imagine, according to his power that is at work within us, to him be glory in the church and in Christ Jesus throughout all generations, for ever and ever! Amen. (Ephesians 3:20–21)

God's willingness and ability to do immeasurably more than anything we ask or imagine is one of the reasons Paul gives Him praise. It's an essential part of His character and gives us cause for worship.

The Message translates this same passage so powerfully:

> God can do anything, you know—far more than you could ever imagine or guess or request in your wildest dreams! He does it not by pushing us around but by working within us, his Spirit deeply and gently within us.

If you ask God to fulfill a need, watch out as He amazes you with the abundance of His affection and provision. Bring along some baskets for the leftovers!

Believe He Will Be Glorified

Jesus' question, "How many loaves do you have?" highlighted the shortage of supplies. There was no question about it. The disciples didn't have enough. So, how would they solve that problem? Jesus watched as the disciples considered their options. He wanted to know if they would struggle to solve this problem themselves or turn it over to Him.

What if the disciples had managed to solve the food shortage with their incredible managerial skills? Suppose they whittled a fishing pole, caught some fish, started a campfire, and baked bread over the hot coals? What if they collected money from everyone in the crowd and trekked into town to order takeout? What if every attendee had packed a little snack and the disciples had pooled the resources to form a buffet line? Then this gospel account would have been about their skills or hard work or Jesus' leadership ability and not at all about God's compassionate and miraculous provision.

It was the insufficiency of the boy's gift that allowed Jesus to be glorified.

What happens when we strike out on our own and try to be sufficient in our own strength? We steal God's glory. This is my propensity. Is it yours also? Do you tend to rely on your own strengths and abilities rather than turn to Jesus for help?

Many times we don't pray for God's help until we've exhausted every other option and finally realized we can't handle things. Despite the disciples' best efforts, they would never have found, made, or bought enough food for the crowd. Likewise, we can't be enough in our own strength either. If we're relying on our talent, skills, hard work, and ingenuity, we'll just fail. Our only hope is to give our all to Jesus and trust that He will multiply our insufficient offering for His glory.

God never expects us to be sufficient in our strength and abilities. If we are strong enough, together enough, talented enough, smart enough, or equipped enough in our own strength, there's no room for God to show off in our lives and receive the glory

He deserves. The gifts we bring become less about Him and more about us.

God is glorified in our insufficiency. Our weaknesses ensure that people can't look at us and marvel at our problem-solving abilities or our strengths. Instead, they see God working in impossible ways—all eyes are on Him! That's what happened when everyone saw the leftovers and knew how small the boy's lunch had been. "The people realized that God was at work among them in what Jesus had just done. They said, 'This is the Prophet for sure, God's Prophet right here in Galilee!'" (John 6:14 MSG).

God promises us in Psalm 46:10, "Be still, and know that I am God; I will be exalted among the nations, I will be exalted in the earth." "Be still" doesn't mean have a quiet time or listen to some softly playing praise songs. It means stop worrying and fretting. Don't try to do things on your own. Don't arm yourself to fight your own battles. Rest in the assurance that God will be glorified and exalted in every situation. He will come to your rescue so that He can show off for the nations!

So we can follow the example of many in Scripture and ask Him to provide for us, not for our own sake, but for the glory of His name. Look at how others prayed in the Bible:

- "*For your name's sake, LORD,* preserve my life; in your righteousness, bring me out of trouble" (Psalm 143:11).
- "*For the sake of your name, LORD,* forgive my iniquity, though it is great" (Psalm 25:11).
- "*For the sake of your name* do not despise us; do not dishonor your glorious throne. Remember your covenant with us and do not break it" (Jeremiah 14:21).
- "He refreshes my soul. He guides me along the right paths *for his name's sake*" (Psalm 23:3).
- "Help us, God our Savior, *for the glory of your name*; deliver us and forgive our sins *for your name's sake*" (Psalm 79:9).

- "Set me free from my prison, *that I may praise your name.* Then the righteous will gather about me because of your goodness to me" (Psalm 142:7).
- "Lord, listen! Lord, forgive! Lord, hear and act! *For your sake,* my God, do not delay, because *your city and your people bear your Name*" (Daniel 9:19).

Perhaps you are tempted, as I often am, to pray for specific solutions to your problems. You might say, "God, here's the amount of money I need, the job you could give me, what I want for my kids . . ." Just name the problem and we probably have an ideal solution all worked out. All we need is for God to sign off on our perfect plan and give us what we want.

Consider trying a radical experiment in your prayer life. When you have a need or a problem, pray, "God, please be glorified in this situation. Work in such a way that all eyes will be on you. Show up in all your majesty. Be awesome in my life. Let people see how you take care of your children and allow me to give testimony to your faithfulness and abundant love." Let Him decide how He can work on your behalf in such a way as to be glorified.

Believe He Is Consistent in His Provision

Has God ever had to teach you a lesson more than one time? He certainly has to refresh my memory often enough. I'm so thankful our God is patient because otherwise He'd have given up on me long ago!

He was patient with the disciples, too. After Jesus fed the crowd of more than five thousand, He was teaching another large crowd one day and it grew late, long past dinnertime. Jesus called the disciples over and once again prodded them into faith. He said, "Look at all these people. We don't have enough food and it's late. What should we do?"

His disciples missed it again. Immediately they searched for practical solutions and asked, "But where in this remote place can anyone get enough bread to feed them?" (Mark 8:4).

They are so lucky they never met me because I would have popped them on the head at this point! Not long ago, Jesus fed more than five thousand people. Now He's looking at four thousand men plus women and children and these guys don't immediately think, "I bet Jesus could feed them!" They're still coming up with practical solutions that will inevitably fail.

Really?!

Jesus exhibited so much restraint. He didn't lecture them, but He did jiggle their memory a little bit. He asked them the exact same question as the last time, "How many loaves do you have?" And, you guessed it, He did the exact same miracle. He gave thanks. He distributed abundant food. The people ate until they were full and the disciples gathered leftovers.

We humans just seem to struggle with memory problems. We so easily forget what God has done in the past when we face a new crisis. You can journal or scrapbook or write poems or testimonies or songs or whatever you can imagine, but you must find ways to record how God has been faithful to you. You need physical reminders that God has rescued you, that He's provided, that He's healed, and that He's comforted you. I talked about this in more detail in chapter 5 when I wrote about Sarah, but I feel the need to emphasize this again.

Jesus was so serious about our need to remember what He has done for us that as He handed around the Passover bread during the Last Supper, He told the disciples, "This is my body given for you; do this in remembrance of me" (Luke 22:19). Most of us hear our pastors say these same words as we take communion, or the Lord's Supper, in our churches today. We have been called to remember what the Lord has done.

Psalm 136 exemplifies the discipline of remembrance as well. This psalm is a responsive song of praise to God. The leader declares the good things God has done and the chorus responds with, "His love endures forever." As the worship leader tells the people how God created the world, rescued them from Egypt, led them in the wilderness, defeated their enemies, and provided for them, the people answer, "His love endures forever." They say that twenty-six times in this one psalm.

This is the psalmist's way of declaring, "Look at all the amazing things God has done for us," and the people respond with the declaration that God's love didn't end with any one of those miracles. Instead, His love endures forever. God delivered us before. He will do it again. We know this is true because "Jesus Christ is the same yesterday and today and forever" (Hebrews 13:8).

So What Will You Believe?

Jesus multiplied a meal not once, but twice in Scripture. Obviously it's a lesson He wanted to make sure the disciples understood. He asked the worried and overwhelmed disciples, "How many loaves do you have?" and then transformed their insufficient offering into abundant sufficiency for the crowd.

That same God asks you a similar question. He's searching your heart when He asks, "How much do you have?" It's not so we can frantically search for our own answer to the problem or feel the weight of our inabilities. He's waiting for us to throw up our hands and admit we're not enough. Whatever we've got, whether it's finances or brains or ingenuity or energy or tact, it's just not sufficient.

But our insufficiency is the best backdrop for Him to reveal His glory to others, and that's what we should seek. His glory should be our heart's cry and our deepest motivation. Be glorified, Lord! Be glorified in my life and in my troubles and in these triumphs.

Give thanks for all He's given to you and hand everything you have over to Him, believing in His ability not just to satisfy your needs, but to do abundantly more.

How many loaves do you have?

Philip and the Disciples

Make It PERSONAL

- Describe a time when you prayed for something and should have waited for God to answer but didn't. What did you learn from the experience?

- In what areas of your life do you feel insufficient?

Make It CONNECT

1. The disciples saw the facts of their situation:

   a. A crowd of five thousand hungry men plus women and children.

   b. No nearby places to eat.

   c. No food to give them.

Jesus saw an opportunity to give God glory. List some facts about a situation that you are in. Do you believe God could work in a surprising way to help you and bring glory to himself?

2. Jesus asked Philip, "Where shall we buy bread for these people to eat?" We're told that Jesus "asked this only to test him, for he already had in mind what he was going to do" (John 6:5–6). Did Philip pass the test? Would you have passed? Why or why not?

3. In the same way, Jesus promised the woman at the well "living water." Why did this seem impossible to her according to John 4:11?

4. Jesus said, "With man, this is impossible, but with God all things are possible" (Matthew 19:26). In what areas of your life do you need God to do the impossible?

5. Have you ever heard people say, "God won't give you more than you can handle?" Do you think this is a proper interpretation of 1 Corinthians 10:13?

6. How did the boy with small loaves and fish demonstrate his faith by offering his meager lunch to Jesus?

7. Do you normally thank God for His provision before He has acted on your behalf?

8. The insufficiency of the boy's lunch gave Jesus the opportunity to be glorified. Our insufficiency can give God glory, too. When was the last time God was glorified in your weakness?

9. In Matthew 14, Jesus fed the crowd of five thousand. In Matthew 15, the disciples had to feed a crowd of four thousand and they were still bewildered by the challenge. Jesus asked the same question, "How many loaves do you have?" What lessons has God had to teach you more than once?

Make It REAL

- This week focus on giving thanks in all circumstances, even before God has answered your prayers. Keep a list of what you're thankful for.

- When you pray, ask God to be glorified in each situation. Trust Him with the when and how of your deliverance.

Make It LAST

Memory Verse

Now to him who is able to do immeasurably more than all we ask or imagine,
according to his power that is at work within us,
to him be glory in the church and in Christ Jesus
throughout all generations, forever and ever! Amen.

Ephesians 3:20–21

Journal Prompt

Like the little boy with the lunch, offer God 100 percent of your resources. Don't hold anything back. Acknowledge that it's not sufficient, but that He is enough.

Do you love me?

Eighteen

How We Love Him

I love *Fiddler on the Roof.*

I love how the main character, Tevye, talks to his horse and argues with the other men in his small Russian town. I love how he struggles to hold onto his Russian Jewish traditions while around him the culture and community is rapidly changing. I love how he reluctantly allows his daughters to marry for love instead of arranging their marriages like business deals.

But one of my favorite scenes in this musical is a song that Tevye sings with his wife of twenty-five years, Golde. As they talk about their daughters, he nudges her and asks an embarrassing, impertinent, probing question, "Do you love me?"

She sings her answer, deftly avoiding the real question for much of the song. Golde sings, "Do I love you? For twenty-five years I've washed your clothes, cooked your meals, cleaned your house, given you children, milked the cow. After twenty-five years, why talk about love right now?" And finally, after considering in song all that they had been through together, Golde declares, "I suppose I do."

What strikes me about this song is that Golde doesn't check her feelings when Tevye asks her the question. Instead, she looks at her actions. She considers whether her behaviors and experiences show that she loves her husband. Despite all the nagging and picking at each other, despite having an arranged marriage themselves, she does indeed love her husband.

What would happen if God asked us, "Do you love me?" Would we check our emotions to see how in love with God we feel as we sing worship songs on Sunday morning? Would we consider how emotionally charged we feel after a great sermon or even the warm fuzzies we get when we sponsor a child from Africa?

What if how we feel isn't the gauge of whether or not we love God? What if instead of consulting our emotions, we check our actions and behaviors?

Isn't that what Peter did when Jesus asked him not once, but three times, that piercing question, "Do you love me?" That question dug deep into Peter. Before Christ was carried away, beaten, and killed, Peter had "insisted emphatically, 'Even if I have to die with you, I will never disown you'" (Mark 14:31). Those were his feelings talking. He was passionate and excited about what he thought the future might hold.

Standing around the fire outside the temple during Jesus' trial, though, Peter's actions told a different story. Three times he denied even knowing Jesus, much less being a follower or even one of Jesus' closest and most trusted disciples.

He messed up.

But Jesus didn't leave Peter full of shame and feeling defeated. Instead, after Christ's resurrection, He sought out Peter and restored him, not just to relationship, but to leadership in the burgeoning church.

It was around a fire that Peter first betrayed Jesus. Now here he sat with Jesus around another fire. As Jesus talked, Peter could have looked at the flames and heard the crackle of the wood, powerful reminders of his past betrayal. Then Jesus asked him three times, "Simon son of John, do you love me?"

He could ask the same question of you and me. Do you love Him? Does your life reflect that love or is it something we say and sing but never truly mean?

Do I Mean It?

There's a song we sing at church with these lyrics: "Jesus, lover of my soul. Jesus, I will never let you go." I love that song from the worship band Hillsong. Sometimes I can sing it with my whole heart, unreservedly, because I believe that I really mean it. "I will never let you go . . . No matter what the obstacles or circumstances or challenges, I feel certain I would continue to follow Jesus."

I'm sure you sing songs at your church that declare how much you love God, how you'll surrender anything to Him, and how you'll never fall away in your faith. Do you mean it or are you just reading the words from the hymnal or off the screen?

It's not something you can just decide once. It's a matter of continual growth. You surrender "everything" to God, and then He asks you to step closer and you have to choose to surrender more. He reveals another area of your life that you haven't surrendered to His lordship and He asks you all over again, "Do you love me?"

Peter's answer to this question was tested. He had been singing passionately all along, "I love you, Lord. I'm never going to leave you. Even if the whole world abandons you, I won't." Then he had to prove it. When the worst happened and he felt as if his faith could endanger his life, suddenly it was safer to deny Christ. His actions didn't match his words.

There around the fire, when Jesus asked, "Do you love me?" Peter searched his soul. The memory of his mistakes was fresh and still painful. Jesus didn't ask Peter this question to hurt him or to dredge up past sins and shame Peter all over again. Instead, Jesus asked Peter out of love for the disciple and as a way to move Peter beyond the past and forward into ministry.

Peter could have felt unworthy of leadership in the New Testament church. Hadn't he been the one to deny Christ? Hadn't he failed Jesus? Here by the fireside, though, Jesus showed Peter that he was forgiven and was still an important part of His plan for the church.

When we read about their conversation in Scripture, we miss so much because our word "love" doesn't convey the different types of love Jesus and Peter were talking about. Our language is more restrictive than the original. Jesus and Peter use two different words for "love" as they talk. The first two times, Jesus asked Peter, "Do you love (agape) me?" He was asking, "Do you unconditionally love me in the same way that God loves you?"

Peter, his heart still tender from his betrayal of Christ, knew that he couldn't promise that unconditional love. He thought he loved Jesus in that way, but then when circumstances grew tough, Peter had denied Christ. So instead of saying that he agape loves Christ, he answered, "Lord, you know I love (phileo) you." He says, "I have tender affection for you, just as if you were my brother." He was honest. No more impassioned rhetoric that proves false when put to the flame.

When Jesus asked Peter the same question again, John writes that "Peter was hurt because Jesus asked him the third time" (John 21:17). But this time, Jesus matched Peter's language. He asked, "Peter, do you love (phileo) me?" He accepted Peter's honesty, knowing that Peter was making sure he said only what he could match with his actions.

Christ asks for honesty from us as well. Do we love Him? Are we willing to obey Him no matter what? Does what we sing on Sunday morning match our actions Monday through Saturday? Do we love Him with our families, our finances, our callings, our relationships? Are we willing to walk in radical obedience? Are we ready to go where He calls us to go?

If we were dating a guy who constantly told us how much he loved us, we'd expect him to be faithful, unselfish, considerate, and generous toward us. His actions in our relationship should match his fancy love-talk. If that sweet-tongued sweetheart cheated on us, we'd know that he wasn't honest about his affection and we'd dump him. Words are meaningless if they aren't matched with action.

God expects the same from us. In John 14:15, Jesus says, "If you love me, keep my commands." For Peter, Jesus was even more specific. He followed up every question about Peter's love for him with a commissioning to a specific ministry. He told Peter to "Feed my lambs . . . take care of my sheep . . . feed my sheep." Peter could live out his love for Christ by tending the New Testament church.

It's important to state that this isn't about legalism or works-based faith. Our salvation is not contingent on our own merit or how good we are in this life. Obedience is our loving response to the love of our Savior. When my husband tells me he loves me, I say the same to him. When a friend writes me an encouraging note, I am reminded to pray for her or look for ways to return her affection and care. We respond to love with actions of love. Our response to God's love is to obey Him.

Do you mean it when you say you love God? When you sing on Sunday mornings, when you wear your Christian T-shirts, and when you post your Christian statuses on Facebook, do you really mean it? Are you walking in obedience and doing what God has told you to do? That's the test that Christ gave Peter and the command we are given as well.

Loving God without a Prenup

Sometimes we do love God . . . with certain protective clauses built in to maintain our comfort and the life we want to have. We love God if He meets our expectations. We love God if He blesses us. We love God as long as He doesn't ask anything too hard from us. We love God if He gives us what we want. If God doesn't live up to His end of the agreement we've made, then we feel released from that relationship, free to go through the motions of Christianity without any real commitment or life change.

Peter had been so sure that he loved Jesus, so sure that he meant it when he said he would die for Him. But that was when he thought Jesus was coming as a triumphant Messiah who would overthrow the Roman oppressors and establish a powerful Jewish kingdom. That's when he thought Jesus was a conqueror and he and the other disciples were riding Christ's coattails to victory.

Jesus didn't meet Peter's expectations. Instead of achieving great military victory, Jesus was battered and bruised by the same oppressors Peter hoped to overthrow. When Jesus died, Peter and the other disciples were confused by this apparent failure. Had they followed a faker after all? Had He been just another religious fanatic claiming to be the long-awaited savior of the Jewish people?

Often we create expectations for God just like Peter did for Jesus. Since we're Christians, we expect to be blessed—to get the job and the promotion, to have the nice house and car, to have the perfect family with the faithful, loving husband and the wonderful kids who always behave and do well in school. We expect God to give us the good life in exchange for our expressions of affection for Him.

What happens when He defies our expectations—like he did for Peter? We can look at Scripture and see what following Jesus sometimes costs.

234

In 2 Timothy, Paul writes his final epistle before his execution. Unlike his first imprisonment in Rome when he had his own place and could have visitors and people to care for him, this second imprisonment was lonely, cold, and painful.

Not that Paul was a complainer. If you read 2 Timothy, you have to read closely to glimpse the setting. He writes:

- "So do not be ashamed of the testimony about our Lord or of me his *prisoner*. Rather, join with me in suffering for the gospel, by the power of God" (1:8).
- "That is why I am suffering as I am. Yet this is no cause for shame" (1:12).
- "You know that everyone in the province of Asia has deserted me" (1:15).
- "When he [Onesiphorus] was in Rome, he searched hard for me until he found me" (1:17). Note that no one knew where Paul was being kept!
- "For which I am suffering even to the point of being chained like a criminal" (2:9).
- "For I am already being poured out like a drink offering, and the time for my departure is near" (4:6).
- "Do your best to come to me quickly, for Demas, because he loved this world, has deserted me. . . . Only Luke is with me" (4:9–11).
- "Bring the cloak that I left" (4:13). He must have been so cold!
- "At my first defense, no one came to my support, but everyone deserted me" (4:16).

Can you imagine? At his trial, not one person stood up to defend Paul. *Not one.* After a life filled with ministry and sacrifice to others, no one came to his defense. He was cast into a prison and his friends had to struggle to find him.

Beth Moore writes in *To Live Is Christ*,

> Paul was held under conditions like those of a convicted killer. He was bound by heavy chains—the type that bruise and lacerate the skin. He was almost 60 years old and had taken enough beatings to make him quite arthritic. The lack of mobility greatly intensified any ailments or illnesses. He most likely was reduced to skin and bones. The cells where the worst prisoners were chained were usually filthy, wet, and rodent-infested dungeons. Paul was cold. He wanted his cloak and begged Timothy to do everything he could to come before winter.[1]

Despite all of this, Paul never questioned his call, never questioned his faith. He trusted God no matter what. When he said he loved Christ, he meant it. His actions, including his martyrdom, tested and proved his love, and he loved Jesus without expectation. Even in hardship and even in the face of death, he did not renounce his faith and alter his affection for Christ.

Nineteen

How He Loves Us

I wonder if God sometimes feels like I do as a young mom who works from home with young kids. All day long, filling demands, meeting needs, listening to requests, helping with problems, cleaning up messes, tying shoelaces . . . well, that last one might pertain only to me, but the others seem to fit.

My work days go something like this:

- Get everyone settled and sit down at the computer to write.
- Help child put clothes on her doll.
- Sit down to work.
- Get a drink for another child.
- Sit down to work.
- Spell "Pocahontas" for older daughter who is systematically drawing every princess she's ever heard of.
- Sit down to work.
- Change baby's diaper.
- Sit down to work.

- Break up fight between older girls who both want to be the same princess.
- Sit down to work.
- Get snack for children who declare that they are starving and will die if they don't eat something now instead of waiting for dinner.
- Sit down to work.
- Get lemonade for the children who forgot that they were also thirsty and not just hungry when they asked for a snack.
- Sit down to work.

You get the idea.

In the midst of meeting all those demands and filling all those needs, one of my daughters will appear at my feet, wrap her arms around me, and say, "I love you, Mom." My baby runs over about once an hour to lay her head down on my arm so that I can stroke her head and kiss her. Then she's off running again to dump out all the blocks and pull every book off the bookshelf.

The beauty of love like hers is that she doesn't love me because I fixed her a snack or dressed her baby doll in another outfit. I'm loved because of who I am, her loving mom. Likewise, I love my children not for what they do but for who they are. God demonstrated His own love for us so clearly with the cross, a sacrifice we didn't deserve or merit. Yet, we don't love Him only for what He does for us; we love Him for who He is. He is our God of abundant grace; He is our Savior; He is our Redeemer. His actions simply revealed His character.

Even though I *know* my daughter loves me for who I am, at times being a mom can make me *feel* like I'm only loved for what I do and not for who I am. Perhaps sometimes you feel the same way about your role at work or church. You're overwhelmed by the needs of others.

Sadly, so many days, I treat God the same way, as a Wish-Fulfiller. I go to Him in need. I ask Him for help, encouragement, intervention, provision, healing. All day long, I pray for myself, my family, and for others. And He longs for us to bring our problems to Him. It's not that our requests tire Him or He grows weary of our constant coming. We aren't meant to try to fulfill our needs on our own or try to handle our problems apart from Him. But sometimes we forget to enjoy the beauty of relationship and time in His presence unmotivated by need or a prayer list. Sometimes we don't come to Him unless we need a prayer answered.

Peter initially treated Jesus in just that same way. He thought Jesus came to set the Jewish people free from the oppression they'd endured for hundreds of years. He loved Jesus because of what he thought Jesus would do for him.

Yet how precious are the moments when we come into God's presence not asking Him to help us with anything or fulfill our expectations, but just because we are pleased to have His company. That is when we show that we love Him and not just what He does for us.

Psalm 131:2 says, "I've kept my feet on the ground, I've cultivated a quiet heart. Like a baby content in its mother's arms, my soul is a baby content" (MSG). In the NIV, this description is of a "weaned child with its mother." The image here is of a baby content to be with her mother, not because she's looking for food or the fulfillment of a need, but just because the mother's presence brings comfort.

It's part of the maturing process in this Christian walk. God weans us so that we don't just look to Him for help, but we also respond "to Him out of love . . . for God does not want us neurotically dependent on Him but willingly trustful in Him," writes Eugene Peterson. It's not that God no longer cares for us or sees our need. It's not that we've become independent or learned to thrive on our own. We still look to Him for our provision and help in every situation. It's that we seek after relationship with God for who He is and accept His gifts to us as signs of His faithful love.

He asks us to trust His love for us so much that we can lay our burdens at His feet and leave them there, choosing to focus on God himself rather than our troubling circumstances. We see His love and not our empty bank account. We look to His faithfulness and not our illness. We focus on His might and not our broken relationships.

In his book, *A Long Obedience in the Same Direction*, Eugene Peterson goes on to write, "Choose to be with him; elect his presence; aspire to his ways; respond to his love." This reminds me of Psalm 42:1–2: "As the deer pants for streams of water, so my soul pants for you, my God. My soul thirsts for God, for the living God. When can I go and meet with God?" It's a cry for relationship rather than a desperate plea for help. It's a call to enjoy God's presence for who He is, not just for what He does for us.

When Jesus sat by the fireside with Peter and probed the disciple's heart with his question, "Do you love me?" He was asking if Peter had put aside all those expectations and prerequisites for his affection. In that same conversation, Jesus predicted Peter's martyrdom. He was telling Peter that sometimes loving Christ is costly. Jesus didn't preach a prosperity gospel in which Christians get an easy life in exchange for saying we love God.

Jesus asked for Peter's love despite the hardship and sacrifice his future would hold. Peter responded, "Lord, you know I love you." He committed to loving Christ, not for the good things he'd get out of it, but because of who Jesus was and all He had done for him. Peter loved Jesus because Jesus loved him first, which flowed from who Jesus was and is.

Loving Him because He First Loved Us

Peter could see the scars in Jesus' hands as they sat across the fire from one another. He had felt the full weight of Christ's forgiveness.

While Jesus was being interrogated by the Sanhedrin, Peter stood in the temple courtyard and denied even knowing his Lord. When Jesus hung on the cross and died for Peter's sins and yours and mine, Peter was nowhere to be found.

Then Jesus had exited the tomb after three days and triumphed over death and Satan. Instead of condemning Peter and ostracizing him or pushing him into the same category of traitor as Judas, Jesus forgave Peter, restored him, and commissioned him for ministry.

How could Peter, in light of the greatest act of sacrificial love ever, not love Christ in return? The disciple John later wrote, "love comes from God. . . . God is love. This is how God showed his love among us: He sent his one and only Son into the world that we might live through him. This is love: not that we loved God, but that he loved us and sent his Son as an atoning sacrifice for our sins. . . . We love because he first loved us" (1 John 4:7–10, 19).

We love because He first loved us. This is how it must have been for Peter as Jesus asked him repeatedly, "Do you love me?" Jesus didn't even address the past with Peter. He focused solely on the present and what He was asking Peter to do in the future. The past had been erased by the cross.

Scripture tells us that God is singing over us with joy (Zephaniah 3:17). He loves us enough to sacrifice His Son so that we could be with Him forever in heaven. He is the bridegroom joyfully and with great expectation waiting for His bride. He's overflowing with passionate love for us—for me—for you.

He loves us. Sometimes we need to hear that over and over and be reminded of the magnitude and weight of His love. It's especially true when our circumstances are difficult and we feel like we're sinking. Remembering how He loves us is even more necessary when, like Peter, we realize just how much forgiveness He has offered. We can rest in His love, praise Him for His love, and trust His love, rather than worry, fret, or be held captive by shame.

When we take the time to truly meditate on God's amazing love for us, we're changed. It's impossible not to be. Our focus shifts from our failures or fears or what-ifs and fixates instead on His love.

Consider how your everyday life would change if you walked around fully aware of God's love all the time. All your self-condemnation would cease. Your worries would end because you'd know that God loves you enough to care for you and not abandon you. You would love other people more unconditionally because of the grace you yourself have received. You wouldn't question God's plans for you because you'd trust His loving direction.

Your life could be transformed. I know mine would be. Peter's certainly was. He was forgiven and restored and raised up as a leader in the church. This man who denied Christ in fear would deliver a powerful sermon on Pentecost and bring many people to faith. He would perform miracles, even the raising of the dead. He would testify before the Sanhedrin and escape prison and ultimately die a martyr's death for the sake of Jesus Christ.

Paul also reminds us that our life changes when we live in the knowledge of God's love for us:

> I pray that you, being rooted and established in love, may have power, together with all the Lord's holy people, to grasp how wide and long and high and deep is the love of Christ, and to know this love that surpasses knowledge— that you may be filled to the measure of all the fullness of God. (Ephesians 3:17–19)

The Message translates verse 19 this way: "Reach out and experience the breadth! Test its length! Plumb the depths! Rise to the heights! Live full lives, full in the fullness of God." Our lives should be full of passion and joy as we respond in love to the God who loves us so.

Amazingly, we've done nothing to earn this love and we can do nothing to end it. Paul writes in Romans 5:8, "But God demonstrates his own love for us in this: While we were still sinners, Christ died for us." He loved us in our sin, with all of our mistakes and failures, with our lack of trust and our self-focused lives. He loved us when we didn't have anything to offer in return. He loved Peter even when Peter denied Jesus three times.

Rest in this today—He loves you. And He asks you the ultimate question, "Do you love me?"

Twenty

Continuing the Search

It's been almost a year since I began feeling the nudge of that initial question on my heart. *What do you want me to do for you?* That's what I heard God asking me when I finally sat in silence before Him, finally stopped pestering Him with questions long enough to hear what He was asking. Now here I sit and still I feel the weight of that question, as well as the others God has asked me on this journey. The searching of my heart continues.

What Do You Want Me to Do for You?

The first question that I felt God ask me in this journey wasn't designed for me alone. Jesus had asked it before—twice. In Mark 10, two brothers and a blind man both came to Jesus with requests. Just like us, they brought their petitions to Jesus. There's nothing wrong with that. He is the one who can supply all of our needs. He wants us to bring our requests to Him and to pray over all things.

Yet, instead of performing immediate miracles or making instant promises, Jesus asked them this searching question. It all began with James and John, the fiery sons of Zebedee, who started out tentatively, "'Teacher,' they said, 'we want you to do for us whatever we ask'" (v. 35).

Jesus was no fool. He asked for specifics: "What do you want me to do for you?" (v. 36). What could their request be? What was their deep-down, true desire? What motivated their service?

For these two brothers, the truth was an ugly one. They desired self-exaltation and personal glory. "They replied, 'Let one of us sit at your right and the other at your left in your glory'" (v. 37).

In other words, they said, "We serve because of the attention and praise it brings. We want to be told how great we are and to feel proud of being your followers! We want to be your right- and left-hand guys, with all of the power and status that entails."

Jesus denied their request, teaching the disciples that God's kingdom doesn't function with the same hierarchy as on earth:

> Whoever wants to become great among you must be your servant, and whoever wants to be first must be slave of all. For even the Son of Man did not come to be served, but to serve, and to give his life as a ransom for many. (vv. 43–45)

Does a desire for attention and praise motivate us in the same way? If God asked you that same question right now—*What do you want me to do for you?*—how would you answer?

Would you want material provision?

Would you want physical comfort or worldly success?

Would you want to feel like the best mom, wife, employee, daughter, and friend?

Would you desire ministry impact? If so, for what purpose? To feed your pride, make you feel valued, or give you special status in God's kingdom?

Please linger a moment on this question and consider it in light of all that you do because this question of motives covers every aspect of our lives. Be honest. Brutally honest.

Are you making your child an incredible birthday cake because you love him or because you want your other mom friends to know that you're the best mom on the planet?

Are you on the worship team at church because you desire to help others praise God or because it gives you a chance to shine on the stage?

Are you serving meals at a soup kitchen because you love people with Christ's love or because it makes you feel spiritual and holy to do so? Maybe even because you know others think you are a great person for being so humble?

Are you living for your own glory?

Or do you desire His glory? Do you desire greater intimacy with God? Do you long to see Him?

That's what blind Bartimaeus wanted. Just a few verses after Jesus' motivational chat with James and John, Jesus met this blind beggar. When he heard that Jesus was in town, Bartimaeus cried out loudly in desperation, "Jesus, Son of David, have mercy on me!" (v. 47).

"Have mercy!" That means, "I know I don't deserve anything from you, but I ask because you are compassionate." Daniel prayed in this same way when he said, "We do not make requests of you because we are righteous, but because of your great mercy" (Daniel 9:18). From the beginning, Bartimaeus's request was different than that of the brothers, who asked for status because they felt their service merited it.

Bartimaeus, however, knew that we don't earn God's gifts to us.

So the blind man screamed for Jesus' attention and Jesus, hearing his cries, called Bartimaeus over. He asked that same question: "What do you want me to do for you?" (Mark 10:51).

What was it Bartimaeus wanted? A place in Jesus' kingdom? A seat near the throne? A place in Jesus' inner circle? No. "The blind man said, 'Rabbi, I want to see'" (v. 51).

Immediately Jesus healed him because of his faith. Then Bartimaeus did the only thing possible when Christ delivers you; he followed Jesus down the road.

So we have two answers to the same question. The brothers wanted status and personal success. Bartimaeus wanted to see Jesus.

What is it you want God to do for you?

Are you seeking God's glory in all things? Are you longing and searching to see God in every situation? Or are you asking God for what you think you need, for what will fulfill you, for what will make you happy, and for what will satisfy your pride? What is your motivation?

It All Comes Down to Grace

Unfortunately, most of the time the question of motives hurts. That's because we're plain old, sinful human beings. We're not perfect. Sometimes—well, lots of times—our pride gets demanding. Sometimes we long for a little attention. Sometimes we don't know how else to live.

The hurt is Scripture doing its job, just like the writer of Hebrews said:

> For the word of God is alive and active. Sharper than any double-edged sword, it penetrates even to dividing soul and spirit, joints and marrow; it judges the thoughts and attitudes of the heart. (4:12)

While the truth sometimes comforts us, it also can shake us up. It reminds us of ways we need to change and calls us to repentance.

When we read God's Word quickly, glossing over the Scripture passages so we can check off our Bible reading for the day, we miss out on the conviction and the power of God to change us. When we monopolize our quiet times with a one-sided monologue—asking God questions, telling Him how we feel and what we need, never stopping to listen to Him—we're preventing spiritual growth.

When the author of Hebrews tells us God's Word is sharp, he means it might hurt at times. The Word of God is wielded as a scalpel by a Master Surgeon, cutting into our wounded places, separating what is healthy flesh from what is diseased, dead, and necrotic. The Surgeon doesn't dissect in order to bring pain, though it might be a consequence of His work; He cuts deep to bring health, healing, and wholeness.

If we never feel the sting of the knife's blade or run our hands over a scar left in place of the wound, then we've never allowed His Word to clean out the pockets of sin buried in hidden places of our hearts.

It's not that the Bible is never an encouraging or comforting word. It's not that Scripture points a finger in our faces and dumps burdens of shame on our backs. Not at all. Romans 8:1 promises us, "Therefore, there is now no condemnation for those who are in Christ Jesus."

Scripture reminds us of our mistakes but accompanies that with the offer of grace. It's always a package deal.

Ezra, the high priest of Israel, and Nehemiah finally finished rebuilding the temple and walls of Jerusalem after returning from exile. They gathered "all who could understand" into the square while Ezra read aloud the Book of the Law of Moses. The crowd listened in silence, except for their weeping as God's Word revealed their disobedience.

Each day the people stood for hours, morning until noon, while he read, and they fasted and donned sackcloth and dumped ashes on their heads in sorrow for their sin. Theirs was the natural response of people who were attentive to God's Word. In the midst of their distress, their hearts brought low in shame, they declared, "But you are a forgiving God, gracious and compassionate, slow to anger and abounding in love" (Nehemiah 9:17).

Oh yes, truth hurts sometimes. If it's never painful or uncomfortable, maybe we've tuned it out or accepted watered-down adaptations. Even as we wince with pain, though, we know that the One yielding the scalpel does so with grace and compassion, pouring out a healing balm of forgiveness that washes away the signs of sin.

So, if you've come to the end of this journey through God's questions and you're tender in places, I understand. I'm a little sore myself. Yet, in the middle of that is grace. The truth is that regardless of any sin or misplaced motives, any doubts or hidden fears, God always loves us.

It's that very love that moves Him to question our hearts' desires, our motives, and our attitudes. He wants to clear all that is tainted so that our relationship with Him and our ministry for Him can be pure.

God's Questions

Perhaps God is asking, "Where are you?" just as He did for Adam and Eve. He's seeking out whether you're walking with Him in obedience or covering yourself with shame because of your past sins. Have you left His side and wandered away to pursue your own agenda or are you trusting His purpose and plans for you?

Perhaps God is asking you, "Where is your brother?" just as he did for Cain. God reminds us that this Christian walk involves relationships. We can't head out on the journey alone and ignore the brothers and sisters in Christ that God has given us. Sometimes people get hurt along the way. Churches fight. Ministries break apart. Friends stop calling one another. Are there relationships that require your attention and maybe need forgiveness? Are there people you need to work harder to love and behaviors you need to stop because you're hurting those around you?

To Hagar during her flight into the wilderness, God asked, "Where have you come from, and where are you going?" We can trust The God Who Sees to know right where we are, to know all we have come from, and to lead us in the right direction at the perfect time. Are you willing to let God change your plans and alter your course? Do you trust Him with the direction of your life?

About Sarah, He asked, "Why did Sarah laugh? Is anything too difficult for God?" It was unbelief that caused her silent chuckle in her tent. It's no easy task to believe God when circumstances tell us it's impossible for Him to fulfill His promises. It's hard to wait year after year for God to do what He said He would do. It's bitterly painful to see others blessed while you feel overlooked. Still He asks us to have tenacious faith because God always keeps His promises.

To Jacob, as they wrestled with each other long into the night, He asked, "What is your name?" He desires to know us intimately. He sees not just who we are and all the baggage we carry with us, but also who He is transforming us into. He longs to give us a new name so that we can throw off our old identity and be new in Christ. Do you long for a new identity in Him? Do you truly desire for Him to know you in the very depths of who you are?

To Moses shifting awkwardly from foot to foot at the burning bush, God asked, "What is that in your hand?" He held nothing but a shepherd's staff after forty years of mundane sheep tending in the wilderness. God, though, saw so much potential in this fugitive from Egypt. When we obey Him in humility, He will transform our insufficient offerings into powerful tools for His service. Are you willing to give Him whatever tools and gifts are in your utility belt?

To Elijah, who battled suicidal depression in the wilderness, God asked, "What are you doing here?" If you're fighting dejection and a season of sadness, what has brought you to this place? Have you abandoned your friendships and accountability? Have you neglected your physical health or allowed self-pity to distort truth? Without judgment, but with a desire to minister to you in your need, God asks, "What are you doing here?"

To the disciples as they despaired over not having enough food to feed a hungry crowd, Jesus asked, "How many loaves do you have?" The truth was, they didn't have nearly enough for the task at hand. But that was unimportant, because Jesus was able to multiply their meager offering into abundant provision for their need. Through that miracle, they learned about seeing through eyes of faith and trusting that God can do the impossible. He can do abundantly more than all you ask or imagine also.

To Peter sitting at a campfire with the resurrected Messiah, He asked, "Do you love me?" We can profess our love for Him over and over, but the question digs deeper than that. Do our actions show that we love Him? Can others look at our lives and see that we love Christ? After all, He has poured out His life in love for us.

No matter what question He's asking, you can know that He searches your heart with that same unconditional love and grace that He displayed on the cross. Isaiah promises us that "The LORD longs to be gracious to you; therefore He will rise up to show you compassion" (30:18).

As you meditate on God's Word and spend time listening to what God has to say, don't ever forget that He cares about your well-being. He's not sitting on His throne monitoring the condition of the planet but not really caring about you personally. Don't allow yourself to become blasé and apathetic about God's love for you. Instead, remember that God's great desire and His passion is to show grace to you. He stands up in heaven when He sees you in distress, rising from His throne in order to show you compassion. He loves you, my friend. He loves you regardless of your answers to these questions.

So, like David, we can pray, "Search me, God, and know my heart; test me and know my anxious thoughts. See if there is any offensive way in me, and lead me in the way everlasting" (Psalm 139:23–24). It may seem like a dangerous prayer, one that could dig deep and reveal things we want to keep hidden away. Yet we can trust our God to lovingly lead us ever closer to Him as He searches our hearts. That's really where we want to be, after all—always moving forward "in the way everlasting."

Do you love me?
And beyond

Peter and us

Make It PERSONAL

- What song(s) do you sing that challenge you to surrender all to God and love Him with your whole heart? Do you truly consider the words as you sing them?

- What's easier for you—to declare that you love God or to accept and believe that He loves you?

Make It CONNECT

1. Why do you think Peter disappeared for a time after he denied knowing Jesus? Would you have done the same?

2. Jesus asks Peter, "Do you love me?" three times. Why the repetition?

3. Do you consider your love for God agape love or phileo love?

4. If someone says he or she loves you, what kind of behavior do you expect from that person? What does Jesus expect according to John 14:15 and what did He ask of Peter in John 21:15–17?

5. Psalm 131:2 says, "I've kept my feet on the ground, I've cultivated a quiet heart. Like a baby content in its mother's arms, my soul is a baby content" (MSG). How easy is it for you to be content in God's presence (like a weaned child) and not expect something more from God?

6. Now that you've finished this study, look back and decide what question has searched your heart the most. How can you allow God to continue the search? How can you avoid forgetting what you've learned or moving on unchanged?

7. Hebrews 4:12 states, "For the word of God is alive and active. Sharper than any double-edged sword, it penetrates even to dividing soul and spirit, joints and marrow; it judges the thoughts and attitudes of the heart." Have you experienced the painful truth of Scripture before?

8. Nehemiah 9:17 says, "You are a forgiving God, gracious and compassionate, slow to anger and abounding in love." If this journey through the questions of Scripture has been convicting for you, how does this Scripture verse give you hope?

Make It REAL

- This week pay attention to whether you are living like someone who is loved by God. Are you full of self-condemnation? Are you a worrier? Can others lose your love because you love them conditionally? Do you regularly question God's directions for you? If so, consider how you can make radical changes in your life.

- Don't walk away from this study unchanged. Choose at least one question from Scripture to write on an index card or in your prayer journal and contemplate it in the weeks ahead. Ask God to search your heart with that question and change you in revolutionary ways.

Make It LAST

Memory Verse

But God demonstrates his own love for us in this: While we were still sinners, Christ died for us.

Romans 5:8

Journal Prompt

In the course of this study, what has changed in your life? Now that you've finished, what do you want to change? Did anything in your heart surprise you, embarrass you, or encourage you?

Notes

Chapter 3

1. Eugene Peterson, *A Long Obedience in the Same Direction* (Downers Grove, IL: InterVarsity Press, 2000).

Chapter 9

1. Beth Moore, *The Patriarchs: Encountering the God of Abraham, Isaac, and Jacob* (Nashville: LifeWay Press, 2005), 67.

Chapter 10

1. Jennifer Rothschild, *Me, Myself and Lies* (Nashville: LifeWay Press, 2008), 108.

2. Eugene Peterson, *A Long Obedience in the Same Direction* (Downers Grove, IL: InterVarsity Press, 2000).

Chapter 11

1. Beth Moore, *The Patriarchs: Encountering the God of Abraham, Isaac, and Jacob* (Nashville: LifeWay Press, 2005).

2. Eugene Peterson, *A Long Obedience in the Same Direction* (Downers Grove, IL: InterVarsity Press, 2000).

3. Beth Moore, *The Patriarchs: Encountering the God of Abraham, Isaac, and Jacob* (Nashville: LifeWay Press, 2005).

Chapter 13 1. Priscilla Shirer, *One in a Million: Journey to Your Promised Land* (Nashville: Lifeway Press, 2010), 188.

Chapter 14

1. M. Mitchell, "Cyrus," in C. Brand, C. Draper, and A. England, eds., *Holman Illustrated Bible Dictionary* (Nashville: Holman Bible Publishers, 2003), 377–78.

2. Chuck Swindoll, *A Man of Heroism and Humility: Elijah* (Nashville: Word Publishing, 2000), 113.

Chapter 18

1. Beth Moore, *To Live is Christ: The Life and Ministry of Paul* (Nashville: LifeWay Press, 1997), 214.

Note to the Reader

The publisher invites you to share your response to the message of this book by writing Discovery House Publishers, P.O. Box 3566, Grand Rapids, MI 49501, U.S.A. For information about other Discovery House books, music, videos, or DVDs, contact us at the same address or call 1-800-653-8333. Find us on the Internet at www.dhp.org or send e-mail to books@dhp.org.

About the Author

Heather King is a busy-but-blessed wife to James and mom to four precious children. Born in Maryland, she and her husband have settled into life in rural Virginia where Heather serves as a women's ministry and Bible study teacher and worship leader.

Heather holds a B.A. in English from the University of Maryland and an M.Ed. in Educational Leadership from Regent University. After teaching English in Christian high schools, she transitioned to life as a stay-at-home mom, balancing life at home with ministry in the church and writing.

Heather is a regular contributing writer to online Christian magazines, has had articles published in *P31 Woman Magazine*, and writes devotions at http://heathercking.wordpress.com about applying the Bible to everyday life with all its mess, noise, and busyness. She would love to hear how God is at work in your life! You can visit her on her blog, find her on Facebook (Heather C. King), or follow her on Twitter (@Heather_C_King).

17.00 US
45.90 EC

THE AUTHOR

It is now over 40 years since John Caldwell completed his Desperate Voyage. He and his wife next travelled to America, where he graduated from the University of California with a degree in Sociology and became a social worker. A yearning for the sea soon led them to buy a 36-foot yacht, *Tropic Seas,* on which they set out with their three-year-old son, Johnny. Their second son, Roger, was born in Tahiti, and from there they sailed to the Fiji Islands and a joyful reunion with the people of Tuvutha, who had saved the author's life seven years before.

After 18 months at sea, they returned to Sydney, where John Caldwell donned suit and tie for an office job. But the sea still beckoned, and he and Mary spent two years of their spare time building a clipper-bowed ketch, which was launched with a case of beer and named *Outward Bound.* They spent a year amongst the Barrier Reef islands, survived a three-day thrashing from 30-foot waves off the Seychelles, then sailed via the Red Sea, Greece, Italy and the Canary Islands before arriving in the Caribbean. For five years they were employed there in full-time chartering, voyaging amongst islands, reefs and endless white beaches.

Struck by the shortage of palm trees, especially on the beaches of the Grenadine Islands, John Caldwell took coconut plants on most trips, planting around 8,000 in five years, and becoming known in the islands as Johnny Coconut. Coming to anchor at last, they leased Prune Island from the St Vincent Government, renamed it Palm Island, filled the swamps, cleared an airstrip in the jungle, and built a 24-room Beach Club resort, which for 16 years has been their home.

SAILING CLASSICS

SEA STORIES by Joseph Conrad
ROUGH PASSAGE by R. D. Graham
THE CRUISE OF THE ALERTE by E. F. Knight
THE CRUISE OF THE KATE by E. E. Middleton
ACROSS THREE OCEANS by Conor O'Brien
SAILING ALONE AROUND THE WORLD by
    Joshua Slocum
ONCE IS ENOUGH by Miles Smeeton
ENDURANCE by Alfred Lansing
BECAUSE THE HORN IS THERE by Miles Smeeton
SURVIVE THE SAVAGE SEA by Dougal Robertson
THE LONG WAY by Bernard Moitessier
CAPE HORN: THE LOGICAL ROUTE by
    Bernard Moitessier
DESPERATE VOYAGE by John Caldwell
THE CRUISE OF THE AMARYLLIS by
    G. H. P. Muhlhauser
SOPRANINO by Patrick Ellam and Colin Mudie
THE SEA WAS OUR VILLAGE by Miles Smeeton
THE BOMBARD STORY by Alain Bombard
THE RIDDLE OF THE SANDS by Erskine Childers
SUNRISE TO WINDWARD by Miles Smeeton
THE SEA IS FOR SAILING by Peter Pye
THE VOYAGE ALONE IN THE YAWL 'ROB ROY'
    by John MacGregor
A MAINSAIL HAUL by John Masefield
THE JOURNEYING MOON by Ernle Bradford
MISCHIEF AMONG THE PENGUINS by
    H. W. Tilman
LAST VOYAGE by Ann Davison
A WORLD OF MY OWN by Robin Knox-Johnston
MISCHIEF IN PATAGONIA by H. W. Tilman
SOUTH SEA VAGABONDS by John Wray
THE WIND OFF THE ISLAND by Ernle Bradford
THE MISTY ISLANDS by Miles Smeeton
THE CRUISE OF THE TEDDY by Erling Tambs
VENTURESOME VOYAGES by J. C. Voss
SAILING WITH MR BELLOC by Dermod MacCarthy
THE ROMANTIC CHALLENGE by Francis Chichester

DESPERATE VOYAGE

JOHN CALDWELL

GRAFTON BOOKS

A Division of the Collins Publishing Group

LONDON GLASGOW
TORONTO SYDNEY AUCKLAND

To Mary

Grafton Books
A Division of the Collins Publishing Group
8 Grafton Street, London W1X 3LA

First published in Great Britain by Victor Gollancz Ltd 1950
Paperback edition published by Granada Publishing 1985
Reprinted by Grafton Books 1988, 1989, 1990

British Library Cataloguing in Publication Data

Caldwell, John, 1919–
Desperate voyage.
1. Pagan (Ship)   2. Voyages and travels
3. South Pacific Ocean
I. Title
910′.09164′8   DC122

ISBN 0–246–12708–2

Printed and bound in Great Britain by
Hartnolls Ltd, Bodmin, Cornwall

CONTENTS

CONTENTS

Diagrams of
Pagan

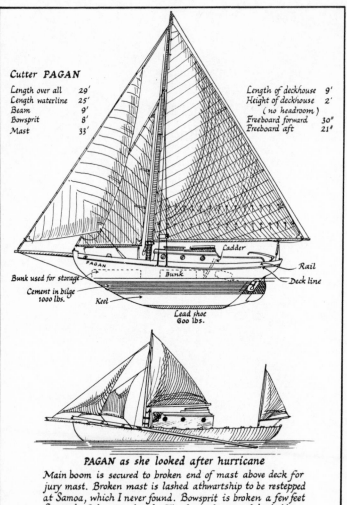

Cutter PAGAN

Length over all	29'
Length waterline	25'
Beam	9'
Bowsprit	8'
Mast	33'

Length of deckhouse	9'
Height of deckhouse	2'
(no headroom)	
Freeboard forward	30"
Freeboard aft	21"

PAGAN

Ladder

Rail

Bunk used for storage

Bunk

Deck line

Cement in bilge
1000 lbs.

Keel

Lead shoe
600 lbs.

PAGAN as she looked after hurricane

Main boom is secured to broken end of mast above deck for jury mast. Broken mast is lashed athwartship to be restepped at Samoa, which I never found. Bowsprit is broken a few feet forward of the stem head. The forward part of the deckhouse is smashed. The cabin ports on side shown are out. Ports on starboard side are intact. Rails have carried away at the deck. Sails are makeshifts recut from the original main-sail. An oar is stepped aft as a jigger mast. Estimated speed one knot.

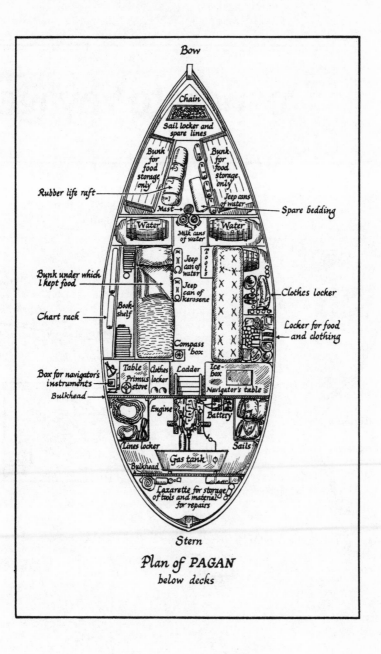

Bow

Chain

Sail locker and spare lines

Bunk for food storage only

Bunk for food storage only

Rubber life raft

Mast

Jeep cans of water

Spare bedding

Water

Milk cans of water

Water

Tools

Bunk under which I kept food

Jeep can of water

Jeep can of kerosene

Clothes locker

Book-shelf

Locker for food and clothing

Chart rack

Compass box

Box for navigator's instruments

Table

Primus stove

Clothes locker

Ladder

Ice-box

Navigator's table

Bulkhead

Engine

Battery

Lines locker

Sails

Bulkhead

Gas tank

Lazarette for storage of tools and material for repairs

Stern

Plan of PAGAN
below decks

Desperate Voyage

—— *by his sloop PAGAN*
·—·—· *by Copra Ship*
xxxxx *by Army Bomber*
— — *by Bus*

$\frac{3}{4}$ *inch = approximately 300 miles*

Bryant

New Guinea

Solomon Is.

Santa Cruz Is.

Vanuambalavu

Samoa

Coral Sea

Fiji Is.

Nandi

Exploring Isles

New Hebrides

Tonga Is.

Tahiti

Carolin
Ato

Hurricane

Noumea

New Caledonia

Sketch of Main
Fiji Islands

Vanua Levu

Taviuni I.

Exploring
Isles

Brisbane

Australia

Nandi
xx

Viti
Levu

Goro I.

Goro Sea

Vanuambalavu

Sydney

Suva

Tuvutha

New
Zealand

Tasmania

P A C I F I C

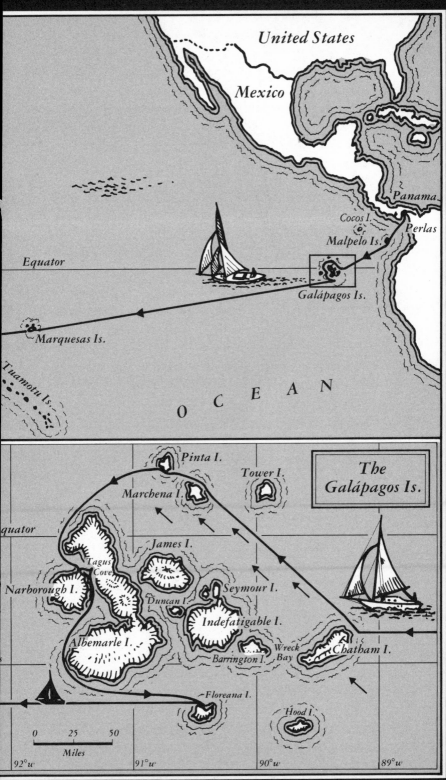

United States

Mexico

Panama

Perlas

Cocos I.

Malpelo Is.

Equator

Galápagos Is.

Marquesas Is.

Tuamotu Is.

O C E A N

Pinta I.

Tower I.

The
Galápagos Is.

Marchena I.

equator

James I.

Tagus
Cove

Narborough I.

Seymour I.

Duncan I.

Indefatigable I.

Albemarle I.

Barrington I.

Wreck
Bay

Chatham I.

Floreana I.

Hood I.

0   25   50
Miles

92°w   91°w   90°w   89°w

Desperate Voyage

CHAPTER 1 Preparation

My BOAT was in her trim, and rearing to be off on her long, ill-fated voyage. A voyage from Panama to Australia — 8500 miles of variable seas, reefs, and tropic islands — across the equator, through the doldrums, and into the hurricane seas . . . singlehanded. A voyage of uncertainty, but what could I do? I had been pushed into it by a sequence of compelling events over which I had no control.

I had to go, or so I thought. And I had to do it on the little sailing cutter I had bought two weeks before at Balboa, Panama. In no other way could I get to my Australian bride whom I had married a year before in Sydney.

It was May, 1946; the war had just ended. Ships were scarce and on chaotic schedules. I was stranded. Mary — my bride — was stranded also. She waited in Sydney, waited helplessly for the ship that never sailed: for that matter, for her, wasn't due to sail for another year. There just wasn't enough shipping; it was as simple as that.

I had tried everything to get a ship back to my bride, but everything had failed. I had been half around the world since marrying her, had been full across America, and finally wound up in Panama, and still no ship, so I bought the small boat.

When I first saw my boat, *Pagan,* she was nuzzling to a buoy at the Balboa Yacht Club, in the Canal Zone. In a word, she was trim — that is, she was built to sail. From forward of the stemhead to abaft the sternpost, she tallied a hair short of twenty-six feet on the water line, and twenty-nine feet on her decks. She ran ten feet at her widest beam, and three feet ten inches at her deepest draft. She lay afloat with a yeomanly air: bow up like a snob, her forty-foot stick raking back and up. She was like a canoe, lying low to the water as she did, stirring sensitively to every change on the surface.

Her cabin, about eight feet long, situated between the mast and cockpit, stood eighteen inches above the rail; other than that her decks showed nothing but her standing and running rigging. For her twenty-nine feet she was clean and spacious.

She had an offset bowsprit which ran seven feet out from the foredeck. This balanced her against her lofty mast, and gave proportion to her long boom that stuck past the stern. She was Marconi rigged, and double ended for ease in a seaway.

Pagan, in her lines and carriage, had the look and air of a sailor that not even a landlubber could fail to interpret.

Though I knew little of yachts — I had only visited aboard one small sailboat in my life — I liked her. I was willing to risk the voyage to Australia with her.

She had been under my hand for two weeks. She was stowed with the necessaries for a long sea cruise, her rigging was in order, there was no reason not to be gone. I, too, after my long month of inaction around Panama, was eager to cast off, and give her her head abroad on the sea. The sooner I sailed, I figured, the sooner would I be with Mary.

I knew little of the intricacies of maneuvering a boat under sail. But somewhere was the ultimate of faith that all would come right in its time. The important thing was to be off on the long trip — to be out on the sea, with the sails filling, the prow seeking the southwest, and water hurrying under the keel, bubbling in the wake.

Such a trip would never have concerned me but that I longed to see my bride again. However, I must admit, as sailing time neared I was gripped more and more with a fever for what was ahead. The adventure of it drew me on like a magnet. In three years of sailing on heavy freighters and oilers in the Merchant Marine, I had never been so taken with the romance of a sea voyage. Suddenly I was rapt in the prospect: my own boat to command at my own will on the southern seas.

I stood gazing out along the main road of the channel, to the open, seemingly level water. Unknown to me then were the perils to come out there in the next six months. I couldn't know the ominous twists the cruise was to take. I could only be impatient to be on my way to my wife. I was keen to close the widened distance between us, even if I had to do it on the little boat.

To do so was to take a course of least resistance and most happiness to myself, that is all. To accept the other alternative and give up the sailboat idea was to continue the forced separation from Mary of the past year.

I have always had a quiet yearning for far places. When America entered the war I had hoped to travel extensively while serving with some branch of the American armed forces, preferably the Army Air Corps. But because of a perforated eardrum I was rejected. I turned seaman and took work as a deck hand in the U.S. Merchant Marine.

After two years on the sea, and twice around the world on ships of foreign as well as American service, I tired of stuffy, blacked-out quarters and the boundless swagger of maritime gold braid. I deserted a Swedish merchantman in Sydney in

January 1944 and joined the Royal Australian Air Force. During my year of service in the RAAF I trained in Brisbane, Dubbo (in the interior of New South Wales), Sydney, and Canberra. It was there I met Mary.

At the end of my second month in the Australian Capital Territory it happened. I somehow committed a minor infraction of Air Force Rules, and I was placed on C.B. — confined to barracks for seven days. During this week I was given a number of humiliating tasks such as mopping out the front offices, and so on. The officer who directed my work was a WAAAF; blue-eyed, attractive, pleasant to take orders from.

We announced our engagement shortly thereafter. In a week my flight was posted to Sydney, where, in February 1945, I was "demobbed" in conformity with Air Force demobilization.

The American War Shipping Administration contacted me, hoping I would apply as an able seaman to fill shortages on U.S. merchant ships. Actually, I had wanted to enter Sydney University and recommence my education, broken off by the war three years before at Santa Barbara State College, in California. I was eligible for Australia's Rehabilitation Program. But the need for seamen was more pressing. The war was still on.

Mary encouraged me to join up with the Merchant Marine and though she had already served three years in the Women's Auxiliary Australian Air Force, she intended to continue service so long as her country needed her.

The day following my discharge, I went aboard an American Liberty ship and signed on as able seaman.

The stubby, rusted freighter, shrouded in wartime gray, put into Townsville in the north, then touched at four ports in the

Solomons. She hit at the New Hebrides, made the three main calls of the New Guinea north coast and discharged her final tonnage at Biak and Morotai. She returned to New Guinea for a company of Aussie "diggers," and transshipped them to Borneo. There we received orders to tramp to Brisbane for another consignment of Aussie troops.

When we hailed into Brisbane I had been gone from Mary nearly four months. It was May. In America May is the month of spring; in Australia it is the depth of winter. But love knows no season.

We were married in Sydney, then flew to Brisbane to honeymoon for three days before my ship sailed on a Sunday afternoon.

The makeshift transport was taking more troops to Borneo and would be back in six weeks. It was to be a steady schedule till the end of the war.

Our farewells weren't burdened by the heavy fact of what actually lay ahead for us. We kissed thinking we would be together every six weeks till the war's end; then forever.

The fat Liberty ship wallowed up through the Great Barrier Reef, around the tip of eastern Papua, and began the long haul for Borneo. Somewhere off Madang, in the black of brewing weather, a sudden cyclone swooped upon the overcrowded vessel and battered her ceaselessly. The whole night she was twisted, lumbering much of the time out of control, being pushed at will by boiling sea mountains and high winds. At a few moments before daylight — less than a week out of Brisbane — she rammed herself full speed and bow-on into solid land, just west of the little tropic port of Finschhafen.

Her bow stood fifty feet into the New Guinea jungle; trees

overhung us as far back as number two hatch. The diggers were lowered over the side to form a cordon around the bow, in case we were in Jap territory.

The crew turned to, to save the frowzy ship. Her anchors were dumped into the jungle, the cargo from the forward holds was heaved by the board as jetsam. Towing cables were led aft and veered out to waiting tugs. Gear was piled on the fantail and in the gun tubs to press the stern down so the bow could be worked from its coral grip.

After five days, with three tugs straining and engines full astern, she shook free and limped into Langemak, sister port to Finschhafen, her bows awash. The damage was surveyed and her gaping holes temporarily plugged with cement.

We started her thus for Frisco.

The third night out, the mate on watch sighted what he thought was a beach over the bows. But it was the wake of a PT boat. He threw all machinery in reverse and the terrific shaking of speedily changed engines shivered her as though she were rammed. The cement in the bilges cracked and re-cracked, dropping through the bottom. Bow awash, she put about for Manus, in the Admiralty Islands.

For thirty days the U.S. Navy fetched and carried for the naked gray carcass as she lay shored up in dry dock. Despite the attentions she received, it was almost beyond her to trudge across the Pacific to her interment in an American bone yard.

When I tramped down her gangway for the last time, I took a job stevedoring around the San Pedro waterfront. By stevedoring I kept my finger on the pulse of shipping. In a fortnight I contacted a tanker bound for Melbourne, and signed aboard as able seaman. That night I was on my way to Mary.

Two weeks fell away. It was August. The war had just

ended, and the crew hummed gaily at its work as it toyed with the prospect of living in a world at peace. For many of us this suddenly became our last trip. We were off Samoa, a week out of Port Phillip. Another week and I would be with Mary. It was hard to believe that after three and a half months we would soon be strolling Melbourne's familiar Flinders Street together.

The very night I relished these thoughts, the great wallowing tanker was diverted from her destination by an urgent change of orders to proceed to Manila with our oil.

Two weeks in Manila and we sailed, ostensibly for Texas City via Panama. At Panama we were directed, instead, to Aruba in the Dutch West Indies. We berthed at Orangestadt, like a piglet to a bloated sow, and sucked 125,000 barrels of black oil from the smoking, smelling refineries. As directed, we reported at Honolulu and hence to Yokohama.

There two weeks, a week in Nagoya, eight days in Yokosuka, and we were shoving off for Shanghai. Nine days we swung at the hook on the scurrying Hwang-pu watching the tumbled sampans and junks; then steamed down wind to the muddy Yangtze Kiang and thence into the China seas. Twenty-eight days later we fetched up in Panama, 10,000 miles across the Pacific.

A few days in Panama, and the big black-hulled tanker was on the track for Curaçao, sister island to Aruba. From there we made across the Atlantic and into Bristol Channel, docking at Avonmouth, England.

In two weeks, the first of April, 1946, I landed in New York City. My first thought, after signing off the tanker, was to find a ship back to Mary. I started a thorough search of the waterfront — immediately.

The shipping companies had nothing, passenger or work-a-way. The Red Cross listened to my predicament and offered all assistance, but they could find no transportation. The United Seamen's Service interceded on my behalf with their every agency; but to no avail. The hands of the Maritime Unions were tied; only a few ships were plying to Australia; and all of them were out and not expected back for months. "Try Frisco," they suggested.

I hit the road to the West Coast, hitchhiking. I thumbed my way, because, first of all, I could beat the bus or train; and secondly, by so doing I could afford to pay my fare to Australia more readily. I had with me nearly sixteen hundred dollars, roughly half my pay-off from the tanker. The remainder of the money I had banked.

The story from shipping sources around the Frisco waterfront was much the same series of doubts and speculations as I had found in New York.

Four days later I was shouldering my sea bag down populous Canal Street in New Orleans, with the dust of six states in my hair. Once again I started the search for an Australian-bound ship. For two days I tramped the rounds of shipping offices and seamen's unions on the river front. The best I could do was procure a banana boat for Panama as passenger, in two months, provided I could get a visa!

Finally, I caught a pierhead jump as scullion on a troop ship bound for Panama via Puerto Rico. In the Canal Zone, I packed my gear, and in the wee hours of the morning sneaked it through the tight customs guard thrown around the wharves. My purpose in coming to Panama was to catch a British steamer in transit for Australia; or in fact anywhere in Australasia from whence I could make for Sydney.

This scheme fell through miserably. Shipping was dead. I asked along the wharves from Cristobal to Balboa, but found no flicker of encouragement. In the end I was caught stowing away on a Dutchman bound for Indonesia. It was pure bad luck I was caught. The ship was steaming out the main channel and the whistle suddenly clogged. When the engineer came up to the funnel to repair it, he ran unexpectedly into me, crouched as I was just inside the tall, dark shell. He flashed his light on the loaf of bread and bottle of water under my arm — an uncommon sight on a passenger-less ship.

I was put over the side with the pilot and hauled before the stony immigration authorities. There was no interest in my plight. Nobody cared about my problems. I was hustled into the compound to await exportation as a crewman on the next undermanned vessel to pass through the Canal.

It was in the clink that I met George. George was an Aussie and, like many men one runs across in out-of-the-way places, he was desperate. He burned with a desire to get home. He had missed an Australian ship in Scotland and, unable to pass the physical requirements for the British Merchant Navy, he had no means of working his way back home. He was broke, so he had stowed away on a British tramp.

He also was caught and when the freighter arrived in Panama he was turned over to the Canal authorities and stowed away in the compound. When I met him he was soon to be returned to England to stand trial as a stowaway.

George and I were desperate men. We racked our brains that first day to unearth some means of escaping our predicament. I was to be placed aboard the first ship to loom up short of crew. The chance of that ship's going to Australia, or remotely near, was flimsy; it was more than flimsy — it was nonexistent. I could picture myself pushed aboard some rusty scow outbound from Panama to any odd corner of the world.

When George suggested we get a small boat and "sail the bloody thing across," I fell in with the idea; and in no time we were making wild plans. I knew of a small boat for sale at Balboa, having heard of it on the *Wind's Will* — Kim Powell's yacht, which I had come upon when stalking the waterfront. Kim, a veteran of Caribbean and Isthmian waters, and a sailor of judgment, said he liked the boat; that was enough for me. I told George about it and we decided to buy it.

That night, we scaled the back fence of the compound and found the owner of the craft. The boat was on the block for a thousand dollars. The owner was keen on a sale, but had compunctions about passing it off for such a harebrained escapade. I elbowed George and explained that I had sailed out to Honolulu on racing boats and "all up and down the California coast."

I explained that George had battled across the Tasman Sea to New Zealand as navigator and mate on a ketch. After higgling till two in the morning we came away glowing inwardly and outwardly, the owners of a boat.

The next morning I announced to the authorities that I was a yachtsman — that my craft was anchored at the Balboa Yacht Club, and that I must get back aboard. In due time, I told them, I could produce papers and show reasons and funds sufficient to warrant sailing out on my own to my wife. They dissented at first, and then, when they saw I was determined, agreed to free me if and when they could verify the facts. In the meantime, I was to languish in the compound.

George and I planned that I would go out and ready the boat — which as yet we hadn't seen — for sea, then at the last minute he would come aboard, and off we would go. That night we went over the fence to have the first look at our craft.

At the Yacht Club a small shadow in the dark, near the pier, was pointed out as the *Pagan*. We rowed to her and flashed our lights over her decks, and into her rigging, and down below. Twenty-nine feet never looked so short before, and it seemed to strike George the same way. In fact, when we had been aboard awhile and had become more acquainted with her limitations, he talked less about the boat and more about his coming trial in England. He hoped the sentence for stowaways wasn't too severe. I didn't embarrass George by asking him, when we went back that night, if he intended to go with me.

The next day the Immigration Authorities rather hesitantly gave me the nod.

By then I was in the newspapers. People came and stood on the pier watching me at work, and they always shook their head when they discussed *Pagan*. But I was oblivious of their comments. I owned a boat; it was mine, I was too busy working on her getting her ready to sail.

I noised it about the waterfront that I wanted someone to go with me, particularly someone who could navigate, because I knew little of navigation; but toward the last I didn't care who came along — anyone would do. There were three bidders.

The first was Jim, a discharged Marine. He too had married overseas. His bride was in Melbourne, and he hadn't seen her in seventeen months. There was no transport for her to come across in. His search for a ship, like mine, had broken down. He was seriously planning to fit out a lifeboat and set out on his own. Then he heard of me.

I met him, as arranged by phone, in a bar in Balboa. He, like me, hadn't sailed before, but, as he put it, "There's nothing two Americans can't do. What one won't think of, the other one will."

Jim couldn't wait to see *Pagan,* so I suggested we go out.

I should have kept my big mouth shut and taken him aboard just before sailing time. He thought I was kidding when I pointed out *Pagan* — he was looking at the fifty-footer anchored near by.

Finding no "kitchen" and no "bathroom" he chewed his lip and looked blank. When Jim left that night, I didn't expect him back, and he didn't come.

I didn't learn the name of the second applicant; he didn't stay long enough. He said he was looking for "adventure," but it was the kind he was used to enjoying as an officer in the Merchant Marine. I haven't seen a Junior Third Mate yet with less gold braid than the captain of the *Queen Mary.* And this one was no exception. He was lavish in praise of the fifty-footer and wondered when we would be getting under way. I told him my boat was the twenty-nine-footer on the other side, and we would sail as soon as he got his gear aboard.

What he couldn't understand is that a twenty-nine-footer is roughly only twice as wide — at her beamiest part — as an ordinary bed, and just a little more than four times as long. Not much room for "adventure."

The third bidder was twins, and they wanted to sign on to do no work at all, just loaf and enjoy the South Seas. I signed them on at sight, and I couldn't have made a better choice short of a round-the-Horn windjammer captain. The twins were kittens, castaways from a near-by machine shop. They had a way about them that took all the burden out of setbacks and disappointments when they came. They were better than a crew.

I was hoping the write-up in the Panamanian paper would attract a sailor of experience, or even one without. All I wanted was a companion. Whether he was black, white, red, or green didn't matter. However, regarding the latter, I didn't want him so green he would want to turn back the first day out. When, by May 24 — two weeks after I had bought *Pagan* — no callers came, I loaded the last stores, cleared away the decks, and watched for a seemly change in the weather. Time was skidding on. Out on the Pacific, skies were smiling on the sea, and would do so till October, when the hurricanes prowled. I had four months to outrace the hurricane season to the Tasman Sea and Australia; sufficient time for an easy passage, if I could get under way quickly.

I shook hands around the waterfront. Last minute comforts of books, magazines, food, cooking utensils, and crockery were piled on the wharf for me by well-wishing Isthmians.

When I stepped down the companionway for an early night, the air was clear, the night was clean, and a fresh wind was in the south.

CHAPTER II Departure

My DESTINATION, as the hour of departure drew close, was to be one of the outer isles of the Galápagos group about 1000 miles southwest from Panama. And, if I missed the Galápagos — and since I hadn't yet had time to learn navigation I expected I might possibly pass them before I learned — I was going to make the Marquesas, 3000 miles farther westward, my destination.

The maneuver of getting under sail, and pushing off safely into the steamer channel, had been in my mind a score of times. Over the last week, as departure time for my trip approached, I grew fluttery in the chest whenever I thought of the first encounter I was to have with the sails. What does a boat do when you heave the sails aloft?

I had a book on *How to Sail*. Every day I went through it and memorized names and mentally practiced the ritual of getting under sail. The whole thing made me shrink a little, and feel very small. So I planned the set-off in minute detail: casting away from the buoy, the set of sails — everything. I would be on deck at daylight to cast off. Once adrift, I would hoist the jib, then staysail, then mainsail . . . as the book directed. With the wind from the north quadrant I would run down mid-channel before it. And if it was southerly, I would cast off on the port tack, run to the bar on the right of the channel, then come about to the opposite bar. Thus no matter what the wind, or what my nautical shortcomings, I felt prepared.

The time to go had come. It was Saturday, May 25. A light breeze slid in from the south. My boat and I were as ready as we would ever be.

I was on deck at six. I wanted to be under way before the yachtsmen were out for their day's sail. I didn't want them seeing me make my first tries at the sails and tiller. It was for exactly this reason I didn't take a trial run around the harbor to acquaint myself with my boat. The armchair sailors in the Yacht Club lounge — with their yachting caps on — were ready to guffaw "saltily" at every move that didn't conform to their dainty code.

I pulled my little seven-foot dinghy aboard, lashed it in its place on the starboard rail against the deckhouse. I unfurled the sails, led the halyards free, and ran the sheets out. I coaxed the engine into motion, and the propeller turned over slow ahead. I danced to the bow and fidgeted with the shackle which joined the anchor chain and buoy. In a moment *Pagan* was free, moving slowly ahead. I jumped back to the tiller and pointed her up to the channel.

I decided on the spur of the moment not to use the sails since the engine performed so agreeably. I lashed the tiller, and sprang to the bow to ready the anchor in case I needed it. It was tangled with its chain, which was strewn across the fore scuttle.

I took up the anchor, heaved back on the folds of chain to clear them, and made to lay the anchor beside its hawsehole. The deck tilted ever so slightly — I stubbed against the traveler. My foot slipped. I went over, back first, clawing upward.

I was under in a second, dragged by the anchor. I dropped it, and groped to the surface.

When I could see again, *Pagan* was a length away, sliding eagerly on toward the moored yachts. The anchor chain was rattling through the hawse.

The chain drew taut as the anchor bit in, and *Pagan's* bow fell off, sailing in a long circle around the anchor. I struck out toward her. She passed within a span of a buoy, slid very close to a near yacht, then fell away noticeably down tide. The anchor was dragging. Beyond, to where she drifted, were boats, moored closely bow and stern.

I broke into a hard swim, head down. I didn't look up, I pounded at the water. When I looked *Pagan* had fallen farther away. Then, what she did stopped me short.

She struck a buoy, or rather glanced off it, and turned directly toward me. I swung aside; the curl under her forefoot slapped me gently. When the chain plates came up I took a grip on them and pulled myself over the rail, onto the decks.

I pushed the tiller down and she swerved cleanly away, making for a clear spot where I wanted to stop her and relax a minute.

Then she fetched up with a jolt to the end of her chain, and twisted, doubling back toward the cluster of boats. In a panic I cut the engine and wished I hadn't. The anchor, I asked. Will it hold?

Pagan dragged back and back. The boats loomed. I thought of the engine — I was deciding to go below and crank it. We slid past a mooring, then past the first of the boats. Then I remembered the sails.

I leaped along the deck to the mast and dragged down on the mainsail halyard. The heavy white canvas whipped and

rustled while it climbed — then it filled, bellied out, and by
its force slacked off the sheets. I ran to the tiller. *Pagan* was
moving, in fact she was scudding before a quartering wind
on the starboard side. I jiggled the tiller to clear the boats.

Quite suddenly, I forgot everything I had learned about
sails from the book. I froze as it were, and sat searching in
the rigging for the logical thing to do. I was confused, I
guess, by the sudden speed and my inability to reason with it.
Just then *Pagan* came to the chain end. She stopped where
she was for a moment, strained mightily, then jibed. The
heavy boom flew across with a swoosh from the starboard to
port side. I saw it coming and ducked, or I would have been
knocked sprawling into the harbor. I ran forward, broke the
anchor loose, and drew it on deck.

I heaved on the sheets and *Pagan* fell off on the port tack,
reached up to the wind, and skidded out of the yacht anchorage and into the main steamer channel. By now the pier
was peopled with sailormen out early for the day's cruise.
These "harbor circumnavigators" practice a hard scrutiny of
all things of the sea. A few had seen my glaring amateurism.
I wanted to redeem myself by a seamanly show as I crowded
into the wind, making for the open sea.

I stepped lightly forward and hoisted the staysail and
sheeted it flat. I hurried back to the tiller, to tend my course.
In a minute I stepped up and sent the jib fluttering into the
rigging. *Pagan* took on a more balanced feature in her looks,
in her pull, and in her angle on the wind. She sped along at
what I judged to be about five knots.

As she approached the sand bar on the rim of the channel
I put the helm well down, as it explained in the book, to
bring her about. She turned jerkily up to the wind, luffed

her sails for a brief moment, but fell back on the port tack.

When she had gained sufficient speed, I thrust the helm again to leeward. She rounded into the wind, faltered, and fell off the same as before.

Again I resumed speed on the tack. Then suddenly, and almost imperceptibly, *Pagan* eased to a noiseless halt. She swayed smoothly as though balanced on a wire, except that she was heeled at an unseamanly angle.

My kittens were clawing uphill over the tilted decks. I tossed them below to the safety of my bunk.

I doused all sail, started the engine, put her full astern. No response. I stumbled to the bow, plunged from the low deck into the shallow water and fitted my shoulder against the stem. I lunged at it — again and again. I rested a few minutes, watching the falling tide as I did, wondering how long before I would be high and dry! And in view of the Yacht Club!

I climbed to the deck, wilting as I climbed, cursing the bar with everything I could lay my tongue to. Then it came. The wake of an outbound steamer passed under her, wafted her high, then dropped her roughly on the sandy bottom. I gave the engine full throttle astern, leaped over the bows, and in a moment of joyous strength, aided by a surge of wake, shoved her free.

I dragged myself over the bows and struggled across the sail-strewn decks to the tiller. I moved *Pagan* into mid-channel, and taking no more chances with the sails I headed her outbound to the wide gulf, where there was sea room for my experiments.

When Panama saw me last, the decks were flowing their overload of sails and sheets into the water, the boom jerked from side to side, and halyards flew at loose ends in the rigging — but for all that, *Pagan* rode happily out to sea.

ᔓ   ᔓ   ᔓ

Day was gone. I was alone with the night sounds of the sea. *Pagan* pushed through the damp blackness slowly, as though feeling her way. I was straining eye and ear toward the bows for hints of land. In my lap my dainty kittens slumbered placidly, unmindful of my deep anxiety.

I drooped over the tiller, yearning for a guiding light to wink out of the black. I was lost. Three hours before I had felt certain I knew my position, but now I was steering a jigsaw course, and hoping for sight or sound of a haven where I could anchor and rest for the night, and think. The day had posed perplexing questions.

As near as I could figure I was some fifty or sixty miles off shore; somewhere near — I hoped — the little island of Pedro Gonzáles in the Perlas Islands.

It was ten o'clock at night. I was limp from hunger and from the work of practicing all day with my sails. The full long day I had hoisted and dropped sail, had maneuvered my boat on every angle to the wind, had even reefed and double reefed the sails, and had drifted and butted aimlessly over a large circle of the sea. In the end I knew my boat better, but I was left in confusion. I didn't know it well enough. Then unexpectedly dusk had swooped in. I found myself in the busy steamer channel, and grimly in need of a night of deep rest.

At dusk Pedro Gonzáles had been a blue smudge on the horizon which night quickly enfolded. Had I then used full engine with the sails, I could have soon closed in enough to make a night landfall with ease. But I held off. I had expected the breeze to build up soon after dusk and push me in just as quickly. Instead, I was becalmed on a glassy sea with sails slatting, blocks creaking, and *Pagan* rolling listlessly.

I left the sails up but put her under power and groped uncertainly forward. Suddenly the quick rush of seas came to my ear, followed by regular intervals of near quiet. I leaned closer to the night. A blackness blacker than the night reared up ahead, and soon the surf was louder.

I could see only the towering edge of the jagged isle where it blotted out the stars. Sometimes the seas, pounding against the blunt shore, sounded closer than at other times.

An outjutting of the shore loomed up ahead. I turned off, rounded it to starboard, and sighted another shaggy shadow on the port beam. I swung around and bore down between the two, hoping to stand in close where I could cast the lead in search of anchorable water.

As I crept along the seas grew louder. Close by to port was a curling line of gray surf — somehow it seemed it should be farther away.

Ahead I could see dollops of water splashing over the rocky shallows. The air was damp, as though there were spray in it. You don't acquire the mariner's instinct for imminent danger in a day of sailing! I flashed my light across the water and blinked it.

Suddenly, voices boomed from out of the black: *"No pase par aquí! Piedras! Peligroso!"*

Rocks! In a hair-raised moment I flung the tiller to port. *Pagan* jibed. Gleaming gray water flashed from all sides. I cut the engine. I raced to the mast and cast loose all halyards, clawed down the mainsail. In a trice I had, almost unknowingly, thrown the anchor out and made it fast at ten fathoms. Rocks were awash practically at the forefoot. On either beam the slush of water over shoal heads kept me on deck, heart abeat, for over an hour, as *Pagan* settled peacefully to anchor.

Mestizo fishermen rowed out in their frail *cayucos*. They swung aboard in the beam of my flashlight, grinning from stubbled faces, assuring me that my position, though precarious, was safe enough; and went away.

I sat on deck, eying the rushing water, hearing its ominous sounds — in a confused reverie. I thought back on the day filled with lessons, and I tried to look ahead to what was in store when I should be alone out on the ocean. The longer I pondered, the more I was convinced of my total inexperience for the trip I was undertaking. I didn't know my boat. I couldn't handle her. The day had shown it.

It was practice I needed, at least a week of it, if not two. I needed to work and live with my boat as I had done that day. Then I would know her, would be able to predict her behavior, could control her.

I thought of practicing in the waters off Pedro Gonzáles, using the isle as a base, and I thought of using the whole Perlas chain as a practice ground.

I flashed my light over the Perlas chart and saw in the tight-clustered arrangement of isles ideal grounds for my purpose. There were suitable bays to practice anchoring in, and there were close channels to beat through, and there were shoals and reefs and small islets to practice avoiding. In a revealing moment I decided my liking for them, and fig-

B*

ured on getting to work when daylight came. When I went below I was relieved of an unsureness that had been a part of me for days.

Now I could practice in a proper way. I could learn what I needed to know, and then sail out on the blue, easy of mind.

Throughout the day of working the sails and maneuvering my boat I had eaten little, and suddenly my stomach was squeezing and unsqueezing itself. For preparation of meals on *Pagan* I followed no organized menu. When it came time to eat I always glanced through the stores list and struck off whatever suited my mood and fancy. Then I rifled through the food lockers until I found it. I made it a point to keep a close tally on my stores, so I could readily know the exact state of my supplies.

When I outfitted *Pagan* in supplies I had the same idea you would have if you were going on a hunting trip. Hunting trips, however, are usually short-lived, whereas I had stocked up for well over four months.

When I provisioned for the trip it was a compromise — a compromise with foods I enjoyed eating, foods that were inexpensive, foods easy and quick to prepare, foods that would keep. I took aboard a gallon each of the following: rice, flour, oatmeal, corn meal, hominy grits, tea, coffee, honey, jam, oleomargarine, and sugar. The reason I say a gallon is because the only things I could find around the Yacht Club to store my staples in were a dozen one-gallon cider bottles. I couldn't afford to buy sealed containers to store food in, so I filled each of the bottles, screwed the lids on tightly, wrapped them in blankets, and stored them under my bunks. Because I had twelve bottles, I filled two with sugar.

For bread, I carried a five-gallon tin of hard, heavy sea biscuits. Housewives around the waterfront gave me a number of quart jars which I filled with dried prunes, dried apples, and dried peaches. From the ceiling of the cabin hung a huge bacon and a ham. They swayed with the roll of the boat, and freshened the cabin with a richly sweet smell.

The bulk of my food stores centered in a heavy load of canned goods — 248 tins in all, mostly large-sized cans. I liked the big cans, they were the right size for a meal; a few twists with a can opener and I had the quickest meal possible. There was everything in the selection from canned ketchup to canned fish for the kittens.

Of all my provisions, my favorite was pork and beans. Life on a boat whets the appetite and sharpens the appreciation. The simplest foods take on a zesty flavor. I didn't need, nor had I the means and time for preparing, rich, ornamental foods. My funds wouldn't allow anything more than simple, life-sustaining fare. Moreover, I was in glowing health, and had virtually no food dislikes. It was quantity rather than quality with me.

A small, low table on the port side in the after part of the cabin served as my galley. On one corner of the table was a little Primus stove — an intricate affair which worked by compressed air and kerosene. It gave a healthy flame in quick time. It made masterful fish stew.

Isthmian housewives had given me an array of pots and pans and odd tableware, no two pieces of which matched. It all amounted to an effective "kitchen," and when, on occasion, I wished to dine other than straight out of a cold can, I was able to set up an impressive formal table.

Means of storage for water had been a grave concern from the very first. One of the yachtsmen gave me two ten-gallon milk cans which I filled and lashed to the mast in the cabin. Someone gave me a ten-gallon oaken breaker, and someone else a little four-gallon oaken keg. I found a fifteen-gallon airplane gas tank in the rocks on the harbor edge. I bought six five-gallon jeep cans at fifty cents each — one I used for kerosene, and the other five for water. I bought two ten-gallon oaken breakers from the Commissary at the heartbreaking cost of five dollars apiece. From quart jars housewives gave me, I managed another three gallons which I stored in the forward bunks. When I sailed I carried a little over ninety-five gallons of water.

My fuel supply for the little Kermath marine engine consisted of eighty gallons of gasoline. There were twenty gallons in the built-in tank just forward of the lazarette. I had six five-gallon cans in the cockpit. Two five-gallon cans were strapped to the mast on the foredeck, two more were secured to the sternpost, and one was lashed to a cleat on each cockpit coaming.

Aside from the supplies of food and fuel there were other items. There were an army first-aid kit purchased from war surplus, a large cosmetic kit and other gifts such as nylons for Mary, flea powder to delouse the kittens, two brand-new suits of clothes — complete with overcoat and hat — in which to meet my wife upon my arrival in Sydney, a pneumatic life raft for emergency use, and two cheap feathers and a shark spoon with which to fish for extra food. I had a small library aboard, about twenty-five books in number, almost all of which were given me. Many magazines were brought down to the wharf for me, including comic books. The latter I would have discarded except that I felt I could pass them off to some appreciative native peoples along the way.

In the way of luggage aboard I had my personal belongings packed into my sea bag — my carry-overs from the Merchant Marine. I had seven suits of khakis, odd shirts and trousers, shoes, and foul weather gear.

I had a number of navigation instruments aboard which as yet I knew very little about. I was waiting to get out to sea where I would have time enough and ideal conditions for learning to navigate.

My total stores, according to my rough estimate upon departure, were sufficient to keep me in good supply for at least four months. If I was lucky at fishing, as I hoped to be, or able to collect island fare along the way, I figured I could sail for five months. This afforded me a wide margin of safety, since I expected to be in Sydney in just under four months.

CHAPTER III   Practice

THE PERLAS are a low, thick-wooded group seemingly at anchor in the southeastern quadrant of Panama Gulf. A scattered mestizo population of Indian, Negro, and Spanish inhabit its quaint semicivilized villages. They eke out a meager living from the uncultivated tropical fruits and vegetables, and abundant fish off the shores. Their "pueblos" lie on the leeward sides of their tangled islands and usually front small bays.

I had anchored for the first night in Perry Bay at Pedro Gonzáles Island.

The next morning early, I made sail. A brisk wind, wetted by torrents of rain, sent me east on my quest for a safe bay that I could work into and drop my anchor. Close by, in the lee of Señora Isle, I found a sandy spit and maneuvered up close to it. I guided myself in by standing on the stern, manipulating the tiller by foot, and sounding the depths, as I crept closer with the hand lead line. When I thought it fit I brought the bow into the wind with tiller hard alee, and sails luffing. I pushed the anchor off the rail and freed the chain to rattle out the hawsehole. I loosened the peak halyard and clawed in the main. I threw staysail and jib halyards loose and doused the staysail with a jerk, and teetered out on the bowsprit to pull the jib into a neat lump. I was anchored . . . and it had

been easy, I felt confident. I thought I would go below and
enter it in the log. Then it happened: I could sense through
my bare soles on the deck that the keel was thudding against
something.

In the tight anchorage I had neglected to stop off the
chain; it veered out full length, putting me stern first ashore.
The rain poured so heavily it stood solid on the decks before it could run off. The sea gurgled with its patter. When
I saw I was aground in this bleak, uninhabited little island,
the rain for the first time felt cold.

The tide was ebbing speedily. Two hours later *Pagan* was
on her beam ends. I sat on the top rail, drying in the new sun,
trying to picture a solution. My kittens moped about my feet,
wet to the skin and small as rats, echoing my hopelessness
as they scratched along the canted decks.

I saw my voyage at an end where I sat. I could hear voices
saying, "I told you so." I thought of my wife, and I thought of
going back to Panama without my boat. I watched for hours,
hoping a boat would round the bend and tow me off. The
tide was coming back and the bow was beginning to waver
about. She would either fill with water or ride higher on the
beach. I watched the tide seep higher around her, licking
and exploring. I got angry, and though I wasn't sure what to
do, I resolved to fight back.

I piled much of my heavy gear on the shore with the kittens. When the bow floated, and she righted a little, I shored
her up with a water barrel. The tide marched higher. I heaved
tight on the anchor chain and fired up the noisy little engine,
gunning it at high speed.

The tide crawled upward and I hoped it would crawl on
till it floated her. I jumped into water up to my thighs and

strained against the heavy sternpost. The bow was buoyant but the stern was fast in the sand.

I shifted weight from the afterpeak into the forepeak. Still no change. The tide had stopped rising — it was now or never. I put the throttle full down and jumped in again, pushing against *Pagan's* three and one half tons with every last ounce of strength.

She eased an inch, two inches — and stopped. I rested a minute and tried again. Another inch and another, then she slipped two inches. I was amazingly tired. I threw my back against the stern, pushing till my heels dug in. She stirred and slipped, then slid clear. My boat was saved.

Running aground was not my only blunder as my practice sailing continued that first week in the Perlas Islands. I made errors of navigation such as the time at dusk I mistook a sand cay off Viveros Isle for a smudge spot on the chart, and put *Pagan* bow first high and dry on it, where she lay on her beam ends for two tides before I finally hauled her out to deep water.

Then there was the time at Casaya. I saw a good spot to cast anchor for the night, just under the village, in the lee of a grassy spit, in two fathoms. Here is where I erred: in waters where the drop of tide was sixteen feet, I anchored in two fathoms!

At a monstrous hour of the night I was tipped gently from my bunk. I struggled over the sloping floor, through a jumble of strewn stores to the hatchway — then I knew. *Pagan* lay slumped over, her beam deep in the stinking mire.

All I could see was an eerie mass of shadows, except where a faint moon glinted in the morass. There was work to be done. It meant stamping about knee-deep in smelling slime and fetching and carrying to make my boat tight against the returning flood — and at the same time make her light so that she would float before she would sink.

Three hours later found me naked and mud bespattered, checking by flashlight the result of my emergency labors. I had nailed down the cabin door. I had dogged all hatches and ports. I had dug away from under the rail and lashed my two purposely emptied water casks close against the bilges. Inside I had shifted heavy lockers of food from the port side, on which she lay, to the starboard side. Much of her heavy gear I had carried ashore.

Later, when the lapping water licked upward on the planks, I slogged about in the slush and hip-deep water, straining my back as my jaunty little craft strained hers in sucking from her fast grip as she rose to the occasion.

But the most humiliating blunder I made came off in the bay fronting the junk lumber village of San Miguel on Del Rey Island. I let my anchor go when its chain end wasn't made fast to the deck and it flew out and disappeared into the harbor as I stood there watching it. *Pagan* was adrift, heading for the rocks. For some unaccountable reason I couldn't start the engine. Then *Pagan* was knocking against a shallow ledge, and that left me only one thing to do: hop in my dinghy and tow *Pagan*, by rowing, away from the ledge. But row as I would I couldn't fight the current, so I set up a wild scream to the villagers for help and they came out in their *cayucos* and hitched on, and together six boats of us towed her off to mid harbor, where I leaped aboard, filled my sea bag with tools, and used it for a jury anchor that night.

Another error I made: I offered a dollar in the village next morning to the man who would dive for my anchor. Seven men pulled out onto the bay to search for it, and strangely enough, despite the fact that they were scattered in their quest over a hundred-foot circle, all seven discovered the anchor at once; and they all claimed the dollar! It was worth seven dollars to have the anchor and chain again.

Hardly a day passed that I didn't make some sailor's blunder. But the more mistakes I made, the more skillfully I learned to sail, and the better I came to know my boat.

In the end I lost my anchor. It happened in the ideally protected little basin off Saboga. A great haziness surrounds the loss of that anchor. I entered it in the log as "The mystery of the missing anchor." The mystery is still unsolved. This is how it all happened:

I made an early afternoon approach to the village. I was sighted when still well out — and boats put off from shore to meet me. This welcoming party rather aroused my vanity, and I found myself shooting into their presence with a daring maneuver or two in the offing. The Saboga anchorage is windless; I pointed in under full power, with all sail up. I saw where I could sail between two close lying boats and impress the islanders with my skill at the tiller.

Pagan was footing it fast. The stem parted water with a satisfying gurgle. I grinned beforehand over the neatness of what I would do. But in the final moments, as I bore closer, my enthusiasm for the trick fainted away and I decided too late I didn't want to do it. Sailboats don't stop with brakes, nor do they make hairpin turns that greatly resemble hairpins; at least *Pagan* didn't.

I pushed the tiller hard over and screamed inwardly for a ready response. When the natives saw my bow waver, they too began to waver. Their paddles churned the water, and instead of spreading they closed, and instead of avoiding me, they drove into me.

Or so it seemed. I couldn't see. The headsails hid everything. I felt the thud when we struck, and heard the wood splintering, and heard the swearing in Spanish.

I ran forward expecting to see one of the boats badly scarred, but when I saw them both stove in and sinking, and their occupants thrashing in the water, I didn't know what to think.

The first of the natives pulled himself aboard. His face was candid with severest pain; a pain of hugest inconvenience. The others came and stood dripping beside him, fumbling their small pouches of wetted tobacco. Then the words flew. I was cursed and ranted at as only the Latin tongue, waggled by an outraged Latin, can do it. I could only stand flat-footed and mumble.

They demanded ten dollars for each boat. It was like asking a hundred dollars for a broken shoestring. It was especially heartbreaking to me because I was down to my last twenty-five dollars, what with paying for the anchor and purchases of bananas and smoked fish and a few lopsided pearls, the only kind found in the group, for Mary.

I offered them five dollars for the two *cayucos*, and they were ready to revolt. We quibbled back and forth with our limited language, refusing to understand each other till dusk was gone and dark come. Finally they left in a huff, taking with them my little clinker-built dinghy given to me in Panama as compensation for their "hollowed logs." I gave it to keep peace in the village, and to ease my conscience.

It was that night the anchor disappeared. How it disappeared, I don't know. All I know is it was gone when I went on deck at daylight.

I made the usual preparations to sail, then heaved in the heavy chain, heavy enough in itself to hold *Pagan* in a quiet haven such as Saboga. I knew the anchor was gone when I first pulled, but I thought it had merely slipped its shackle. I started the engine and moved back and across the air-clear water, peering over the gunwale, seeing the same moss-grown rocks and coral formations. About midmorning some of the natives rowed out and helped me.

By noon my suspicions were wakened enough to suspect thievery. There was no anchor on that bottom. It was a mystery I could best settle by getting under way before something else disappeared. I readied *Pagan* to sail.

I dumped my tools back into my sea bag and made it fast to the chain as a jury anchor. I ran the sail up and shoved off for Pedro Gonzáles Island.

It was June 1; I had completed my first week of practice. I had visited bays and inlets on all islands of the Perlas Archipelago except San José, which was quarantined by the Army. I had flogged my boat through narrow channels. I had fought upwind and upcurrent in tight waters. I had sailed my boat on every conceivable angle to the wind. I had lain flummoxed in the long, recurring calms and had made errors enough to win a give-away checker game.

My confidence was sharpened. I was learning. I could say I was beginning to understand my boat. In every emergency I had got myself out of what I had got myself into. I had now the feeling of a sailor — if not the prolonged actual experience.

Through it all my sprightly little cutter had proved herself a stanch sailor. Whether on her beam ends ashore or

butting clumsily into a reef, she bore an unaffected decorum
and grace.

My boat could take it. I liked her. I was beginning to think
of her as an individual. However, despite my liking for
her and confidence in her, I couldn't move myself to make
the jump off into the Pacific with her quite yet. I thought
of it, but shrank from it. I needed more training. At the
same time I realized I couldn't prolong the preparation much
longer. Another week, or ten days at most, was all the time I
could spare. I had less than four months to race the hurricanes to Sydney.

CHAPTER IV Confidence

As my eighth day of practice hauled around, I decided to do something more impressive than "playing around in close." So the morning of June 2 saw me cleared away for a "long distance" cruise around the whole Perlas Group. With my kittens wide-eyed and capering on the cabin I stood out to south from Perry Bay.

I could, by a nearly rectangular sailing pattern, make the entire trip in a twenty-four-hour day. But I hadn't counted on the uncertainties facing the seaman in the Gulf of Panama. Between calms, which were relieved only by impotent winds, I coaxed *Pagan* at a snail's pace.

I coasted around to the south of Del Rey, past Punta de Cocos. East of Pacheca Island (the last island in the string), and with the little isle bearing west by south, I turned northwest, and prepared to heave to for the night.

It was my first night on the water. I was eager to know what my boat would do, how she would express herself with a lashed tiller all night, sailing under her own free hand, while I was below in the bunk.

I didn't know exactly what to do, so I left all sail up. *Pagan* struck a northwesterly course with the wind playing at west of north. I lashed the tiller slightly aweather and eased the mainsail. As the wind billowed *Pagan's* sails, she tended to move her bow into it. Thus, close on the wind, the mainsail luffed fruitlessly. Jib and staysail barely pulled, but pulled enough to give the slightest headway. Then at the rudder's command she fell off west of north, with sheets straining and a few ripples in the wake. Thus, backing and filling, I left her to bide her night.

Somewhere late at night I awakened to the raucous whipping of headsails, the screech of wind in rigging, and driving rain. Gusts from a squall were beating her down. Gunwale to the water, she was flying into the night.

I hadn't yet handled *Pagan* in a squall; this was my first one. To get the extreme angle out of her decks I pulled down the belligerent main. She righted, as I hoped she would, and squalls suddenly lost their terrifying reputation. One thing was important: get the mainsail down. The jib and staysail could take it.

Dawn found me west of Saboga, with a light wind bearing to northwest. I swung to a heading of southwest and crawled along a lee shore under the beam wind. *Pagan* steered herself under a lashed tiller all day with nothing untoward happening. The afternoon was especially calm. My fishing luck was in the doldrums too, because I failed to catch my mewing cats their usual afternoon fish. They fretted on the foredeck, hiding under the anchor, refusing to be friendly.

Later, though, I hooked a beamy yellowtail, big enough for all three of us. Fried fish with strips of bacon, slack-baked corn patties, washed down with coconut milk went well for an early dinner. One nice thing about the crew on *Pagan* was the lack of complaints with the food.

The day was waning. I was standing well off the southeastern tip of San José. My course was shaped easterly; Mafafa, southernmost Perlas village — a good two hours' run — was my destination. It would have to be a night approach, but I wasn't worried, now that I had some "experience." I could make it all right by rounding Punta de Cocos in time to sight something prominent in the village, then steering through the dark by compass.

Punta de Cocos is the rocky end of a fingerlike peninsula that juts southward off Del Rey. In the crook of the finger of land lies Mafafa. Once I passed round the point, I could see the village.

The enclosing dark was outsailing me to the point. In one of those reckless moments, I decided to cut in hair close in rounding Punta de Cocos. I could see, every so often, a number of growling rollers crash onto the point, where a fast shoaling ledge threw them up. Seas were piling on it suddenly and toppling onto themselves, throwing white arms of water upward. If I timed my approach carefully I could shoot past the point at the interval between rollers. If one could rely exactly on the actions of natural things, wouldn't it be a dull world?

At the moment I changed *Pagan's* angle to cross Punta's bow closely, two big combers bore down on me from abeam. *Pagan* got a deck washing I shall never forget. It came so suddenly, and at what seemed a peaceful moment, that I was overwhelmed. The mast from the hounds down was awash with spray. I froze to the tiller and watched the water scurrying over the decks — the first water I had seen there. The solid rock wall was a heave-line toss away. Another roller rammed her, and crowded aboard; this one had broken farther out and came aboard in a surge.

I thought of the engine and the mistake of not having used it.

Pagan was thrown so close to the rocks that I could see crabs clinging to them. My decks were water-loaded. When I looked out to see if I could fend the boat off, I saw the cats swimming aft along the flooded deck rails, only their heads in view, wild-eyed, pawing through the water.

Pagan was about sixty seconds from the closest fists of rock. I slung the tiller alee and grabbed the kittens, ready to toss them high onto the rocks. A counter sea rolled back from the rock face, killing the effects of the next roller. *Pagan* steadied, filled away, and pulled off a few feet. But the next sea caught her where the first had. In a smother of foam she fell back. I could see nothing I could do. Cats in hand and tiller underfoot, I waited petrified. A fourth sea boomed broadside against her, spilled over the rail, and rapped her sharply against the first line of boulders.

As the jolt ran up from the keel I was terrified lest her mast jump out and fall over me. Without looking directly at it I could see the mast was swaying wildly.

All this time the tiller had been hard down. Her bow had twisted away from the rock face and bow-on she met the next sea. As she slithered a few feet sternward, I could visualize the rudder and propeller smashed into the rocks. But somehow she lost little way. She rose to it, foundered momentarily, and battled on. With her bowsprit thrown sky-high one minute and immersed feet deep the next, she slowly pulled away from the angry cape. Her sails were pulling with all force or she would never have made it.

She slipped away to smoother water, but my eyes were

glued on Punta de Cocos, where the seas charged against the rocks, and where I had nearly lost my boat. I had brought her off safely, and I felt a flush of kinship with what sailormen call seamanship. I had saved my boat — had acted sensibly under duress.

I smiled happily to myself. At last my confidence was thoroughly built up, I was ready to go; the Pacific beckoned. I looked at the darkening horizon, beyond which was my patient wife. In the morning, I thought, in the morning I'll be on my way.

But when morning came I was interrupted at my breakfast by rapping on the deck, and the cheerful voices men have at dawn. I came up to find a rowboat of soldiers tied alongside. They were from an Army Weather Station in the same bay. They climbed aboard.

No matter what their rank, they took me for what I was — a sailor boy caught in the rush of after-war.

They were greatly interested in my boat and the proposed trip. They evinced a hearty desire to help me "get ready to go." So I decided to stay another day.

We pitched in early, the six of us; and what a job of work we did. We painted the mast and spars. We did the decks and deckhouse and cockpit in a lurid design consisting of the four colors of paint I had aboard. We oiled the standing rigging, puttied portholes against seepage, and sewed bolt ropes onto all the sails.

One, who was a mechanic, dismantled the little marine engine, and at the end of the day he explained a host of benefits performed. Something about plugs cleaned, carburetor adjusted, feed line cleared, generator overhauled, valves ground, and so on.

Another, electrically minded, wired *Pagan* so that a flip of this switch or that set her cabin ablaze with light from my engine battery. Even her running lights were wired for emergency use. The same GI by performance of his magic transformed a junk radio I had wanted to "give the deep six" into a useful instrument.

Another boy, exercising a hidden talent awakened by army ingenuity, did me an outstanding service by building a large locker, half the width of the starboard bunk and its full length, from the deck beams down. The value of this, only a boat owner can know. Another lad designed and built in a bumkin for *Pagan's* transom to stay the tall mast in case of heavy weather.

Thus, ten days after my arrival in the Perlas, I was ready to go down to sea. From jib tack to mainsail clew my little cutter was at her fighting best. Time to weigh anchor and shove off.

But the soldiers . . . there's nothing too good for a soldier. By way of thanks for their generous assistance I proposed a trip. I admit I was reluctant to do it. I wanted to be on my way to Mary. But I had to show my appreciation to the isolated soldiers.

We sailed around Del Rey's southeastern bulge to San Miguel that day. It was the bright spot of *Pagan's* life under my hand. We returned at dusk the next day to the little bight around from Punta de Cocos. *Pagan's* last service as a pleasure yacht had been rendered. From now till her ill-fated demise, her work was to be serious — and finally grim and relentless.

That night found me outfitted for sea: water breakers filled and bunged, lockers stocked, and gear lashed and tied.

There was even a supply of canned fish aboard for the kittens, a gift from the soldiers.

One thing I was convinced of — my boat could take it. Ten days of hard usage had proved that. She had a history that made those ten days possible, and made all that she went through out on the open sea possible.

Pagan was Norwegian designed and built. Her planking, decking, ribs, knees, and timbers were from the weather-tested far northern slopes. She had blunted the challenge of turbulent Scandinavian seas for many years as a supply boat for lonely Baltic lighthouses.

In 1934 *Pagan* arrived in Panama after an Atlantic passage from Poland. Aboard were four Poles ostensibly headed for Australia as settlers. They had outlived hair-raising escapes and a discouraging series of bruising gales, after which even tropical, rainy Panama looked better than the prospect of sunny Australia.

They promptly sold *Dwaja* (spirit), as she was then known, and there followed for the little gaff-rigged sloop twelve years of peaceful "harbor circumnavigation." Light harbor sails, bellied by soft harbor breezes, were bent to her spars. From Colón to Balboa she luxuriated in the peace and quiet of yacht club atmosphere. A yachting pennant swung from her masthead. Gay parties took place in her cabin. She became well known as the "original" *Pagan*, on both the Atlantic and the Pacific sides.

At some time during her twelve years' career as a coastwise and harbor playboat her sail plan was redesigned to the Marconi rig, and *Pagan* became a sharp, fast cutter. She was regarded as one of the fastest little vessels on the Isthmus. Rail down, there were few who could match her.

The boat I was to sail with was fast and sturdy, and after my numerous experiences aboard her I knew her, I had confidence in her, and so I had confidence in myself — what more could I ask?

I stepped out into the cockpit and flashed my light through the rigging and across the decks, and found everything as it should be. I was pleased. I went below, where I lay a long time before I slept, thinking into the low ceiling, glad the time had come to be going.

CHAPTER V

Sunk!

EARLY ON THE MORNING of June 7 I lashed my little pneumatic raft to the base of the mast, heaved my sea bag of rocks aboard (I had taken the tools out of the bag when they showed rust, and substituted rocks), and sailed for deep water. Under a hard easterly breeze, sharper than usual for these waters, I put her immediately on a westerly course and made for the open sea.

My destination was once again the Galápagos Islands, the lonely volcanic group lying on the doorstep of the southeast trade winds.

My first stop would be Seymour Island, where an army weather station was located. That is, it would be my first stop if the army base wasn't closed down. The last word I had received before leaving Panama, from fishing boats recently in the Galápagos, was that the Army expected to be out by July first. This gave me twenty-one days to make the transit — more than enough time; I figured I could make it in eleven days.

My plan was to haul up there for a week, check my boat for her running and standing gear, and for her hull, then shove off into the southeast trades and race nonstop across the ocean to Sydney. With the hurricane season crowding me for time, I had no alternative, unless I holed in somewhere en route for three or four months till navigable weather returned. In case of necessity I had charts and sailing directions for likely island groups along the way. If trouble came it would be easy enough to put in for repairs or send a cable.

When the Perlas had faded from green to blue, and from blue to gray, I began thinking of what course I should steer to make my destination. I was in somewhat of a quandary about what to do, but remembering that the shortest distance between two points is a straight line, I laid a ruler flat on my chart and drew a straight line connecting the Perlas and Galápagos Islands. This line was my true course. It lay southwest. All I had to do now was to sail straight down it, and after a certain time, lo, there would be land. I soon learned that in deep water sailing theory is one thing, and actuality an astoundingly different thing!

The fresh easterly breeze began to wane by late morning. But it had enabled me to make a good offing. The Perlas were low down on the horizon astern. Off to starboard the Panamanian mainland was a thin, foglike shadow.

I whiled away the morning on the deck with my feline crew. The tiller was lashed and *Pagan* swayed gently and sailed smoothly as beam seas rolled under her. My native hat toned down the sun and my comfortable rope sandals kept my soles clean. I was stripped to shorts. About midmorning I cast out the fishing line, baited with the tail of a yellowjack I had hauled aboard the day before, and in twenty minutes I heaved a throbbing Spanish mackerel over the transom for the kittens.

They were the most antic little devils I have ever seen with a flapping fish. Hardly a day passed that I did not see them in battle with something I pulled up. The act was the

same every day, but it never palled. At first they approach
the fish with a cat's normal curiosity. A sniff tells it is a sort
of crêpe Suzette, cat style. They jump viciously upon the
powerful fish, growling for a tooth hold. With a violent flip
the fish sends them bowling across the deck, and they scatter
wild-eyed, tail flying, to the foredeck. In a moment the rich
smells begin to torture them anew, and they come creeping
cautiously back, innocent faced, hopeful looking. They move
up beside the victim, crouch low as if to eliminate themselves, and sniff distantly, then bunch up tightly for the
spring. I drop a hammer behind them — and trigger-quick
they fly scampering to the bow.

They wait a moment or two, then peer wonderingly
around the deckhouse corner with round, bright eyes. Down
the deck they descry their quivering dinner. Once more they
slink slowly, belly down, along the deck, range up beside
the delicacy and sniff deliciously. Throwing caution to the
winds they pounce athwartships of the fish and growl wolfishly. Like a desperate cowboy they cling for a few wild
jumps and again scurry away — spitting as they go, tumbling
over each other.

Patience is a game that is never taught; it is learned. Much
to my entertainment these goofy little cats never learned it
where fish were concerned. Right up to the day that I tear-
fully parted company with them, they were a riot of humor.

About noon the fresh breeze of the morning waned per-
ceptibly. This was the first weather item recorded in my log.
I was using a notebook for a log. It contained ninety pages;
with a page for each day's reckoning, I figured I would just
be filling it when I hove in sight of Sydney Harbor. Not knowing the proper procedure for annotating a log — if there be

one — I just jotted, "June 7, 11:00 to 12:00 A.M. Wind slowing up." Thus the voyage began.

For lunch I had island fare: an avocado, the butt end of a pineapple, two bananas, and coconut milk. Tied gaily to the mast were two stalks of bananas. Rolling along the decks were coconuts, avocados, mangos, papayas, pineapples, taken from the abundant jungle before I sailed. These, I figured, would be the last fresh foods before Australia.

Often a meal was nothing more than a can of beans ripped hastily open and eaten from the tin. Meals were fancy or simple in turn, depending on how I felt and a lot of other things. Sometimes I shared the cats' daily fish, and at others it was easier to lie out in the soft sun sleeping the day away than go below for the can opener.

Later in the afternoon the lagging wind veered to north-west and suddenly stiffened, kicking up the first white caps of the trip. At nearly sundown it was stronger and had hauled around to where it blew out of the west, causing a confused sea. A scud was flying in from over the horizon. *Pagan* had a considerable tilt to her decks, and I found myself wondering at what precise moment does one decide to reef, and when one does, how is it done? I had played at reefing down in calm weather, but now, with wind beating at the bow and bow beating at the sea, it was all so different.

I went below and perused my handbook on *How to Sail*. Alas, it was designed for harbor sailors and those who haunt protected waters; not one word breathed it of the reefing ritual.

I handed my way out of the sloping cabin onto the wet

C

decks. I searched the low, louring clouds for a hint of the extent of weather; nothing I read helped me. "So this is the Pacific's stormy greeting," I thought. I looked around and saw that the lee rail was awash; *Pagan* quivered lightly, her timbers creaked. The wind was definitely higher; a welter of water was surging under her, beginning to hiss and howl in the way of mounting seas. I wasn't sure that now was the "precise" moment to reef down, but I concluded it was a darned good one to do it.

How to get the sail off? How steady the spar in such a wild setting? The Indians say the best way to do a thing is to do it. But on a boat there is a proper way. One doesn't unbend the halyard, then heedlessly allow the wind to whip it from hand . . . as I did. Such negligence is dangerous because the sail spills its wind and flails wildly at loose ends. The sail can be split right down the center, the Marconi clips ripped from the luff, and four or five seams strained and rent so quickly as to leave the sail in six shapeless parts in a matter of seconds. The reason I know is that that is just what happened.

In the brief minutes that I clutched at the wind-whipped halyard, my sail flew to spare parts. I raced to it and fought with its threshing ends. The unruly boom swung across and across with maddening persistence. I clung rashly to it as I made to put the sail in stops, and in the twenty minutes or so required to lash down the sail I must have seen each side of the deck a thousand times. When I finished there seemed to be more lightning than before, and the spray stung more.

I discovered that in dousing sail I should have eased the tiller accordingly; for now I was footing it before the wind in all haste toward where I had used the day in coming from. In a questionable maneuver I worked her around — and suffered a few heavy slops of water as she broached. But I managed to heave her to on the starboard tack, with tiller lashed slightly to windward and with headsails aback.

I watched her point hesitantly into the gathering night. Now and then a heavy sea caromed off the bow, throwing it high; a comber curled under her, dancing her about. So this was all there was to heaving to in a storm. Child's play. Just let the mainsail blow to pieces, leave the jib and staysail up, lash the tiller aweather and hit the sack! Expensive, but simple.

As I stared into the night I began to feel a flutter in my stomach and the faintest hint of lightness in the head. I flattered myself by calling it weariness and went down to my pitching bunk. *Pagan's* cabin was having hell's merry time. There were the rattle and clank of gear gone adrift; the frantic to-and-fro race of water in the bilge; the vexing warmer temperature of the cabin; the weak whine of the wobbly cats as they fumbled about sickly. Finally the wash of angry water against the planks, gurgling suggestively as it does, became a liquid knell to whatever peace I had thought I felt.

I groped full-jowled out into the screeching night. On my knees and clinging to the shrouds, I "fed the fish."

The wind was intoning a terrifying whine to resounding crashes of thunder and sea growls, and between "feedings" I grew increasingly conscious that I was in a rising gale. More darts of lightning flashed and more wetness was in the air, smacking of heavy rain and nastier weather. The jib was bellied out to maximum. Since it was an old one I instinctively felt it would soon go. The staysail was standing the gaff; the main boom was snug in her crutch.

I stretched out in *Pagan's* lee waist and a bilious nothingness completely enshrouded me. I could think a little, and feel a little, but beyond that I was nothing. I knew the jib was straining; that any minute it would rip out from its fittings. She was shivering by the leech, and quaking the decks beneath my stomach. I turned numbly onto my side and watched the grim, hopeless match between boundless nature and man-made trivia.

The jib shivered mightily as a man will do under a withering load. A hank parted company at the luff; there was an intensity of already frantic motion. The aged fraying boltrope snapped, followed by a stringent rip of the sort fat boys make when they bend too far. At the bat of an eye the hapless sail was in tatters and its bits were whizzing off astern with the driving seas.

I attempted to pull myself together and view more sternly what was happening. The wind was still on the upgrade; the sea, growing angrier, was swept into foaming windrows. Lightning had grown to the intensity of daylight, and flashed on and off like house lights. The air was laden with bursts of rain. With staysail aback, *Pagan* was holding her own but floundering. Now that I had pulled myself to, I was sensible enough to be scared — plenty scared.

The staysail, I could tell, had reached that "precise moment" when a reef was required to save it. I loosed the halyard — but clung tightly to it and dropped the frantic sail to where I could get at the reef points.

Reef point by point I tied in the unruly strings. Staysails are uncomfortable members to deal with. You mustn't even

consider reefing one down in heavy weather unless prepared
to take at least a dozen buckets of water in your teeth. Then
there's the sail itself to contend with. It pounds madly
about your ears. The bow rears and plunges wild-horse like.
With all sail off, the boat rolls. And upon the foredeck
there is nothing to which you can hold. No wonder I once
heard a yachtsman refer to his imperious wife as "my
staysail."

I studied the screeching night airs before going down below, and what I saw didn't improve my seasickness. *Pagan*
had incorporated a wild roll in her behavior and the swelling
seas were beginning to bounce her about. She was falling
off before the wind; it made me wonder where land could be.

Down below, I put on my life jacket and squeezed the cats
between it and me, at my chest. Such tight quarters displeased them, so I took them out. I cut open an old-type life
preserver and removed its cork floats. To two of these I attached a string; and to the end of each string I tied a kitten,
by the hind leg. Then I went on deck and tried to feed the
fish. But I had what is called the "dry heaves." The more I
strained the worse I felt. I felt so useless I looked at everything and said "So what."

Sheets of spray whipped over the weather bow. The wind
screamed in the rigging. A raging sea was coursing astern.
The staysail had a press of wind that set her aquiver, affecting
the whole boat.

"What the devil do you do next?" I thought, and went
below. The cats were in a bewildered ball of legs and corks
and strings. I sorted them out and sat on my bunk with them
in my lap, disturbed by the noises I could hear and by my
imaginings. I remembered someone's saying, at Panama, that

the best place for a storm sail was the mainmast. I didn't have a storm sail . . . but . . .

I cut a dozen small lengths of one-inch line. Dragging out my aged spare staysail, I toted it lamely up to deck. The short lines I bent loosely about the mast. To each such "ring" I attached a clip connected to the leading edge of the sail and heaved the sail aloft with the main halyard. Because of her loose foot she strained considerably, but she did the work of a storm sail, and *Pagan* reared up and about less often. I dropped and furled the staysail, and hurried below.

The cats and I had dozed off into a questionable sleep when I was disturbed by the obstreperous beat of a rent sail. I found the little storm sail split from foot to peak, her frayed ends pointing to leeward. *Pagan*, of course, was wallowing violently.

What to do? Lightning was throwing the night into brilliant confusion. A series of squalls was lording it over us. It is said first things are worst; and this was my first storm. I was beginning to fear my little boat was heading for the port of missing ships. Such moments as these, when one doesn't know what to do next, are enough to make one vow to take up harbor sailing.

Pagan was lying in the trough of the seas. Boiling water, breaking over her beam, threatened, I thought, to turn her turtle. I hastened to unfurl the staysail — as a last resort. A heavy lump of water pitched into my ear, nearly knocked me sprawling into the dark deep. On an impulse and a fear I heaved my sea bag of rocks outboard and crawled into the safety of the cockpit and wondered what the effect would be. The bag sank but at the same time it dragged, and *Pagan's* bow swung smartly upwind.

It was deep into the hours of morning; seasickness, weariness, anxiety had chafed at my reserves. I trudged down to my bewildered kittens — and sleep.

At close on daylight it happened. Luckily the wind had abated — though the seas were running high — or it might have been worse. A sledgehammer blow smote *Pagan* on her keel. We were wrenched from sleep and flung to the floor. The cats yowled. I jumped to my feet and stumbled before I could walk. A rattle of displaced gear and rending timbers, like Satan's pitchfork pounding on the cabin.

I started for the hatchway, but I was knocked flat almost instantly. *Pagan* heeled dizzily and a dozen noises fought for supremacy as she shuddered from the shock. In a moment she righted, but another thump on the keel sent me sprawling again. I was sure we had run onto a sea-pounded shore.

The thought reeled through my head: "Wrecked!" I was glad I had my life jacket on.

I groped for my cats, for I feared I would have to make some desperate leap onto jagged rocks — and I didn't want to leave my crew to perish in the hold. In the melee they had dived for cover, but I fumbled upon the cork squares, so I ran on deck, cats a-dangling.

I had expected to see the towering shadow of land leering down upon me, and a shore of bristling rocks reaching for *Pagan's* tender planks. But I didn't see this at all. Instead, at my very feet, was what seemed the body of a mammoth whale, its tail roiling the waters off to the right.

And on the other side another whale, only smaller, was churning about lazily. I had heard of whales attacking small craft — but the absurdity of it in a storm!

I was petrified lest the monster erase me with a sweep of

that broad tail. Then the outlines of "that broad tail" took a clearer shape, and I made it out to be, not the tail of a whale, but the limbs of a drifting tree. A tree whose girth was such that its lumber would have made two or three or even five *Pagans*.

Its bole lay beneath the surface, its limbs awash, and the whole of it rose and fell with each sea. Evidently making sternway in the storm, I had come backing off the crest of a wave and landed atop it. I shoved the yowling kittens below, and made to fend the obstruction off with the boat hook. My efforts against a limb were of little avail. *Pagan* was pivoted athwart it, reeling with side-to-side motions and thumping with rebounds that were too much to take for long.

Heavy rollers crashing onto the forest giant twisted it beneath the keel, exerting a shifting pressure against *Pagan's* timbers. She groaned deep in her parts with the whole-souled complaint of a wounded man.

When a dozen seas had pounded us, and the keel had wallowed an inch at a time its full length across the tree, it worked away and we floated free.

I hurried below and searched by light for seepage or hint of damage. I could see none. However, I saw something flash silvery in the bilge well, under the ladder. I strained my hand through the water till it struck something slippery, fleet, full of life. I pursued it and caught it, and tossed it on the floor boards. A squid! A live squid in the bilge! Full two inches long, a half inch around.

I immediately thought of a leak somewhere in the hull, large enough for him to slip through.

I went out into the cockpit where the bilge pump jutted up from the after end of the cabin and pumped *Pagan* dry, and, observing the bilge, I watched a determined trickle of water flow rapidly into it. Another search over the ribs and planks in the cabin, and below the water line, revealed nothing. She had sprung a leak deep in her timbers, possibly somewhere along the keel and its adjoining strakes. I decided on the moment to head for the closest land. I could only think of Del Rey.

I pumped the filling bilge dry and put *Pagan* about. Unshaking the reef from the staysail, I hauled it aloft and belayed it. I pulled my sea-bag anchor aboard. In greatest haste, and perspiring in spite of the cool wet wind, I uncovered my good jib and lugged it topside and strung it. I regretted that I had been so careless as to blow out my good mainsail. I needed it badly. Under staysail and jib she ran off before the wind, pushed helpfully by stern seas.

I put her on a course of east by south, assuming that during the day and through the storm she had slipped a little north. One part of the sky was darker than the other; the sun was rousing from its bed; the headsails, higher up, were catching the faint light. I made the Perlas Islands dead ahead.

I pumped the bilges and thought I observed that they had filled a little more quickly than before. As a precaution, I started the engine and gave her full throttle ahead. Even in the short time I had engaged the engine, the bilge had filled. I worked the pump till it sucked dry — a sound dear to the heart of a seaman on a leaking vessel. But even as I finished I could look into the well and see it refilling defiantly.

Pagan was making fast time, but it wasn't fast enough. I thought of the spare mainsail in the sail locker and what it would mean to have it flying. I started below to break it out. A disturbing sight met me: the bilge had filled and overflowed; an inch of water was standing on the floor boards.

I jumped back to the pump and pumped till I tired . . . and the bilge was dry. I stared eagerly over the whitecaps at the colorless land, and it seemed a long way off.

A half hour went by. I never took my eyes off the islands except to watch the bilge fill.

Del Rey was about eight miles distant with Punta de Cocos still farther. On the port beam San José was about five or six miles off. I must have stared too long at the land for when I looked down there were at least three inches of water washing over the cabin floor. The leak was growing.

I took to the pump and worked it at an aching pace. I changed hands several times and still water gurgled in the bilge. When at last the pump hissed dryly, I sighed and peered anxiously over the long miles to Punta de Cocos. I could hear the splashing of new water in the swaying bilge, so I took to pumping again. After pumping a seemingly over-long time, I found that I hardly gained on the rising water. And in the time taken to peer below, I had lost the gain.

I jumped to the tiller, unseized its single lashing, and changed *Pagan* to a course of due east. I was now scudding her toward San José, three miles to leeward. Once more I stood by the pump. The water inboard had risen alarmingly, its slopping had wetted down the bulkheads, and my cats, curled and shivering in my bunk, eyed the rising water disdainfully. I pumped furiously to outpace the water. Ahead was an open beach. At its extreme left end stood a jagged promontory behind which was a protected shore. I had no alternative but to put *Pagan* on it. I heard that seamen under compulsion had often run their craft ashore for repairs or scraping and painting.

I altered course three points to port and stood bow-on toward shore. I worked madly at the pump, afraid to look at
the distance yet to go. Suddenly the motor sputtered, coughed
raucously, and fizzled off to silence. I took a quick look at
the engine — it was covered by water. I leaped back to the
pump and worked it fitfully. I was hoping *Pagan's* momentum
would carry her well in, because the tiny headsails barely
pulled. Slowly, slowly the shore closed in. I jerked still more
wildly at the pump, but *Pagan* was settling. Water lapped at
the gunwales. Below, the cats were crying mournfully; I
knew that they had been washed off the bunk.

I expected to see *Pagan* dip her rail under and sink at any
moment. Then, ever so lightly, the keel scraped bottom and
she steadied, losing her way. The kittens swam out the hatchway into the cockpit, towing their cork blocks. I tossed them
atop the cabin and hurried to the work of dousing the headsails. Then I busied myself with making *Pagan* fast to the
shore.

The decks were awash and the insides were afloat. I un-
dogged the fore scuttle, dropped up to my waist in the hold,
and fished out a two-inch hawser. This I clove-hitched to
the bitt; the free end I fastened about my waist.

I grabbed the kittens and gave them a toss shoreward.
They splashed about twenty feet from the sand. I dived from
the bow and came up near them, and saw them as they attempted the impossible — trying to claw atop the bobbing
corks. I took their corks and towed them the few feet to the
beach. Leaving them to shiver beneath the cold sky, I led my
line to a mangrove stump and secured it with a round turn
and double half hitches.

My feline mariners, with "salt in their eyes" — which is to

say, shipwrecked — tottered weakly up the beach, weary of the sea and its vicissitudes. Suddenly they saw the towering jungle loom up blackly and glare down over them with all its silence. With minced steps and yowling complaints they swore at their seaman's lot and squatted back on their haunches to berate their wetness and fright.

I scooped up my sea mates consolingly. Poor little sea-weary blokes.

Up till now my only name for them had been "kitty." But under present circumstances a name for each naturally evolved. The little blond female I named Flotsam, and the darker tom, Jetsam. Unfortunately their name day wasn't a joyous occasion. They spent it under a bucket on the beach, out of danger, so they wouldn't stray to the jungle to become table d'hôte for a crocodile or a boa.

I sat on the damp beach and viewed the dreary picture of my boat, foundered to her scuppers on an uninhabited isle. Right before my eyes she heeled over and settled to her beam on the watery bottom. Her port rail cleared the surface, and the mast appeared about three feet away, slanted skyward at an unseemly angle. It told the story of shipwreck. Still drooping from it was the tattered storm sail.

CHAPTER VI   Castaway

THAT MORNING, seated on this unfriendly beach, and staring at *Pagan's* sunken hulk, represented for me very nearly the low point of the entire trip. I concluded it was hell to be a greenhorn.

What a laugh. "Sydney or bust," I had said when I pulled out of Panama. Now, 60 miles away, my boat was on the bottom — only 8440 miles to go! The cats seemed to sense my rancor and snuggled deeper in my lap.

I swam back to *Pagan*. It was heart-rending to stand on the sloping decks and muse over the hopelessness of the situation. I had thought I was in a bad way the day I had run aground at Isle Señora. I proved myself every inch a seaman by the foul language I used that morning. I cursed and ranted with all the invective I could lay my tongue to, and when I finished, strangely enough, I felt infinitely better.

Seated as I was on the one dry spot, the upraised beam was a familiar experience. Thus far I had almost as much sea time aboard *Pagan* on her beam ends ashore as keel-down in deep water. The trip that everyone had deprecated because it would be "too boring" was getting a little too exciting.

I had gone aground at half tide. In an hour most of the deck was uncovered and water was lapping around the keel, knee-deep. I climbed down and waded about the scarred hull, searching into her every scratch.

Under my hand the little boat had taken a considerable roughening. She had proved her mettle. It was sensible to presume that if the spunky cutter could possibly be repaired and floated, she could easily run the Pacific traverse. My introduction to sailing, at *Pagan's* expense, was easily read in her scraped and scratched under-timbers. I opened the portholes to free some of her inside water. And as the tide fell lower I submerged head and shoulders into the engine compartment to unscrew the little seacock in the curve of the bilge.

The inside cabin was a frowzy raffle to delight a junk dealer. It was a headache I refused to consider for the moment. I was interested in *Pagan's* leaks; I didn't have to go far to find them.

The garboard strake on the port side had sprung at the stem, exposing the cement-filled bilge. Much of her calking had worked out of the seams, and through this fissure mainly the seepage had come. But there were other injuries beside this. The rudderpost had been wrenched from its keel seat. A few of the planks seemed disturbed where they fitted into the sternpost and stem; and a propeller flange was bent.

I noted the defects and noted they could be remedied. From inside I searched out a hammer, screwdriver, nails, and an old shirt. I nailed the strake flush in place against the keel and into the stem and sternpost. Using strippings from the shirt I calked the seams temporarily with the screwdriver and hammer. Of necessity I worked fast. The tide would soon be flowing back. I drove myself, so she would be ready to take the water when it returned.

I met the approaching tide as I crawled from under the last of my temporary repairs. There was only time now to secure her against leak on deck: to batten scuttles, ports, seacock, and seal the companionway off.

The sea marched up the beach, encircling my boat with lapping fingers and feeling at the repairs as if to escape through them. I watched.

Pagan lifted buoyantly on the flood as she had done beneath me before. Her leaks were only a driblet of what they had been; I offset them with a few turns at the pump. At full tide, well after dark, I drew my jaunty craft as close into shore as possible and moored her tightly with her keel thumping on the steep sandy floor and the bow pointing into the jungle. Wearied with labor and anxiety, I trudged up the beach to my wailing starvelings. In all the excitement I hadn't touched food or drink all day. I was so thoroughly jaded that even the thought of going back to ferret out a can of fish for my mates from the morass aboard was an abomination. "In a few minutes I'll go," I said. When I got up to go it was daylight. The cats were gamboling about. It was a fair day; the tide was ebbing; my boat lay parallel to the beach line. The work at hand beckoned. But first . . . we were ravenous, the crew and I.

On board I found that all labels had washed off the cans. So potluck it was. I reached among the rows of cans and grabbed two. They turned out to be diced pineapple and spinach. The cats, forced to face the ups and downs of a sailor's calling, whether they liked it or not, had diced pineapple for breakfast. For me, that morning, cold spinach from a can beat ham and eggs all to blazes, and the pineapple dessert was better than any cup of coffee I had ever tasted.

For the next ten days I lived the life of a royal Bohemian. I wore not a stitch; for a hat there was my matted crown, long since in need of cropping; I had not shaved since Panama and, for that matter, I had long since vowed not to shave until I was with Mary again. Barefoot and golden browned I lay to on my little boat, mending her scarred and strained timbers for a return bout with the sea.

My food was potluck, fished cold from a can; and the selections, as they turned out, were usually monstrous. But I rounded off my diet with fruits and vegetables from the jungle. Hard by were a grove of bananas and an abundant mango tree. Farther on I found avocados and green drinking coconuts, and papayas. I responded wholesomely to the fresh foods. My work showed it, and my full sleep and my appetite and my exuberance.

I bunked in the sand under a lean-to rigged from my staysail and oars. Such sleep, such appetite, such brotherhood with life as I felt in that rustic period, I have not known before or since. There was but one thing missing — Mary. But had she been there, there would have been no haste with repairs. There would have been no repairs. . . .

During those ten days I worked long and hard. When the tide was out I strove at *Pagan's* hull with what tools I had at hand. When the tide was in and my stanch little cutter was pounded about on the beach, I pieced together and patched my battered mainsail, sewing up its three big tears, and making of it a new sail, stronger than before. In addition I patched and strengthened seams in all my sails, resewed boltropes, spliced cringles anew, and attached the hanks and slides more securely.

The job of cleaning house and stowing most of the gear

on the beach at the foot of the jungle was a day's work. It was the work done before any other, and it left me with only my boat to repair . . . and, as I hoped, sail out again.

The garboard planks I ripped off, plugged the old screw holes in strake and keel, drilled anew and rescrewed them more securely than before. I calked the seams with special calking cotton brought along for the purpose, using a screwdriver for a calking iron. I covered the seams with lead patching full length, puttied and painted over all.

I put a lead patch down each side of the stem, overlapping where the planks joined in . . . likewise the stern.

I thoroughly scraped and painted her down to the lead shoe on the keel bottom. I reset her rudderpost and hammered the propeller blade into plumb. And then I was ready to think of horizons again.

By far the weightiest problem concerning *Pagan* was the means of refloating her and kedging her off the beach. I had no anchor. So I concerned myself with this matter first.

It was apparent from the beginning that I must make an anchor of sorts since I had nothing I could use in its stead. My sea bag of rocks was useless as a kedge; what I needed was something that could grip the bottom offshore — something toward which I could pull *Pagan*, if I were able to get her afloat.

I felled a scrubby tree on the jungle edge and dressed it down to two suitable timbers — one long and thick, the other short and thin.

The largest and strongest I used for the shank of my anchor. Diagonally across its end I fitted the shorter piece, four feet in length, as its arm. On the ends of the arm I nailed long flukes that would sink into the sand no matter how the anchor lay. Such an anchor needed no stock or ring, but it had one weakness — it floated. I remedied this by binding to it two slabs of lead sawed from *Pagan's* keel, one at its crown and the other at its upper shank.

I stood looking at the sea and my stranded boat, and estimating the distance between. My former experience of going aground helped me. In the beginning I laid in *Pagan's* bilge and on her floor boards a number of heavy stones to steady her by their weight against pounding at high tide. The strategy to float her now was: await the tide and, since most of *Pagan's* heavy stores were ashore and the stones on her floor were heavier than they, toss them quickly over. Accordingly the little craft should bob up. I could then kedge her away and anchor her. I inflated my pneumatic rubber raft to carry the kedge anchor off astern into deep water.

A half-dozen rods offshore I eased the hand-hewn anchor from the raft and watched it gulped from view. I rowed back ashore and sat beside *Pagan's* cache of stores on the jungle fringe. Flotsam and Jetsam crept into my lap, and together we watched the first investigating lips of the inbound tide nibble at the keel.

In a while, *Pagan* shifted about uneasily, thumping her beam on the sand, tending to skew around. When the tide had flooded sufficiently, I tautened the kedge line and seized its bitter end to the traveler. My boat floundered between her desire to rise and the press of the weight in her bilge. As fast as I could, I heaved the rocks over the side. *Pagan* buoyed up beautifully. I heaved on the chain, the kedge held, and off I went to anchor.

My chief concern was whether mv boat was leaking. If she

was leaking it meant I must run back to Panama for repairs. If not, I was determined to press on.

I went below and flashed a light along the planking and into the bilge. Everything was tight. Not a drop of water issued from the outer sea. When I came on deck the bow was pointing out to open water as though instinct had pulled it there and as though a prayer had been answered.

The same wicked intuition that had inspired me to sail alone from Panama now egged me on to make for the open sea.

It was late afternoon. I was anxious to be going. I pulled my rubber raft up to the transom, stepped into it, and rowed to where the tide tinkled on the strand and *Pagan's* gear lay heaped beneath a sail, and where Flotsam and Jetsam yowled beneath their bucket, the very bucket that was later to save my life. For the next three hours, I moiled with transporting the gear from the beach to the decks. At dusk I made my last trip, with the affrighted kittens staring innocent-eyed from atop the last of the stores into the blackening water.

In less than an hour I was lashing the little rubber raft under the staysail boom forward. I heaved the freak anchor aboard and secured it on the forepeak. *Pagan's* sails were spread; and billowing to a soft breeze, she stemmed out of the little bay. Something intuitive told me that this time it was real; I was on my way into the "vasty deeps" of the Pacific. Of course, I thought of returning to Panama to check my repairs. It was the wise thing to do. But when in an hour not a drop of water showed in the bilge, and when I reflected on the near month I had already lost, days, even hours, became precious in my race with the hurricane season across the Pacific.

The very fact that *Pagan* was again afloat, and making her own way, made me feel a thousand miles closer to Mary.

At midnight, when I had made a safe offing, I set the prow on a track of southwest by west, lashed the tiller, and turned in to my warm bunk with my mates.

CHAPTER VII   Adventure

From Perlas to Galápagos there are 900 miles of ocean to cross. I had been told in Panama that sailing craft had taken anywhere from seven days to eternity to make it. That was about all the actual information I had.

Even men who had sailed over this vexatious stretch of water couldn't lay their finger on anything much that could help me. When they talked about it they looked off at the ocean and frowned. "Work into the Galápagos from the east," they said, "don't get west of them; you can't fight back against the trades and the current."

So that was my plan: work south till I could shape up for the Galápagos by steering into them to westward. Someone said that once I got to the Galápagos, the rest of the voyage to Australia was all "downhill." The trade winds were the thing. It was the trade winds I was after, and as vexations piled up on themselves I looked toward the trades as a salvation worth fighting to.

To limit the conditions of weather in the area between Panama and the southeast trades to such a simple word as bad or terrible is crass understatement. What makes it bad here is that disturbances are general rather than particular. No type of weather is dominant. Rather, one encounters every conceivable annoyance — not to mention their combination.

I had been in one gale, and a squall in the Perlas. And I had thought them bad at the time. But when I nosed out into Panama Gulf and farther, Pandora's box threw wide its lid and hell was a-poppin' from the start.

I didn't meet any really severe weather conditions — that is, harsh storms. But I should rather have the weather flay me a week at a time, then waft me along for a day of sailing, than do what it did.

Almost every night I was double reefed at the main and hove to. Otherwise I was in a flat calm or in a wind too gentle to enable me to make effective headway against the current. Sandwiched between these three perplexing weather habits was the unpredictable appearance of tropical squalls. Usually their only indication was the whir of wind or the cry of a rent sail.

These waters are undoubtedly the sharpest bone a sailor can have in his throat. Three uncongenial ocean currents meet here and claw at each other under the keel. There is the Mexican current dropping in from the north with its cool flood from Unalaska and the coasts of Japan. Out of the west comes the equatorial countercurrent, torrid and forceful, bringing tropic warmth and tropic life with it. Up from the Antarctic, along the South American coast, flows the cold stream called the Humboldt Current. When these varying waters meet the same thing happens that can only happen when brunette, redhead, and blonde come seeking the same man!

In the midst of these variant upsets an unsteady, one-minute-vicious and one-minute-calm, southwest wind added the final touch of mayhem. For it was to the southwest that I wanted to ply . . . straight into the eye of the wind. So I had to tack; first to south and then to west, fighting the current which was trying to suck me back to Panama — and it was succeeding at times. Some days found me hours on end in nerve-racking calms. Then a gale of wind would prod me in the ribs, causing me to heave to and fall back for most of the night. The morning would find me in a dead calm beneath a deluge of rain and rumbling clouds, or in an electric storm, the sky frightful with lightning.

On the first afternoon out I was in a rising south wind with one reef tucked in and pondering whether I should drop sail and tie in the other, when suddenly the wind dropped away to a void. Great smooth rollers ran under me and away to sternward. In twenty minutes a behemoth of a cloud swept down on me from directly behind. I could hear it talking as it came. By rights I should have doused all sail and gone below. But I was too desperate to make a few feet of southwesting. All day I had beaten to and fro across the same acre of water, into the same forceless head wind. A stern wind was a boon. I held to my hat and sat tight. The squall roared up and very crassly gave me the equivalent of a kick in the pants. In a moment I was flying before it at about seven knots! It was just what I wanted.

Imagine footing it at that clip and plowing head on into the oncoming rollers? *Pagan* was flying off the top of one into the center of another, a great spray cannonading upward and wetting the rigging to the masthead. Waves of water sluiced along the decks and spilled over the stern. A thump would herald her fall from the back of a smoking wave, and a thud would tell me that she was plowing into the base of another. At one stage I grew a little apprehensive and determined to bring her about and shorten all sail. "Nuts to it, we're going somewhere," I called out; and let her fly.

The squall lasted about forty minutes, then fell away to nothing, leaving me in a highly confused sea.

⌒   ⌒   ⌒

The next day I saw my first tide rip. In a moment — out of nowhere — the sea became an acreage of numberless cone-shaped bouncing wavelets. It rose and fell in an endless dance, licking at the sky with unnumbered fingers. I sat looking at something I had never seen before. It was amazing to see the uncanny epilepsy. It actually jumped aboard, but ran harmlessly out of the self-bailing cockpit. Under the keel two contrary currents had met; and redhead and blonde were tearing out each other's hair.

⌒   ⌒   ⌒

Another incident was unique in its way. The day had been one of weak and vacillating ladies' winds. I had used the engine several hours during the long hot day, in a futile search for a breeze. In midafternoon I gave up and decided to do with what I had. But as night drew on I found myself quite suddenly in a gale — in fact so suddenly as to be unable to pull down sail immediately. By the time the mainsail was reefed and double reefed the storm was down around my ears in earnest. Frothy seas were piling up, and *Pagan* was pitching savagely. The time had come and gone to hazard the bowsprit and doff the jib.

Staying atop a heaving bowsprit in a gale is like balancing

on a rolling barrel. Every time the sprit goes down, you are past your knees in swirling water. About every fourth time, you come up with water in your pockets — your vest pockets!

You cling like grim death to the topmast stay and work at the sail with your free hand. On a dark and stormy night it doesn't pay to fall off. So you hold tight and work fast — but not too fast. You get careless. That's what I did!

I had been out on the bowsprit several times in the Perlas and I was approaching the jaunty stage. But sailboats are marvelous devices for impressing the need of constant vigilance. *Pagan,* in her own inimical way, heeled over, pitched full down and then came up, tossing her bowsprit at the sky. With the grace of a circus clown I floundered end over end into the reaching dark waves.

I fought instantly for the surface. A series of seas clouted me, knocking me sternward somewhere behind the transom. The bumkin was a bare foot out of reach — and I knew I must soon get hold of it, or something, or the next heavy roller, would sweep me down wind. My fiercest swimming was barely enough to enable me to hold my own against *Pagan's* slow slog to windward. Sea water was impairing my vision and stifling my breath. In this desperate moment I struck something: at first I thought it the rudder edge, but it was a pair of pants I was dragging astern to wash in the wake. I pulled myself by them up to the rail and clung to it for a moment while I rested.

The sea gave tremendous pulls — impressing me with its unlimited power. In four years of the Merchant Service I had not realized its infinite strength. From the decks of great freighters one is on the seas but not of it. One is cradled between sturdy bulkheads of steel. One just sees the sea. When a merchant seaman gets a salt spray on his lips, it's an adventure.

As I trailed in *Pagan's* spuming wake, too spent to pull myself aboard, I learned the need for some sort of line dragging from the stern, something to grab onto if I fell over again. After I got aboard I went to the bowsprit and wrestled in the jib. But before doing so I lay on the poop, staring soberly at the retreating columns of the sea. Like brutes they ran from under *Pagan*, growling into the night. It's natural that I reflected on what could have happened. The danger for the lone sailor is what I had just escaped. I had been lucky. Next time I might not be so lucky. I felt a close part of my boat, an inseparable part of it in the battle with the hungry sea.

I wondered if I would have begun this trip had I known of the actual uncertainties to be facing me, as I was seeing them now. Yes I would, I concluded. What I was doing was fun, it had thrills. Despite the danger, I loved it. There was an appeal that every man feels — the appeal to adventure. And besides, it was taking me to the one girl in the world.

The morning of the fourth day out was like any other, except for one thing. Daylight found me standing east of south, bent slightly before the wind, making laggard time. As usual there was something untoward about the sky — but that was nothing more than I was learning to expect. I had been deepreefed the night before. To make the most of the day I had risen early and hoisted full sail. But it was useless; the wind was falling steadily off to a calm under a leaden sky.

I cranked up my talkative engine and ran her for two hours before I came upon a light breeze. It was southwest as usual and mild enough to fill my sails but faintly.

During these first five days I was in the process of learning celestial navigation which heretofore I had been too crowded with tasks to get to. While learning the celestial, I figured my daily progress by dead reckoning, using the bubbles rushing off the end of the keel as an indication of my speed through the water. So far I had estimated my gait to be a modest seven knots! — placing me approximately halfway to the Galápagos.

At 10 A.M. I found a new interest.

A great blunt-faced shark was lazing alongside *Pagan*. He eyed me with tiny pig's eyes and sidled quickly in to thwack the bilge strakes with his ponderous body.

Seeing and hearing this activity of sharks was an old story to me. Many times in the night or day I have heard them thump the planking. They do it to scratch themselves — or maybe they are vengeful. The first time I ever heard it was when I was sailing in the Perlas. It was night. I was hove-to near Saboga and down below asleep. I was awakened by a sinister thump, which shivered the boat. I bolted to deck thinking it had struck a reef, because I wasn't sure of my position. My first thought was that I had come about and run back in to shore. But mostly I thought of a reef. On deck I could discern nothing. The air was static and overcast. *Pagan* was scarcely swaying. For a long time I was perplexed. Then from an oblique angle a silver wake of phosphorus marked the track of an approaching object. At my very feet it banged into the side, scraped eerily a few feet, and slithered away. It was a shark.

I couldn't have that. *Pagan's* planks were only one-inch oak and they were twenty-six years old. Too many back scratchings by hulking sharks and I would be swimming in my bunk. I broke out a spear and when the big shark lumbered in, I reefed it into him. With a startled twist he broke my hold and plunged speedily. Lost: one good spear. After that I tied a bowie knife to an oar — and when they ranged near I gave them a tweak in the ribs with six inches of cold steel.

But to return: the shark which filliped *Pagan's* hull that morning of the twenty-third was a whopper. I couldn't help but marvel at him. He was all shark. He had the swagger of a brute bully; he was half the length of *Pagan,* and had teeth the size of fingers.

When I saw those staggered twisted teeth I wanted them . . . to show what I had seen. I wanted Mary to see that crushing jawbone, to hold it in her hand.

I brought my heavy sport reel and pole on deck, and attached my largest steel shark hook. I baited it with a fat yellowjack partly gnawed at by Flotsam and Jetsam. When the shark came near I dangled it before him and dragged it away before he could look it over, a simple bit of classroom psychology which, as it whetted him, angered him. Next time he nuzzled it, and arrogantly swept it into his jagged mouth.

I heaved back with all the strength I had. The hook lodged unmistakably in his bold jaw, and with the burn of cold steel he tensed, then, slashing about with a startled suddenness, roiling the water, sent a wave against the planking and made off to beamward.

Threshing in agitation with his slow main strength, he battled away from the boat, making the reel hum. When he ended his run of sixty yards he turned on the hook and flailed the surface, gleaming silvery as he twisted in foam.

I braced myself against the lashed tiller for a ringside view of the most fascinating struggle I had ever seen.

The massive thing tore at the surface of the water, bending violently, from U shape to S shape, champing viciously. Sometimes he appeared astern, then on the bow, always with a smear on the quiet sea. He turned on his back and threshed fitfully, or spun in great full circles abeam and close aboard, followed by his pilot fish.

At one time he was more than a hundred feet down straight under me—so deep in fact I could see nothing in the limpid water. His most spectacular effort came about a half hour after he had been hooked. He had fought the line to its end, dead astern. With dorsal fin cleaving the surface he sped in fury full around the boat, threshing mightily as he went. Spray shot above him and a long wake rolled away behind him. He ended his circular run, paused a second, then sped fifty feet toward the quarter, swirled about, and raced away as though he would wrench his head off with the impending shock at the line's end. Barely before he reached the line's end he thrust himself from the water, and twisting on his back he sent a shiver from head to tail that, had the line grown taut — even if it were boltrope — would have snapped it like spaghetti. After that his defiance fell completely away. He struggled only pettily as I towed him to the rail.

The teeth I saw were unbelievable. They lay in two uneven rows, each two inches long and thicker than a pencil. They jutted at rakish angles, looked unmercifully sharp, and were wielded by a jaw mammoth enough to crush bone.

My envy of his power, coupled with the animal instincts of the victor, induced me to lean over the rail and punch him in the nose. I found it about as hard as *Pagan's* decks.

The great jaw, the jagged teeth — they were fascinating. But how to get them? My wicked intuition that all was well prodded me. Pull him aboard; cut his head off; boil the flesh away — it's simple.

Flotsam and Jetsam, with paws on the rail, could smell the fishy stench of the beast's breath and were fidgeting and mewing eagerly for a feast. I decided to pull him aboard.

First, I naïvely tried to lift him by direct pull, but only budged him scantily. He weighed hundreds of pounds. I fastened the main halyard to the gaff hook fitted in his gill and with desperate heaves dragged him an inch at a time over the transom, into the cockpit. What a monster. His head lay in the cockpit and his tail hung over the stern. He stirred faintly. I took the hatchet and buried it in his spine to end his tremors. A spurt of blood sprayed over me.

At the same moment the big body quivered violently. Flotsam and Jetsam went racing to the bow. I watched them. I heard a resounding scuffle and saw my tiller, splintered loose at the rudderpost, go flying into the sea.

All hell broke loose around me. The great shark came completely to life, threw himself in wild assault. With great sweeps of his tail and butts of his head he swept my legs from under me, almost knocking me overboard.

The great tail was pounding up and down like a sledge-hammer, splintering, slamming, erasing. The gas-tank hatch disintegrated in a flash and the brazed copper tank went flat, spilling its load into the bilge. I clung to the rail, horror-stricken. The cockpit coaming rumbled, shattered, and flew at me, and if I hadn't ducked it would have gone down my throat.

In the meantime the hatchway sliding door had been popped through to the cabin floor and the rear porthole cracked. The bottom of the cockpit was giving way. *Pagan* was bouncing as though pounded by great fist blows.

I darted as close as I dared, grabbed up my hatchet, and chopped away at the heaving spine. Again he set to beating with sinuous motions. The partition between the engine compartment and cockpit screamed and split away. The cockpit deck itself broke through, the gasoline drums rumbled into the engine compartment, and the shark lay head down on the motor. I jumped in and struck again, burying the blade, and burying it again.

The destruction went on.

Pagan was being blasted apart before my eyes. I hacked with the hatchet like a wild woodcutter. I opened gashes in the head, and in the back. I had chopped his dorsal fin half away. Still he mauled my boat. I was afraid he would work his way into the cabin and rip it down or endanger the mast. I struck the harder. I went after him like a madman — blood bespattered and desperate.

He mangled the engine with side movements of his head, bending the sparkplugs down and tearing the wiring away. He fell beside the motor, threw himself around athwartships, and lying on the propeller shaft throbbed till it bent out of line. I was terrified lest he should work his way against the ribbing and smash the hull open. I lay on my side atop the engine, eased close, and notched a great hole in his stomach and lower jaw.

He jumped spasmodically. I moved after him, lost in the

bloody, death-dealing strokes. I cut his eye completely out and opened a hole from his gill to his shorn dorsal fin; still he lashed like a whip.

I sidled closer, drawing my legs up so that I could fit into the confined space, and turned more on my side to apply all my strength. Aiming for his nose — a supposed Achilles' heel — I laid it open bone and all, as far back as his front teeth. Still he throbbed dangerously. Moving closer — inches from him — I hacked into his vital stomach organs.

I was so far gone I was hardly nicking him. But it suddenly didn't matter; he gaped at the mouth and lay still. I lay for a long time beside him, watching him, hoping he wouldn't move, because if he had, I would have been in his way and too tired to shift. Everything about me was either smashed or coated red. I was caked with blood.

Before I could consider getting the battered carcass over the side, I had a few jobs to do. I had to pump gallons of gasoline, battery acid, and clotted blood from the bilges. Then I washed the gore from the decks, cabin, planking, and ribbing inside. After that I cleared away the splintered and broken lumber, piling it in the cabin.

The cockpit was a gaping hole. In the midst of it, the kittens were growling hungrily over the shark; chewing tastily with the corners of their mouths. I cut them a sizable meal and placed them with it on the fore scuttle.

Cutting into the shark's stomach, I found a motley of tragic creatures which had wholly or partly contributed themselves to his meals: two whole squid, a large Spanish mackerel, a mass of predigested small fry, the yellowjack I had baited him with, and several chunks of flesh and bone torn evidently from a very large fish.

After such a contest to subdue the shark, I considered his jawbone more a prize than ever. I cut his head off and later cleaned and scraped the bones and yellow teeth — a gruesome sight.

To heave the carcass over the side I had to cut it into two pieces and tussle with it by main strength. As to the wreckage — most of my spare time for the next two weeks was spent in rebuilding the stern.

Because of the shark I added another moral to my list: don't haul sharks aboard!

The engine was useless unless I turned back to Panama to have it repaired. As I look back now, I realize I should have turned back and put in at the Mechanical Division in Balboa for the work. In the long run I would have saved time. Too, I probably would have had a much hastier and most uneventful and dull trip across the Pacific.

The principal reason I didn't do an about-face was the state of my exchequer — it was low; only twenty-five dollars. And that wouldn't pay the docking fee. Also, my navigation by dead reckoning indicated I was making from eighty to a hundred miles a day. I expected to be in the Galápagos in a week — once there I wouldn't need an engine. The southeast trade winds, I was told, begin there, and with their power and constancy motor power is unneedful.

So I bore on, strictly under sail.

CHAPTER VIII

Overboard

THERE IS ONE GREAT HAZARD above all in singlehanded sailing, as I had learned, and that is, if you should topple over, there is no one to turn the boat about and pick you up. This was always before my mind, and I was forever cautious to guard against it.

The day after the shark battle I rigged a life line of about sixty feet, which I dragged astern — something to grab onto if I should fall over. Sometimes I bent a hook to its end baited with a stripping of white rag, and caught a fresh meal for the crew and me. Or I tied on a dirty pair of pants or a shirt to launder themselves in the wake. I used it also for a log line to indicate my speed. Primarily, though, its purpose was that of lifesaver in case I should fall over.

But one morning even my lifesaver nearly left me afloat on the sea.

The sun was barely up before a tumult of wind was down on me from the southwest. The sea picked up into a churlish, slapping hand, and I was banging into the teeth of it. The mainsail and staysail were reefed. I hesitated about pulling the jib, thinking conditions would abate.

Getting dunked and even dragged off the bowsprit now and then wasn't discouraging any longer. *Pagan's* bowsprit was too long — about seven feet — and very small around.

Taking in the jib in a gale was an activity for which I was never able to formulate an exact process. Never once did I doff it satisfactorily — so to the end I was practicing with it. But to get it in I usually proceeded something like this: First I crawled out and loosened the lanyard. I crawled back and slacked the halyard a foot or two, dropping the sail. Out again to snap loose a couple of hanks, pull the clew in, and pack it behind the rail at the forepeak. Slack away at the halyard again; unsnap several clips and pull in more of the sail from the grasping water, and stow it on deck.

Invariably I always left the jib to the last minute before tugging it in. Because it was clumsy to handle, it made little difference whether I grappled with it in a mild gale or a full one.

On this morning of high wind I was preparing myself for a bout with the jib by the usual cursing and swearing beforehand. When I got out on the bowsprit, I found that the turnbuckle of the stay was almost unscrewed. I twisted it by hand to tighten it, but must have turned it backward — suddenly it parted. I grabbed a handful of the sail, and hung to it as the wind filled it.

The next moment I was in mid-air dangling from the billowed sail. I was fifteen feet up and the same distance off the beam. I had a death's grip on the sail luff and I was wondering if I would be thrown too far out to swim back if I should let go. I decided to hang on.

Suddenly the sail spilled its wind and I swung inboard, crashing into the mast. Before I could think to let go I was blown back into the air again. The wind was whipping at the sail. I was being shaken back and forth as a terrier shakes a rat. Then the sail slipped loose from the stay, lost its wind, and folded as it splashed onto a sea.

The knotted halyard end caught in the block and I was towed astern. I was clinging to the stiff sail and wrestling with it as I clung; trying to gather it into a bundle, hoping I could somehow save it by gaining the deck with it. The canvas resisted stubbornly. Then the halyard slipped through, leaving me adrift: I had only the sail to hold to. *Pagan* moved away. I had the sail in a close grip, and swam to the life line astern. But sea slime and small rubbery sea animals had grown to it; and hanging to it, while clinging to the sail, was like holding on in a slippery pig contest.

I was determined to save the jib. My spare jib had been blown out in the storm off San José. The one I was fighting to save was my last. I needed it badly. A jib is a vital sail when working to windward.

In a minute I knew that fighting my way up the slimy rope with the sail still in hand was impossible. I managed to edge a few feet ahead, only to be thrown back by the wash of a swell.

I was deeply mindful of the cruel steel shark hook at the line's end. When I stopped to rest, I found that the line was slipping steadily through my hands. Not all the pressure of my grasp would counter the drag. The hook was near my feet, and threatening to snag them. I was slipping helplessly. The sea, pulling on the sail, was sliding me back and back.

The sail was bundled loosely on my stomach. I freed my hold on it and let the water devour it. I hated to do it, but what could I do?

Pagan, double reefed and heeling deeply as she pushed into the teeth of the rising wind, had a plucky look about her partly denuded spars and exposed hull as her trim lines battered the rough edges of the swelling seas, thirty feet ahead of me. She was wreathed in spray. I could hear the bow cleave the oncoming rollers.

I started the long haul up the slimed-over line from handhold to handhold, fighting each sea and the bubbling wake.

I crawled onto deck and lay watching the churning seas, crested with foam, racing away to the horizon, rumbling like trains as they went.

Lying there thinking morbidly over what might have happened, I noticed, as my eyes wandered astern with each sea, a ripple on the water's surface. I could see that it was my sail, and that somehow it was fouled with the end of my life line, and towing behind.

I gathered in the line, hoping the sail wouldn't disentangle. It didn't. When it neared the transom I saw that the shark hook had barbed the sail at the boltrope. One chance in hundreds.

I later entered the occurrence in the log as "taking in the jib the hard way."

CHAPTER IX Malpelo Isle

THOSE FIRST NINE DAYS I figured my speed by approximation. Each evening I plotted an estimated position on the
chart. It was marvelous the distance I had covered. The water
was sweeping beneath the keel at a rate of at least seven
knots, I figured. According to my dead reckoning I was hard
by the Galápagos; but was I? I wondered. Someone in Panama had said, "Don't go to Galápagos by dead reckoning; it's
suicide." I was beginning to get uneasy the day I tried my
first sextant shot.

It was a shoddy affair. I spent the day capturing the shifty
sun in terms of an angle, and working out a questionable
noon sight from a maze of figures. Late that evening, after
juggling ciphers and sights all afternoon, I arrived at a position which put me somewhere inland in Central Panama.
I gave up for the night.

On the next two days I arrived at consistent figures — but
what figures! My wearisome computations, no matter what
number of times I checked and rechecked them, came up always with the same result: they placed me only some 350
bare miles from Panama. The figures said I was near a barren isolated rock called Malpelo Isle. I refused to believe the
figures. I stuck with my dead reckoning estimate which put
me some 900 miles from Panama.

But as the morning wore on I rechecked the figures. Unfailingly they established me as somewhere near Malpelo. Finally I scaled the mast and searched the horizon, and saw nothing more than the monotonous sea. It was dirty in the southwest. A hazy curtain hung over the water.

There were birds around and they led me to believe land was near. But there couldn't be land; the Galápagos were a day away . . . unless . . . it could be Malpelo. Then, as midday rolled around, from out of the sea eased the loom of land. Dead ahead the crag floated, about ten miles off, barren, solitary, unmistakable.

This meeting of boat and sea-swept rock out on the pathless ocean came as a sort of miracle to me. For eleven days I had sailed and searched and had lifted no more than a steamer's smoke. Then suddenly figurings and jottings on a squared sheet of paper said land would raise itself across the bows now . . . and it did! The land was before me in the form of an indistinct blob of rock, small, and frothed at its base where the sea charged.

Seeing it there brought a flood of relief. Navigation suddenly became a game of fun, all the uncertainty I had felt over it glimmered, and I quickly looked upon it as simple, where for years I had fidgeted in awe at the mere thought of it.

Before I bought *Pagan* I used to think one had to know differential calculus to navigate a peanut across a dishpan. Too, I had looked at Bowditch, Dutton, and Cugle's and walked away blubbering to myself in a navigational fog. That's the way it was when I first went aboard *Pagan*. In the front of my mind was the prospective trip out onto the sea and in the back, haunting me, was my ignornace of navigation.

The devil of it was, while in port before I sailed I hadn't a spare hour to study it, the whole two weeks I owned *Pagan*. I had such a high respect for its complexities that I didn't want to put forth from Panama knowing the little I did of it, which was only visual pilotage from flying. But what could I do? Time was against me . . . I had to get across the Pacific before the hurricane season set in over the Coral and Tasman Seas. There was no time, as I saw it, to attend a fortnight of navigation school. The moment cried that I go.

When I sailed, I had exactly this navigating equipment aboard: one sextant, given to me by Captain Baverstock of Balboa. A pocket watch, exceedingly reliable. A cheap compass, that came with the boat. A hand lead line. A copy of Bowditch, given to me, though I didn't need it; I used it once — to light my Primus stove. A copy of Warwick Tompkins's *The Offshore Navigator*, $1.50, and worth its weight in gold. A copy of Hydrographic Office Publication No. 211, 90 cents. A small cardboard protractor, 10 cents. A six-inch rule, 10 cents. Good charts of likely island groups along the way, $4.00. Sailing directions and light lists for the waters I was to cross, $2.30. Total cost, $8.90.

If you will navigate, take what is listed here and sail away. When, after ten days of study and stars, you can't fix your position, turn back and take up harbor sailing, for you will never navigate. Any sensible person who can see the sun or horizon plainly can use these tools to go round the world.

ٮ   ٮ   ٮ

To me Malpelo meant nothing. I was not on a sightseeing trip. But if I had been, I would not have come there for scenery. The isle is so wind-, rain-, and sea-swept that not even the guano from its host of birds will cling to it. Around its base are a few toothlike rocks. Otherwise it is sheer and uninviting. I was glad to see it for what it meant to me as a check on my navigation, but it was a setback to learn that in eleven days I had traversed only some 350 miles.

I laid my slow progress to inexperience and the host of frustrating weather conditions which had beset me. Also there was no certainty regarding the speed and exact set of the currents. But the main factor in my poor showing was the loss of the engine. The use of an engine in a calm, even for an hour, can often move the craft into an area of wind.

By nightfall I had made a good offing from Malpelo into the south. But a little later it fell calm. I dropped the main to avoid hearing it slat aimlessly and went below for the night. At daylight of the thirtieth I found that the current during the night had pulled me off to the northeast of Malpelo. The calm still held, and I fished from the deck to while away the time till a bold young breeze should whip me past the lonely rock for the second time.

Around midmorning a lusty breeze sprang up. I stood away to the west till I had cleared Malpelo, then shoved around to south and beat away toward the equator. Through the afternoon I bounded into a making wind till at nightfall I was deeply reefed and ready to heave to. Malpelo was far behind. In the face of a line squall I' doused the main and put her in stops, and heaved to for a stormy night. Before I went below, out of the weather, I had what I thought to be a last look at Malpelo.

Dawn came with rain pelting the cabin like bird shot. I got up to as morbid a bit of weather as I have seen. Visibility was nil; the wind high; a lump of sea running. It was a day of perpetual dusk. Not even the ubiquitous sea birds were out. I didn't dare put up a stitch of cloth. I stayed below.

Though I couldn't see it I knew the deformed island was somewhere near. For three days now I had been in its vicinity, and I grew sober whenever I thought of my helplessness before the weather.

At noon sea and air were still unchanged, except that off to starboard I could catch the recurrent hollow boom of pounding seas. At first I thought a ship was somewhere about. But there was no blast of foghorn. After a while I realized I was falling back before the storm, past Malpelo.

Deep in the night the winds abated. I climbed out of the warm sack and showed on deck. Stars blinked in patches; the sea was still rolling in heavily; the air was both bold and weak as it is in moments of change. But it looked as if some sail could stand. I tied a reef into the mainsail and ran her up. In a few hours I passed Malpelo for the third time, looking gray in the early dawn.

The breeze freshened as the sun climbed. Late in the morning I tied in the last reefs and pulled down the jib. In the early afternoon the wind veered to a little north of west. A heavy swell set in from the south. Shortly cross seas were at work and *Pagan* was rolling and yawing wildly. Malpelo hid herself in the falling clouds. By dark I was hove-to properly.

The cats were tottering weakly on the bunk with *mal de mer*. I tucked their drooping little bodies close by me where they would be warm, and made them feel in their misery that they had an understanding friend.

The wind was backing slowly to its wonted position. Cross seas were worsening. Above the noise of wind in the rigging and rumbling of sea crests I could hear occasional proofs of seas breaking on Malpelo.

Long after I had bedded down I was awakened by the nearer crash of seas on a shore. I knew before I uncovered myself that it was Malpelo. Damn this island; wouldn't I ever get past it? On deck I reached with eye and ear into the wet night of drizzle and made the crash and hiss of the surf dead astern more or less. I couldn't risk falling back farther, so I strung up the staysail to see if *Pagan* could stand off a lee shore.

In an hour the roar was louder. It was no longer difficult to hear or make out its bearing. *Pagan* could hold her own with the wind, but it was the current that was sucking her back. I reefed the staysail and put up the double-reefed main. For the remainder of the night she held her own.

At daylight — five days after sighting the island — I found Malpelo leering at me a hundred yards down wind, and the wind was stiffening! She was directly in my wake, and reaching closer with each squall and gust. I was gravely in need of the engine. A scathing wind was on. *Pagan* had no business with sail up — still, I didn't dare take in a stitch.

At times it looked as though she might ride clear of the isle if I should drop sail and let her drift. I was tempted to back her around and risk clearing the island by running before the wind. But in such a sea I was afraid of being broached-to by veering too sharply into the wind, or pooped by shipping a wave over the stern. With *Pagan's* cockpit still not fully repaired from the battle with the shark, I didn't dare hazard it. The more I watched the jagged spire the more ominous it became.

A cold wind swept the clouds from the air. The blue dome

of the sky, across which a cool sun worked up to high noon,
looked down over me as I grew furrowed at the brow. There
was no need for a noon sight; my exact position was impressed on me by every minute.

I could easily have tossed a sea biscuit onto the closest
rocks. The roar quite suddenly grew deafening. It's a wonder Malpelo isn't toppled right over by force of driving seas,
so greatly do they slam against her. I slipped as close to her
weather-worn sides as I dared, still hoping the wind would
abate, or that *Pagan* would work away.

At this juncture I did the only thing I could possibly have
done. But first I pushed my little pneumatic life raft off the
foredeck and led it aft to secure it to the bumkin, in readiness
against the moment I might need it. I tied the cork blocks to
Flotsam and Jetsam and stuck them in a corner of the cockpit. Then, knife in hand, I cut the lashings and reef points
away along the boom, freeing the sail, and jerked the strained
canvas hastily up. It filled, and *Pagan* shivered. The lee rail
went under the sea and a froth swirled against the deckhouse.

I jumped to the tiller and pointed *Pagan* as far off the wind
as I could without broaching her to. She heeled more steeply
and the rudder kicked. She breasted each sea jerkily. Holding
the tiller was real work. Great lumps of sea bombarded the
windward rail. Spray landed on the cliff face close abeam.

I knew the sail wouldn't hold long, but a few minutes'
sailing would drive me far enough to clear the rocks. If the
sail flew out at the seams right away — I had only one resort,
the rubber raft. Flotsam and Jetsam were unmindful of my
weighted concerns. They sat close together like a furry ball,
looking calmly ahead.

In five minutes I peered down wind and thought that even

then I could clear the isle. Then the slides ripped from the luff of the sail. They screeched and the sail pounded at loose ends. I shoved the tiller down. *Pagan* rounded to into the wind, and fell before it. I knew she would pass close to the rocks if she passed at all. And close it was. Spray from the battered stone fell over us. It reminded me of Punta de Cocos. Flotsam and Jetsam shivered and crawled up to my lap.

The same night I drifted far to northeastward of Malpelo. At dawn the wind was still high, a lumpy sea was still rolling — and *Pagan*, under staysail and jib, was hove-to far to leeward of the horny rock. Overhead was the clearest sky I have seen on the Pacific; not a cloud showed, only a depthless blue. A fierce unvarying wind blew the full day, driving cresting seas onto the decks. I was seated in the chill cabin at work with palm and needle on the tattered mainsail. She had pulled loose at the seams, and had frayed a bit at the ends. Here and there was a rip which demanded a little attention. I noted that only the seams sewed by machine had split; those which I had stitched in at San José were good.

As I worked I thought, Why go on fighting uselessly against the fitful winds overhead and the redheads and blondes at loggerheads around the keel? Six days on one small field of water. I was for turning back to Panama, for a rest and repairs and a new start. The more I thought of doing it, the more sensible it sounded. Then my wicked intuition lulled me, telling me the trade winds were hard by, and coaxing me to push on. Mug that I am, I listened.

Late in the afternoon I completed the job and spent the time to dusk fretting before a porthole. Through the night the wind held, and only with the dawn did it moderate to where I could put on the sails and start the long beat into the wind toward Malpelo for the fourth time. All morning I worked sail and tiller. At noon I was close by the rock.

Throughout the afternoon I sailed under a halcyon sky, hoping the friendly wind would hold till the night. I was beginning to think of Malpelo as a jinx. If only I could pass out of sight of her once, my troubles would be over. As I passed her I stood at the shrouds and loathed the sight of her hornlike crags in the belated twilight. At ten o'clock, with wind still holding fair, I tied the proper angle on the rudder and called it a day.

For the first few hours of the next morning I could see a tuft of rock on the horizon astern. What an unburdening it was to imagine not seeing that grotesque shape again. Late in the forenoon, I saw again what I had not seen for eight tiring days — a landless expanse of sea.

CHAPTER X

Navigation

For the next few days there were equable breezes. Old Phoebus came out from his grizzled curtain and washed the sea warmly. It was wonderful to be on deck all day. No line squalls, no nightly gales, no ladies' winds. I made strange entries in the log those days. Something about blue skies, sunny days, warm tropical nights.

I was able in those few soft days to put the finishing touches to the deck work on the stern. I lengthened the cockpit, by eliminating the lazarette, so that it extended to the rudderstock, making it capacious enough, if need be, to sleep in. Since the engine was now ballast, I lashed it down to its bed and extended the forepart of the cockpit right up to the hatchway. When I completed all, the stern was infinitely altered — from the lazarette to the hatchway, it was one long roomy cockpit.

The shark had slammed away the sliding hatchway door, and since then I had done with a towel tacked over the opening, which I untacked each time I came out from below. This too I repaired. I built in a pair of small, swinging doors which opened outward, and which — so I thought in my boundless confidence — were a vast improvement over the thick, heavy, sliding door.

Between the engine compartment and the main cabin I

installed a watertight bulkhead. This I had wanted to do before leaving Panama but couldn't spare the time. The watertight bulkhead afforded the degree of safety I had long wanted. I am thankful I built it as sturdily as I did — it saved my life.

In only a few days after leaving Malpelo, all the deck work was finished. There was time to be devoted to the cats, to fishing, and to perfecting my navigation.

ᔐ   ᔐ   ᔐ

Navigation was done wholly by the sun. On several occasions I experimented with the moon and stars, obtaining a dusk or dawn "fix" with simultaneous sextant readings on two bodies. In the end I found it needless work, and stuck to the simple sun method.

The slow speed was ideal for navigation totally by sun. I soon narrowed my daily navigation down to less than an hour's work.

At noon I took what is called a noon sight, or meridian altitude of the sun. This established my latitude, or distance north or south of the equator. I used only the sextant with a few figures added and subtracted to come to a hasty, accurate computation.

In the afternoon — about three-thirty or four — I took a shot of the sun. From its altitude I quickly and easily (as explained by Mr. Tompkins in *The Offshore Navigator*) determined a line of position, at some point on which I was located. Simply be estimating my latitude, according to distance and direction traveled from noon, and applying it to the line, I had my position. Anybody can do it.

To determine my speed, I used my life line as log line. To

the end of it I connected my bucket. Tossing it over, I set off the second hand of my navigating watch, and stopped it when the line drew taut. If it took ten seconds, for instance, it was a matter of going sixty feet every ten seconds. By simple multiplication and division, I could soon ascertain my hourly knottage. But the exactness of such a calculation would depend on a steady wind. Since I was interested in a close approximation of my speed between noon and four o'clock, I usually tossed the bucket over several times and took an average of the results.

As a rule I made a point of calculating my position each day. But if I was having a good time watching the cats, or had a fish on the line, I overlooked navigation occasionally.

Around the middle of the morning each day I caught my eager cats their rations. I used my large sport reel mounted on a strip bamboo pole. Despite a limited assortment of flies to choose from, I rarely found it difficult to please the mood of the fish. My fishing equipment, aside from my sport reel, consisted chiefly of a fishing kit which came with my little rubber raft. I had a dozen hooks ranging in size from very small to large enough to catch a dolphin. There were two hand lines, a large white fly, several leaders, and two kinds of bait. I had also the three angling items I purchased in Panama: a large spinner for sharks and two smaller flies for red snappers and yellowjacks.

In these waters, rich with fish, one doesn't have to lure catches; often I made them with nothing more than a piece of cloth for bait.

As a rule I could take a delicacy from the water in an

hour's trolling, or, if caught in a calm, in only a dozen casts. Then the fun would begin as my impetuous sea mates tackled the catch. They brightened my day as they charged and countercharged their flapping victims.

What hilarious wrestling matches I have seen on *Pagan's* decks. I have seen my doughty cats tackle everything from three-inch flying fish to a nine-foot marlin, with equally heedless ferocity. A thousand times I have seen them high tail it to the bow, after a severe drubbing. In a moment they would marshal their forces, and with a technique that never varied — yet never grew dull to watch — would slink soft-footed and fierce-eyed back to the tiny war.

After gorging themselves, if the weather was favorable, they often curled up behind my homemade anchor on the bow. Sometimes they slept in the shade of the lee waist, or if the sails were furled they climbed into the folds of the staysail or the main. All afternoon they made pilgrimages back to the catch, thus fulfilling what ordinary house and alley cats spend a lifetime dreaming of. Though Flotsam and Jetsam often had to tolerate the horrendous emergencies of sea life, all in all I am sure they wouldn't have missed the trip for a ton of mice.

It was about this time that I noticed in *Pagan's* wake a small school of a dozen dolphin — blunt-headed, sleekly designed, and wily. I must have picked them up at Malpelo. Every day they were there idling along in the shadow of the keel or shooting out ahead of the bows, preying on the hapless flying fish or the silvery shoals of small fry. I was glad of their company and often tossed them bits of fish scraps from my catchings. They spurted hurriedly to the scraps, but remained stolid and unmoved if anything hinting of a hook showed. However, one, a little dumber than the rest, succumbed to a fly one morning.

I'll never forget the morning I caught him. I had heard fishermen describe dolphins in their death throes, but I felt their imaginations had inflated what they had seen. When I pulled my first dolphin from the deeps I saw something truly amazing. He lay there quivering and gasping deeply as I unrooted the hook. Then I saw what the fishers had told me of. Instantly his ordinarily blue-greenish color changed to blue in a shimmering wave like grain fields before the wind — then ranged between the hues of purple and gold to greenish brown, gray-brown, silvery, and finally to a startling silver, spotted with blue; then came an abrupt reversion to his familiar pastel shade.

The greatest fun of fishing these waters was that I rarely caught the same species twice. Sport varied with each catch. Sometimes I caught Spanish mackerel, albacore, tuna, wahoo, and several species I was unable to identify. These waters from Panama to Galápagos are the richest sport fishing grounds in the world. They literally teem with fish. Long ribbons of birds pounding tirelessly into the water on every hand testify to the abundance with which they are sustained.

On the surface there floated small, brownish jellyfish trailing a brown, stringlike tail. There were white dollar-size organisms floating in myriads. Several varieties of seaweed showed up. Avenues of fish eggs, from horizon to horizon, keel deep, and wide as *Pagan*, fed the fish and gave birth to fish which would be food for fish and yet would prey on other fish — life-and-death battles that I saw every day. In a handful of the water itself were dustlike particles of infinitesimal life on which shifting schools of fish, looking like sunken reefs, fed themselves. Harassing the frantic shoals of fish were packs of wolfish sharks, schools of picturesque dolphin, and the sea birds.

Every few days a great sea bat would shoot up from the depths, make a full turn, and land flat with a trenchant resound. Occasionally a shark would bump against the keel, sending me on deck with my knife lashed to an oar end, or schools of porpoise would frolic before the bow. Often I saw the geysers of whales; and once I caught a glimpse of the tall sharp black fin of the brute killer whale slicing the water.

One morning a sudden heavy soughing noise startled me at my daydreaming. Looking off over the bows, I saw a great round hump, like a ship's keel, about fifty yards ahead. It was a huge whale lazing on the surface.

The bluff of *Pagan's* onrush must have frightened him. Quite gruffly he flourished his great body in a sharp twist, and pounding the water with his wide glistening tail he plumbed. *Pagan* breasted the wave of water he set off. As we passed over the spot I stared into the greenness. And there he was, like something out of *Moby Dick*, moving in giant spirals, trailing a heavy wake of churning water and bubbles, plunging into the vast deeper darkness.

Late one afternoon, I sighted the spouts of three small whales sporting on the horizon. How many times had I seen whales similarly on merchant ships! My stolid old captains had seen them too. But to be a captain, one must be lost to the world of nature — and resigned to a world of tare and tret.

How often I had wished I was in charge of the helm. I would have visited every puzzle of the sea. So it was only natural that I should come about and run amidst the cavorting pack. Two of them plunged when I was the length of the boat away. The other, bolder, hung on. I didn't know he was asleep. I pressed the tiller down and swung up. *Pagan* cast a shadow over him. And then the bow nicked him a side blow. The sails rustled from the soft shock. In the terror of sudden awakening, he whipped out with his great fluke, flipping a dollop of green seas over the rail into my teeth. The round head grew suddenly from the lather and a snort of spray blew out of it. Then it plunged and another wave spilled into the cockpit up to my knees. Behind the stern, as I pulled away, a widening white circle eddied and shifted across the wake. Later I saw other whales, but I didn't investigate.

Another morning I hooked onto a splendid swordfish. After a tiff of two hours wherein I saw every antic the sleek swordsman of the deep could contrive, I wound him into the rail. I left him gaffed at the scupper with the grappling hook, till I was certain he was good and dead. Then I hauled him onto the boards and looked him over in detail, and made a sketch of him for the log.

From his bony falchion right back to his powerful tail which gave him the superb speed and bursts of spirit unequaled, he was a study in streamline. He was the only swordfish I caught, but after such sport, he'll not be my last.

After dissecting him and probing among his vitals, I cut myself a sizable steak and a tidbit for the cats. As an afterthought I sawed off his sword, dorsal fin, and tail. The sword, I nailed to the bowsprit end. I tacked the dorsal fin atop the cabin and nailed the flared tail to the bumkin. Salty old sea dogs have said this keeps a sailor up in his luck.

For three days, following my weathering of Malpelo, blue skies and fair winds held. I reeled off an average of forty-five miles a day. In the log I made happy entries. Considering that I had no engine, that contrary currents were opposing me, that the wind, almost hourly, died completely for a few minutes, that I was hove-down about eight hours each night — I was doing well.

Gradually I nibbled away at the distance. Sometimes I grew unfathomably discouraged. Hard, wet ropes; inclement, capricious weather; the small wearisome reef points — but most of all the desire to go faster made me gloomy. And when gloom smote me hard and the sea miles wore me down, I went below, and with my dainty crew in my lap found solace reading from among the worn letters I had received from Mary during our long separation. They chased the gloom and the wornness, and inspired me to patience.

But always there was the pleasant thought of the southeast trades. "When I get to the trades it'll all be different," was my hope. I imagined wind abaft the beam, steady dependable wind and seas running with me, no squalls, no opposing currents. I was creating a roseate paradise for myself down in the trade winds — it was what kept me going south.

The three days' respite from foul weather south of Malpelo was like a reprieve. But soon, as though these waters were taking a final crack at me before I should go dancing away from them before the trades, a thoroughly familiar weather pattern set in. There were two or three squalls a day, gale winds at dusk, and early morning calms.

CHAPTER XI

Crew

THE MORNING OF JULY 8 I came on deck as usual, threw my eyes into the rigging to check on things, then gazed around the horizon at the sea. There was a fresh wind up. Off to starboard was something that made me look again. It was a dense curtain of cloudlike air, arm-shaped and bent, reaching from the sea into the clouds, and marching over the water. It was a tropic waterspout.

How many waterspouts I had seen in the Merchant Marine! How many times had I leaned on the rail peering wistfully into their mystery and wishing I was captain! And now I was captain: and I did what I always said I would do, if I saw a waterspout from my own boat. I loosed the lashings from the tiller and set *Pagan* on a track that put her straight for the center of the waterspout.

I have heard a lot about waterspouts during my time on the ships. Some have said they suck solid water into the clouds, and to put a ship through their center is to take it into a waterfall. Others have said they have hurricane winds inside. And others have said they mother a great whirlpool at their funnel-like base that can suck a ship under.

I have studied dozens of waterspouts from the rails of ships and I have always held that they were harmless. I have argued again and again that they are only large short-lived whirlwinds. And now I was going to test my arguments. I tossed Flotsam and Jetsam below, dogged the ports, and slid the companion hatch shut.

Pagan was deep reefed at the main from high winds of the night before. She crept in upon the towering dark wall of whining air. I lashed the tiller down and raced to the bow for a closer look, to see if it might not be wiser to change my mind about going on. Then suddenly the spout shifted and headed directly for *Pagan*. I ran to the mast and clung to it. *Pagan* was swallowed by a cold wet fog and whirring wind. The decks tilted. A volley of spray swept across the decks. The rigging howled. Suddenly it was dark as night. My hair whipped my eyes, I breathed wet air, and the hard cold wind wet me through. *Pagan's* gunwales were under and she pitched into the choppy seaway.

There was no solid trunk of water being sucked from the sea; no hurricane winds to blow down sails and masts; and no whirlpool to gulp me out of sight. Instead, I had sailed into a high dark column from 75 to 100 feet wide, inside of which was a damp circular wind of 30 knots, if it was that strong.

As suddenly as I had entered the waterspout I rode out into bright free air. The high dark wall of singing wind ran away. For me another mystery of the sea was solved. I shook out the reef in the mainsail, hoisted all sail, and went below to write my adventure into the log.

⌁   ⌁   ⌁

The next night I was hove-to — riding at sea anchor. I was slumbering peacefully: *Pagan* was dogged down tight. She had a terrific roll on, and not a stitch of sail up.

Unknown to me, my ten-gallon water breaker, secured into the starboard bilge, had chafed away its lashings. Suddenly it lurched from its position. It bounded to the floor, followed through on top of me, then careened into the port ribbing. Before I could arise, it bounded back and knocked me with it to the floor. Several times it used me battering-ram style. It jumped and rolled like something alive; there was no holding it. My weight was as nothing before it. When I rose to scramble away, it caught me at the ankles, toppling me under it, and proceeded to roll over me. I jerked my mattress from the bunk and thrust it between us. With my pillow and blankets and a life preserver I wedged it in, and trapped it between me and the bunk side. It's a wonder it hadn't broken some bones or wrenched a few joints, or for that matter it's a marvel it hadn't done extensive damage to my boat.

What had happened to the cats, I didn't know. Presently I heard their just complaints. They were part of the wedging material — certainly a job their harsh contract hadn't included. At expense to my bruised elbows and knees, I freed them, and relashed my cask.

But I wasn't the only one aboard to be severely treated by the sea's caprice. One noontime the cats and I were enjoying the midday sun. I was lolling in the cockpit and Flotsam and Jetsam were flouncing about the cabin top. They were playing cat's games on a box I was intending to paint when it dried. The wind, from southwest, was weak and unsteady, except that every now and then it bent us over gustily.

A gust of wind hit us of a sudden, knocked us out of plumb and pitched the box to the deck, bouncing the cats off the rail into the clutching sea. At first I wanted to pitch in after them and return via the life line. But the likelihood of getting both of them, or even one, was remote. I heaved my life jacket near them to mark the spot, and hastened to put *Pagan* about. Every foot I moved from the spot where they fell over was crucial. An object on the surface of the sea is well hidden at twenty-five yards. Once a seaman fell from a ship I was on. A life ring was thrown him. He was seen to grab it. By the time the ship turned about he had disappeared among the crests. Two hours we searched, in two lifeboats, with powerful binoculars. We never saw man or life buoy.

I had this in mind as I slashed the ropes on the tiller, put her helm hard aweather, and threw off the jib sheet. As she jibbed around, the sheet rings screeched across the travelers and the whole boat jumped under the blow. I sheeted the jib home, eased off the main, and bore down on the spot as I remembered it.

I ran for what seemed an unconscionably long time. Seeing nothing, I thought it meet to turn back and zigzag the area.

I brought her up into the wind and dropped her over to the starboard tack, on a reach. Standing on the cabin, gripping the mast with one hand and the glasses with the other, I scanned every drop of water. At a suitable moment I came about on the port tack and searched the crests both up and down wind. Nothing. I was lapsing into despair. Those poor little scamps, floating on an unfriendly, lonesome sea. And if they were seen, who would bother about cats?

The searchings I made on the billowy sea had a depth of compassion behind them. I made two more long tacks, covering a wide range, but the hiding sea wouldn't give them up. Hours must have passed. With last looks over the curling waters I turned to my former course. Suddenly my life jacket heaved into view aport. I felt sure I could find the cats now if they hadn't drowned, or swum too far from the preserver.

When the yellow life jacket came in view again it was practically dead ahead. But there were no cats near it. I searched the immediate water with my glasses and saw nothing. I scrutinized the top of each sea, jerking the glasses here and there to examine each unfamiliar splash. Only the impersonal sea, but no unfortunate kittens struggling on the surface. In a moment I saw why. As the jacket appeared, there they sat, atop it, blending into its unruly surface, and wailing as only lostlings can wail.

The looks they gave me, as I scooped them in, were ample clarification that they were wholeheartedly grateful. Three hours on that pulsating frothy floor had left them wringing wet and bedraggled, shivering helplessly. This, to them, at least for the moment, was the last straw.

I took them below to dry off and sleep safely in warm wool blankets.

Soon after this, one of the large variety of sea birds landed aboard *Pagan* — probably a gannet. He took a position on the cabin and regarded me airily when I came near to be friends. The first time I picked him up he vomited a mass of tiny, partly digested fish on me and jabbed at me with his long, dull bill.

Later, we became firm pals, when, after discovering he was ridden with lice, I dusted his feathers with some of the kittens' flea powder. And when I took him out of the heavy weather at night, and perched him on the handle of the tool kit in the peaceful cabin, he became my outspoken buddy. Whenever I came near him on deck thereafter he would squawk raucously — evincing his happiness at being a part of the crew — fan the air with his long wings, and nestle contentedly under my petting.

Each day he flew off a few hours to feed, but finally gave up the struggle for existence when I included him with Flotsam and Jetsam each morning in apportioning the fish I caught. But the new passenger hated the kittens. The first time they met was at a fish feed. A knock-down drag-out brawl was the result, with Flotsam and Jetsam taking a drubbing. I came out when I heard the scuffling. The kittens were spitting and arching. The sea bird was attacking them in turn, flailing them with his wings and pecking circles around them.

Thereafter I had to keep them separated.

I named him Gawky, because he was a living monument to the word. I got the idea when he toppled off the boom onto the cabin and bounced over the side when I playfully sneezed in his face.

So Gawky took his place as a boarder "on the house" along with the cats and my school of dolphin. The leader of the dolphin, a battle-scarred old veteran of thousands of successful contests with lesser and greater fry than he, I named Old Death. He didn't forage out ahead as the others did — he stayed in close, lazing under the shadow of the hull, darting out with murderous speed on unsuspecting victims, making his kills within a boat length of the keel.

One morning I saw an unbelievable thing aboard *Pagan.* I had been splicing a jibsheet fair-lead at the fish plates. Upon finishing it, I started below. And there, beside my bunk, under the chart rack, in startled quiet, was a large gray rat.

He was longer than either of the cats. His eyes, like tiny

black agates, were fixed on me; his whiskers wigwagged nervously. Beside him a thick hairless tail formed a thin gray wake, showing where he had turned as I startled him. He made a motion to go, and I grabbed and tossed the first thing my blind hand touched — my alarm clock. Glass and spare parts flew around the tiny cabin.

I was sorry I had startled and threatened the poor devil — "Live and let live," I thought. I figured he would be a welcome part of the crew, along with Flotsam and Jetsam and Gawky. Out here on the high seas, in a tiny bobbing world, what mattered it who was aboard.

It was an amazing thing — this rat aboard — when I sat down to think it out. How and when had he come aboard? How in all these weeks, in so small a space, had we avoided each other? Not a sign of him had I seen. What about the kittens — why hadn't they detected him? Where had he gotten his food and his water?

I jerked bolt upright at the thought of the latter. Had he gnawed into my water breakers? I checked instantly each of my oaken casks, turning them around, searching their whole area. No sign of tampering.

I searched into my food stores beneath the cabin bunks, in the lockers; and found droppings he had left behind, which I hadn't seen before. There was no possibility of his eating into the tins or the jars or jugs. Then, as I crawled under the forepeak, and rummaged in the starboard bunk, I found where all these weeks he had secreted himself.

In Panama I had stored a few items in a lemon crate, tacked it over with canvas, and painted the covering. It was into this he had gnawed in search of the cheese, salt pork, and prunes inside. As to his source of water, I can only assume he licked up my spillings during mealtime, or he licked up the over-spillings from the milk cans.

One thing I quickly learned — the kittens knew of his presence. When I brought them down, they went directly into the forepeak to stand a patient vigil at the small opening they couldn't get into. In the weeks since leaving the Perlas, I had been too busy working my boat to see the grim drama below decks.

Stowaway, so far as I can conjecture, must have come aboard when I ran aground at San José. Just possibly he had crept from the jungle into my supplies on the beach and had somehow become trapped in the gear as I reloaded it.

Judging from what is told of the sea from old, of rats not boarding an unsound ship, I was flattered by the compliment of his presence. So Stowaway, as I named him, became a part of the cruise — another mouth to feed in my little Pacific household.

Each night I placed a morsel of food and a thimbleful of water at the base of the mast for Stowaway. I wanted him to be fed and watered, so that he wouldn't be up to such rat's pranks as gnawing into my water breakers. In my spare time I sawed up and hammered together a small shelter, somewhat like a bird house. I lashed it to the mast at the floor, with the door directed forward so that our diffident passenger could come and go in secret. Though he rarely made a public appearance, he never failed to draw his rations.

He evidently felt at one with his abode because several times I caught the cats snooping around it. They had that eager look which usually possessed them when I flashed a fish under their noses.

They had many a struggle at its front door, a small round

hole. It was easily large enough for Stowaway, but Flotsam and Jetsam could get only their eyes in. What a tantalizing place for them that box became. I can still see them there, each with a fierce paw clawing through the opening, laboring like tiny lions and voicing mightily their ego and thwarted desire.

Since Flotsam and Jetsam were confirmed seamen and adapted to a regimen of fresh fish, I was surprised they would concern themselves over a mere rodent. But despite the salt in their blood, they stalked Stowaway in a fashion to do a landlubber justice.

And so life went . . . a succession of simple events to detract from the bane of tortuous miles. The plainest things were of the greatest interest.

Many have asked me if I was bored out there in a wooden world whose length was that of most kitchens and the width of most bathrooms. Life is never boring to me, never was, no matter where I have been. My early life was such that I was forced upon myself, when I wasn't working. I learned early to fill those hours with my own diversion.

Aboard *Pagan* I found plenty to do, even at the most static times. My main preoccupation — aside from working my boat, which took overwhelmingly of my time — was with reading. I had a varied library aboard, everything from "who dunnits" to Darwin. And I read all. Now a mystery, now a novel, now politics, now philosophy, and now poetry. The ones I liked were De Maupassant's *Short Stories*, Carey McWilliams's *Brothers Under the Skin*; Harold Laski's *Reflections on the*

Revolution of Our Time, and Will Durant's *The Mansions of Philosophy.*

Another thing I did, I spent time thinking. Often I sat for hours gazing out across the water to the sea rim, chewing mentally at whatever wished to ease into my mind.

Often my thoughts turned on my past life, and I relived completely all that had gone before. The oldest of five sons and a daughter. The loss of my father at fifteen . . . during the depression. Four years of work helping my mother support the family. Factories, mills, and sweatshops — for a boy who wanted to go to school.

Remarriage of my mother to a kindly stepfather. For me, freedom from the yoke of a large family. All I earned, my own now. But I didn't want to earn: I wanted to learn; to rise above the factory. So off I went — broke, with a ninth grade education — to college. I had no alternative. Who, at twenty, after working four years in the "open" shops of Los Angeles's south end, wants to go back to high school . . . with the kids?

Santa Barbara State College: I begged my way in and they let me stay. I borrowed money from the Dean of Men — a swell guy. I worked my way through. Played football. Class prexy in my sophomore year. What should have been my junior year was spent on merchant ships. I wanted to fly a bomber but I had a hole in my eardrum from childhood T.B. — 4F in the draft; no service would have me but the Merchant Marine.

Two years in the Merchant Marine. Twice around the world. From Reykjavik to Cape Horn. A year in the Royal Australian Air Force. Marriage — to a blue-eyed Aussie girl, the greatest event in my life. Again in the Merchant Marine, this time more than a year. The war over, Mary and I caught in the shuffle, separated by circumstances.

And now, bobbing on a splinter of wood uncertainly across the Pacific.

Some of the time I worked ship — depending, of course, on the weather. Each morning I trolled for fish. I navigated. If the cats were in a playful mood, we sported about the decks awhile. Or I had a long talk and a genial boxing match with Gawky. Many hours I watched Old Death and his boys slipping through the sea attacking the flying fish. A few hours a day I read.

Of principal importance was a letter I was writing Mary, to be mailed at Seymour Island. I added a few lines each day to it. It grew as my dreams and desires to be with her grew.

At times Mary seemed an unconquerable distance away. Soon it would be two months since I sailed from Panama. At such a rate it would take a year to get to Australia. According to my original timetable I should have been at least half across the Pacific. I would have to hurry now to outrun the hurricane season. Each day the prospect of constant trade winds pushing from behind became a brighter encouragement. Each day I found myself a little nearer them. Each day I sloughed off a few dragging miles.

With the noon sight of July 15, I pin-pointed myself at 1° south latitude and 85° west longitude; roughly 300 miles from the Galápagos. I hauled around to a course slightly south of west. From now on each day's sailing counted for the maximum. At last I was making a steady course of west. *Pagan* became a happy boat. The logbook, nearly two-thirds filled, had its first optimistic entry "12:15 P.M. Turned finally west. I can smell the southeast trades!"

The cold Humboldt Current, diverted westward by Cape Pariñas on the South American western bulge, was now helping me along. The wind had shifted into the south; a fairer face was on the sea; and a set of comfortable circumstances set in that were almost mystic in their wondrousness.

After a month of beating back and forth to a destination that lay dead to windward, such sailing as this smacked of peculiarity. But I was making time, I was killing distance, it was wonderful. Three hundred miles on the bow lay the Galápagos, athwart the equator. For the first time I eased sheets a bit, watched the life line straighten out astern in the frothy wake, and sailed as one reads it is done in books and yachting magazines.

For the next few days, I felt not a squall; not a drop of rain; not a disordered cloud. It was so unearthly serene that the cats and I bedded down under the stars in the cockpit. Even lazy old Gawky roosted out with us. He had his special position on the lashed tiller, and we rode so smoothly over a halcyon sea that not even he could fall off a perch. We gave Stowaway the cabin to himself.

In the fleet time before sighting my first land, I hastened to finish the long letter I was writing to Mary. By this time it had grown to sixty-two pages on both sides. In it was every warm thought a young man could crowd, who was in process of transit to his love, as I was. It took every bit of sixty-two pages to say what I felt. . . .

I planned to mail it at Seymour Island, a fistlike outjutting on the north end of Indefatigable, where an army weather station was located. I intended to stop only a day or two — long enough to check over the gear, and have a night or two of soft sleep; then push off.

The last 300 miles to the Enchanted Isles I reeled off in less than four days. On the forenoon of July 19, Chatham Island reared herself above the sea as a dark shadow, one point on the port bow. The first landfall; the first leg of the trip over; 1000 miles of sea behind me; 7500 miles yet to go.

CHAPTER XII

Unenchanted Isles!

On a sunny afternoon, I stood atop the deckhouse, leaning against the mast and peering at the northern tip of Chatham Island on the eastern rim of the Galápagos group. On Chatham lies Wreck Bay, the anchorage of the seat of the government. Ecuador owns the archipelago — the Enchanted Isles, as they are known. But I wasn't making official calls. My desire originally had been to pull straight for Seymour; and at the Army Base give *Pagan* the once-over posthaste, store a few fresh supplies, and pass on my way. But the calms, the storms, the adverse currents, the loss of my engine had thrown my timetable off, and now, arriving in the Galápagos after July first, there was no Army Base to go to. According to my information it was to be moved out by July first. However, I could see no loss in going to the site on the off-chance that the move had not yet been made.

The wind was holding at south; but it had toned in strength. My interest was taken mainly with ascertaining my set to northward by the strong current sweeping up from southward. I watched the north tip of the island, and saw it, as I suspected, shifting to south of me.

I shifted the angle of rudder, turning the bow to southward, and set myself for a broad reach that would stem me into sight of Seymour late at night — and assure me of an early morning arrival. I passed Chatham before dusk. I noticed that my driftage to northward had been considerable despite course corrections. I reset the straining tiller and went below to read.

I had a few pages to go with the "Paradise" of the *Divine Comedy,* so I wandered a few hours among pleasant words, peering out occasionally into the black. At nine I ended the mystic tale and went on deck to ponder its soul-stirring aspects. I found that the wind had petered out and *Pagan* was jolting in a confused sea. The sails were slatting and the running gear was banging as the disjointed rollers jostled her. "Bolts and shackles," a calm.

All through the night the flat air held, and the sea slapped and smacked along the bilges. I had no idea with what speed I was drifting north. Some places on the chart showed two knots; others three. There was no certainty. The chart was an issue of the British Admiralty — of excellent artisanship — but it was old, the only thing available on the Galápagos. I conjectured all the night on what my position was, on how long I had been drifting. North of my track somewhere were three small islands: Tower — Marchena — Pinta. According to the chart they were barren, waterless, seared lava. I cupped my hands to my ears, listening for the pounding of seas on rock face.

Deep in the night the sky clouded over and there were no more stellar reflections in the black water. Darkness closed down over me like a fog, and I began listening more intently. Another hour dragged past — several times I thought I heard something. Finally I shipped *Pagan's* ungainly oars, fitted them into their rowlocks on the gunwale, seated myself in the cockpit . . . and waited. *Pagan,* because of her shallow draft and low tonnage, was movable under oars; in fact, to a degree she was maneuverable. An eerie silence pervaded everything, not a whisper escaped that massive pond of reflecting water. I placed the cats beside me in their abandonship box I had built them after Malpelo. It floated. In it were provisions to do them till they could reach land. We listened with ears strained to north.

Much later a puff of wind stirred out of the southwest for a few unsteady minutes. It fell to a void before I could trim the sails. Left again alone with my imagination and the dark night, I fell into a series of wild speculations. That wind from the southwest — what did that mean? Where had the wind sat when I was reading? From the southwest? I couldn't remember having looked at the compass once during the time of reading. The lethargy of the past three days had led me to trust the wind in the south. Had it shifted? Had I actually been sailing northwest when I had thought I was sailing west?

I sat another hour, quieter than I had sat for days.

Hardly an hour later I was startled awake, by the unmistakable thunder of seas on a closed shore. I made the sound dead to west of north; about two miles off, as I could reckon. It was the din of water breaking against solid cliffs. I bent to the ungainly oars and brought *Pagan's* bow off to the east and labored her into the black night. In a short while the roar had grown considerably.

The air was dead. *Pagan's* sails slatted from side to side on each light swell, popping with a maddening persistence. Blocks rattled, sheets dragged in the sea and tossed water indiscriminately across the decks.

I was thinking of the day at Malpelo, and wishing I had a fine gale on now.

The first streaks of the new day were overdue. So I leaned more heavily on the oars. Hard by to starboard, a ragged, towering shadow was making up. At its base a gray surf was surging to and fro like heartbeats.

I could faintly observe a clear alley of escape in the weakening dark, around a hump in a bulge on the eastern coast. I pulled to clear the stomach of rock and at daylight I sat fascinated, as barely two boat lengths away the escarpment, breasting the seas rolling out of the windy south, moved away. Fore and aft, the full length of the island, great beetling cliffs, underwashed by the bristling sea, glowered on me.

My chart showed that it was Marchena Island, cliff-bound and unreceptive. I was nudging along with the current. So far as I could tell, all ahead was clear. A little to the north was Pinta, as yet not in view — small and easily avoided, according to the chart. I had only to drift around the northern tip and await a wind.

Overhead the sky had become a grizzly curtain, the sea was as smooth as a dance floor. With daylight I expected wind; but as late as when the sun first showed I was still in a void. Shortly afterward, I drifted off the low end of Marchena, only to find Pinta, twelve miles distant, lying more or less in my track. The peculiar thing was that I couldn't decide whether she was astride my path or not. One moment it appeared so, and the next it was questionable. The bowsprit, along which I was attempting to sight the island, was circling like a nervous finger.

I presently concluded that whether Pinta was in my line of

drift or not, I should start rowing. The current was shifting me toward the little isle at two knots or better.

On her southern end was an active volcano at the water's edge. It rose a hundred feet and from its blunt summit a broad column of thin smoke hung in the dour air. Its base lay in the sea; and I somehow felt that the water would be hot there. Beside it lay a shingled beach which ran onto a parched hill topped by another crater. The land everywhere had a naked, withered look. I thought of the word "dry" as I looked up the hostile slopes. Here and there was a cactuslike growth, seared gray-brown bushes, and stumpy, hungry-looking trees. Totally uninviting!

I started the rowing when I was yet a long way off, but soon wished I had started earlier. I was rowing to west because I felt it would succeed more easily than fighting the current east. There was easily eight miles of rowing to do, so I spent the first few hours at regulated long stroking. At first I judged that I would easily clear the island, and doubtless lost much valuable time when I relaxed to half-stroke.

As I drifted closer I saw a pack of seals sporting in the water. When they saw me, they stopped, with eyes showing above the water, staring from their shiny heads, looking first like boulders, then like apparitions.

One, not suspecting my dire straits, came up to offer friendship. He swam in unusually close, often ducking under the oars. I am sure we would have become great pals if I hadn't been so frantically at work. I would have loved to catch him a fish and feed him by hand. And I'm sure he was all for it.

Suddenly, I found that I was closing at a quicker rate . . . an alarming rate! I was midway across the island, and no longer in the lee of Marchena; the full current had gripped me and was thrusting me as if I were in a millrace.

Though I was clear of the volcano, I could feel its hot breath and sense its hostility. I rowed the faster, not looking up, till my arms cramped.

I looked up to gauge my progress and what I saw actually refreshed me with the terror it held. I was less than a hundred yards offshore and it was easily several hundred yards to the point of the projecting land up the coast. An impossible contest. I stroked with such wild haste that, dipping short, I missed the water altogether and flopped heels skyward onto the hatchway step. The oars went flying beamward, out of reach.

I thought of plunging in to retrieve them, but on hearing the lapping of water licking over rocks I knew it would be in vain. There were still three oars in the cabin. My first thought was to break them out; before going down I took a look, and prospects looked so grim I didn't bother to go below.

Ordinarily I'm not one to give up, but what I saw made me quit thinking of trying to save my boat. I was seventy-five yards from the pockmarked wall of lava, and hundreds of yards from the point. There was nothing to anchor on; nothing I could do. I gave up. I had to save myself.

I strained my faculties for the next thing to do. The cats. They were in their floating box; I tossed them into the rubber raft and pushed it off the rail. I made ready to cast it adrift and climb in.

Land was less than a hundred feet away. The sea was washing against it with subdued thuds, but with force nevertheless.

I stared quickly about for the last thing to do. I thought of water, food, clothes. But I thought of the fight back upcurrent with small oars to the shingled beach, and the need for an immediate start.

Then, for some unknown reason, but most likely because I was grasping for last threads, I raced to the bow and plopped my rustic anchor into the placid water. Bubbles trailed it where it plunged. It ran to its chain's end. The chain hung up and down in water empty of a chance ledge. There was nothing for the anchor to snag against. I turned to run to my raft to make away while there was still time. Then a darkening line showed on the water, ruffling it and closing in on the port beam. I hardly had time to grab the tiller before a squall raced aboard *Pagan*, enclosing her sails in shrieking arms, pressing them flat, whipping them with a faint rain.

Pagan heeled sharply to the flurry. I whooped and hollered exultantly as she worked off the now roaring shore and bit into sea room. In a scant twenty minutes — well clear of the scorched land — I rounded up to the wind and dropped the mainsail. Before tying in a reef, I pulled the pneumatic raft to the counter and handed out my despondent cats. They strode stiffly below, disclaiming for the moment the sea and its abruptnesses. I massaged them briskly in a fuzzy towel and folded them into an army blanket. To smooth their outraged humors, I took my pole to the deck and cast a singing, well-baited line off the quarter.

Gawky returned to the cabin top after having deserted us in our moment of peril. I shoved him below, out of the weather.

I made the course southwesterly, to clear the threat of other northerly island groups. I forgot about Seymour since it was back to southeast, and pointed for Albemarle, the largest and westernmost island in the group. It was my intention to make for the leeward side of the great sprawling island to rest and collect myself, but mostly to sink into restful sleep for the night.

The wind was stout and *Pagan* stemmed the tide ideally, for now we were heading south fighting the current. At dusk I noticed a gray wash of sea along an extended ledge off the north of Albemarle. It jutted out a good mile. There is nothing more frightful to a seaman than shallow reefs kicking up a growling surf.

Halfway along the ledge I could make out the cold-looking bones of what looked to be two wrecked vessels. In a foot or two of water they sat, lonely and stark, awash and helpless. They were evidently incautious fishermen who had rounded the point too sharply, or had been swept there by the current, or by one of the frequent tidal waves native to the Galápagos. I gave the whole cape healthy clearance.

The sight of the tortured hulks made me jittery. I decided not to pull into the lee of the cliffs and anchor — instead to shape a course down the northwestern shore, tack around the western point, and beat into Tagus Cove, probably on the morrow.

By now *Pagan* was much fouled on the bottom with shell-fish. I was wishing I had some high tides and sandy beaches as in the Perlas. I needed to careen her a tide or so, to scrape her and paint her. I thought of returning round to Seymour where the Army might be. But I chased the thought away because of the wrecks on the point. Too, I was afraid some unavoidable delay might crop up which would jeopardize the safety of my trip. Seymour wasn't a necessity, so I decided against going there.

Floreana Island was about a hundred miles distant. I thought seriously of going there to do the hull work. The chart accredited her with a beach and sandy shore; also, there is a postbox there. In that way I could kill two birds with one stone, by doing the hull and mailing the ponderous letter I had written to Mary. Besides, doing the work alone, I could be done all the quicker and be sooner on my way.

Post Office Bay at Floreana, I had learned in Panama, is an ancient mailing station. It was created by whaling ships of old, outward bound to their hunting waters. In passing they dropped off letters to folks at home — at the same time procuring fresh water and fruits and vegetables as well as the great land tortoises (*galápagos*) for fresh meat.

If another ship happened in on the way home, she obligingly picked up and delivered the mail found staked on the beach in an old box. Today a barrel stands there. Occasionally, even now, a northeastern-bound fisherman, or in fact anyone clearing the island for the mainland, cleans it out and deposits the load in a post office in Panama or San Diego. Amazingly enough letters posted there — whether stamped or not — have been known to arrive as addressed . . . in time.

After a night of intermittent naps, and steering mostly by guess, I wound up at daybreak negotiating the strait between Narborough Island and Tagus Cove. I passed into the embayment and rounded up for the anchorage. An hour later I went below for a "nap." I slept the day out and all that night.

CHAPTER XIII

Post Office Bay

I FOUND TAGUS COVE an unusually snug protection — in fact ideal, except that there were no means to do the hull work. Not that *Pagan* was direly in need of it. But since I was planning a nonstop run to Sydney, I felt I wanted her clean before setting forth.

To the west of me lay more than 7000 miles of ocean. There were a little over two months before the hurricane season would set in. If I was to cross these waters in safe time, there could be no stop enroute. Therefore I esteemed it a saving in time to do the cleaning here, where I had a sufficient tide, and safe harbor such as Post Office Bay. And I could get Mary's letter, in a manner of speaking, "on its way" by the antiquated postal system. So I resolved to beat around to Floreana the next day. But first I wanted to check the standing and running gear thoroughly.

I rigged a bosun's chair to the main halyard and hoisted myself aloft. By midafternoon I had painted the thirty-five-foot mast and tightened the screws in her slide. In addition I had renewed all halyards, put up a new shroud, and painted the boom. I overhauled my main boom blocks and greased their reluctant shafts. I shifted the traveler and tried to fit it more securely, but to no avail. It had never been the same since the shark had torn it out, but it was serviceable.

By evening all was shipshape, not counting the hull and a few bits and pieces I could perform in my "off watch" hours at sea. The jaunty little cutter was straining at her tether, longing for a less peaceful element.

I had managed my time through the day with such circumspection as to even include catching a mess of fish for the cats and Gawky between chores. Gawky was getting so spoiled that he refused to go out and forage any more. But while we were anchored in the circular cove he flew out for a constitutional among the towering ledges, leaving the decks safe for Flotsam and Jetsam.

My cats, gorged and thoroughly at peace in dreams, lay curled in the folds of the mainsail. Occasionally they bestirred themselves and waddled back to their "pottie pot," a sandbox I had built for them on the fantail. After, they would saunter, as though accidentally, upon the fish, and in a manner of saying, "Oh well, there's nothing else to do," they would gnaw languidly on each of the two varieties.

After this came experiments in luxurious ways of sleeping: they sprawled on the warm decks; they relaxed in the shade of the rail; or they wandered below to the cool of the forepeak. Those cats were rotten spoiled. Heaven help them if they should ever have to go back to civilized life and table scraps.

◞   ◞   ◞

Though I wasn't on a sightseeing tour, I was completely taken with the uniqueness of Tagus Cove. Why it isn't a famous scenic spot I don't know. It is roughly a hundred boat lengths across; shored in by precipitous cliffs. In its lofty seams, queer species of birds nest themselves and echo each other in a constant chorus. The cove is really the crater of a dead volcano with its seaward wall washed out.

Tagus is lonesome and mysterious. In her clear waters swim sharks, seals, mantas, sea lions, sting rays, sailfish, eels, and penguins. Yes, penguins. I saw a pair of them — and I have since been corroborated by a fisherman who has seen them there. They were smaller than ones I have seen in Capetown and the Falklands.

They swam beneath the keel, squirming with necks stretched, after fish. They bobbed up several times but were too busy to notice the new arrival in the cove.

Another attraction of Tagus is the arrangement of names painted in various positions over her riven surface. They run into dozens and reflect the ever-constant quest of adventure, long considered dead — and erroneously. I can remember, even yet, a score of them easily. It is obviously a tradition for boats visiting the archipelago to autograph, in some peculiar spot, the challenging walls of the cove.

I had promised people in Panama I would display *Pagan's* name in bold hull white on a prominent ledge, and I set about finding an appropriate spot.

At the far end of the cove, on its northern rim, I saw a rocky platform, behind which appeared footing secure enough to wend up onto the high ledges. I climbed into my rubber raft and rowed over with the light metal oars. From the low ledge, shoaling sharply into the water, a young sea lion waddled and dived and watched me with eyes above the water in the same way people stare at foreigners. He didn't appear frightened, in fact he climbed back onto the ledge close behind me, as, bucket and brush in hand, I began the ascent into the deformed lava clefts.

Well up, I came upon a flattened space. A few feet above it was the shapeless, barren terrain of the island. Towering over and away off to my right was a great lopped-off crater apparently burned out.

Looking back through the tight walls of the crevasse, I could see my little boat fetching snugly to her makeshift anchor. Like a peanut in a washtub, she was foil to the placid blue and gnarled varicolor of the cavernous walls.

From the corner of my eye I saw a jerking movement near my feet. A jagged spiny rock rolled over. With ghostlike mysteriousness it moved. It waddled smoothly over the rocks and then stopped as if in death. A great black eye stared blankly from its head held high, a notched tongue flicked from its jagged head. Suddenly, with the quickness of a cat, it turned and spat at me from a black mouth. The black tongue flicked again. It looked like a lizard, but more like a dragon; it was easily five feet long. It was spiny along the back, gruesomely wrinkled, had fingerlike hands and a long listless tail. It perched, not moving a muscle, glaring at me.

In all my life I had seen nothing like it. I could only remember what I had heard in Panama. Someone had said that in the Galápagos were "prehistoric species of animals."

A man named Darwin had come here once and pronounced them "different." Whatever it was he said they did, they did. I believe it; I was looking at one of the results. I wouldn't have been surprised had this thing coughed fire — I would only have stumbled more clumsily than I did. For in confusion and bewilderment my step went awry and I fell all over myself; but mostly in the bucket of paint.

The very response to fear engendered fear; and I went slipping and falling down among the sharp volcanic boulders.

I nearly landed aboard the sea lion as I ran out onto the ledge; in horror he hurtled himself into the soft water. In a fury of oar stroking I was beside *Pagan* and aboard.

No sooner on deck than the cove lost its appeal. The walls looked foreboding. What a place to be alone in! Even the cats sensed my uncertainty. They squatted in fuzzy balls, jerking their whiskers nervously.

The sun was behind Narborough; the cove was becoming a shadow; it was so still it shrieked. "To the devil with this place," I said to the cats.

Then I saw it. Beneath the keel it went, a slimy, ghostlike shadow in the paling day. The same lizard or a creature similar . . . swimming! Its arms and legs were folded to its body much as you would hug yourself. It propelled itself solely with the long tail, in a wavy motion, and it slithered with the ease of a snake. That was enough for me.

I threw off the stops from the sails, hoisted them to the full, grappled the heavy anchor chain into a lump on deck, and dumped the clumsy wooden anchor atop it. As dark crowded close, I passed from the placid waters of the sinister cove to the piling whitecaps seaward. I pointed away from the mammoth volcano of Narborough, making for sea room to the south.

Dinner that night, potluck as usual, was a can of diced carrots, gulped wholesomely from the can. I ate at the tiller, steering by foot. *Pagan* danced on her tacks to southward. Within three hours, I estimated I had cleared Narborough to southward. I trimmed sails on the port tack and filled away close-hauled into the southwest on the long leg that would clear the lower western bulge of Albemarle.

The ponderous island lies like a dividing amoeba on the meridian of 91° west. I planned to tack around her in the night, so as to catch some "shut-eye" during the broad reach to Floreana the following day with tiller lashed and sails trimmed.

The morning sun, one hour high, found me well under Albemarle. Floreana, seemingly near but far away, was a gray hump forty miles on the starboard bow. I wanted to be fetched up to the anchor by dusk in Post Office Bay. There was a current to buck, and despite a nice wind it meant a day cram-full of work at the tiller, without sleep. I crowded on full sail and settled back for a day of "yachting" along the southern reaches of the Galápagos.

Late in the day, with the last of twilight to pilot myself into the quiet harbor, I rounded its northern point and opened up Post Office Bay.

This peaceful harbor is a crescent of water about a mile deep and the same width. To the left, as I came down its central road, lay a clump of islets. Ahead a sandy beach; slightly back of it an ugly disintegrating shack. A little way along resided the famous white barrel attached to a stake. Beyond the beach grew a motley array of scraggly barren bush, and the remnants of an ancient trail with which I wasn't interested.

I dropped the hook fairly close in, and rowed ashore immediately. I hastened down the beach to the parched ornamental barrel, and inserted my bulky letter to Mary. Attached to it was a five-dollar bill by a rubber band. Five dollars from my small remaining funds was a lot; but I wanted Mary to get that letter, and if five dollars would insure it — and I felt it would — then the money didn't matter. I stood by the traditional landmark for a moment wondering if the letter would ever reach Mary. Night was crowding in. *Pagan* was a blur in the water. I didn't like it ashore here any more than at Tagus.

As I rowed out to *Pagan* I was oblivious to the dismal countenance of the surroundings or the growing cold. My mind was across the Pacific. It was also with the letter in the barrel. An unholy melancholy was on me. I was swept with the futile remorse of great desire, hindered by need of lengthy patience, and burdened by uncertainty.

I went to bed early, and silenced my quarrels with circumstances by a full night's sleep, knowing that the next night would find me rushing "downhill" to westward.

Along about noon the following day my work was finished on *Pagan's* hull. She lay careened on the short beach, partially shored up by a water cask. Her shapely hull was scraped free of marine growth and coated with the last of my boot topping. The slack tide was crawling up the planking. As the keel shifted uneasily on the hard bottom, I tested my kedge, and prayed that she would hold. In a few moments my boat was borne up, and she eased away to anchorage.

I hastily hanked on the jib and cleared all lines for the one-man scramble necessary to trim *Pagan* for departure. I took one final look around at the somber anchorage and turned peremptorily to my halyards and sheets, anchor line and tiller.

CHAPTER XIV   Trade Winds

BY DUSK OF JULY 23, I had made a good offing from Floreana. I stood due south of the cluster of lifeless cones on Albemarle. Sometime around midnight, I expected to nose free of
the westernmost point of charred lava forms and push into the
sea stretch to westward — 3000 miles of open water to my
next landfall: the Marquesas Islands.

The wind was in the south: *Pagan* slid blithely over a be-
neficent sea. The end of the Galápagos bird squadrons bent
their homeward course around the mast and swooped away
sternward. Darkness curtained off the last glimpse of the
"ash heap" I suppose I shall ever have.

The heavens cast themselves with a measles of guiding
lights. A waning moon softened the night. The ocean un-
dulated lightly, at the behest of a fresh breeze. The spill of
wind out of the sail made my skin tingle. The night was made
glorious in the thought that I was nudging into the locale of
the trade winds: that I was starting across the big ocean to
Mary. The seas ahead of me were well known for their tran-
quillity. The current, though setting to northwest for the
nonce, would soon straighten out and shove me due west, at
an average rate of 30 miles daily, free of charge. With the
wind expected to push me at a rate of 90 to 100 miles a day I

would be amassing a daily average of 130 miles — wonderful for my purpose of speed across the ocean.

That night was the most roseate of the whole voyage. A letter was on its way to Mary, explaining all. The hull was clean, and sliding blissfully through the seas. I had gaffed a great sea turtle early in the afternoon. I would have fresh meat for three days. After that I would have dried meat — sun-dried after the style of Indian jerky — for the full passage to the Marquesas. The weather was lovely. What more, excepting the presence of my wife, could I ask?

Unhappily, my bliss was to be short-lived. I had overlooked the fact that first I would have to find the trade winds. In the Eastern Pacific, the trades don't always reach as far north as the equator. They are where you find them. In between is an airless patch known as the doldrums.

Trudging across the doldrums into the trades is a sore-footed task. When you pick up a cat's-paw for a few hours, you think you're in the trades. Then suddenly the wind elopes; and the ensuing glassiness of the sea, its silence, the boat's unending clatter, run roughshod over your nerves. A slatting sail, rattling blocks, slapping halyards, slack sheets have an indescribable nuisance value. Each calm found me drifting with the current to the north.

Not once did a fresh wind curve the sails and bend *Pagan* to her work but that I felt it was at last the trades. Again and again, however, the wind died away. In a few days I found myself north of the line. The tremendous letdown of the trades was doubly exasperating since I had expected such a sterling performance from them.

My intention had been to stay close to the equator in sailing west; to avail myself of the strong westerly current near it. Even seventy-five miles south of the line, the extra push on the keel slacks off a dozen miles daily. Better to go south and lose some force of current than to stay up here in constant calms, on a heat-reflecting sea. Reconciled to the wisdom of a steady wind rather than a stronger current, I waited on the next wind. It came not at once and not steadily but in faltering episodes. Each time, under flattened sails and a neutral tiller, I hauled into the southwest.

With each puff of wind I added to my southing: with each calm I drifted back north again. The doldrums played with me as a cat devils with a mouse. Hours on end I drifted under spars stripped to the standing rigging, unable to bare the monotony of flapping sailcloth and clattering tackle. I couldn't read, I couldn't nap, I couldn't think; I could only grope with slit eyes hour on hour for a hint of wind on the polished water.

At the onset of a stir of air I ran up every square inch the rigging could hold and nurtured every pulse beat out of the sky, pushed doggedly on in search of the diffident trades.

On the afternoon of July 27, four days out of Galápagos, irritation aboard reached its climax when Gawky, after several weeks of languishment on *Pagan*, suddenly soared from the deckhouse and made a bee line for the horizon to eastward. He departed with too much energy and determination for it to be a routine flight. I watched him to the last, to the point where he sparkled in the white glare, then dropped below the horizon.

That night I made a sad entry in the log.

Still three more days ground painfully on my hopes. An occasional sky breath teased me. I sat out the days on deck, gnawing at dried strips of the turtle and playing at patience. Then quite suddenly the wind in a summary movement jumped out of the southeast. I eased away the sheets for the very first time and caught the breeze astern and, with way on, ran down the wind. It was a pleasure to see *Pagan* actually running off before it. I put her on a course between west and west southwest so that she would make the traverse, arriving off the Marquesas in 9° south latitude.

That night I exultantly entered the momentous news in the logbook — the first happy entry in seven days.

My noon sight for August 4, the twelfth day out, put me 1010 miles offshore — a greater distance than I had traveled in the thirty days from Perlas to Galápagos. Hereafter followed 2000 miles of the pleasantest sailing I probably shall ever experience. For days on end, the boat sailed itself. The only times I came on deck were practically of necessity. *Pagan* ran off before the wind, chasing columns of wind-pushed rollers and wind-driven clouds that never varied — in short, she sailed it as "harbor circumnavigators" do it on yacht club verandas. Life those days ran on an amazingly even keel.

At sunup I always came topside to collect the night's catch of flying fish trapped on deck. During the night the prow, slicing open the water sent them skittering like quail from the wave tops and often they flew blindly into the sails and expired in the waists or on the forepeak. Never a morning but there was at least one. If more than one were found, I enjoyed fresh fish, otherwise the hungry maws of my Flotsam and Jetsam yawned.

The flying fish is delicious food. I found them bony but worth the pains incident to enjoying their soft sweet meat.

I liked them best boiled in salt water and eaten with ketchup and crackers. They were delicious fried in bacon fat, too. Many was the time, with only one fish found on deck, I regretted having my hungry kittens aboard.

Out there I had lots of time on my hands, far more than from Perlas to Galápagos. Keeping my plucky little cutter eating at the westing was routine work of a few minutes each day. With sails curving full and the tiller lashed slightly aweather, *Pagan* floated along unheeded and free at a laughing speed. Each morning and night I glanced at the compass; at some time in the day I sauntered over the sloping deck from stern to bow and back with eyes aloft, searching out a weakness that might interfere with the peace and purpose of my little Pacific world. Here too I usually found all okay. No more work till next day.

I altered the lashings on the tiller but a very few times the whole crossing. Not once did I lower sail or reef down. The only real work of the cruise was with chafing gear on the shrouds to protect the sail from wearing through. I know there is a way of using rope yarn to make chafing gear, but being a greenhorn I didn't know how it was done and I couldn't figure out how to do it, so I ripped up my two bed sheets into one-foot strippings and wrapped them around the shrouds as a sort of padded sleeve. I bound each pad with string at top and bottom and middle; then scaled the mast and slid them up the wire where the sail chafed and made them fast to the shroud itself with line again. They did me yeoman's service; my sails right to the last were as good as the day I swung round before the southeast trades.

The weather was ideal. The days were warm and fresh, bathed by sun and the purest air. The nights were cooled by the chill current under the keel. The cool of night was a sleep-inducing cool, just enough to need a blanket and clothes on deck.

I came often on deck of biological necessity. This I took care of by use of the bumkin spread. I kept a board with a sizable hole in it on the stern. When the need arrived, I laid the board on the bumkin arms and straddled it saddle style, with the sternpost for a horn.

About the only other time I came on deck was to navigate or bask in the sun, watching the dolphin at their kill, or to play with the cats. Now that Gawky was gone, they had free run of the boat. For hours they would romp over the canvas-covered decks. I would crawl along the cabin top spying on their kittenish whims and gambols.

When Flotsam and Jetsam were out on deck, I always spent time below making friends with Stowaway. He was a most reluctant fellow, and no wonder. The kittens were in constant prowl around his abode — things had come to such a pass that I was forced to place his food and drink inside his house, so seldom was it safe for him to venture forth for it.

I tried painfully to teach him to nibble from my fingers, but with the kittens aboard it was a lost hope. He was trustless: the poor fellow had gone cynical; he was disorganized; he considered friend and enemy alike, and chose to fritter away his life in isolation.

Since I was only on deck a few hours each day, the remainder devolved to whatever suited my fancy. I perused everything from crossword puzzles to Shakespeare and Mary's old letters which I always kept in my sea bag. When I tired with reading, I pieced together the same jigsaw puzzle over and over again. For fun I turned it over and did it the hard way. These days of peace and speed were dreamlike in their constancy.

I was never bored: it is impossible for a person with an active mind to be bored with his own company. The days went too quickly. I hadn't time to do all I set out to do each morning. Besides, my early days of work had forced me upon myself, and the aloneness was something I had known before.

An average day went along something like this: I awakened usually with the first graying of dawn, inspected the course from the compass beside my bunk and went on deck to check the tiller and sails and to look for flying fish that might have landed aboard in the night. If there were two fish — and nearly always there were — I gave one to the kittens in the morning and one in the afternoon. If more than two, it meant fresh provisions for breakfast — either fried in bacon fat or boiled in salt water.

Invariably breakfast consisted of a cooked cereal. I mixed about six parts of fresh water with one of salt, boiled it on the Primus, and stirred in the cereal — corn meal, oatmeal, and such — with a heaping spoon each of powdered milk and sugar. I ate most of my meals out in the cockpit in the wash of the tropic air.

I whiled the morning at reading, at playing with my crew, at coaxing my hopeless passenger, or at watching the death chases out ahead of the bows.

Lunch was the simplest meal of the day. It was only a matter of marking an X on the stores list, then selecting a likely-looking can from the former icebox. The thing I liked about the noon meal was the surprises I often got when I opened the wrapperless cans.

In the early afternoon I napped; in midafternoon I took a sun sight and pin-pointed myself on the chart; in late afternoon I sat on the cabin peering around the sea rim in hope of a smudge of smoke or a sail. Or I sat watching the lonely, impersonal sea birds who glide their lives away over the barren Pacific wastes.

My night meal was a warm one. I fried a slice of bacon or ham and heated something from a can. There was always a pot of coffee or tea with which to wash down a couple of hard sea biscuits. Often I made a kind of stew with leftovers and a bit of salt pork or fish.

In the evening, after checking the set of the sails, and the lashed tiller, I lay on my bunk to read for an hour in the dim light of my barn lantern swaying from the overhead. When I tired, I merely pulled up the blanket and blew the lantern out. I didn't have to undress for bed; I didn't wear clothes in the tropics.

But one day I was jostled from my settled world. I found during my daily inspection that the bobstay had loosened at the stem and that the chain was dragging free from the end of the bowsprit. It was a job of the type a novice knows nothing about, but which cries out to be mended. I looked it over and started repairs with my usual trial-and-error methods. I lowered myself into the water and fidgeted and tinkered, trying to join the connections of stay and stemhead, while the rollers of the trade winds skewed me from side to side of the bow. In two hours of futile fidgeting and cursing under water, I decided to give it up.

But it was a thing one couldn't give up. The bobstay bolstered the bowsprit; it in turn supported the topmast stay; which in turn secured the mast against rearing backward and snapping off. I couldn't hazard being dismasted out on these lonely wastes. So back to work I went. It turned out to be a job more distasteful than shoveling fertilizer. Need is a harsh driver. The need to repair this impediment drove me to a merry ride, hanging onto the bowsprit and clinging to the stemhead. But working under water on the dancing object was worse. Eventually I got the ringbolt fitted into the cutter's stem . . . and dragged myself over the rail.

The jib rattled up the head stay; other sails were soon atrim and curved to the wind, and with laughing heels *Pagan* tore away to the blank horizon.

There then followed more days of peaceful sailing. *Pagan* scudded on before the southeast trades, with hardly a variation in wind and sea. Ahead, shoals of flying fish sprinted from the sea and floated away to port and starboard, slipping into the wave tops one at a time, or en masse like bird shot. And what masses of flying fish they were. I was amazed as every hundred yards, day on day, a gleaming squadron of them flashed into the sun and glided horizonward in a dozen directions.

Harassing them from dusk to dusk was Old Death and his lesser dolphin, who prowled ahead of the bow and streaked into the unsuspecting schools. For two thousand miles now, I had watched this game of stalking and hunting: a vicious circle of dog-eat-dog, among the creatures under the sea. The dolphin has a blunt, stolid face trailed by a beautifully lithe body. Along his back lies a weblike fin which ordinarily lies flat but which he flares into use in the hairpin maneuvers employed against the flying fish.

I have sat on deck hours on end watching these fascinating creatures give the flying fish the chase. Singling out a lone flyer, the dolphin will stay on his tail for five hundred yards before giving up. As the flying fish clears the water in mortal haste, his apt enemy is just behind and below. The stalk is on — a stalk of speed and thrills where a single slowing or stopping by the flying fish means death. Occasionally the dolphin sails free of the water for a twenty-foot leap to see his victim.

Spotting his game ahead in the air he returns to his element and with a few powerful thrusts rides up under him, eying him, waiting for the drop into the water. As the flying fish falls from his glide, he is set upon, and there ensues a terrifying encounter of champing teeth, flaring fins, swirling wakes, and the dolphin comes away grinning.

I have seen this tragic episode a hundred times, and only a dozen feet away. Once I saw a flying fish nipped neatly in half by Old Death. In a flash it was done — in fact with such suddenness that the fish didn't suspect what had happened. Another dolphin took him in on the run before the poor flying fish had time to realize he was already half eaten.

Once, a huge squid bolted from the water off aport and glided a hundred feet in toward *Pagan*. On plunging he espied a grim assassin close behind and threw himself, horror-stricken, twenty feet straight up into the air. The dolphin spun around and with a terrific thrust hurtled himself up out of the water. They met in mid-air: the dolphin shooting up, the squid falling. The shock of impact nearly choked the dolphin. What was left of the squid fell thirty feet away, and was gobbled up by another dolphin as it hit the surface.

Another time one of the largest flying fish I have seen, and judging his size a veteran of many a fracas with death, soared out of a wave far ahead. I watched him soar on the wind, making a clean half circle that only the wariest pursuant could follow. He slowed himself in mid-air and made to plop into an oncoming sea. What he didn't know was that he was followed: not by one, but by four dolphin, shouldering one another aside for the choice lead spot.

He settled lightly in the water. There was a rush, a flurry of fins and flukes, the chop and smack of spiny teeth, then confusion so great that it seemed the dolphin themselves didn't know which one had snared the prize.

Another day a shoal of flying fish were flushed very near the bow. As the dolphin streaked among them in their ber-serker way the flying fish literally went crazy. Some of them leaped straight up only to fall straight back. Others, in their terror, only stumbled along the surface, unable to break into flight. One small squadron bolted off the water straight into *Pagan's* sails. Twelve of them. Old Death and his crew often helped me out like this.

One day Old Death ran short into a small flying fish. They met face to face, then the chase of death began. I could see them from where I stood on the cabin peering into the air-clear water. The little fish skittered to his wings and soared in toward *Pagan's* beam. The gnarled old killer flashed in pur-suit. He lunged into the air and struck the fish as he sailed, upsetting him, tumbling him into the sea. A scrimmage for life ensued, and the little fish got somehow into the air again. Old Death, in a rage, was close behind. Suddenly the flying fish saw he was gliding straight into *Pagan* on the beam. He wavered in flight. Beneath him was the inexorable hunter, ahead *Pagan's* hard, dry decks. He could have dropped to the water and jockeyed for a new take-off — but he didn't. He knew the outcome. I am sure the decision was his to smash his head against the cabin and drop quivering to the deck.

Not a day passed but that a number of such deathly encounters occurred an eye distance away.

On numerous occasions, when an overwhelming desire for a change from flying fish obsessed me, I sought to harpoon the dolphins; but I landed only three of them the whole trip. They are explosive energy keyed to high sensitivity. Hardly does a spear near them when they thrash away. I speared Old Death at least ten times. Each thrust into his ancient sides proved only another tattered scar, and didn't diminish his love of *Pagan's* company a jot. He followed me to the very reef where I nearly drowned.

Those of the dolphin I speared I cut into strips and dried on strings tied between deckhouse and traveler. The meat kept indefinitely if redried often enough. I alternated this with my decreasing supply of turtle, which too I had to keep drying over and over again.

During this time, about a week out of the Marquesas, I fell often in reverie . . . with the past . . . the future . . . the present. I reacted on the immensity of watery wastes by seeking an escape through thinking. Long hours out there lent themselves to retrospect and iteration. I fell to thinking of the days of crowded happiness of my romance with Mary, our courtship, our marriage. The whole panorama of unfortunate circumstances that had kept us apart but which I was now overcoming in crossing the Pacific.

I sat on the cabin, lounging under the sun and breeze, listening to the slap and smack of water against the planking, and watching the ripple thrown out by the bow. Sitting so, it was easy to think. Thoughts came uncalled for. What I thought wasn't important, but the fact that I thought was vastly important.

The morning of August 18 found me an estimated three days out of the Marquesas. My ninety-page logbook was nearly filled — I was eighty-five days out of Panama and this was just five days from the day I had expected to arrive in Sydney when I sailed. Mary was expecting me. I hoped my letter from the Galápagos had reached her telling of the upset to my timetable and explaining the new arrival date.

My sights at noon of August 20 estimated my position at 9°5′ south latitude, 138°50′ west longitude. The Marquesas were hard by. I climbed the mast often and swept every horizon for an object grayer than the clouds and stiller than the rearing seas. By nightfall land hadn't hove in sight. There were plenty of land birds around: bosun birds, gannets, gooneys, man-o'-war birds, terns. I was certain that not too far south of me was the lush tropical island of Hiva Oa I had heard spoken of in Panama. And somewhere near, probably just under the horizon on the starboard bow, was Ua Huka, and just to westward, Nuku Hiva.

That night I came on deck often to sweep the frail horizon to starboard for land and listen for the hollow boom of trade-wind seas on coral reefs. I neither saw nor heard anything, but I knew it was there.

Daylight found me under the shadow of land to the north . . . land after twenty-nine days.

CHAPTER XV

Devilfish

THE FLAT GREEN ISLAND near by to starboard was Nuku Hiva. Back on the starboard quarter was the graying dome of Ua Huka and distantly visible on the port beam was Ua Pou. Nuku Hiva is the main island and port of entry for the French-governed Marquesas Islands. I stood about two miles south of Sail Rock on her southeast point. The wind- and sea-laved rock was white with the foam of relentless rollers advancing before the seasonal trades. Behind it, and blending with it, was Cape Martin.

On Nuka Hiva's southern shore you find three excellent harbors, Comptroller Bay, Taio Hae Bay, and Tai Oa Bay. I idled along the coast at a wistful distance and peered into each inviting anchorage. In my lap lay spread the chart of the island. I explored each part I passed. I was nearly tempted to steer into one of them.

Taio Hae from the sea is dark green, seamed with cool valleys and topped by a benevolent cloud, a valley as soothing as fresh linen. But I wasn't on a sightseeing trip, I had no visa, and I had no clearance papers for the port. My exchequer was down to twenty dollars, and I had no way of knowing, if I did go in, if I had enough money to get out.

But most important of all, I couldn't afford the time. Hurricane weather would be setting in on the Tasman Sea in less than six weeks, and I had to be in Sydney before then. It meant hard sailing: there were more than 4000 miles of sea yet to cross. Furthermore, *Pagan* was in need of nothing. Food I had aplenty and there was three months' water supply on board.

Morale of passengers, crew, and escort was high, especially so since I was nearing 145° west longitude, the halfway mark to Sydney. Flotsam and Jetsam were thriving on the life. Stowaway, though I seldom saw him, was in fine fettle. Old Death and his mob, despite the fact that they had lost three of their number on the traverse, didn't appear to be affected by 3000 miles of day and night swimming at five knots. The whole gang was with me to a man: "Sail on," they said. So I glided along the southern extremity of the famous island that has figured so strongly in romantic literature and the lives of adventurous men in the South Seas.

Later the same day I wished I had gone into one of the quiet embayments. The mainsail halyard suddenly parted, chafed through at the peak block, and I found myself with the nastiest repair job known to the seaman, which is to say, scaling the mast to tie a splice into the becket. Throughout the voyage I had dreaded the onset of such a task. To this end I had replaced all halyards before leaving Galápagos, hoping they would last out the voyage to Sydney. The hard usage of the trades had worn the weak sisal rope through where it rode in the block.

Such a repair on the smooth waters of a basin is one thing, but in the unceasing seaway of the southeast trades it is decidedly another.

I got no farther than the hounds before I realized that what I was doing was impossible in the nude. I slid back down the swaying pole, minus a few minor chunks of flesh and smarting where I had met the mast and shrouds. I donned trousers and shirt and commenced the exhausting climb again.

This time I got well into the rigging before I encountered serious difficulties. Hanging on was a superenergetic job. I was puffing before I reached the first set of hounds. I had both legs and one arm locked tightly about the mast. With my free hand I cut away the old halyard at the becket, and barely managed to reeve the new line into the block, when I became aware that no matter how desperately I clung, I was being torn from my grip. I pulled the line through the sheave. My strength, in the maximum effort demanded to clutch the lurching spar, was deserting fast. I could hang on, I knew, only a few seconds at most. My holds were slipping, I was going.

I expected I would fall from the swinging spar and crash on the deck. The next land down wind was hundreds of miles.

It would be impossible in that sea to pass the line through the main peak block and splice it then to the becket on the topmast block. I could only hope to get safely out of the mess I had got myself into.

I made a movement to glide to deck thirty-five feet below. My leg unwound from its hold and was flung sharply away from the mast. I was thrown out of balance. My other leg followed. I was tossed against the shroud and against the mast. I could neither hold on nor work my way down without plummeting to the deck.

Below me *Pagan* looked like a canoe. Her headsails were

bellied to the wind. Each roller that passed under her counter pitched her steeply and rolled her to the rail. Up here I was looking down on first one side of *Pagan's* decks and then the other.

Unable to hold longer, I cast loose and kicked away as best I could. I fell as little boys fall from trees: completely out of control, legs kicking, arms flying. But I landed on the hard water — how it happened I don't know. Until the moment I sucked water into my lungs, I thought I had struck the rail.

I clambered on deck and lay atop the deckhouse gasping for breath.

It was evident I couldn't splice the halyard into the becket. I gave up the use of a peak block altogether and used the single purchase with one block. When I was rested, I hooked the sail on and pulled it up. It was harder to handle but it worked. *Pagan* was under full sail and showing her heels to the Marquesas.

Noon had gone. The islands were still in sight. I was resting and smarting from my labors on the mast. *Pagan* was doing her work nicely; she was shaping slightly south of west. The afternoon was passing like any other, except that I was enervated from the morning's exertions. I was sitting in the cockpit with the kittens purring their pleasant way, asleep in my lap. Slightly abaft the beam and about a hundred yards out the sea surface rippled, then it rippled again.

I stood up and watched, expecting to see a school of porpoise. The splashes and eddies drew near. Then, breaking water near by, and gliding smoothly beneath the keel, came a giant devilfish. He approached *Pagan* as though he hadn't seen her, and when he passed, he turned and slipped deliberately back, coming close enough to touch the planking, eying me with black protruding eyes. His head was the end part of a slightly humped and heavy body. His mouth was a black hole and either side of it were short armlike growths that he used, I suppose, to cram his victims into his black maw. The wide meaty wings moved with rippling motions, thrusting the tons of his weight along by the merest movements. Trailing behind him, like a life line, was a short thin tail.

The sea bat moves in utter disdain of whatever passes near him. He is remorseless in his power; confident as a peacock; more arrogant than a shark.

I wondered, as I watched him coast along, if I dared challenge him. And I did dare, because I knew that if I was careful the advantage was mine. With the experience I had gained from the shark near the Perlas, I felt I could outpoint his great weight and strength. It was simply a matter of hooking him and letting him play himself out — then I could pull him in close to the side and examine him at close quarters. This was another thing I had often dreamed of doing from merchant ships.

The size of him would necessitate a heavy line; the life line from the mainsheet traveler would do. I pulled it in and bent to it twenty feet of steel wire. I worked hastily, keeping my eyes on the huge fish as he boldly slithered beneath the keel and treaded water on the port quarter. On the end of the wire I spliced my two heavy shark hooks and baited them with a large bluefish I had caught in the morning.

This tidbit I dropped practically in the big brute's lap as he sauntered by. He deployed himself for a moment to consider it; then, with a great thrust of his batlike wings, fell on it in a rush. At the same moment, and with the same motion with which he took the lure, he plunged. I watched the line go down and come taut with such violence that the stern was pooped, and ran about three inches of water.

I watched the quiver of *Pagan's* stern and the stress against the line. I was ready with my knife to cut it away at the traveler if the strain against it threatened destruction. My idea in hooking him so was that the short line with *Pagan's* heaviness at the end would all the sooner wear him down. I was eager to finish him off and drag him to the stern where I could hack his jawbone out and add it to the shark's for Mary to see.

The line slacked for a moment, then tautened to the port side with a force that veered *Pagan* three points off course. I went sprawling into the cockpit. By main force, my boat had been stopped in her fix. She was making no headway. She merely strained where she sat. Her stern was pulled around till the wind was threatening to jibe the sail. I bounced to my feet with a decision to cut the line.

Pagan was being jerked about at will. I stepped out of the cockpit, wondering what next. As though a mule had kicked me between the shoulders, I went tossing headlong onto the lazarette. *Pagan's* decks trembled as she was jerked off course. The terror of thought gripped me; my body went cold; everything stopped. I scrambled to the stern, groping with my knife.

I heard the splintering of wood. I looked up to see the traveler being ripped away on the starboard side. It was made fast to both deck and rail by heavy screws, and yet it went as though it were tacked on. It twisted upward at a grotesque angle and bent farther as the line tightened. The strain was beginning to splinter it loose from the port rail.

I rushed to cut away the line. Something swooshed over my head. *Pagan* shivered mightily as she jibed and rounded up on the other tack; she was a half circle off course.

I looked at the sea and saw the devilfish was off the starboard quarter. He was on the surface and in his rage he was lathering the sea to a froth. His great wing tips were cleaving the surface, threshing like a wounded bird. *Pagan* was bouncing like a rowboat in a bad chop. The full weight of pull was now on the traveler where it connected to the port rail. It was now or never. I touched the taut line with the knife blade. The line snapped, unraveled, and flew at me.

There was only a swirl on the sloping wall of an onrolling wave where the devilfish had sounded into the tippled depths. *Pagan,* free of the restraint, quickly picked up speed.

I dropped the main immediately and pitched in to repair the twisted traveler and the splintered rail.

What a day it had been. As soon as the repairs were made, I was glad to get sail on, lash the tiller alee, and hit the sack, too tired to enter the day's events in the log.

The next afternoon Flotsam and Jetsam added a merry note to what had been a dull day. This was one of the few days that there hadn't been a flying fish on deck for them. Also my trawling had been to no avail. My potluck meals had netted me a can of spinach for breakfast and pineapple juice with a can of corn for lunch, not a suitable substitute for catnip.

By one in the afternoon, I still hadn't caught them a fish. I was on deck pondering just what to do in such a weighty predicament. A rule of the sea reads that one's sailors should eat sufficiently. Besides, morale demanded it. My crew was on the verge of mutiny. I heard a growling and scuffling unlike anything my charges had ever engaged in before. I jumped through the companionway, whence came the fracas.

There, under the forepeak, in a deathly encounter, grappled Flotsam and Jetsam — claw and fang into our passenger Stowaway. Stowaway heaved with kickings and twistings. My young lions, with claws bared and teeth dripping, jockeyed for better bite holds. Taking each of my grim starvelings by the tail, I spread them from the would-be feast. Stowaway, bruised and minus a few patches of fur, darted to his refuge.

Flotsam and Jetsam became highly indignant that they had been denied the passenger as fresh rations, and slunk into the forepeak to continue the toothsome search.

I could feel their hurts deeply, and I wanted to do right by them. So I searched among my stores of unlabeled cans for sign of a tin of fish. The cans in the lockers and in the icebox — some twenty cans in number — gave no hint that they contained fish.

According to my stores list I had 86 cans of food stored beneath the starboard bunk. To this point, I had eaten 139 of my original 248 tins of food. When I looked, I saw a sight to set one's nerves on edge. Something was wrong. I could tell it instantly.

I had known all along that it was damp in the tight space beneath the bunk, but I had no idea that in so short a time the dampness would infiltrate into the cans. I examined each swollen, seeping tin and found all of them puffed with gas and fermented soppy liquid. Not one of the whole storage was eatable. They had putrefied to a can.

Almost I decided to put about and try to gain back against sea and current to the Marquesas. Quickly I checked through the remainder of my stores. Thus far on the trip I had devoured over half my staples. The ham, bacon, salt pork, sugar, corn meal, peaches, prunes, and cheese were gone. Of the remaining staples — oatmeal, rice, oleomargarine, hominy grits, flour, jam, and honey — there was anywhere from one fourth to three quarters of a jug of each left. I counted 150 sea biscuits, a quart of dried apples, a gallon can of ketchup, a quart of peanut butter, plenty of tea and coffee and 23 cans of food. A check on my water supply showed just under 50 gallons aboard.

Since the bulk of my food stores had been centered in the canned goods, the loss suffered under the bunk had hurt. However, on paper I shortly estimated that it was possible to extract 107 meals from the remaining supplies. I also estimated that with forty days of hard sailing I could finish off the trip to Sydney. It had to be this way: in only a month hurricane weather was due. This meant that I must ration my food, cut down to two meals a day, and eat a little less at mealtime than I was accustomed to. It was that or try to win back to the Marquesas and suffer the possibility of holing up over the hurricane season. There wasn't time to turn back; I voted to go it to Sydney in one hard sail.

I was due to pass Caroline Island, a lonely volcanic and coral atoll, in a few days. My wicked intuition that all was well urged me to press on to the little isle, to stop long enough for coconuts as an addition to my larder.

It was about this time that I began to sense a subtle change in the weather pattern. I didn't worry about it because there was little effect on my timetable — but I certainly didn't like the looks of these growing changes. They argued that I speed on, that I crowd my boat to the maximum . . . that I get to Sydney as quickly as possible.

～   ～   ～

Overhead were split-tailed tropical birds; out forward shoals of flying fish flitted briefly, and in the wake were large sharks — all sure signs of land. On the morning of August 29 the loom of land raised across the bows, "right where it should be."

With the sun's rising I made the land — Caroline Island — to be seven miles distant, and shaped a course slightly north of South Island. On the starboard bow were a number of low mounds washed heavily by the sea.

According to the *Sailing Directions*, South Island is the main point in this tiny archipelago. There are supposed to be a few natives, a lot of fish around, and water ashore. A U.S. Solar Eclipse Party had been here in 1883, it said.

I sailed *Pagan* on a bowline for the readiest approach to the anchorage: I wanted to get done what I could before dark, so I could be on my way. I pointed up into the southwest corner of the weirdly shaped island. I donned my army fatigues and shirt; pulled on shoes and socks, the first since the Perlas; combed the salt out of my beard and hair, and took the tiller.

Not mentioned in the *Sailing Directions* is an active volcano, trailing a flow of smoke like a passing steamer. I kept the smoky crest on the bowsprit and dropped my homemade anchor in front of the reef-bound harbor. It took an uncertain hold and occasionally slipped. I found I had to keep my jib and staysail backing and filling to maintain a hold. *Pagan* rode easily, lying close under the land, catching the breeze falling from the summit.

Across the reef and over the placid lagoon I could see the shore line was planted to coconut trees. The rest was dark green jungle veering up into the heights.

Soon a sail put off from what appeared to be a small wharf. It glided over the protected bay and bounced across the thundering reef and closed in, its occupants smiling gleefully. I saluted them in as friendly a style as possible and encouraged them to moor their outrigger to my halyards.

At the helm was an old man, accompanied by his aged wife, two young men, a young woman, and two devilish looking boys and a girl. They were dark-skinned, and I am sure they were apple-cheeked under their burnt faces. They were more a Polynesian type of people — tall, brown-skinned, with long straight hair, Caucasian looking — not so squat and Negroid as the peoples I had seen farther west during the war.

They didn't know how to take me; though they smiled, they held back. I motioned them aboard in as friendly and disarming a manner as possible and indicated seating room on the cabin and rail.

I saluted each barefoot visitor with a friendly, informal handshake and nod as he stepped aboard. The men were clad in loose-fitting lava-lavas tied at the waist and extending to the knees. The two little boys were naked. All the women were robed with lava-lavas which began at the chest. The clothes of all were worn looking; they showed holes and ragged edges. I had the feeling that even these had been put on for this special occasion. Isolation showed in their faces.

The old man styled himself promptly as chief. He indicated my boat with a sweep of his gnarled hand and smiled admiringly. He spoke in a type of French unlike anything I had heard in Algiers or Quebec during the war. We quickly contrived a sort of *bêche-de-mer* centered around key words such as "boat, sea, wife, man, you, me, come, go, Australia, America" and so on. He pointed out his wife, his sons and grandchildren.

The youngsters stood somewhat in awe of me, the first white man they had seen. My blond bushy beard, growing since Panama, and by now some three inches long, alarmed them. My hair by now had cropped out over my ears, was extending toward my shoulders, and was down to my eyes in front. I tried to act in such a way as to show them I was no different from other men, except that I was luckily born white and fortunate to be partly educated.

The chief glanced below decks. Seeing no one he inquired after my crew. It was difficult to explain that I was alone and the reasons for it. Somehow I put the story across; and the men especially became quite impressed, but I'm sure they didn't believe that it was all for Mary.

In their youth the chief and his wife had lived in Papeete, the main anchorage at Tahiti. The whole group had been isolated, he explained, since the beginning of the war. When I told them the war was ended, all nodded agreeably and looked pleased, but I am sure they had no idea of who was fighting.

They fitted their mood to mine and reacted as I did. If I was amused, they were amused; if I listened very gravely to something the chief said, they in turn pondered it profoundly.

The younger men, around my age I would judge, were keen about *Pagan*. They were tall, square-jawed, with lean biceps and a spot of curled hair on their wide chests. They fingered the turnbuckles at the shrouds and the Manila halyards approvingly. I brought my sextant, compass, and pocket watch out. The watch fascinated them. The whole group drew in a close circle and emitted Oohs and Aahs when I unscrewed the back of the watch and displayed the intricate workings.

As I gained their confidence much jollity ensued — even the youngsters warmed up to me. A great happiness sprung up among us, and I forgot about my shortage of food and brought out nine unlabeled cans. As I gouged them open with the now rusted can opener, amazed exclamations went around. The old chief explained proudly, however, that many times before he had dined from tins.

We enjoyed our snack taken from the open can with our fingers. I ate the can of spinach that was opened because I was afraid their tastes might not appreciate it. They smacked feelingly over corn and beans, peaches and carrots, beets and applesauce, tomato soup and asparagus. Much dipping of fingers in various cans went on. While we ate I tried to explain the reason for my rustic anchor which one of the men had spotted in the shallow ice-clear water. It was difficult to tie up the modern conveniences of my craft with its incongruous ground tackle.

At this point a near riot occurred. The two boys, shuddering and jabbering, bolted from the cockpit and stumbled against the rail, falling onto the outrigger. The little girl and the young woman leaped across the row of legs to the foredeck, shrieking distractedly. Then from out of the hatchway into the cockpit sauntered Flotsam and Jetsam, padding sleepily, blinking at the unusual crowd.

The chief was the only one of the elders to recognize them as harmless, since the others had never seen a cat. My doughty crew was soon swept up by loving arms and such cooing and gushing went on as the kittens had never heard.

I invited the party down below decks to give them a clearer picture of my boat. Nine people make a cabinful on a twenty-nine-footer! But it was pleasant to hear voices in the little house that so long had been silent except for my voice talking to myself. I was satisfied merely to sit and listen to their appraisal of the fixtures, the portholes, the tools, the lantern, the mattress, my library, and the Primus stove. I took the stove down, pumped it up and fired it for them, and let them feel its fierce blaze. Anything to keep them talking.

When the young woman evinced interest in the milk cans, I offered her the empty one and she was pleased. One of the boys scrambled out of the cabin into the outrigger and returned with a huge black fish which he plopped on the deck for me. The old chief smiled magnanimously, and told me there were more ashore. It was about this time I decided to get rid of much of the junk that for a long while had littered the cabin. First I cleaned out my clothes locker. To each of the men and boys I tossed a pair of khaki army pants and a shirt. I cleaned out my tool case of extras I could do without. I heaved three empty jeep cans into the outrigger. I dragged out the spare lumber from under my bunk and set the boys to passing it up on deck. I gave them half my fishhooks and flies.

I could see the women were disappointed that I had not offered gifts in their direction. I fished in my sea bag and brought out several tablecloths my grandmother had crocheted for Mary. I explained to the ladies that they would make good dresses. I gave them my signal flags, which I had never used, for the same purpose. I gave them two of my four sail needles and a roll of twine. And I handed each an offering from the cosmetics case I had bought for Mary, but, as sane women should be, they were more appreciative of the half dozen jars with lids I gave them.

To the kids I dished out my magazines, comic books, and the jigsaw puzzle.

They took my house cleaning as a show of generosity and a greater cordiality grew up. They became willing to talk about their life ashore. They caught their water, they explained, from rainfall off their roofs, or trapped it from streamlets on the crater. They lived on taro, mangoes, and breadfruit from the interior of the island. They also domesticated pigs and chickens and caught sea life in the lagoon. I visualized the ordinariness of the life they must lead ashore with only a small patch of land under them surrounded by a monotonous sea.

Under safe circumstances I would have gone ashore as they invited, and, despite my haste to be under way, have relaxed for a day in their miniature village. But the holding power of the quickly shoaling bottom was precarious and *Pagan* was wantonly exposed to any shift in the weather. I pointed these things out to the group. One of the tall silent young men volunteered to stay aboard to guard against contingency. It was out of the question; it was the same as expecting me to be efficient with the intricate outrigger.

The afternoon was wearing on, the sun was well down toward the horizon, and I told the chief that I would soon be casting off. At a command from him, the outrigger, under the hand of one of the husky young men and the boys, shot over the reef and glided across the coral lagoon to the beach. In a little while it returned, lightering some water, pawpaws, breadfruit, tarl, about fifty drinking coconuts, and two small pigs and two chickens. I was overwhelmed at the generosity of an island that could ill afford to give much. My gifts, which I could easily afford, looked paltry in comparison.

I put the chickens under my bunk for the time being and turned the squealing pigs loose in the cabin. They promptly jumped all over everything. In a last-minute burst of generosity I tossed some line, some pots and pans, a can of nails and screws, an American flag, and a pair of shoes into the outrigger. These things were received happily enough, but somehow there wasn't the spontaneous reception as at first. The children especially looked at me longingly as I prepared to go. And when Flotsam and Jetsam, with paws on the rail, peered innocently and wide-eyed upon them they melted with wistfulness and no longer concealed their desire. Then I realized . . . and it hurt to think of it. I couldn't imagine *Pagan* without the kittens. They were more than a part of my boat, they were a part of my life. But still these people had precious little. I handed them into the outrigger into the happy arms of the little girl. I felt it would be cruel to deny these lonely people the company the kittens and their future generations could bring.

The time had come to go, and I must admit it weighed heavily. I knew I would soon be missing the voices, the laughter, and the warm company. It was cruel to force myself to return to the fight with the sea when here was a cool desert isle where I could put in for a rest. How many clerks, lost in a maze of office files, office routines, and the littleness of an office desk would have welcomed my opportunity?

The serious business of my leave-taking prodded me. The sun was half under the sea. I offered my hand around the sober circle and patted the young heads with whom I had established a close rapport. The old man clung to my hand; the sagging muscles of his face quivered as he passed on last-minute advice about the weather, the set of the current, and islands to westward. The young men looked wistful, and I am sure that if they had been a little more bold they would have asked to go along. Flotsam and Jetsam had found a fish in the bottom of the outrigger, and they didn't see my preparations to go.

The last of the islanders stepped off the decks by aid of the shrouds and settled themselves into their loaded craft.

I put my tiller over alee, shook the anchor loose, weighed it to the hawse, and grappled it aboard. The mainsail fluttered up the mast; all sails bent to their work; and in a few minutes my offing was made. I turned to wave a last good-by to my friends and my kittens. The outrigger hadn't moved; the islanders were standing and answering my wave. Then growing dusk closed them in and took them away, the distance blotted out their farewell calls.

The next morning I awakened in a calm, the first I had experienced since leaving the Galápagos, more than a month before. A little bit after daylight curtains of water driven by high winds closed around me. At first I thought it was only a series of squalls; but by noon I was heaved-to under storm sail in a gale of wind out of the south. All in one day!

I spent the day in my bunk gnawing pork joints, since I had subjected one of my piglets to his purpose the night before. That night the gooseneck broke, and I went out into the storm to wire the boom to the mast. By midnight the wind hauled around to south of east and modified. I set all sail, lashed the tiller, and made a course south of west.

After leaving Caroline Island I had a run of foul weather very like some of that I encountered on my way to the Galápagos. Always there were early morning squalls. There were occasional short calms. The wind shifted often and varied in strength. Cloud banks were heavier, wetter, and closer to the sea.

The weather was depressing. I had hoped to be making top speed over this area — instead my daily runs were lagging. I got lonesome without the kittens. I missed them snuggling in my lap when the weather deviled me. I missed their daylight capers, and when I ate the flying fish the taste wasn't the same as when the kittens ate with me.

I tried to tame the chickens, but they were disinclined to be tamed; so I ate them. The one remaining pig squealed every time I offered friendship — so he too got the pot. There were now only Stowaway and I aboard — and he was still a confirmed crank. Old Death and his boys were around but, as always, the simple things of life didn't concern them; they were concerned only with making a kill and gobbling it. Life on *Pagan* had lost the thrill of the days of Gawky, and Flotsam and Jetsam.

With the supplies I had picked up at Caroline, I looked forward with relief to the last month of the trip. Five days out from Caroline I was still gnawing pork bones and eating loads of fresh fruits and vegetables. I wanted to fatten on these perishables before my two-meals-a-day ration set in. And it was a good thing I took every available bite as I did, for even at that moment I was on the brink of the most climactic and nearly disastrous event of the trip.

The next day was Thursday, September 5, 1946 — I shall never forget that day. It started like any other in this area. I woke up at daylight to find a mild southerly breeze. In the neighborhood were four squalls, and I sat at the tiller riding between them. By the time the sun was an hour high I had run off from under the slanting wet curtains and was reaching for the clear sky beyond and a good day's sail. I was expecting to fetch land any minute in the Suvorov Islands. I had no intention of stopping; I merely wanted to bounce off them as a check on my navigation. I scaled the mast a time or two, and looked toward where the reefy group should break the horizon.

At nine o'clock the wind palled, and soon I was slatting in sticky air. Almost immediately a slight swell set in from — of all places — the north. I noted this most critically and attempted to reason out the oddity. I didn't like the implications. They pointed to a wind somewhere in the north. The weather of the past week came back to me. I glanced over my charts, my sailing directions, my information on storms. I knew what a northerly meant in these waters but I didn't mention it to myself.

By noon great glassy swells were crowding upon each other, still out of the north. *Pagan* was broached-to in their troughs; galley utensils clinked and clanked; the boom pounded where it was lashed; the blocks creaked and rattled. The sky had censored itself with a deep, gray mantle. *Pagan's* unsettled groanings seemed wasted on the immensity of the outer stillness and monotony.

By three in the afternoon it had grown darker, and, it

seemed, stiller. The heavy swells were gathering speed. They were larger, closer together, more purposeful. Off to the north an audible soughing whispered along the horizon.

Pagan's sails — except her staysail — were in. She was stripped to her standing rigging, looking nude as she rolled on that indifferent sea. I lashed the boom double secure to its crutch, clinched the halyards down, and cleared the decks. I battened all ports and hatch dogs. I nailed the fore scuttle to its coamings with heavy spikes, a precaution against deep seas boarding my decks. Down below all was shipshape: gear was stowed and lashed; lockers were packed tight and strapped down; a life jacket was on my bunk. From the bunk's edge dangled a number of short lines, to lash myself down when the need came.

On deck I sat atop the cabin . . . and waited, searching the horizon, the water, and the sky.

CHAPTER XVI   Hurricane

CAT'S-PAWS dappled the round crests of the hurrying rollers as a light air whisked out of the north. The breeze was strong enough to steady the staysail. It had a dampness that hinted at rain and it stirred a heavy cloud to motion, which soon proved to be a squall. It came on, closed over me, and wrapped me round with wind and rain. I stayed on deck despite the wet. Inwardly I felt apprehensive; and I couldn't go below.

In a way I was wishing I had a barometer so I could have some proof of what was afoot. As it was, I was now suspecting that I was being stalked by a hurricane. But at what rate, or from what precise direction, I couldn't know; only a barometer could tell me.

The area north of the Cook Islands, where I was, has a notorious reputation for cyclonic disturbances. If there was a hurricane in the locality, there was nothing I could now do but sit tight. I couldn't counter it. I was glad I had no barometer. Knowledge of a falling glass would only have verified a foregone conclusion. As it was I could sit minimizing the unmistakable symptoms, and hope to the very last that my fears were ungrounded.

My hands were tied, there was nothing I could do to avoid whatever it was that caused the northerly swells. Conditions of the sea and weather were not such that I could move profitably under sail. And I didn't want to be caught with my sails up, so I doused them, put them in stops, and watched and listened . . . denying every ominous sign.

I was soon encountering a series of nasty squalls, lowering skies, and hurrying of seas. Hours later still nothing definite could be read in the skies. I was forced to wait.

I strained at every nerve to know what was coming. I read from every shift of wind, every lessening of distance between the seas. I recalled everything I knew, little though it was, of hurricanes and their peculiarities.

A hurricane is greatly like the little whirlwind which dances along the street on a summer day, only it is infinitely larger. Its small round center is an area of low barometric pre. ure and calm air. The outer reaches of the disturbance have a high barometric pressure. As the barometer falls you know you are nearing the "eye" or center of the storm. Working from the outside of the hurricane, in a circular motion, are prodigious winds which intensify right up to the edge of the calm inner area. The whole system of terrific winds and calm central sector is usually little more than three hundred miles across. The duration of a hurricane depends upon the speed it travels — anywhere from five to thirty miles an hour.

A striking peculiarity of the hurricane is that in the northern latitudes its winds are counterclockwise, and in southern latitudes they are clockwise. Also, the portion of a hurricane nearest the equator is generally its least violent part, the portion farthest from the equator being especially dangerous because cyclonic tracks tend away from the equator, and thus advance across anything in its way. The thing to avoid is the center. If you face the wind in southern seas, the center is on your left. The dangerous semicircle would depend on the path of the storm's center.

⌐   ⌐   ⌐

By evening the last of the squalls had passed and the worst of my fears took shape. Rain poured heavily from the jagged, lowering clouds and a mild gale-force wind set in, whipping the seas so that they charged down around me. It was no guesswork about the hurricane. I was certain that I had one right in my lap. I took my anchor below and lashed it to the mast and made a last check of all gear to see that the precautions I had made against the storm were in readiness. I unlashed the rubber raft from the mast, pushed it off the foredeck, and strung it from the stern . . . just in case.

Gray tooth-edged clouds raced past barely above the mast top. They unburdened themselves of torrents of stinging water. The wind had steadied in the north; and the fact that it hadn't changed direction in an hour disturbed me. I rigged my storm sail on the mast, sheeted it flat, and crammed the staysail below. My last move was to cinch the tiller down doubly secure. I went forward, seated myself on the deckhouse, and with arm locked about the mast watched over the bows for what was coming.

Night closed in and heavy rollers, growling a flashing gray, were the only indication that the night was anything else but wind and rain. I went below to lie in my bunk, stare at the overhead, and wait.

About an hour later, *Pagan* commenced dancing nervously. Instead of rising gently to the oncoming crests she broke abruptly into them. Instead of a quick roll before the more forceful seas, she made a sharp lurch which found her often heeled over far enough to throw me. In my bunk I was forced to grip its sides. It was obvious I was in the center of the gale winds which lie just outside the perimeter of the on-coming hurricane winds.

After a while more occasional strains shivered the boat when the storm sail cringed before the wind. The brewing hurricane was slamming with ever greater intensity. I checked the watch and saw it was just before eight. That was the last time I looked at the watch; from then on there was too much excitement, too much violent motion.

Opening the hatch doors, I peeped into the garrulous night. Hissing rollers worked with a heavy swish beneath my boat and ran growling into the blackness. The wind pursued them with the persistence of a bully. *Pagan* lay as though still; now on a hillock, now in a ravine of water . . . as yet not pitching, but rolling mightily.

She was no longer riding comfortably. Her bow was lying five points off the wind, which still persisted from the north. The port rail was under, and the windward bow was throw-ing spray high into the rigging, and beating into the seas. Rain was the heaviest yet. It was impossible to look straight into that wind and rain.

With the wind holding for so long from one direction, I was certain that the track of the hurricane lay directly over me. I could figure on three phases of behavior from it. The first: the infernal winds of its dangerous semicircle. The second: the lull of the hurricane's center where winds from a dozen directions send great rollers crashing into a small, crowded arena. The third, and least vicious: the navigable semicircle or tail end of the storm.

Seeing that all was well as could be expected on deck, I pulled my eyes in and closed the hatch. I braced myself against the low overhead, and flashed my light over the airless interior. For the first time I lashed myself in my bunk and waited.

Two hours later *Pagan* was slapped by severe bursts of wind and sea that rattled her like sudden earthquakes. I was sure now that I was entering the first of the hurricane winds.

At a hidden hour, sometime later, *Pagan* heeled mightily, yawed and pounded. I loosed the hitches across my chest and legs and peered into the thick weather. The storm sail had failed to hold its own in the high wind and had blown to loose ends.

It meant going on deck again. I set my sea anchor — a home-made job, rigged coming over from the Galápagos — and veered it out on a hundred feet of line. *Pagan* rounded up successfully, though she was taking heavy, noisy water over her gunwales.

Below decks I lay lashed in my bunk once more listening to every creak and groan that shot past the hollow din of shrieking rigging and rumbling seas. I could hear the churning water surging over the decks. When the heavier gusts struck, I listened deepest. I was alert for any structural defects. I had learned to know my boat by the very feel and sound of her. After sleeping for more than two months with my ears tuned to her every murmur, I knew what each sound meant and from where it came.

My great concern was for *Pagan's* twenty-six-year-old, aging, tired timbers. It was hard to believe as I lay there that night listening to the inside sounds of a small craft under extreme stress that the planks surrounding me had been spreading water for those years. But *Pagan*, for all her age, was a well-found boat.

Along about two in the morning I heard a quivering shriek — the loose ends of a snapped shroud. It whined like something wounded. I opened the hatch and peered out. Giant wind-whipped seas surged to port and starboard. The wind, growing harsh and harsher, had the force of solidity.

Pagan was falling away laboriously. Her mast was describing a widening arc: she heeled to such an angle under the heavier gusts that the mast nearly lopped off the wave crests.

She pointed in a fast glide down the back side of a moving mountain. She plunged bow-on into the base of the next, submerging the forepeak, and quaking under the load of tons of green water. Pitching her bow out of the water to the keel, she sent a rivulet rail-deep cascading along the deck and pouring over the stern.

In the deep trough formed by the hills of sea, the wind was unable to strike; and *Pagan* righted abruptly. As she neared the curled peak on the climb up the oncoming roller, she once more encountered the blast. She careened before it. I couldn't stand. Too, she was struck by the thundering wind-driven comber which broke in a heavy continuum atop each hurricane swell. It was then *Pagan* pounded most. Her bow was pitched up as though dynamited, and she yawed wildly until heavy seas, boarding her, weighted her down so that she wallowed clumsily, her lee rail out of sight. Then she would shake herself free of her load and go reeling down the back side of another great, rolling swell of water.

The broken shroud — the forward one on the starboard side — was flailing like a whiplash. It cried the danger to my thirty-five-foot mast jolting at the storm blackness with only one shroud holding it on the starboard side.

The wind snatched my close-fitting watch cap from around my ears and threw it into the venting clouds. In a second I was drenched to the shoulders by flying spray.

I stared into that disjoined sea and saw instantly the uselessness of my life jacket. I stripped it off.

Before jumping on deck I bound a heavy line around my middle, and made it fast to the handrail on the deckhouse. I awaited a moment when the decks were water free and leaped out of the hatchway, closed it, jumped into the windward waist, and lay flat, facing up deck. The prying fingers of the wind caught the loose folds of my shirt, filling it at the front, tearing away the buttons, and ripping it down the back and sides. It hung by tatters. My full strength was required to lie flat on deck. I didn't dare stand into that wind, or even sit. When I looked into it for a second, I could feel my eyes depress; I could feel my hair whip against my cheeks.

I had strung a life line above the rails — from the bow to the shrouds and to the sternpost. Two more life lines lay strung on deck from the forward bit along each waist to the rudderpost. These latter lines had double knots tied in every two feet: and to these I clung each time a swirling sea charged along the deck.

I pulled myself ahead a few feet and locked myself, feet and hands, around the knotted line. When the decks spilled themselves of eddying water, and when for a moment I could expose myself, I freed my waistline on the handrail, moved it forward a length, and slid up under it. Movement was slow. It had to be. Thus I worked my way to the starboard shrouds to examine the damaged member.

I found that the turnbuckle on the after shroud had loosed. The shocks of the mast, reeling in a wide arc, had been absorbed by the forward, weaker shroud, weakened in the encounter with the devilfish, and it had parted.

The mast was held only by the one shroud, and it wasn't tight as it should have been, since the turnbuckle had unscrewed. The load on it was terrific. It couldn't sustain that tremendous load for long. Each time *Pagan* pitched her heel clear of the water and twisted over into a flat beam roll, the mast looked as if it would jump out of its stepping. I could feel the timbers in the deck beneath me crawl.

I tightened the turnbuckle as well as I could by hand. But it wasn't enough. The single shroud couldn't hold out alone. There was only one desperate move I could make to save the mast: loosen the forestay at the stemhead and bend it to the chain plate as a jury shroud.

As the next heavy sea went crashing around my shoulders and over me, I made ready to loosen my body line and fasten it a few feet ahead so that I could snake my way to the bow. I moved slowly and carefully across the open deck. Between seas I shifted my line from one secure fastening to another — and more than once, but for the line, reaching green waters would have snatched me over the stern.

Scrambling from the mast across the fore scuttle to the bitt was a risky business. It was then that I was clinging only to the deck lines, having nothing to which to attach my waistline. I watched the seas overspilling the rails, and timed the intervals . . . then jumped. I made it. The seas growled unhappily and continued to be unhappy, sniping at me as I worked. I loosened the forestay as quickly as possible and, gripping it fiercely, slithered back to the shrouds.

I lay on my back on the blown decks working with only my hands and forearms in the wind. I took my time; thought carefully over each job before I did it. When I finished, *Pagan* was bolstered by full shrouds and I was eased of mind. The decks, aheave and awash, didn't seem so bad with the mast safely held. The job completed, I made the gross error of sitting up to check it. An explosive wind bent me to a helpless angle. A flurry of bubbling water lifted me bodily and bounced me against the deckhouse and into the shrouds, then whelmed me over the rail onto a churning sea.

The line was around my waist, fortunately. The pull of the sea spun me upside down, wrenched at me, and tore. *Pagan* submerged her rail and I found myself clawing in a surging froth, closing my throat against the water. I was hard against the hull, being slammed against it, one minute under water and one minute not. A heavy sea dropped down on *Pagan* too perpendicular to be climbed. I saw it curl over, towering before me. *Pagan* had just heeled obliquely, throwing her windward rail high. I was yanked from the water, and had it been possible to stand in the wind I could have walked down the hull. Above me I could see the curling lip of descending water.

My tiny craft, caught between sea and wind, sank bodily beneath the impact of her decks. I was glad I wasn't on the open deck, as the flood engulfed the bow and rolled heavily against the bulkheads.

Another drink of salt was choked down me as the boat was dragged by main force before the ungovernable sea. My arms and legs were thrown at will. She sidled and broached about as though she would wallow and founder.

The high strain of fighting back had pared my strength

away in a few short minutes. I was choked with water in lungs and stomach, and flopping against the hull had set my head to spinning. I was giving it up, I knew it, but I couldn't resist longer; the thing was I didn't want to resist longer. I could see *Pagan* close by and I could see the gray loom of seas, but I couldn't reach toward one or lean away from the other. I relaxed. I became part of the sea. I could hear the singing siren.

Pagan's white hull was only a foot or two away, looking like a high wall. I wanted to touch it and climb over it. I closed my eyes, wondering what would happen next. A dollop of seas whirled broadside onto *Pagan*. I struck the rail and floated against it. The deck tilted steepily; I slipped somehow inboard and brought up against the deckhouse. *Pagan* came out of the hollow between the seas cringing before the winds.

I knew immediately that I was safe on board. I remember vomiting the water I had swallowed, and tugging faintly at the hard wet knot on the handrail. The next thing I knew I had toppled through the hatchway, had somehow closed it, and had tumbled in a heap on the cabin floor. I was too sick and weak to care what happened next. For long hours I rolled to and fro on the floor knocking against the bunks as *Pagan* tilted high. Finally I crawled into my bunk and bound my lashings over me.

CHAPTER XVII

Dismasted

WHEN I AWAKENED, it was daylight.

I didn't waken because I had slept enough, or because the daylight had caught my eye. Not forty-eight hours of sleep would have been enough. Not a searchlight could have disturbed my profound sleep. I wakened because of *Pagan's* sudden change in behavior. Her pitching and rolling became suddenly beyond what I had ever felt before. She inclined to flatness on both beams; and pitched so high that it seemed incredible she didn't jerk her keel off.

I thought at first my boat must be turning over and over. But I could see the overhead remain near where the overhead should be — and I tried to explain to myself what was happening.

Most perplexing was the absence of the storm's noises. I had passed out with the hurricane shrieking in the rigging. Now, aside from the wash of water in the bilge, a pounding on deck, and an occasional swish of sea, there was little else . . . strange.

The combination of quiet and violence scared me.

Unbinding my lashings, I wavered to the hatchway, barely able to keep off the plunging bulkheads. I opened the hatch doors a foot and pushed my eyes above the cabin. I saw a vast circle of foam upshot with rearing cones of water . . .

but not a breath of air stirred. There were no rollers or combers as such, only peaks of water shooting up and falling away flatly.

Instantly I knew I was in the lull of the hurricane; which is to say, the airless central circle around which revolve the cyclonic winds. Pushed into this diabolic arena were thousands of wind-churned seas from countless directions to collide and intercollide.

I don't know how to explain it, unless I suggest that you visualize yourself on a crag, surrounded by numberless other such, then, at a given signal, they resolve themselves to liquid and each sets upon the others as would hunger-crazed beasts.

As far as I could see, great pyramids of water bolted masthead high from the sea surface. Here and there great cross seas crashed into them, dispersed, re-formed, and crashed again. *Pagan* lay to her scuppers beneath a constant deck of water. Her sea anchor was helpless; she danced to all points of the compass, her mast scoring the water on either side. Suddenly she was high and suddenly she was low.

Nausea assailed me. The sickening surge of the boat, and the unstable watery sight, set me to vomiting. I couldn't hold myself up longer.

I stumbled into my bunk and lashed myself down. I realized that I should get up and pump the bilges; also plug the broken porthole — but I was too dead sick to move. I couldn't even brace myself against the lurch; I just lay there, rolling against my lashings.

All morning my head spun as the jaunty craft threatened to fall apart. Not once could I sleep, even fitfully. I lay listening to the noises. I was nervous to distraction as to what could happen to my boat in this constant, violent rough-and-tumble.

Early in the afternoon I nosed into the outer circle of the hurricane. Once again the rigging dinned with the howling winds. This time the wind had shifted into the south and my bunk was on the windward side. One inch of tired oak plank-ing — only a span away — stood between me and disaster-crested seas. Most of the time I was tilted high in the air with the other bunk below me at the bottom of the slanting deck. Water was overtopping the decks and sloshing through the smashed porthole. It wet me down, refreshed me, eased the seasickness a bit.

I was still strapped in my bunk. The seasickness was paci-fied by the more consistent motion of the boat. Now that the wind set upon her again, there was a system in her wild be-havior that was kindred to my experience.

From where I lay, I could hear the bedlam of wind in the rigging, could feel my boat wince before each header. The furiously whipped seas were snarling across the decks like packs of wolves. Because of water slopping through the port-hole, I got up and stuffed a pair of pants in the opening. I realized that while I was up I should go out on deck and cut free the boom, which, flying at the end of the topping lift, was smashing at the stern end. Also the bilges needed pump-ing. But, remembering my narrow escape on deck, I reasoned that the threat of boom and wet bilges was naught compared to the risk of venturing in the open. I remained in the safety of my wet bunk and tightened the lashings over me. Again I waited . . . listening.

The process of riding out a hurricane in a small boat is terribly nerve-racking. It's the sense of futility you feel in the face of imponderable odds. The hurricane is supreme master; you are its trifle — a cork in a tempest.

There is only one safe way to ride out a hurricane on a small boat: flat on your back lashed in the bunk with ports and hatches dogged, and everything strapped down. But lying there strait-jacketed to a mattress is depressing: you always wonder what's going on in the rest of the boat. You wonder if somewhere a leak is breaking, or a repair needs attention. To keep the boat under constant examination is too bruising a job: the prospect of overseeing things on deck is taboo, positively taboo. So I passed the long jolting hours in my bunk . . . waiting, and determining *Pagan's* condition from a distance.

The fact of *Pagan's* years, the fact that she still had her original wood — this was the reason I listened the more intently. She was too old to be bucking up to a hurricane and this thought was cropping up all the time. Another concern which accosted me was my life raft.

It had been trailing astern since the start of the hurricane. When I was last on deck I had caught a glimpse of it, wallowing to its gunwales in the angry froth. But that had been during the lull when I was sick. I could only hope it was still there. If not, I had nothing to escape in, if trouble came. I thought of going to the deck to look for it, but I didn't figure it was worth the risk. There was nothing I could do if I needed it but go out and look for it; if it wasn't there, well . . . that was that.

How many hours I lay there straining at my lashings, waiting for some indication that the storm was abating, I don't know. Night came. More hours dragged. The hurricane was twenty-four hours old. It labored on to somewhere near thirty.

The same violent jerks of the boat, the same roaring wind, crashing sea, clatter of dislodged gear, and slosh of a water-filled bilge!

In the wee hours of the morning of September seventh — after two days of storm — hard luck struck. My first recollection that something was amiss came when *Pagan* broached to and refused to round up into the wind. Great seas were ramming against the beam and combing athwart the decks. She scudded before each tumbler, creaking loudly and inclining more than usual. She lunged as though filliped by a mammoth finger. It was punishment beyond what my boat could take for long.

I unbound my ropes and took a look outside. It was the same wild world as ever: a sea blown to windrows, heavy curlers boarding the decks, volleys of spray flying around my ears, *Pagan* yawing at the will of each disjointed sea and wind.

I could tell without seeing that the sea anchor was gone: evidently chafed at the bobstay. I was thinking of something I could use to replace it. Somehow my boat must be made to face up to the wind. Only a sea anchor could make it do that. With *Pagan* rolling and pitching eerily it was impossible to make one. What was worse — there wasn't time to make one; an hour of this and *Pagan* would break up. To prove my point a swelling billow with a smoking mane sent us lurching on our beam ends. I acted quickly.

There was my rustic anchor lying on the cabin floor, lashed to the heel of the mast. If I heaved it over and let it drift out to chain's length it should drag enough to hold the bow into the wind. It was worth the try. I groped for it in the dark. I wrapped it in the jib, and bound it on the outside with the sheets to make it act as a decent drag. I tied my life jacket to the flukes to prevent it from sinking; and made ready to heave it out of the hatchway into the sea.

The decision to go out on deck was hard arrived at. But I had to go. In some way I got the anchor into the cockpit and crawled in beside it, lying low under the wind. I heaved it overboard, clinging to the bitter end of its line. With just my eyes over the coaming, I watched it float forward. I had now to secure the line to the bow. I waited a long minute before facing the open decks. As she lay, *Pagan* was in a position to pound herself apart, broad-on to the breaking seas.

The windward bulwarks wore an uninviting look; so I jumped into the flooded lee waist. So long as I was alee of the cabin I could crawl. I had to be careful; the rail on the starboard side was gone, carried away by the flood. There was nothing to hold to if I should be washed outboard. When I edged out ahead of the deckhouse into the wind, I lay flat on my face and snaked my way. All the time a line was fast to my middle and connected to a stanch object. In addition I was gripping the knotted line strung over the deck.

I was afraid that heavy seas overrunning the gunwales would raise me so that the cyclonic fingers could roll me overboard. But I made it safely to the stemhead and fastened my waistline to the bitt. At the same time I hitched a hasty bowline with the anchor line to the chain leading from the chain locker. As quickly as possible I slipped back to the safety of the cabin. *Pagan* was yawing badly. If the anchor dragged more slowly than the boat, the bow would fetch up to the wind. I hoped she would answer soon.

Just then the most severe shock of all rocked her — a gust firing point-blank. Piles of water rambled roughshod athwart her to the height of the portholes. She heeled to her beam ends, and creaked loud enough to hear above the storm sounds. In abject terror I fled below.

Another roller struck her more heavily than the other. For a moment the beam planking became the deck under me. The rattle of loosened gear filled the blackness of the tight cabin. Before my little world could right itself, it shivered again beneath an impact. And a moment later again. This time the sea hurtled over the starboard quarter; she had been turned half around by the force of the sea blows. At the same moment a resounding snap of solid timber impinged on every sense of my body, froze me, stopped me short. The mast! I could tell by the feel of the wounded boat.

I knew what a broken thirty-five-foot spar could mean. I staggered faultily toward the companionway. Something heavy pounded her by the stern. Another heavy sea had hit her. Just then — and exceeding quick — the stout little doors dissolved into a sheet of gray. With black suddenness a lump of water shot at me. In the wink of an eye I was sledge-hammered back the full length of the cabin, rolling, twisting. When I stopped falling I was under the foredeck, sitting waist deep in rushing water, surrounded in dark.

In front of me was the heel of the mast. On one side were my mattress and blankets, where they had washed with the sudden inflooding. On the other were the sails, where I had stowed them. In my lap, pinioning me and fighting me, was a fifteen-gallon water cask, swept loose from its lashings. I was helpless to push it away. The surge of the knee-deep water forced it one way and another, against the mast or my chest. In either case it was still in my lap. When *Pagan* pitched, throwing her bow down, the water rushed me, and knocked me flat and covered me.

Pagan took another roller across the stern. More water poured through the companionway. The water rose to my chest and raced to and fro faster in the pent space. I was knocked under more often. It was harder to sit back up.

Pagan's interior was a welter of attacking wavelets. It was like a tomb; it was frightening. With an ocean to drown in I was drowning inside my boat. I fought to get at least on deck. To be licked off by the wind and sea was more fitting than perishing under deck beams, hundreds of miles from a safe shore.

A providential movement of the barrel enabled me to sidle from under it and struggle from beneath the forepeak. The cabin was a nightmare. It ran thigh-deep to water. Three quarters of my gear was adrift. The locker doors were gaping, and their contents were dropping into the brine. The lockers themselves, caught by the shifting water, were in the process of ripping from their fastenings.

I wavered through the morass and clambered into the brimming cockpit. Its coamings were gone, but I was protected from the wind when I lay low. *Pagan* was rounding up nicely to the drag of the anchor; I could tell by the feel she was plunging into it dead ahead.

The mast had snapped; that was definite. I could see it wrenching at the dark sky. I could feel it nearly jerk the planking off at the chain plates, and I could hear it stomping on the foredeck, threatening to break through the deck. The heavy pole was held up by the shrouds and stays. It was trying helplessly to fall. Each pitch, each roll, each twist, endangered the life of my boat. And lying there in the flooded cockpit I could see it all, and I could see there was no alternative but to chop away the shrouds and free the big spar to topple into the sea.

A hatchet was ready to hand in the cockpit. I bellied along my system of life lines, tying my waistline ahead of me as I went. The decks were still awash, and the wind still in high glee. Lying on my back I hacked at the now slack, now taut, wire shrouds. Eventually one cut through; it went singing into the dark obscurity. I chopped away at the other. The stress of the wavering mast would have snapped it, in a little time, without my hackings. It suddenly parted. The high, heavy pole slammed away to leeward and splashed onto a sea.

I cringed against the deck when it went and heard rumbling and splintering after it fell.

Without a mast the little craft lay more comfortable, less affected by the powerful winds. She no longer beat into it, but rose with it, and kept an evener keel. I crawled back close beside the cabin and crept through the breach in the coaming into the cockpit.

The cabin below was a bog. My boat was terrifyingly close to sinking. Water was the depth of hip boots, and was solid from the watertight bulkhead to the bow. Only the fact of that water-resistant wall kept her from foundering by the bow or stern as the water surged fore and aft with each upward lurch and toss of the bow. She had to be pumped out before more seas should crowd aboard her.

But how to pump her out? My bilge pump was aft of the cabin and connected to its overhead. Its position was vulnerable to the wind. I dared not expose myself by using it. But *Pagan* had to be emptied . . . somehow.

There was only one recourse: the bucket. I lowered myself into the hip-deep swirl and fished around till I found it. I commenced the awkward bailing. I braced myself against the carlings or clung grimly to the hatch coaming, while wrestling with the bucket. I bailed till I felt green in the face; and bailed on.

It was easiest to stand in the center of the cabin and heave the water into the cockpit, and when the boat rolled, the cockpit emptied through the splintered coamings into the scuppers. But when it pitched, some slopped back into the cabin. Also the forepart of the deckhouse was smashed in from the felling of the mast, and some big water came in occasionally. The three portholes to windward were out. But by a steady sweat I could gain on the threatening water.

The seasickness of earlier in the storm began creeping over me again as weariness set in. After hours of bailing the floor boards were visible. I took time to plug the dripping portholes and stow a few soggy items of gear in suitable corners. Then I dipped and poured till the boards showed dry.

I ragged my watered mattress onto my bunk and prepared to fall onto it. The floor rose sickeningly as *Pagan* spun before a bank of water. She was pushed off her heading till she lay stern-to, before the seas. I leaped atop my bunk as the first seas crowded aboard and roared around the decks. Braced against the deck beams I watched the floor fill to ten inches of water — an hour's fast bailing and, tired as I was, a heartbreaking sight.

Another sea had at her and more water spilled through the companionway. I bolted out into the overflowing cockpit, hiding under the wind. A third sea overran the transom, licking at me, nearly forcing me back into the cabin. After that *Pagan* broached to and appeared to be coming about into the wind.

I was safer down below bailing than sitting out in the wind. I lowered myself into the watery hold and fished for my bucket. I filled and poured for endless hours. There was no consciousness directing my work—I bailed blindly and dumbly and unfeelingly. In fear of further swampings, and in completest indifference, I jettisoned anything and everything that came to hand. My mattress went by the board; also blankets, tools, dishes, canned food, coconuts, clothes, water breakers, sails — all that encumbered my bailing.

I was fighting for my life in hip-deep water, lightening my boat. Any moment I expected her to dip her stern into a sea and go under. I was fighting to lighten her before that sea came — if it was to come. There was no such thing as bailing just water alone, I bailed whatever I scooped up in the bucket; and I scooped and bailed till it was an effort to lift even the empty bucket.

When I could no longer think or even hope — for I hadn't eaten, or drunk, for two days, or slept — I collapsed on my bunk boards. I slept as I fell. And I slept where *Pagan* rolled me. I wasn't lashed down.

I was totally jaded, sick, and numb. I put myself in *Pagan's* hands. I was aware of nothing. I never knew when the hurricane ended. Maybe it was an hour before I came to awareness or maybe half a day . . . or a day . . . I can't know. I only know that I sat up, and that it was strangely quiet, and that *Pagan* rolled easier than she had done in days.

She was shifting on a light seaway. Outside it was dull and gray, but calm. The horizon mewed lightly in the direction the hurricane had gone — the adaptable sea was already composing itself for the friendly sky on the opposite horizon.

CHAPTER XVIII

Jury Rig

FROM THE TIME I had collapsed on my bunk boards, while the storm was yet on, I slept twice around the clock. I wakened but once in that time for a couple of hours, at an unholy hour of night, to bail out twenty inches of water in the hold. How it got there I didn't know. It hadn't dawned on me that my boat was leaking. I had thought the flooded cabin was caused from a swamping while I slept. But outside there was calm. There were no seas to jump aboard. I was tired, still too tired to reason things out, so I fell again on my hard, wet bunk boards. But now I was aroused from my deep slumber by water slopping over me again.

The floor was flooded. It was dawn, and I was rested. I went on deck for the first time since the storm to pump the bilges, and to see what my boat was like.

Pagan lay in a flat calm. Smooth-crested swells of the afterstorm passed under her. The sky was blue and tranquil — here on this wide field of the sea was little to indicate, for one with Olympian eyes, that a violent hurricane had recently passed under *Pagan's* near-derelict hulk, heaved into view out of a sea valley onto a glassy roller.

It gave me serious pause just to stand and look.

What I saw was a monument to chaos. A dismasted boat is a naked sight; but one in the condition that *Pagan* was in —

battered and bruised, limping as if wounded — is a heart-breaking sight for a seaman. I walked to the bow and stood looking back over the scarred decks of the little ghost ship. She no longer creaked and rattled from tackle and spars. Her tackle and spars were down, and dragging in the sea with her rigging.

The bowsprit was gone, snapped at the stemhead. There was barely a rail on the boat — only slivers and stubs. The staysail boom was gone, its fastenings broken at the bow. My carefully laid deck canvas was peeled away where it had been caught between wind and sea. The forward end of the deck-house was caved in, evidently by the mast and the charging seas. The splintered stub of the mast, a foot high, where the stick had twisted off, was the most unreal sight of all. Only one porthole was whole; all others were stuffed with an array of clothing.

Back aft, the cockpit coamings were broken away. The companionway doors were gone. For the second time Pagan's tiller had been torn off, despite the double secure lashings I had applied before the storm; this time by the boom hurtling at the end of the topping lift. The bumkin was snapped off — this too by the clublike boom. But most representative of the hurricane's damage were the raffled trailings of Pagan's rigging in the limpid water. They hung from the port side and trailed astern like tufts of matted hair, clutching the mast, the broken boom, the bowsprit, and splinters of the bumkin.

She had lived through the storm and stress, and I was glad. I tried to depreciate the extent of damage; but somehow my observations weren't convincing.

My little life raft was still floating astern, partly submerged.

Later I learned that one of its compartments had been deflated, probably in altercation with the boom.

The hold had all the earmarks of an Augean stable; a chowderish mixture of the thousand and one articles of gear I had tucked away in corners, which only an inimical sea could fetch out. It was a fearful sight: a quagmire, one to discourage a battery of janitors. Tools, articles of clothing, oilcans, loose line, crippled fixtures, strips of bedding, shoes, and splintered lumber lay intertwined where they had wrestled during the storm.

The sea was quiet as seas are in the calm, and as I looked out over it, it seemed more quiet than it had ever seemed before.

My main concern was to see *Pagan* under sail as speedily as possible. Before I settled to my work, my thoughts turned to food. For three days and nights I had not eaten; I was ravenous. I found a quart can of tomatoes and a coconut in the debris and broke into them with the hatchet. After gulping them, I looked for water.

My water breakers, I soon found, had all slipped their bungs, so that the water was either spilled or polluted. But strapped to the carling on the starboard side was a small keg of "emergency water" — four gallons. All I had aboard. "Plenty," I thought, and took a deep drink. It would last me to Samoa, what with coconuts and other liquid foods that I could dig out later from the mess in the cabin.

I went on deck and pitched into the work of rigging *Pagan* to sail. This, it seemed to me, was the most important consideration at the moment. There would be plenty of time later, when *Pagan* was once more fitted out and running before the wind, to clean up below and take stock of food, water, and my position. For the nonce it sufficed to know, by re-calling my last determined position before the heavy blow, that I was somewhere in that lonely stretch of the Pacific be-tween the Cook Islands and Samoa; exactly where would be easy to determine when I sought out my navigation equip-ment and took a sight. Before the sun was fully up I had pulled the mast inboard and lashed it obliquely across the fore-deck. I intended to carry it thus to Samoa where I could have it restepped and continue my trip.

The broken thirty-five-foot mast, weighing several hundred pounds, was far too heavy and clumsy for me to set up alone. I thought of cutting off its lower twenty-five feet and step-ping that, but even that much, I knew, would be too cumber-some to handle. I was looking hard and stretching my imagi-nation hard to conceive from *Pagan's* derelict woods some-thing suitable for a mast.

There was the better half of the boom. I fished it in and trimmed it for an abbreviated mainmast. It was small, hardly fifteen feet. It was all I had. My plan, devised fitfully as I went along, was to rig *Pagan* as a yawl. A yawl, roughly, is much like what *Pagan* had been as a cutter, except that a small mizzenmast is located just behind the tiller. Rigged as a yawl she would have a good spread of sail, and would handle easily. I wanted a spritsail, so I cleared away the remainder of the old bowsprit and reset its larger half, but without a bob-stay.

The former shrouds, cut shorter with the hatchet, I used for the new standing rigging. I made my connections at the head of the new mast directly to the main boomdale, using "U" bolts. I sawed out a hole in the deck in front of the broken stump of the mast. The fore side of the stub I shaved flat with the hatchet. I did the same to the after side of the boom, and knitted them together with two heavy bolts and strong lashings. I wedged in the new mast securely at the deck hole. To tighten the stays and shrouds properly I used the heavy turnbuckles at the chain plates.

Thus the storm-ravaged boom afforded a twelve-foot mast, carrying a ten-foot-high trysail. By midday I had rigging up that could hold a mainsail, staysail, and jib.

About this time of day I knew *Pagan* was leaking. The bilge had filled since I had pumped it at dawn, proof, even to a green horn, of a leak. I pumped the bilge and went below. I spent an hour looking for the leak, pushing through the gear-piled floor and into the mess of the forepeak, and finally decided it was somewhere below the cement-filled bilges where I couldn't see it or reach it. There was nothing I could do but pump the bilges hourly and hope the seepage wouldn't grow.

All afternoon I cut and sewed miniature sails from my weather-worn mainsail. For the mainmast I made a trysail ten feet high and seven feet long. She was hoisted on the boom-dale block and belayed at the staysail traveler. One-inch line spliced around the mast served as rings. I sewed each ring into the luff. This sail worked loose-footed, clewed up to an oar stock which I pared down for a jury boom.

I worked the pump from time to time, gushing out the estimated twelve gallons of water that was seeping into the bilges every hour. As I pumped I eyed the full circle of the horizon in hopes a ship might break over it. The hourly pumping, I felt, was a job that in time could grow distasteful, but since I was only some 400 miles from Samoa, by rough guess and assuming that the hurricane had not carried me far from where it found me, I wouldn't be at it long enough to matter.

Staysail and jib were considerably smaller than the mainsail, looking like pillow slips when they filled away. I sheeted the staysail to the chain plates, and the jib to the bitt. By dusk I had three sails in the wind. An occasional bubble showed in the wake. I lashed the broken tiller so that I made a course, according to the star, of due west. As yet I hadn't found my compass, but I didn't worry about it because I knew it was somewhere in the mess below. The important thing at the moment was to get sail up and way on.

Dark was drawing in. I pumped the bilges with a hundred quick strokes. Rifling in the hopeless tangle of the cabin, I came up with a can of peas. It was the first bite since dawn — I had been so busy.

When I had eaten I went on deck. Night had closed in. I sat on the cabin for hours watching the four winds, flashlight in hand, waiting to give a signal. At a late hour I hit the sack — or what I called the sack. I slept on my bunk boards, folded in the one blanket which I hadn't "deep sixed" during the confusion of the hurricane. This was only a temporary arrangement; I figured I could tolerate it till I lifted Samoa.

Daybreak found me out in the fresh morning air shaping my last oar into some semblance of a mizzenmast. A mop handle served for the boom. I had to build on to the splintered remains of the bumkin in order to sheet the new addition.

I used rope to rig it, and set my shrouds and topping lift from a masthead knot tied and nailed in a groove at the peak. It was stepped just aft of the steering post, going through the deck and bedding in the sternpost.

By noon the jigger was sheeted home and carrying wind.

Pagan was converted from a cutter into a yawl, and was limping down wind at an estimated one knot. For the time being I held her on her westerly course, "rail down" for Samoa. The next job was to get the cabin shipshape, take account of the food and water, find the navigational instruments, and grope after my position on the sea.

Before my cleaning job was finished that afternoon I learned some sobering facts. These facts so set me back that I lay awake many long hours that night. I learned, first of all, that I was completely without navigational instruments — not even a compass. Secondly, that I was practically foodless. Thirdly, that the only fresh water aboard was the four gallons in the emergency keg plus a quart of battery water I found in the hold.

On my bunk, in a thin weak line, lay the miserably few articles of food and comfort I had found. There were a bottle of ketchup, two unlabeled cans of food, and a coconut, my total larder!

I could recall that during the hurricane I had heaved many articles out in a frantic haste to lighten my boat — and as I heaved, I realized that items of food were going by the board. But never had I realized I was so completely tossing out my food stores. Further, I had not realized that my jugs and jars, in which were capped my precious staples, were being smashed and their contents mixing with the sea. In the desperateness of the hour there had been no time to so thoroughly think out the possibilities and probabilities of my actions.

Beside my scanty food supply lay my sextant, or rather what was left of it. It had once been a fine precision instrument, but now it was a twisted piece of junk. The index mirror was broken off completely. The telescope was gone. The alidade was bent at a rakish angle and jammed so that it couldn't be moved. The arc was rippled beyond any dreams of repair with means at hand.

Close by lay the compass — what was left of it, that is. The glass was smashed and the precious liquid had spilled. The guts of the instrument were lost in the disarray of the cabin, and it was the more useless in that it was torn from its gimbals, and they weren't to be found.

During the day I found no charts, no *Sailing Directions*, no Light lists; not even my carefully kept log of the voyage. These articles I always kept in the chart rack beside my bunk. When the cabin filled, the rushing water had licked them out.

The tidying process disclosed considerable damage to the interior of my boat: The icebox, lockers, galley, sink board, chart rack, ladder, and floor boards had been torn from their fastenings. They were a mass of amorphous lumber. The crushing weight of the twisting water in the hold had chewed down all my fixtures except the stout bunk.

There were few exceptions to this destruction. Built into the forward wall of the deckhouse, high up, was a small elongated cabinet; of all the inside furnishings it alone was dry. In it were twenty cartons of cigarettes, which I was taking to Mary's dad, some matches, and my navigation pocket watch. The cigarettes were useless because I have never smoked, and near the cabinet, on the starboard bulkhead just under the portholes, there clung the bookshelf; in it a frowzy mixing of wet pages and crumpled bindings.

Pangs of uneasiness set in. I tried to recall every important tenet a seaman should know for such times as he is lost on the sea, and foodless and waterless. Once, during the war, I was in a lifeboat for a short while. But it had been infinitely different from this. There had been the company of twenty men. We had a regular food and water ration, handed round by the old scoundrel, our captain. And we had our officers, with gold braid enough to defy the devil, to inspire us. The greatest difference between the lifeboat and *Pagan* was that in the lifeboat we knew we would be rescued. The Army and Navy were looking for us; so we enjoyed ourselves teasing the sharks and regretting we couldn't feed them!

That night on *Pagan* I detailed for myself a strict regimen to be followed to the letter. Food and water were to be carefully doled. I suggested a pint a day water ration and a few nibbles of the food, something to take the edge off hunger. With Samoa so near, I wouldn't be sorely pressed. A matter of two weeks' discomfort, then port, and the luxury of refitting my boat for the last leg of the voyage. The date was September 9 — five days since the start of the hurricane.

I was lost, that was definite. Five days ago my position, according to memory, had been 13° 21' south, 162° 40' west. I had then been a bosun's roar from the Suvorov Islands, a low, nearly barren, uninhabited coral reef. After a long calculation I figured I was somewhere south and west of the Suvorovs, somewhere under their lee. Not close enough to bother or to risk looking for them. Better leave them be, I thought. Do the safe thing, go on west to Samoa.

I guessed the distance to Samoa at about 400 miles. To be on the safe side I put it at 450; actually it was 480. I estimated my progress with sails at twenty-five miles per day. And from what I remembered of the Pilot Chart, there was a current push of from zero to twenty miles per day on the keel. I conservatively planned on five miles a day help from the current, which would jump my daily coverage to thirty miles.

By simple arithmetic, I supposed that in sixteen or eighteen days I should come upon Samoa, provided I was in the right latitude. If I wasn't, then I would pass by it into landless westward waters. The closest sizable land if I missed Samoa was Fiji, some 600 miles to the southwest. I made up my mind not to miss Samoa, to press every faculty of boat and man to find it. Rigidly rationed as I was in food and water, and at my slow speed, I didn't dare miss it.

I determined to be as circumspect as possible with my steering; to keep a ready eye for all signs of land and commerce on the sea; especially to husband very closely every morsel and drop of my edibles. There was to be absolutely no physical exertion, aside from pumping out. If my body was to stand the gaff of a sixteen days' fast, there must be a minimum loss of energy, with plenty of sleep and rest. Also I must attempt to add to my meager provisions; I would fish, and perhaps catch sea birds.

I thought grimly on each possible precaution that would lengthen the supply of food over the next eighteen days. Before me sat the two cans of food, the bottle of ketchup, and the coconut.

Since I had worked the whole day and was tired, and my body was in pressing need of nourishment, I decided to bolster my flagging flesh and spirits with one of the cans of food. Doing so was contrary to the strict ration I had set for myself, but I needed backing up after three days of grueling work. Maybe I was short on resistance and couldn't face up to the ration; but I like to think there was a real need for that can of food. It would take at least a can; my body felt the need of two or three cans. I hatcheted one of the cans open and found it to be peas. I took them out into the cool night, to dine on the deckhouse, to eat and watch for a chance light. They were delicious beyond belief; there was a sweetness and delicacy I never knew peas could have. I chewed them to a fine gruel before swallowing them, remembering Captain Bligh's advice to his starving men in their open boat.

The night was fresh. Stars were on the march across the heavens, leading *Pagan* west. I checked and steadied the tiller. The bow was set on a planet just off the end of Scorpio, giving a nice westerly course. When the planet should fade below the horizon, I could use the Southern Cross, keeping it on the port beam. A spanking breeze welled up from the south. The mast was bent slightly from plumb. I was making good my thirty-mile-a-day clip. I pumped the bilges, took a last look at the unbroken horizon, and went below.

Sitting on my bunk, I had a light nip of water before hitting the sack. I thought that the best method to conserve water would be to drink only when thirsty, and then just a sip, but taking care never to consume more than a pint a day. With that ration I had water for thirty-two days. I fitted the bung to my precious keg of water and rolled in for the night.

CHAPTER XIX

Lost

THE FIRST THING I did next morning was search out all my medical supplies. I had many cuts and abrasions, and skinless knuckles and joints. I wanted to get them healed before hunger began taking its toll. I salved, and patched over, my dozens of cuts and scratches.

My next move was to take steps to plan out my navigation; to somehow keep a record of my position and my progress along the track to Samoa. I scratched out a makeshift chart on the floor of the cockpit showing the sector between the Marquesas and Australia. I etched the islands in from memory and remained fully aware when I finished that my work wasn't exactly accurate.

On the chart, as closely as I could figure it, I drove in a nail to represent my position, intending each day to shift the nail as I made to westward. Thus, on entering my second day under full sail, I tapped the nail in at a point a little to the south and slightly to the west of the Suvorov Islands. And, since I had no calendar and in order to keep up with the passing days, I managed a kind of calendar that consisted of X's on the wall — knifed in just above my bunk below the porthole.

My fishing kit I never found. But I ran onto two hooks, and some line. I found, too, a small packet of fish bait. It was salted pork strippings. I baited a hook and fed it over the stern, keeping the line fast to my little finger.

For the first time since the hurricane I noticed that Old Death and his voracious boys were still with me. It was heartening to see them; now I had a mobile food supply. They were having difficulties in orienting themselves to the slower speed of the boat. Before the hurricane, when I had sailed faster, they were able to advance at a more favorable clip upon the unsuspecting schools of flying fish, but now the flying fish were able to observe my approach from a distance, and scatter. Despite this handicap my faithful dolphin never deserted me; nor did they trust me, keeping a discreet distance to avoid my spears and ignoring my baited hooks.

Happily, the hurricane had not pitched all my books from the bookshelf just above my bunk. There were nine volumes with which to shorten the hours to Samoa. I spent most of the morning reading. One hour I gave over to a nap. Other than pumping out, and searching the horizon, I did nothing. I avoided the deck in the heat of the day, but as the afternoon waned I came out to enjoy the fresh breeze and see to the steering. At the same time I made a check of the sails and my jury rigging. Everything looked okay.

I remembered that it is a good idea for those living in thirst to bathe the body with salt water. The pores drink in the moisture, and a little of the parched condition is thus comforted. I slipped over the stern and dragged in the wake to my neck. The cool water was delightful, laving over me with soft fingers and washing away my uneasiness. After ten minutes I climbed aboard, refreshed, and dried in the sun and wind.

As yet I had eaten nothing during the day. An intermittent gnawing walked hobnailed around my stomach. I decided to open the ketchup and have a taste — enough to take

the edge off hunger. Working the cap loose, I took a strong
suck from the bottle. I replaced the cap and leaned the
bottle against the curve of the ribbing. The sight of it tormented me, set my juices to working, so I shoved it beneath
my bunk.

By dark, I hadn't caught a fish. I drew in my line. I
pumped the bilges and lay down. My system for working the
pump varied in the day and night. During the day I came
up to pump out every hour. This gave me a chance to search
the horizon a dozen times a day. At night I pumped out as
often as the noise or splash of rising water awakened me,
which was every few hours.

When I arose to greet the sun and found my belly gnawing I went seeking another swallow of ketchup. I found the
ketchup bottle empty. I remembered taking a suck in the
deep of the night, and that's all I could remember. It must
have been deeper than I realized, and it was regrettable, but
the ketchup was gone. . . . I didn't worry about it. For
breakfast I rinsed out the bottle with a part of my morning's
water ration.

My hook was over the transom as soon as I could put it
there. I sat reading on my bunk, jiggling the line tied to
my finger. I dwelt constantly on the remaining can of food
and the coconut. I wondered about the can. I guessed at
what it could contain, and the more I guessed the emptier
my stomach grew.

Hunger pains irked me all morning. Finally I thought,
"Why be hungry when there's food around?" I grabbed the
hatchet; and in a few minutes I was downing a can of sauer-
kraut. I thought as I ate, What an unreasonable thing to be
hungry when there's food around.

The coconut lay on the foot of my bunk.

I was still hungry. My stomach was squeezing and un-squeezing itself. I put the coconut out of sight. But I thought of it constantly. I brought it out, smelled it, shook it, and heard the teasing rustle of coconut milk. I put it back. My throat and mouth turned wet with the possibilities of a bite of the soft white coconut meat. I went on deck, but soon concluded the sun was too hot.

Down below I got the coconut out and sat staring at it, fascinated. "Don't eat it," I said, "be reasonable." "Reasonable my eye," I replied, "if I were reasonable, I wouldn't be here." "It's all the food you've got for eighteen days." "So what."

Ten minutes later I was smacking over the last white morsels of the exquisite coconut meat. My careful plans for apportioning out my food had gone glimmering. What did it matter; I was full and happy. I had no worries. If there was no food, there was no food . . . and that was that. Better to eat and be at peace than stalk and fret over a morsel. My spirits rose. "Tomorrow I'll catch a fish."

I went on deck and basked in the cool afternoon sun. In a while I dropped over the stern and rinsed my body in the fresh sea. After, I went below and read till dark. About seven o'clock I pumped the bilges for the last time that day, had my nightcap — a bare sip of water — and turned in.

All the next day I sat expectantly at the end of my line. Noon came; I had a small drink. It tasted sweet. Dusk came on, dark closed around. I pumped out, went below, and had a small drink that I called dinner. I turned in sorely disgusted. I didn't even bother to haul the fishline aboard: it lay strung out through the hatchway and over the transom dragging in the sea astern, still twined about my finger.

In the middle of the night, I was raised from sleep by something nearly jerking my finger off. Instantly I realized it was a fish and went bounding to the deck, hauling on the line as I ran. From under the transom I pulled a rather life-less-looking fish. When I took the hook from him, he just lay there breathing heavily. Suddenly he flipped himself about with quick snaps and, because there was no rail, splashed into the sea and swam merrily away.

I was stupefied. I turned my light onto the black water but could see nothing. The excitement of possible food had restirred the hunger movements; the sudden disappointment made me sick. I called myself onto the carpet and raked my-self over the coals. When I realized that cursing and fuming was using up my reserves of energy I went below and fell into a miserable sleep that lasted through the night to the dawn.

I put fresh bait on the hook. The old bait, of course, I ate. It was pork rind processed chemically. It was tough and salty and had a peculiar ironlike flavor. But it was delicious. It set my digestive juices to flowing and soon all the devils of hun-ger were tormenting me. For hours I sat brooding over the packet of bait, saying no, and denying the growing call of my emptiness. And I knew there would be no respite from it as long as there was a crumb of food aboard. I decided to have just one of the thin strips of bait. "Just to suck on," I said. By noon, not unstrangely, all but one of the strippings of bait was gone.

I sat and stared at it. It was beautiful to my eyes — I put it aside and tried to forget it. Soon I was back, fawning over it, pondering its destiny. As bait on the hook its value was in-estimable; yet, on the other hand, it could just happen that a fish might steal it, and I would have neither fish nor bait. The fate of the strip of rind became of huge proportion. I carefully weighed its future, thinking deeply on every possibility. Then . . . saying to myself, "a bird in the hand. . . ." I placed the rind on my tongue, and soon I was sucking on it happily. That settled that problem.

But it made me feel better to eat. When the food was gone I relaxed, read, and thought of the good time I would have in Samoa. Water, not food, is the important thing in starvation. This I knew. As long as I had a few sips of water each day, I knew I could survive to Samoa. I was rigorous with my water, knowing that my very life depended on it. I never drank more than a pint a day and I always staggered my drinking through the day and night so that I received its maximum benefit. But eatables . . . I gulped them on sight.

During my life I have achieved ideal health. I knew my body could stand any physical rigor within reason. To go without food for long periods isn't a great test for the human body. So I didn't worry if my impulsiveness resulted in a temporary hardship. The thought of Samoa only two weeks away braced me up.

I caught the same fish again. The moment he tugged at my finger, I bolted to the deck, bristling with sudden hunger. I pulled him quickly over the stern and dropped him in the cockpit. Before he could take a first breath I was on him.

I fell chest first over him, smothering him with my weight. Very gradually I eased off and clutched him with both hands. I felt as the lion feels with a fawn under his claws. The fish's baleful eyes watched me as I beat the life out of him.

I fetched him below; and less than five minutes after being hauled from the deep he was cleaned and scaled. With his

insides gone there wasn't much to him. He was a common
variety of triggerfish, blackish brown, about eight inches long
and half as wide; his head made about third of his body.
Under my bunk was the faithful little Primus stove, and miraculously enough it fired up. I scraped the rust out of the
skillet.

I was at a loss as to how to cook my catch. I couldn't afford
the water to boil him, and I couldn't use salt water for its
effect on my thirst. There was no grease for frying. Then I
remembered the jar of vaseline in the medicine kit.

After drying the fish, I coated him liberally with vaseline
and dropped him into the hot frying pan. As he sizzled and
popped beneath a cloud of smoke, I rolled him over. When
he grew seared looking and soft, I cut the fire and pinched
at him with my fingers. In a few minutes there were only
a few bones to identify what had twenty minutes before been
a fish cavorting in the sea. I kept the bones for breakfast.

The next day dragged by with nothing more exciting than
the hauling of the wind from south to southeast. My line
was still dragging astern, but there had been no bites. Hunger
ravaged my stomach like tank treads. I had been saving the
vaseline in case I caught another fish. As dark closed in, and
my stomach cried out, I cleaned the jar with my finger and
licked it dry. It was greasy and probably contained little or no
nutritional value as fat; but at least it quieted the hunger
call.

A morning soon after I wakened with greediest hunger
because all night I had dreamed of feasting and gorging. I
sipped my morning water ration, which only tormented me.
I went to the medicine chest, and before I could caution myself I ate the only jar of Vicks. And that afternoon when the

devil harried me again, I squeezed one of the two tubes of boric acid down my throat. I saved the other tube and a can of tooth powder for the next day.

I spent the afternoon thumbing through the only magazine aboard — one that had lodged on the bookshelf. As I turned over each page it was the same thing — food. Mammoth advertisements showing food in its most toothsome manner. Great roasts and salads, sandwiches and desserts, stews and cocktails. Hunger cramps started. Each page tortured me. I jumped up and with one sweep tossed the magazine far out on the green water. I felt better.

The next day I mixed half the tooth powder with water, and drank it as a potion. It had a pleasant aftertaste but it made me flinch when it went down. By nightfall, still no fish.

Prospects for the next day looked good. There was half the small can of tooth powder, and the other tube of boric acid compound. I bedded down that night unutterably hungry.

Then came the worst night of all. A night of food dreams. A night of ghosts in the form of chocolate cakes and steak dinners. Through the long hours I writhed between waking and sleeping, and at last I wakened finally and found myself champing at my blanket. I jumped up and fumbled hurriedly into my medicinal supplies. I came out with the last tube of boric acid, squeezed it into a blob on my fist, and smeared it into my mouth. Then I slept.

With morning I suddenly remembered my shipmate, Stowaway. I hadn't seen him since the hurricane, and strangely, I hadn't particularly thought of him. The little house I had built him was gone; it evidently went by the board during the storm.

I remembered Stowaway as I had seen him last, just before

the hurricane, sleek, fat, and beady-eyed. I grew aquiver with
the thought of the nice stew I could make of him. I began
a detailed search of the boat, which took me into its every
nook and cranny. For hours I crawled and squirmed into
impossible places. By noon I found no trace of his recent existence aboard. I had torn away all the inside planking and
ripped up what floor boards were left. I had also lowered myself into the watertight stern section and probed through it
with my flashlight. I finally had to admit that my long-time
buddy had been washed overboard.

But the search hadn't been entirely fruitless. I found several
articles that I could use. There were a chamois cloth, an army
shoe, a box of pepper, a tube of lipstick and a jar of face
cream left from the cosmetics I had planned to take to Mary,
a small box of tea, a bottle of shaving lotion, a bottle of hair
oil, and a tiny jar of fish eggs for bait.

I opened the fish eggs to put fresh bait on the hook. I
baited it and intended to screw the cap on the jar. To explain
what I did next is impossible; there is no explaining it, it
just happened. Before I could get the lid on the jar, I had
gulped the eggs. There was only the empty jar in my hand,
but hopelessly little comfort for the valuable mouthful I had
downed. . . . But they were gone; so I didn't have to worry
about how to resist them.

My hunger went unchecked. When I napped in the
afternoon I fell into eerie food dreams. I had to get up, I
couldn't sleep. I turned to my limited food resources and
experimented with them. I chopped the chamois cloth into
tiny fragments, spilled them into a strong tea made from my
ration of water and some of the tea I had found, and boiled
them for ten minutes. This I seasoned heavily with pepper,

a half can of tooth powder, and a generous dash of the shave lotion. To give it an interesting taste, I tossed in a fistful of salt water and a part of my can of machine oil.

The result was a stew that made my eyes burn and my nose revolt when I ate it. Since the chamois had been used to strain gasoline, it gave the brew a distinctive zip. I ate half of it that afternoon and deferred the rest till the next day.

I got up as on any other day and started out the battered companionway. What I saw on the sternpost paralyzed me. It was a sea bird. He sat there looking absent-minded and wriggling his tail feathers. I could sense his fatness and I was eager to have my hands on him in a death grip.

Instantly I was the primitive beast stalking his prey. I knew I couldn't creep upon him, close enough to pounce on him, unseen. I thought of crawling near and clubbing him, but the mizzen was in the way. Then it occurred to me to spear him. There was my fish spear. Spear in hand, I eased into the cockpit and each time his eyes were away from me I slid a foot nearer. Six feet from him, I dared not go farther. I posed my weapon, took a deep breath, took nervous aim, and jabbed. It was a clean stroke impaling him at the breast.

The bird was one of the small variety of tern which tolerate the Pacific wastes. Defeathered and cleaned he weighed out something less than a pound. The vaseline was gone, so I coated him with machine oil and put him on the fire.

It was a wonderful breakfast. I smacked over the thought of it for the rest of the day. At night when I had failed to get a fish and no further birds had landed aboard, I brought forth the small handful of bones left from the morning feast. Each bone I gnawed and crushed and sucked, then sprinkled it over the side.

The next morning I quaffed off the last of my devilish brew. It made my hair crawl to smell it. It had soured in the night, so I downed it quickly, not wanting to lose its liquid value. Later I became queasy, and lay hove-down with a fever that night, unable to bail out. By morning the water had risen to my bunk top. I realized I had better make some effort to get afoot and pump out, or the decks would soon be awash.

I got up and stood in the knee-deep water. There was nothing to eat. I looked up hoping there would be a bird as on the morning before. There was nothing — only the limitless whitecaps. I drank my ration of water for the day. It made me feel better. I pumped for an hour, lowering the water to the bilge. The growing morning heat was robbing me of my moisture. I lowered myself over the stern and dragged along in the gentle wake. It refreshed me and I came aboard strong again.

I finished the dreaded job. It left me so tired that I went below to bed. I slept several hours but awakened with fitful pangs of hunger. There were only the face cream, hair oil, shaving lotion, lipstick, and army shoes aboard. I sifted through them for something edible.

I took a nibble of the lipstick and found it not too bad. Cutting the red lump loose from its holder, I broke it in two and swallowed each lump. However, the lipstick didn't relieve my hunger. I opened the jar of face cream, and before I knew it had crammed the unctuous mixture down my throat. It left an oil taste in my mouth for hours and made me slightly squeamish, but the inner twistings ended, and I was at peace.

I slept till past high noon and went on deck to work the pump. The effects of my semistarvation were beginning to tell. I began for the first time to labor at the pump. Also, I felt a greater inclination to sleep, and a general drowsiness, and I was aware of a slight fogginess in the head. I had lost some flesh, my arms were thinner, a few ribs showed, and my knees were somewhat knotty. My waistline grew more fashionable every day, it was smaller around than I would ever have had occasion to imagine it could be.

All I thought of was food. Every waking hour was dedicated to it, and every sleeping hour. I recalled great meals where I had sat to table in the past and eaten hugely. And I dreamed of tables in the future where I would sit for hours and glorify food.

While I was pumping I noticed splashes emanating from the life raft astern. It had a shallow layer of water in its bottom, and from there they came. When I took a close look I could see that some sort of fish was trapped inside and attempting to swim in the insufficient water.

Flipping about helplessly was a delicious looking flying fish. He had evidently leaped inside and now he was trapped. He was easily eight inches long. I picked him up and admired his shimmering beauty with drooling glances. I was estimating how tasty he would be fried in machine oil. "But first," I thought, "I'll just have a nibble of his tail."

I bit his tail off and ground it up exuberantly, bones and all. It was savory beyond description. Before I quite understood what I was doing I had devoured the whole fish and was picking scales out of my teeth. All I could remember of the fish was the slightly bitter taste about halfway through.

The fresh meat put me in a scintillating mood. My spirits soared and I felt that I would come on land any minute. By my arithmetical calculations I was hard by Samoa. The

Manua Islands should be appearing presently. Maybe in the night the loom of them would rear up on *Pagan's* bow. I decided to rise as often as possible in the night to pump out — and look for them.

I rose often in the night and searched, but nothing broke the monotonous dim horizon.

Morning found me on deck at the crack of dawn, straining my eyes across the bows. I climbed the mast and peered ahead; but when the little spar groaned beneath my weight, I clambered down. The horizon offered up nothing to encourage me. But the ocean did.

Just under *Pagan's* counter I espied three triggerfish — new arrivals from near-by land, I suppose. I broke out the spear and set to work. Kneeling on the stern, I sighted down the spear shaft and struck. My first thrust was awry. I tried again and again, but learned that striking at so small a target with a single barb isn't easy. Eventually I nicked one of them and he limped off astern. I never saw him again.

The other two played wary and sought the protection of the keel. To draw them out I dropped bits of wood on the water which they sidled out to investigate. Peering over the stern, I stabbed them as they sauntered out, and again when they hurried back.

In time I nicked another of them and he too fled sternward, not to reappear. I realized if I was to get the last one I must make a spear with more than one barb.

Dusk was coming on. I was exhausted and ravenous. There was nothing to eat except shaving lotion and hair oil, and an army shoe. I wasn't desperate enough to stomach those, so I had a last look for land, pumped the bilges, and slipped below for the night — hungry.

The day's exertions had been too much for a peaceful sleep. Food dreams haunted me . . . hamburgers, "Cokes," hot dogs, chocolate sundaes whirled through my mind, causing me to pitch and toss. In the middle of the night I dreamed I was chewing a juicy chicken bone and shouting for more. I awakened, and there I sat bellowing into the black night for more chicken.

A foot of water covered the cabin floor. Outside was the persistent noise of the sea as it lapped against the planks. I got up to do the pumping — an hour's work.

Before dawn I awoke with hunger's sharp stitches in my stomach. I couldn't sleep. The recurrent thought of the spear I had to make was badgering me. In the end I arose early, and began to work at it. I made it from one of the oars given me by the Perlas Indians. I cut the oar blade off square a foot from the tip and drove four nails up grain. Pounding the head of each nail flat, I filed them sharp and into some semblance of a barb. I pared down the oar blade to coincide with the handle, and my spear was ready.

At daybreak I was perched on the stern waiting for old "wobbly fins," as I called him. The triggerfish swims very leisurely and with a lackadaisical flourish of his large fins. In a short time he sauntered out into the rising sun. My first strike missed cleanly. He reared back to note the cause of the disturbance around him, exposing himself broadside. It was a shot I couldn't miss.

Soon he was frying on the fire, smoking like a coal burner. I had to fry him in hair oil since I had used the last of the machine oil on the bird. I ate him so fast it made little difference what he was fried in. And I ate him as I fried him, head, scales, fins, and all. Usually I saved the bones for the next meal, but when I finished there were no bones.

The policy on *Pagan* was rapidly becoming: when there is food, eat it; when there isn't any, forget about it.

With the acquisition of food, I burst into liveliness again. I felt optimistic about land and expected to see it by noon. There were a few signs to indicate its presence. Flying fish were more in abundance than at any time since the hurricane, and Old Death and his boys were giving them a merry chase. Several sea and semi-land birds were in the air, hovering over the voracious dolphin, swooping on the flying fish. And astern, their wicked pointed fins jutting menacingly up from the dark water, was a school of leering sharks.

I stood before the mast all day watching each new cloud. Right up to dark there was a landless horizon. With the ship making so little way I wasn't afraid of beaching myself in the night on something I couldn't see before dark. I pumped the bilges and went below.

That night I had a bad case of "channel fever," the nervous anxiety that plagues the seaman the night before arrival. I slept fitfully and, when I dreamed, I had nightmares. I wakened once shouting "Land ho," and rushed out on deck expecting to see it. Before daybreak I was perched at the mast, watching for a sail or a cone of land.

Light of day brought no gray shadow that could be called land. There were the usual birds of the past few days — and more of them, it seemed.

Two in particular showed the keenest inquisitiveness about *Pagan*. They flew up within a dozen feet of the stern, hovered for a moment, then broke away into a slanting curve that brought them back again. I could see that if I had a weapon, I could knock one of them down as he poised in flight. A bow and arrow, it flashed across my mind, would be just the thing.

I crept below, and after a considerable search decided to rip out one of the oaken deckhouse beams for the bow. It was nearly an hour before I had broken the heavy timber out. Outside, the prying birds were still slanting across the stern, and in fact, now that I was below, they appeared to be easing in a little closer. In another hour I had sawed the beam, chopped it, and whittled it into something resembling a bow. The arrows were easier to fashion. I simply sawed strips from a pine plank, wired a nail to the tips, and prepared to shoot them untufted. I strung my bow with a strand of wire left over from the shrouds.

With an arrow fitted to the string I waited, and watched for the moment when I could shoot. I was standing just inside the cabin, prepared to fire through the companionway. When a bird soared in and hovered a moment, I let fly, but missed. I had many shots and was heartened by an occasional glancing blow or near miss.

The birds grew chary. By noon I had lost nine arrows and the birds were no longer coming quite so close.

Nails — especially after the extensive repairs I had made — were scarce. I made a few more arrows, and during the afternoon I fired twelve, my total supply. Hunger pains and exhaustion, the long hours of nervous anxiety, were beginning to tell. What was worse, there were only a few more nails for arrows, and these were in the foreward hatch where I had nailed it down in preparation for the hurricane. I pulled them and made more arrows. Soon I was shooting at the ungainly frigate birds again.

My aim was getting erratic. Then, unexpectedly, one of my shafts connected. A head shot: he folded limply and tumbled into the water a few feet off the beam. There were pointed fins just to sternward or I could have dived the short distance to retrieve my kill. I pulled the rubber dinghy up, hopped in, paddled to the limp feathery ball, and even as I was stepping aboard *Pagan* again, I was ripping out handfuls of feathers.

Food for two days in a row brought a Christmas-like spirit to *Pagan*. My optimism soared. I would sight land by the next morning; if not, by noon; and by nightfall enjoy dinner at the Naval Station in Tutuila. I also thought of a scheme for making a slingshot from rubber of the life raft. It would be simple enough to knock down a dozen birds in the time it had taken with the bow. That night I had a rosy dream instead of the usual nightmare.

The next morning, after looking fruitlessly for land, I set to work on my slingshot. I wanted to knock down a bird or two to sustain me through the day till land came. After extensive practice in making such boy's weapons as a youngster, doing it now was a pushover. In little time I was ensconced in the cockpit with my new weapon and a small pile of nuts, unscrewed from the engine.

Soon I was getting an occasional shot, but not doing well, because I was overearnest. Moreover the large frigate birds which make easy targets were gone, only the smaller terns were around. They flew faster, were smaller. About eleven o'clock I winged one. He landed off a good way, too far to chance a retrieve in the dinghy; but when I came about and beat up toward him, he took off and limped along to eastward. It was tough luck, but there were plenty more around.

Sometime in the late afternoon I sent another plummeting into the green sea. I jibed ship and flew toward him; but he too got away.

Along about five o'clock I gave up. I poured a few pans of sea water over my body to moisten the dry, dying skin. I pumped the bilges, had a last look for land, and shuffled below. I was dead tired and thoroughly disgusted. The thought with which I went to sleep was, "Tomorrow there will be land, I hope."

The next day was overcast and dull. Overhead, for the first time, floated white bosun birds, short-winged, long swallow-tailed, plummeting from time to time like falling bombs into the sea. They were new on the scene and they were land birds. I had seen them from the Perlas Islands all across the Pacific — and always I had seen them near land. It is said the bosun bird hovers within sight of his land. I watched them float, collapse their wings and tremble downward, and as I watched my hopes for a quick approach to land grew.

Somewhere close was land. The birds bespoke it. I followed them, studying their every movement for hours. Not a hint, not a clue did they drop of where land might be. And there was no trace of land on the horizons . . . until, in the afternoon, dead ahead, it welled up from the sea. I could barely distinguish it in the haze, but it was land, I knew it was land. I raced toward it exultantly. Land after sixteen days of near starvation! I found myself clinging to the mast, shouting and singing. Then it happened. What I had thought was land went racing away along the horizon, changing its shape as it went, and hiding itself in the thick air. I had been hoaxed by a cloud; but I wasn't discouraged, land was near.

The bosun birds were still flying overhead "in sight of

their land." I wished I could see with their eyes. I wished
I knew what they knew. Somewhere near was land. There
were gannet birds in the air and varieties of land terns, besides the bosun birds and the ever-present sharks loafing
patiently around the stern. But where was the land? How
close, how far, in what direction?

I searched the horizon for hours, trying to penetrate the
overcast air. Land was overdue; I should have sighted it two
and even three days before. By calculation I had passed it. I
consulted the figures of my guesswork navigation. If I were
making thirty miles a day; I should be near, or past, land. The
nail, marching to westward over my chart, was sticking up in
the center of the Samoan group. On the bulkhead, above my
bunk, a lengthening line of X's leered at me. I changed my
figures from thirty miles a day to twenty-five — and still I
figured I should be near enough to sight land . . . if it were
there. I decided to wait another day before taking action. I
went out on deck.

A grizzly mantle completely censored the sun. The wind
during the night had been steady from the northeast. Its
habit, in this area, was to veer steadily from the south over
a space of days to the northeast, then suddenly haul back to
south and start the cycle anew. There was no way, with the
sun blotted out, to know the set of the wind, whether it had
changed or not. I certainly didn't want to run before it, with
it on my starboard quarter, if I didn't know its direction, especially if it was out of the south, I last remembered it on the
starboard quarter giving me a westerly course. According to
the stars it had been — then — somewhere in the north quadrant.

The sea swell indicated no change in wind direction. I

decided to play it safe, and doffed all sail but the tiny jib. The work tired me. I went below and slept an hour and came back.

Floating high up were the bosun birds. Their very presence teased me and tantalized me. Land for them was but an hour's flight. I thought of the closeness of land, and of the possibilities of finding it soon, and thought on the deep dishes I would eat. It made my stomach crawl, and I forced it out of mind.

Pagan drifted under a heavy sky. It was painful to have a wind and not to be able to sail; it was worse than being in a calm. But midafternoon hunger was crucifying me. There were several shoes around, only one of which was of undyed leather — an army shoe. I stared at it dejectedly. It smelled like you-know-what; but it was food. I cut the upper part away from the sole, and started chewing its tongue. It was too tough even to be dented. Army shoes are tough customers. I soaked it awhile in salt water, taking it out occasionally to beat on the end of my bunk for "tenderizing." Greasing one sizable piece with hair oil, I fried it, but it only turned black and stayed just as unchewable. Finally I boiled the whole shoe in my precious water ration. I didn't boil it long; as soon as evaporation began to tell on the water content I cut the fire. The soup had an inspiring taste, but the leather was still unbearable. In the end, I cut it into strips, and though I still couldn't chew it, at least I could get it down, and that's all that mattered. I went to bed that night with something under my belt.

Don't eat leather if you want pleasant dreams. For unending hours I writhed in the grip of nightmares about food. I was in a mammoth grocery store running berserk among corridors of food. I wakened in a labor of sweat only to drift back to my horror dreams.

Sometime late that night when I pumped the bilges I caught a glimpse of Canopus, and joyfully established the wind in the south. My hunch had been correct. The wind had shifted. Had I sailed with it on the starboard quarter, I would have been sailing northeast. I trudged to the deck and strung up all sail. Once again *Pagan* was making a bowline to the west.

A wan sun hidden intermittently by mountains of heavy clouds arose and flashed pale beams on a mass of land at the bowsprit end. I watched it closely for a suspicious minute, then I was sure it was land. When I saw it loom up, I nearly went crazy. I jumped up and down on the cabin top and giggled like a child. Grabbing my bucket I ran onto the stern and indulged in a hasty salt bath. The land was closing in at an amazing rate. I dried myself cursorily. Valleys in the land were visible. I went below to get dressed. I donned a suit of khakis, a hat, shoes, and combed my beard.

Coming on deck, I noticed that the land had changed not only its shape, but its direction — in fact, it wasn't land at all, it was a cloud, it was going straight up. I watched it ascend in dejected silence. My heart slumped down to my shoe bottoms. If my body hadn't needed the liquid so badly, I would have wept.

That afternoon, I ran out of nuts to use as ammunition. Everything had been stripped from the engine and its fittings. There was the thousand pounds of cement in the bilge used as ballast. I chipped out a dozen suitable pieces, but by dark had had no success with them.

That night was the grimmest aboard *Pagan* since the

hurricane. Flashlight in hand I sat for hours in the cockpit studying my makeshift chart of South Sea waters scratched in the wood of the cockpit floor. According to my figures I had far overshot Samoa. The next land to westward was the Hoorn Islands, the exact position of which was unknown to me. But to the southwest about 600 miles lay Fiji — some three weeks' sailing time.

It was two days since I had eaten anything substantial. A dread decision was in the balance: go on looking blindly for Samoa, or head south, while there was still time, and connect with the wider area of the Fijis. Covering a wide swath as they do they offered a broad front that would be easier to find than Samoa — but the big thing was to get there; to go for three weeks on two weeks' supply of water, at a half pint a day. It was a decision to be weighed, to be thought on.

If my assumptions were correct, I was somewhere approximately northeast of the Fijis. Unless I headed south soon I would miss them altogether and have to struggle on to the next land, the New Hebrides Islands, over 500 miles from the Fijis. I pondered over the crude map, measuring distances, weighing possibilities. Finally I decided to look one more day for Samoa.

The sleep of that night was woefully unsound. I dreamed I was wrecked on a beach; and I was happy. There was a huge gray whale stranded there. I grabbed him by the tail and started devouring him alive as I had done the flying fish. And I awakened clawing and growling at my bunk boards. It was just as well, the bilges needed pumping.

Before daylight I was atop the deckhouse peering past the wind-filled jib to the landless horizon. It was my twenty-first day under the jury rig. All that day I sat on the fore scuttle, rising often to search across the bows. Overhead were the bosun birds, gannets, land terns, and man-o'-war birds, screaming down on the flying fish scared up by Old Death and his raiders. Land was somewhere, but where? The only times I went aft was to pump the bilges. I kept a daylong vigil that came to naught. As dusk, then dark, closed in I did what seemed the only reasonable thing to do. I stepped aft and changed the angle of rudder, by directing the splintered remains of the tiller to leeward. The bow hauled in upon the southeast breeze and stopped in the south. "Fiji or bust," I said, as I lashed the splintered stub and trimmed the sails to hold me on a new course.

From that moment onward the tenor of my situation changed. I was no longer, as I had led myself to believe, temporarily under duress; I was in a position of extreme indefiniteness about everything. I wasn't even certain that if I did head south I would be able to find the Fiji Islands. It all depended on how far west I had sailed in search of Samoa. It depended on whether I was sailing at a rate of twenty-five miles a day or thirty — or more or less than that — regarding which I had no way of knowing. It depended on the westerly set of the current — that is, its speed. It depended on whether or not I could face another twenty-one days of fast. It depended on whether there were any intervening reefs — and the Fijis are notorious for hidden offshore reefs. I could take a wild stab in the dark and hope for a safe landfall, and that was all.

My most burdensome concern was the weather. Like a sword of Damocles the threat of a destructive hurricane hovered in the offing, I was moving in a widely known cyclonic track, with the hurricane season under way at that!

Pagan couldn't outlive another hurricane, and I hadn't the strength to fight the ruinous winds or bail the boat out for prolonged hours. I closed my mind to the likelihood of any such event, and concentrated solely on the dubious trip ahead and the bout with starvation — the first round of which was over.

The bow of my boat was in the south; I worked the heavy bilge pump for the first time on the new course. I looked off across the stretch of hostile water, took account of my crawling speed, listened to the grumble of hunger in my stomach.

Then an urge struck me that penetrated to my very warp and weft, so I followed it. In such circumstances what else remains to a man but that last unfailing resource, the Great Captain — the Captain of all ships. I bent to my knees reluctantly; for in the last months my sins had been monsters.

From Perlas to Galápagos, and from Galápagos on west, I had uttered such curses as I doubt have ever been heard over the keel of a ship. In every squall, gale, calm, cloudburst, and contrary current, I had unloosed a flood of invective to shame a mule skinner. But more than that . . . in the height of my extremities I had profaned God Himself. On many an occasion I became so bold as to defy Him, deny Him, and swear I would profess atheism all the rest of my life. I even invited Him on deck — man to man — anything but the obstructing persecution of the elements, anything but the slow crawl when I wanted speed.

And now, lost, foodless, without instruments, I humbly bent my knees to the deck and laid my folded hands upon the cabin. With eyes raised I read off a most heartfelt forgiveness and piteous appeal to *Pagan's* real Captain.

CHAPTER XX

Foodless

I SAT IN THE COCKPIT searching my rough-drawn map of the Southwest Pacific. I was pondering the sea stretches I would be crossing and guessing upon the advisability of what I was doing. There were still a few birds from land beating about. I was still sure that land was close, but to go on searching over a trackless sea when *Pagan's* speed was nil, and with food gone, water dwindling, and the next land 600 miles away — no, I couldn't afford to risk another day in vain search. The broad Fijian chain of islands was findable. My only safe recourse was to go there, and take that lesser of two risks.

I had a predominant guide, since the Dog Star Sirius, in its east–west march across the heavens, drives directly over the center of the Fijis. It was my plan to go south till I was under Sirius, then west till I struck land.

There was a beam wind from the east casting up a light chop. *Pagan* sailed easily; now and then she slopped a little water over the rail. The spray for the most part kept me below in the dark cabin.

Toward late afternoon, I remembered a mosslike growth on *Pagan's* leeward side that had grown during the long traverse from the Galápagos. I would have eaten it before now but I was in doubt as to its effects.

I went on deck and examined it closely. Its color varied

between light and dark green, and it was hairlike, growing about an inch long in several spots. I scraped off a fistful of it and squeezed out its salt water. I pushed a part of the salty grasslike wad into my mouth and chewed and swallowed it. It tasted the way grass should taste, sprinkled with salt. It didn't ease the hunger but it eased the mind.

I thought of the half bottle of hair oil and took the weedy stuff below. With a light sprinkling of the oil — and a stretch of the imagination — it had a saladlike taste. But when I had eaten the grassy bit, I found the hunger still gnawing. It wouldn't be quieted.

There was nothing more to eat except the moss. I scraped some more of it from the hull, dripped the last of the hair oil over it, and chewed it down. *Pagan* was foodless. I sipped the last of my ration of water for the day, pumped the bilges, and settled in for the night.

I waked with the worst hunger pangs yet. The moss, without hair oil, was unbearable, but I ate enough of it to quiet my hunger callings. However, in a while they came again and devils tormented me all morning. By afternoon I couldn't stand it longer. I wanted just a bite, just a chew of something to cheat hunger of its grip.

There was a last pair of shoes, but when I chewed on a corner of leather the taste and smell of dye sickened me. I turned to my belt. I took it off and sat holding it in my hands. It was genuine cowhide; I had owned it for years, had worn it in college and all through the war, had worn it through four shipwrecks. Sentimental attachments swelled within me, and I put it back on. There was only my wallet: of kangaroo hide, a gift of Mary's father. Starvation overcame sentiment in its case, and I emptied its contents into my shirt pocket. As with the army shoe, I boiled it, pounded it, cut it into strips — they lasted through the day and the night.

I was sitting on deck just at dawn watching as always for that point on the horizon from which the first birds would come. A small white sea bird, flailing the air with long wings and shrieking loudly, slanted across the bow from what could have been any direction and circled in for a close view of *Pagan*.

I flipped a single cement chunk toward him, more as an afterthought than a serious intent. Bird and rock miraculously converged. A puff of feathers flew up, and the victim plummeted into the sea like a crippled plane, a bare thirty feet from where I stood.

Unlashing its lines, I threw the helm hard down. *Pagan* rounded to, veering into the wind and bearing down on the wad of white. I scooped thé downy creature inward.

What I did next has been unbelievable to me ever since. Crazed by the thought of food, but more crazed because I had food in my hands, I tore the head from the body in one motion. Thrusting the pulsing stump into my mouth, I drank every particle of its life-giving blood. I was an animal who had made a kill; and as the animal will, I went at it tooth and claw. When it no longer yielded a drop, I bit the delicate neck off and chewed it up, bone and all.

Before I could stop myself, the greater part of the bird was gone. Even then I couldn't stop. I bit wolfishly into the mass of feathers, tearing at what met the tooth; whether it was bone or feathers didn't matter. Not one bone of the fowl's body escaped the mill of my teeth. Each one I smashed to fine splinters and ground to pulp and swallowed.

I ate his feet as I found them. Skin and all went down.

When I came to the head, I ate everything "but the eyebrows." His bill chewed like gristle. I plucked the larger feathers from the skin and started gnawing at the down. It resisted like a blanket, but it filled the emptiness and cheated the devils of hunger. When it was gone I wished there had been more.

When I finished my cannibalistic meal, only a few feathers here and there, and among my teeth, showed that a bird had passed that way.

Two days crept tediously past as though they marched on minutes an hour long. I trolled my fishline as ever astern day and night but received no encouragement. The sparse patches of seamoss on the hull were beginning to thin bald in spots. Birds were around and I had a few opportunities to fling missiles at them, but somehow there was no longer the former spring in my arm: my shots fell short or went awry.

One morning as I came on deck I saw a ship. When first I sighted it, I thought it was a rowboat on the horizon. But on closer inspection I made out the top of the stack and the upper reaches of the masts and booms. She was hull down, knifing directly across my bow; a big freighter pitching gracefully into the long swells.

I had joyful visions of being towed to Samoa, to food and rest. I thought of the mast's being restepped, and resuited with sails. I could see myself provisioned anew and setting out again for Sydney, and to Mary.

She was evidently Panama bound, probably out of Fiji or Brisbane. Her superstructure was barely floating on the rim of the horizon, and she was footing it fast. Close though she was I couldn't make out her tonnage or nationality. She was still dressed in wartime gray. Any minute I expected to see her alter course and swing across wind to me.

I scaled the unsturdy mast and blinked my flashlight from the masthead. The mast labored under my weight; I climbed down. Then I raised and lowered the mainsail. All the time I shouted like a madman; I knew this couldn't be heard, but I yelled just the same. But the big ship swept on with graceful deliberation.

Suddenly I thought of a fire. Fires on shipboard are signals of distress. I rushed below and threw a shirt and a dash of the shave lotion into the bucket. I lit it from the dwindling supply of matches and carried it onto the forepeak. The ship had passed from the starboard to the port bow. It hadn't sighted me.

I grew frantic as I realized I wasn't going to be seen. I jumped and waved and screamed, and in between I did everything but sink my boat for attention. I dashed astern and changed course so as to keep in sight of the ship. A thick gray cloud of smoke blew off *Pagan's* decks from the bucket, rising about twenty feet. The mate on watch must have been figuring out his pay or telling the wheelsman what a great guy he was, because a blind man could have seen my signal. I watched helplessly as the ship grew blurry in the distance and dropped below the sea.

I stayed on the southeast course instead of reverting to south. It was midafternoon before I came across a slick indicating the passage of the ship. I changed course to east and beat upwind following in its track. There was one chance in a million that the vessel might stop or turn back. Also there was a chance the cook would dump his garbage.

When dark came on I luffed the bow into the wind and

dropped off on the port tack to my former course. I wasn't too discouraged. When you are lost, land is where you find it. I knew I would find it sooner or later; it was a matter of endurance.

The next morning early, I did something I should have done before. I painted SOS on both sides of all sails. There was no paint to do it with. I used the pitchy stagnant oil from the engine. I also painted it on the foredeck, the cabin top, and in the cockpit, in case a plane should happen over. There were only the haunting sharks or a lonely bird or two to see it, but it was there giving an international message to any craft which might pass in my absence from deck.

I studied the horizon in a slow sweep, pumped the bilges, and stepped through the hatchway.

It was a day of cancerous loneliness. I had long since finished reading the nine books aboard, and I had started through them a second time, but it was wearisome trying to read a mystery when I already knew the murderer. One of the books, however, the Bible, from which I read selections each day, became more purposeful as I reread it. It was the kind of mystery where you couldn't know all the clues, and where the more you knew, the more mysterious rather than more clear became its significance — a mysteriousness which led me to the value of faith, that gift of the Bible. Out there I needed faith, it was the only thread left to cling to.

It was about this time that the more noticeable effects of my starvation struck me fully. My wristbone I noticed first. It stood out like a Ping-pong ball. Veins which never before could be seen, but now were accentuated by shrinking arms and tightening flesh, stood out like miniature molehills. My elbows were gaunt, and my biceps like eggs. Hollows were showing in chest and shoulders; all my ribs could be counted with the eye and my stomach was a sloping valley between chest and thigh. My hips flared out sharply and a deepening cavity was evincing itself on the inside of my upper leg.

Large bony knots stood for my knees. But my feet and ankles had swelled to twice their normal size, probably from liquid seeping down from above. They were heavy, and movement about deck was laborious.

It was also at this time that the last of the moss gave out on *Pagan's* hull. A thorough search of the boat showed that the only eatables aboard were the half box of tea and the half bottle of shaving lotion.

I put a pinch of tea in my mouth each time I pumped the bilges. It helped. The shaving lotion I was keeping in case the water should run short.

The next afternoon the wind changed from east to northeast and grew rapidly in strength. This sudden shift put me on the alert and I watched sky and sea critically. I slacked sheets and for a long time ran before it, making at least two knots. But time came when the danger of being pooped was imminent. I could see a storm was on me; a mild gale was already blowing.

I worked the little ship around to where she faced up to the wind and where she was breasting the onrolling seas. I lashed the helm, unbent the mainsail and stopped it to the boom and mast, and watched her as she stood before the rising weather. She lay comfortably under jib, staysail, and jigger. I pumped her out, had a look into the wild sky, and went below, where I lay in my bunk absorbing *Pagan's* reaction to the making weather . . . and waiting.

After dark, judging from the noise in the rigging and the angle of heel, the wind came up to gale force. But so long as *Pagan* could carry sail she rode easily. I had to pump out every two hours; and it enabled me to keep a close eye on the condition of the sea and wind.

I kept my fingers crossed, hoping the wind wouldn't rise. *Pagan* in her crippled condition, I was certain, could not have weathered another hurricane, even with a hardy crew.

The hours were a nervous and physical strain I could ill afford. I lay lashed in my bunk, straining to hear and interpret every new sound. In the dead of night the little mizzenmast collapsed; I heard it go down. I trudged out on deck not realizing how weak I was till I attempted to retrieve the spindly stick from the sea. In a dozen tries I was unable to grapple it in. The strength just wasn't in my arms.

In the end I pulled it as close aboard as I could by the sheets and passed a double half hitch around the sternpost, securing it. With that effort I was overcome by fatigue. I could easily have slept in exhaustion where I lay, but for the danger of being licked off the railless deck by the sea.

I clawed my way on hand and knees into the cockpit. The bilges were in need of pumping. I could feel that need but I couldn't respond to it. I lowered my tired legs into the confined cabin and flopped onto my pitching bunk. I remember fitting my lashings in place . . . then total blackout.

When I came to, water in the cabin was higher than at any time since the first hurricane — for now I was convinced that I was in another. I was completely drenched. The blanket which I used as a mattress was a sop pad. The cabin was a din of sounds that only water in a confined space can make.

How many hours I had slept I don't know. It was dark.
Pagan was pitching and rolling. I presumed that all sail had
been torn down by winds and that heavy seas had crashed
down upon the stern, flooding the cabin.

A sense of unmitigated futility swept over me, dominated
me. I was ready to give up. Water was nearly washing me off
the bunk. I knew I could never bail it out — I was too far
gone. The hazard of going on deck to work the pump in hurricane winds was suicidal. I felt like lying back and waiting
in desperation for the end.

In complete defeat one rises above fear. The mouse will
fight a lion when chased to the wall. Hurricane or no hurricane I was going to pump my bilges dry. I had to; my boat
would founder if I didn't. I took a heavy drink of precious
water. A refreshed feeling coursed through me. Taking hold
of the coamings I eased my eyes into the night to meet an
amazing sight.

What I saw wasn't one of the treacherous Fijian hurricanes
but a mild tropical breeze of about force three soughing out
of the south. However, a heavy cross sea was running which
gave *Pagan* her antic behavior. My staysail and jib were intact
and the little aftermast was still trailing from the sternpost.

Above me the skies were a patchwork of peaceful stars.
Only the slowly abating rollers gave evidence that a tropical
gale had passed. I took heart immediately and set to on the
pump.

The new southern breeze compelled me for the night to
lash the stub of a tiller with my bow jutting into the southwest.

As soon as I had offered up my morning supplications I
asked the Good Captain that I be excused to tend my menial

tasks on deck. I wanted to get the jigger rigged and holding a pressing sail again as soon as possible.

Seas had moderated. It was simple to pluck from the easy seaway the oar used for mast; and with decks steadied by the lush breeze, stepping the light spar wasn't difficult. With my boat under full sail again, my time was my own. I pumped the bilges and went below to do my daily reading from the Bible.

With a south wind holding, the course stayed at southwest. I didn't tack to maintain a beat into the south, though I needed to make as much southing as possible, for I was still a long way from being far enough south to be under Sirius. Effects of starvation were pronounced. I gave *Pagan* her lead into the southwest. I had to. Even the little work of tacking sail was rigorous labor to me and a drain on my body moisture. To me land was where I would find it: as always my wicked intuition indulged me; it said, "Go southwest."

I hadn't eaten for five days. Five days and no food . . . and I can remember when I bellyached if I missed a meal! The sustained fast enabled my stomach juices to partially hibernate and my nights were less harassed by frightful dreams.

But the quest for food went on. I occasionally got a shot at a bird, but my strength and judgment had ebbed till I couldn't have hit the broad side of a barn if I had been leaning against it. The fishline was ever astern. But Old Death and his wary protégés snubbed it disdainfully. The sharks, now increased to some five or six in number, showed it even less attention. Their interest centered on the limping craft, and in a very strong way I felt they were particularly interested in me.

I was still navigating by the stars and sun, working ever

south till I could look up the mast and sight Sirius dead overhead. When that day came I intended to probe westward for
land . . . whatever reared above the sea.

I went on deck at daylight to be confronted with — of all
things — an island. It was no cloud I saw this time. From the
first glance there was no mistaking its identity as land.

It lay broad on the port bow: a low island, longer than it
was wide. A volcano on the summit emitted a dark curtain
of fast-flowing smoke. Its outlines were bleak because of overcast and a growing wind, which pushed a scud in from over
the horizon.

The island looked prosperous, a sure sign of habitation.
Rescue this time was certain, but I determined from the first
not to be hasty and careless, remembering that infinitely more
seamen have perished in getting ashore than have on the
reaches of the open sea. On the sea a boat can float and it is
safe. But in crossing the reefs to the lagoon or pounding
through the surf to the beach, a boat can be dashed and
its crew overwhelmed and drowned. Also, another manifest
danger to the seaman is the often unconquerable distances
necessary to travel once he is safe on shore — often over entangled, infested terrain — to find help and food. Then, too,
the hungry, thirsty, exposed seaman must remember to nibble
and sip his first food and water or run the risk of violent death
when he is most safe.

All these things I thought of as I gazed on the dark green
paradise that would soon be mine. I thought too of the huge
joy of eating again. I saw myself racing into coconut groves,
clawing down the green drinking nuts and fattening on their
soft meat and cool milk. I visualized groves of bananas growing to the water's edge and I languished on the thought of

eating and sleeping at their roots. Delicious juices suddenly flowed in my mouth as the devils of hunger prodded me.

I changed course, beating as high on the wind as possible, and kept the island on the bow, so it bore directly southeast. I made for its closest point.

CHAPTER XXI

Starvation and Land

I WONDERED WHAT LAND IT COULD BE. I sat before my guess-work map in the cockpit and studied the scratched-out pattern of sea and islands, and by process of elimination I checked off one island at a time until there was left only the possibility of its being some northerly point of Fiji.

It was a most difficult assumption to make because, first, I wasn't certain of the exact positions of the island groups in the area, and second, I knew little of the layout of islands in the groups themselves. It was pure speculation of the crudest kind. It was based on guessed figures of my speed and the speed and direction of the current.

I re-estimated my speed under jury rig at everything from twenty to fifty miles per day — in the end, all things taken together, I settled on thirty-five miles. Thus by figuring my speed after the hurricane at thirty-five miles a day I had covered somewhere near 700 miles in the twenty-one days before turning south. Add another 150 miles, again purely a guess, for current and various kinds of westward driftage in the nine days since pointing into the south, and I was well on toward Australia.

It was sensible to me, then, under these particular circumstances, to assume from my disproportioned chart that a line drawn south from a point 850 miles west of the Suvorovs

would run through the western Fijis, and that this land on
my bow was part of that group. This assumption, as anyone
knows, was a mistaken one, but as I say, under the circumstances that I made it, it seemed valid.

Thus, I figured, the isle before me was the last for another
600 miles to the primitive New Hebrides Islands just east and
north of New Caledonia. Making this island was a matter of
life and death. I doubted seriously whether I could survive
another 600 miles with a quart and a half of water left aboard
and the growing burden of keeping up the pumping. But the
hazard of sailing it with the hurricane season underway was
the most compelling thought of all.

I was about four miles offshore; I shaped my course so as
to reach up to the western point of the island. I was close
enough, from the very beginning, to see tangled vegetation
on the lower slopes. I thought of mangoes and pawpaws and
cool, refreshing, healthful pineapples. Beautiful hunger feelings tingled through me, tickled me and tortured me, and I
had to find something to busy myself with so I wouldn't think
of food. I readied the anchor to be pushed off the railless
decks.

There were hints of palm trees on the shore, but no sign of
a village. I stood on the cabin, holding to the short mast,
searching for a suitable anchorage.

Hours dragged by with torturing slowness. The sun
climbed along its wonted arch to high noon. I had hoped to
be in before then, anchored or beached, and on the quest
for food. There was something amiss with my calculated
approach. I was not closing in properly. After six hours of
sailing I should have been through the reef and safe in the lagoon. Instead I was directly west of the island beating hope-

lessly into the wind. It was evident that my sail area was too small to make any headway. I was actually falling back from the island, losing ground.

By late afternoon wind and current had driven me well back. I climbed to the masthead searching for a sign of life to appeal to, but saw nothing. The shore line was no longer visible. The vegetation and barren upland spots began to blend as one. I was hoping that someone yet might sight me and set off. I retouched the SOS signs with the foul oil from the dead engine. Up to dark no sails broke the horizon. When night closed in, I could see no lights.

For hours I lay on the useless course blinking my weakening flashlight into the low clouds overhead and in a full circle around the horizon. There was always a chance that my spark of light might be picked up and an answering flash bob up on the horizon.

Finally, when my light grew so weak that I could hardly see it myself, I gave up. The island had completely hidden itself in the enveloping dark. It was lost to me. To tarry was fruitless and dangerous. There was nothing to do but turn back to my search for land farther west.

I dreaded the thought of having to cross the landless sea west of Fiji to the New Hebrides. That expanse seemed endless, as I envisaged it in terms of sips of water, hours of drudgery at the pump, and a wet sack. "It's your own fault," I told myself. "You didn't have to come out here, nobody pushed you out of Panama, so shut up."

I set a new course of west by south, that I felt should get me to the southern New Hebrides with good weather in fifteen or sixteen days. I pumped *Pagan* out and went below, wanting day to come so I could consult my map. Also I cut the ration of water to less than a half pint.

At daylight I was on deck for a look at the crude chart etched in the cockpit floor. The next few hours I spent in conjecture over my chances of making the grade with a quart and a half of water. There was water for eight days, possibly nine. I was fifteen days from the New Hebrides, that is, if I could make it in fifteen days, which meant I would be at least six days without water. Humanly impossible.

For the first time in my life, I had a long-term look at death. I had never before had an opportunity to look it in the face.

But now it was before me; and I had a whole week ahead of me to get chummy with it. To my way of thinking — now — death isn't really a dread beast unless you have time to think about him. To be in the presence of death and to have a long-term contract with it are two different things. You can be torpedoed on a ship and be in the presence of death. You can be bombed and set on fire and be in the presence of death. You can be strafed in a lifeboat or under sub attack in a convoy — a lot of things can happen where you are in the presence of death.

But death in such a presence hasn't a sense of finality, or a sense of this-is-the-end; the extreme activity and excitement of action deprive it of that. One can't conceive of death unless it is actually distant.

Strangely, I never once really believed I was going to die. However I will admit I used often to stare stolidly over the restless floor of blue ocean and ask, "Am I going to perish alone out here on the sea?" If I thought of death seriously it is because I toyed with an idea new to me. It never pressed me. My desire, my strength to go on living, was too strong — I had too much to live for. I had overcome too many obstacles.

"I am too young to die," I said . . . and believed it! My new faith in God and prayer — thus my new faith in myself — made life something I wanted badly enough, like wanting to see Mary.

Coming on deck in the morning I saw a seaman's nightmare. *Pagan* was dismasted again. Only the mizzen stood. The main and headsails were down across the decks, the shrouds, stays, and mast trailed in the water like bedraggled hair. The rigging, evidently taxed to extreme in the day of beating vainly into the wind and sea for the island, in its tiredness had collapsed in the night. The hard work of restepping the mast, of refitting the rigging, loaded my mind. Working constantly at the pump had fined me down at an alarming rate. I dreaded the work it all smacked of. But I took a sip of precious water and got started.

I dragged the old mast aboard and sawed it flush where it had snapped at the deck, and shave it flat on one side at the base for restepping; it was now only ten feet long. I shortened the shrouds and stays, and made the little mast ready to be stepped. The effort so depleted me that I was forced to lie down before continuing.

After resting I started the arduous task. I raised the mast as nearly straight up and down as strength would allow and thrust it toward the opening in the deck to step it. It missed by an inch, sliding against the cabin, overbalancing me, and crashing from my shoulder. Again I rested.

The next attempt to stand my mast found me atop the cabin staggering beneath the clumsy spar. I tried to drop it straight down into the opening. The closest I could manage the butt end of the top-heavy stick to the deck hole was six inches. My strength was gone: the exertion left me too weak to stand. I slumped to the deck and lay in a heap, puffing with short breaths.

I thought maybe if I shortened the spar it would be lighter, more manageable. I decided against it, because I needed maximum sail up. The mainsail, even on the twelve-foot mast, was nearly as small as the jigger; which looked like a pillow slip. I went below and fell on my bunk.

When I came out again I felt fresher. But in two tries to step the mast I failed miserably. The last effort missed the hole by a foot. Dejection and fatigue swept over me anew. I went below to rest. I intended to make one more try before shortening the mast.

I awakened sometime in the afternoon still weak from the labors of the morning. I took a sip of water. As it coursed down my throat, I felt a return of strength. Putting the water flask back, I saw the shave lotion. I opened it, sniffed it — it was unbearable. Throwing my head back, I downed a hearty portion of what remained of it. As I capped it, I felt an electric sort of surge through my body.

The next thing I knew I was walking over the deck and before I realized what I had done, I had jerked the mast off the deck, had pointed it up like a broom handle, and it was stepped. Everything I did in the next hour was effortless. I lashed the mast in place at the heel; set the shrouds and stays; hoisted all sail; lashed the helm alee. I felt boundless; I even felt like diving over and giving one of the sharks a bad time!

Under her shortened sail *Pagan* took more time to move. She was sluggish, but as she was driven, and as she gained her cruising speed, she tilted slightly before the southern wind. Soon I was plodding along at something less than a knot.

For the next two days I slept eighteen of each twenty-four-hour period, rising only to pump out, or to sip my drops of water, or read from the Bible. Bad dreams slacked off as general apathy set in; I was a broken robot capable of only a few simple actions.

When I finally did come out of hibernation, it wasn't because I returned to my old self. I never felt the same again after the strenuous day with the mast. Working the pump henceforth became a trial — a far cry from the days when I dried the bilges in fifty long quick strokes. Now I had to pump with one hand for a dozen strokes, then with the other. A hundred movements often failed to clear out the leakage. Halfway through each pumping, I lay sprawled in the cockpit to rest.

Each day I read the Bible more assiduously; found more and more solace in prayer and gave more time to it. I learned the Twenty-third Psalm by heart, and spoke it every rising and sleeping, and often in the night as I heaved at the pump. As well, I learned the Ten Commandments and many other Scriptures. My Bible — a gift of my grandpa when I was a boy — I had never read a chapter of. Aboard *Pagan* I read it cover to cover twice, devouring its words, searching out its comforts. I should have gone insane had I not had the comforting solace of my Baptist teaching. Men who sail small boats know the verity of the Good Captain who piloted my boat.

Atheism with me had been an old story. I picked up a good background for it at college. Later, in the war, my experiences at sea, and in particular the invasion of Algiers in 1942, strengthened my unbelief. I saw strange and bewildering things. I shall never forget the trains of wounded soldiers in

Algiers just after its capture. German, French, English, Italian, American, all together, their wounds making them brothers. Air raids, submarine alerts, and miles of white crosses — all in a few days.

Aboard *Pagan* the petty arguments of "college" atheism dissolved in the light of faith and the crucial practicality of Godly love under the touchstone of vital need and vital want. The test proves; the argument only conjectures. The test is a full measure, the argument a half measure. I smile when I meet atheists.

All my experiences of civilian life in depression America, and in the war, proved a pattern — a direct groundwork for my meditations alone in the vast Pacific. I cannot agree with Laplace that there is no need in this world for the hypothesis of a creator.

That afternoon of October 12, while I slept to fortify my thinning bones, I heard a heavy thud on the starboard hull. It felt solid enough to be the lip of a reef. I thought I might have clipped a part of it, in skirting it. I hurried feebly out on deck and looked around.

Near the bow, and on the sea surface, plowed a high sharp fin. A new fin from any I had seen before: a new arrival to the school of sharks that loafed constantly in the wake. He turned back to the stern and slid fearlessly along the hull, a foot off, pushing himself with a single effort.

He glided amidships and swung his ponderous body gruffly against the planking. *Pagan* shivered. He wandered gracefully off abeam, then came again. Seeing me moving on deck, he waddled close in and eyed me almost humanly with small pig's eyes, only a few feet away.

There we were, eying each other, each wondering how to

eat the other. He, the picture of tropical violence, and I, gone scrawny and desperate.

A most wonderful feeling crept over me. Here was my chance. None of the smaller sharks had dared venture so close. His careless nearness gave me every advantage of the harpooner. The trouble was I had no harpoon. My little fish spear would only tickle him. But I was full of ideas.

If there were only something aboard to make a heavy spear from. I knew that if I could get something big enough into him in a vital spot, he was mine. There were meat and blood enough in him to see me through to the Hebrides. There was at the very least a quart of fresh blood I could draw out of him — enough to last five days. I relished the strength it would give me. I could dry his half a ton of meat, and with plenty to eat I could make out with a quarter pint of water daily. It would be a tight squeeze: but it could be done.

In the bilge, I found an old steel file; under the forepeak was my hacksaw — rusted over, but usable; beneath my bunk lay an eight-inch strip of cold rolled steel, one inch wide, a quarter inch thick. From the workable piece of soft iron, I envisaged a wicked killing spear. How long would the making take, and how long would the shark be around? The work, as I cut it out in my mind, could be done the next afternoon if my endurance could hold. As for the shark, if he were like the others in the wake he would be hovering close astern for days.

The material I was working with was comparatively soft; however, I realized that hacksawing and filing it into shape would wear down my last reserves. The whole venture was a vast gamble — a gamble I was fortunate to have.

I marked the rough outline of a heavily barbed spearhead

on the section of steel. I commenced the long task of driving the saw, stroke by stroke, along each mark. I watched the ceiling as I worked so I couldn't see the slow progress of the cutting. Each time I looked down I tried to be surprised at the few hair widths I had bitten away. My thoughts turned to the kill I would soon be making and the heavy feast to follow. Hunger juices flowed and the dryness of my throat eased. The devils of appetite returned to *Pagan*.

It was late afternoon before I finished cutting out the rough outline of the spearhead. I took a recuperative sleep. Before I could work in the afternoon I had to overstep my ration of water: I drank a half pint. But I felt it a worthy risk, since a heavy feast of meat and blood was in the offing.

By nightfall I had notched in four small niches on the upper part of the·spearhead so it could be screwed and bound to its handle. I was too worn and weak to begin the filing of the spear point; that would start the next morning. I went to bed early, to sleep hard so that I could hasten my labors on the dawn.

But it wasn't easy to sleep hard. Exquisite hunger played tricks with my dreams and horrible nightmares set me to rolling in discomfort on my bunk. My stomach knotted up and wouldn't leave me in peace. It needed food, and if not that at least something that could be swallowed. Every last edible was gone. I thought of pages from my books — but I had tried that before and it had created unbearable problems of the bowels. Then I remembered the oil in the engine.

I groped out into the night, down into the stern compartment, and loosed the plug to the engine crankshaft. I drained off what seemed a half pint of gurling liquid and returned to the cabin. With my finger I stirred the thick gritty liquid that had seen many trips through *Pagan's* engine, and made ready to drink it down.

There are people who wonder and doubt how far a man will go when he is hungry . . . they are those, I claim, who have never been hungry. By hungry, I don't refer to the food-lessness of a day or even a week. Desperate hunger doesn't come until one has starved for at least two weeks — and this is best achieved after about a month of semistarvation.

I turned the pan up and drank deeply and quickly. My throat was outraged. My stomach revolted. I blustered and nearly vomited. My head spun in a light swim and I grew faint and drowsy. I remember settling back; and I remember the knots tightening in my stomach and the faraway ringing in my ears that seemed to come close and go away again. And I dreamed I was in the cockpit peering over my roughly hewed map. I was estimating my position anew; and when I shifted the nail and pounded it in, I found myself in Sydney Harbor. There were the harbor bridge, the skyline of King's Cross, and the Manly Ferry steaming into Circular Quay. Then I wakened; the same darkness, the same slapping of water in the bilges, the same soughing of wind in the rigging, the same feeling of a weak stomach.

Before daylight, though I felt slightly queasy, I pumped the bilges at the regular interval, then I stayed out on deck to work. In the waning dark I scraped at the spear point with my small file. Hour on hour I wore away at the weapon, sprinkling mites of steel on my swollen feet. By midmorning it showed a cruel, knife-edged point and two jagged flanges. Before noon it was a formidable weapon, heavy, unbreakable, sinister. I looked past it to the shark whose fin lazed carelessly above the water and who periodically glided up to the bilges and thwacked them sharply.

I had nothing at hand for a shaft to use as a helve for the spearhead. The last of the oars had gone into the mizzenmast. Shark spearing at the moment had priority over sailing; so down came the little mizzen.

With four heavy screws, I tightened the spearhead to the long oar handle. In addition I bound it with a wrapping of shroud wire. In the opposite end of the shaft I drilled a hole with my knife. Through the hole I passed and secured fifty feet of line, bending it to the heavy cleat at the cockpit coaming.

I was ready to spear my shark, but first I went below and slept a few hours.

The shark was off the beam basking on the surface. I stirred the water a bit. He spread the top of the sea with his heavy fin, thrusting it high, and sped straight in for me. Seeing me, he pulled up short, and gave me the once-over. We sized each other up and squared off.

With a thrust of his powerful body he moved up within a few feet of the planking. He stopped in utter defiance, nosing at the hull, loitering purposely. He turned lazily and moved a foot or two toward the bow. Exposed to me was his whole side. A greater favor the harpooner couldn't ask.

I swung the spear high up, ready to drive it down. I braced myself for the shock that would come. I saw a likely point midway between the dorsal and ventral fins. Bone, flesh, vital organs lay there — everything to bed a spear in.

I glued my eyes to his open flank, and drove the spear hard down. The blade hit what felt like rock, but it penetrated.

The shark lurched in a spasm. I was shoved upward, off my feet. I held to the spear and thrust it back. The great fish threshed and writhed. I felt the spear push deep into his flesh. My hold weakened and I lost it. I crumpled into the cockpit.

I saw the rope paying out into a frothy wake that broke beamward for sea room. He lunged at the end of the line, tautening it with a slam. He spun around — plunged, and I couldn't see him for the boiling he made, but I could feel his might as the decks jerked.

He flailed the surface white. Tail up he fought his way downward, curving back toward the boat. As slack showed in the line I took it in and twisted it around the cleat. The shark shot under the keel, coming up on the opposite bow.

When he flailed in that quarter he plunged again. I sat down watching his useless battlings against death. I knew the spear had a killing hold in his vitals. When his blood gave out — he would come to terms. I waited and watched for weakness.

In a moment I saw its sure signs. He lay on the surface wallowing gracelessly. I led the slack line between two cleats, wrapping it round and round and taking in slack whenever I found it. The shark was stirring only feebly as I dragged him in. Suddenly with explosive fury he shot to the end of the line. I held the line I had taken in so it couldn't pay out. In a moment he grew limp; I was pulling him in again. He felt like dead weight.

Then again he came to life, or so it seemed, and in an explosive movement bolted away, and then again quite suddenly relaxed. I watched him closely as I towed him in. Another shark was entangled in the line; the other shark was towing him. The other shark couldn't untangle himself.

I tried to pull in more line, to get another bite on the cleat. Then a second shark fouled himself with the line. Once more the line yanked tight. At that moment I saw everything. The sharks weren't entangled in the line. They were tearing at the carcass of my shark — eating it!

A third and fourth shark darted in to the death feast. I heaved frantically, and whenever the line showed slack, I wrapped it with mad haste around the cleat. I grew so weak I had to sit down, but I still worked at the line. Every pound of flesh the gluttonous pack was tearing off the carcass was vital to my chance of life. I was fighting for my life. I worked the great shark to within twenty feet of the rail.

One of the greedy pack bit into the tail of my shark, spinning him around in a half circle and racing with him to the bow till the line flew tight. There I could hear a terrifying snapping of jaws as the four set on him, ripping at him, and hastening to rip again. Great holes showed in my shark as he was thrust and pushed and torn.

I worked the mutilated mass of sagged flesh as close in as possible. The thing now was to hook him at the gills and somehow get him on board. I went below for the grappling hook, and hurried back.

The four sharks were jaw deep into the carcass — each thrusting back and tearing from side to side, pulling in opposite directions. The big shark was bent S-shaped. Rusty, blood-filled water nearly hid the heads of his attackers. Like hungry hogs, they were eye deep into the killed victim.

I jabbed my little barbed fish spear hilt deep into the head of the shark nearest me. He was oblivious to the sharp, cold steel. I tried to fit the grappling hook into the gills of the dismembered victim, but weakness felled my arms to my sides.

The grisly feast dropped down to keel depth; and then it dropped beneath the keel to *Pagan's* other side. The line was short, the oar caught against the keel and planking. The extreme pressure was bending it. Through the sole of my feet on the deck boards, I could feel the vibrations of the strained oar. I peered over to see what was happening.

From out of the water came a muffled snap. My oar bobbed to the surface. It had snapped off just above the spearhead.

I moved to the other beam in consternation and below me, gradually sinking into the hiding waters, was the gory feast. I watched it glimmer, and when it no longer glimmered I fell back on the deck boards and lost myself in remorse. I have never been at a lower moment in life.

I reset *Pagan* on her westward course, labored with the bilge pump, and went below. I slept all afternoon and all night.

Two days of sore trial slid past. Nothing more exciting than the change of night and day occurred. Physically I spent them as a vegetable would have, except that I pumped the bilges and stared for pained hours at the shapeless horizons. Mostly I slept or talked to myself. I was tired of the silence: I spoke to hear my voice.

There was an inevitable morning I dreaded to see come. I awakened with less than a half pint of water aboard. One day's ration. After my usual morning prayers I wet my tongue and crawled on deck to do the pumping. I discovered, as I watched the slow motion of my hand at the pump, that I had lost my wedding band. My fingers, thin as reef points, were too skinless to hold a ring.

I struggled with the pump and went below to read the Bible, but soon found that the exertion and excitement of the shark battle had overtaxed me. I was still so overcome that my feeling, my seeing, and my thinking were fogged over.

I could no longer remember what I was reading. What I read I couldn't recall, not a single thought, or a word of it. My mind was blank. I couldn't think straight. I wanted only to sit and stare out the one good porthole. In fact I got so bad that I couldn't even philosophize about the tough time I was having. And that's bad. But I managed to get out every hour and pump the bilges.

By late afternoon I had taken several sips of water to tide me through the day. There was one sip left to see me through pumping out in the middle of the night.

That night a high wind sprung out of the east. For hours I drove along before it to westward. In the early hours of the next morning it grew ungovernable. I took the last sip of water, crawled out to drop the main, and lay hove-to on the starboard tack.

Water was gone. There were hundreds of miles yet to go to land — nearly two weeks' sailing time. But there was a flame still going inside, burning on the skimpiest fuel.

A low scud sailed overhead. It left a dampness in the air but no real promise of rain. I wasn't discouraged; I knew that something would come along — either rain or an island or a ship to tow me to a safe harbor.

Later in the night the wind abated noticeably; the skies cleared. I crawled to the foredeck and hoisted the tiny main. Clambering back, I swung my boat on her former course. The effort weakened me so much that I was unable to pump out. I went below to a wet bunk. At daylight I managed to get the bilges dry. I was never able, not once, after that to work the pump long enough at a single stretch to see *Pagan's* bilges dry again. Thereafter I could only pump till I was tired, then quit.

I looked into the cloudy sky. No hint of rain. During the night I had thought of a scheme to condense fresh water from salt. I had a small oilcan with a spout. I filled it from over the side, fired the Primus, set it on to boil. The hole in the top of the can was capped so that steam could issue from the spout. If I could somehow trap that steam I would have fresh water.

I rigged a curved sheet of tin so that the steam could strike it and give off the yield, if any, in a dish. Eventually a drop fell in; I blotted it up with my dry, swollen tongue, and awaited the next.

In an hour my Rube Goldberg contraption netted many dozen offerings. A tablespoon of water for an hour's agitation and futile hope. I held doggedly on throughout the morning. By noon I was worn ragged; but my mouth was no longer dry. The worst was over till the next day. I pumped the bilges awhile and crawled into my blanket for the afternoon.

Then, unexpectedly, rain came. I heard it beating on the decks. A heavy black squall moved with the slacking wind from the east. I knew what it meant and ran on deck. I spread my woolen blanket over the deckhouse and cleaned the dirt from the cockpit.

The squall, not the first I had seen, but the first that had touched me since the hurricane, worked directly over me. Large droplets hosed down the boat. I washed the crusted salt from my skin and out of my beard. I drank hoggishly of the water standing on the decks, scooping it into my mouth by handfuls.

When the blanket was saturated, I twisted it dry, clearing it of salt. I let it soak again, then squeezed it over the bucket.

I had time to wring it twice before the squall passed; a half gallon of water. There was a gallon lodged in the cockpit. A gallon and a half of water! I felt like a king.

I put myself instantly on a ration of a pint and a half per day. It seemed wasteful to drink so much water in a day.

The high wind held for all day and night, and blew itself out with daylight when I hit the corners of two howling squalls that set me bouncing. Once they passed, I was left drifting in a flat calm.

The sun came up on a glassy sea. I said my long morning prayers, and turned to my Bible reading. But despite an increased ration of water, my mind didn't clear up. I couldn't remember what I had read a minute after reading it. I sat staring out the porthole, waiting for strength and the inspiration to pump some of the water from the bilges.

Finally I went on deck and found a comfortable spot in the shade of the mizzen and watched the sharks and dolphins. Out on the beam, flapping over the windless sea, was a cluster of birds. I thought I recognized land birds among them, but since I was at least 200 miles from land, I discarded the observation. Some of the birds came in close. A chronic exhaustion, too enervating to permit me to care about the birds, had hold of me. I couldn't move to challenge them. My dead brain couldn't produce a means to challenge them. I dared not exert myself in another strenuous gamble for food. One more physical strain and I was finished — I knew that.

I worked at the pump till I could pump no more; then went below to sleep. Sleep came simply and easily. I slept in child-like obliviousness till the rising water slopped into my bunk. Then I went out and pumped, till again I could stand no more . . . so it went.

When the calm still held the next morning I decided to cut the water ration to a pint. The calm vexed me and wore at me constantly. "Surely this afternoon there'll be a wind," I thought.

The afternoon aged. Out on the sea the birds screamed for wind. When the wind blows, the flying fish take to the air while chased by the dolphin and their other underwater enemies. During the calms, they seek other areas in which there is wind, where they have a fighting chance. Thus the wind aids many of those living in and out of the sea to thrive. The lean dolphin hadn't eaten in two days. Old Death and his boys spent most of their time discussing the weather, as did the birds and I.

The arrival of the next day, the third consecutive day of perplexing calm, was proclaimed by the plaintive cries of hungry sea birds. I came on deck not believing it possible that it could still be calm. But there it was — the sea was like a placid lake. Hardly a shadow showed on the surface. The sails were as limp as death. Not a breath stirred. I didn't like it. These prolonged calms are often the harbingers of hurricanes.

I pumped for what seemed an hour, till the water was down to the floor boards, and lowered my clublike, weighted feet into the hold to stare out from the porthole onto the impersonal sea, and fret.

When dark came and still no breeze, I went on deck to pray. I took the part of spokesman for the fish and birds. Hands clasped on the cabin, gaunt knees on the deck, and puffed feet protruding outboard — a position and state I never dreamed I would ever be in. I knelt under the stars, unhindered by the pent cabin, reciting my plaintive call for wind and the chance to fight for my life.

The morning following I rose knowing there would be wind — it was another morning of stark calm. A desolate, sun-glaring sea glowered at me as I came on deck. I took one look, murmured "Still calm," and once more cut the water ration, to barely more than a half pint.

Four days of continual dead wind. Twenty-two days since my last morsel of food. Forty-seven days since the hurricane — according to the X's on the bulkhead. And the closest land an estimated ten days away. That was the sober tally I made that morning. I tried to scribble it into the front page of my Bible with the one pencil aboard so it could live to explain in case I couldn't. But I didn't put it in: I tried, but I couldn't. My brain was foggy, the foggiest yet — I couldn't think of a suitable way so I pushed it aside, and stared out the porthole.

A slight swell was rolling in from the south, intimating that somewhere, at least, there was wind. I struggled onto the deckhouse, remembering suddenly that for the last two days I had forgotten to look for land. As usual there was no land — only the sea-fowl screaming dejectedly.

A loud scratching noise came to my ear. At first I thought it was the foot-deep water in the cabin. Then realized that it came from the planking, on the outside.

Over the rail I saw a large sea turtle scratching at the hull with a discolored flipper. He was an olive-green shade, pat-terned across the back with squares. I felt I shouldn't risk my small store of energy in a fruitless contest with him. I stared for a while at his pawings on the planks. I remembered the sea turtle I had harpooned in the Galápagos. I thought of the meat and blood in this one. I threw judgment to the winds and the fight was on.

I crept astern and found the pronged spear with which I

had formerly tried for triggerfish. I trembled with excitement as I made a lunge to harpoon the big tortoise. But my strength was gone; the spear struck, and skidded across his leathery shell. He plunged, swam under the keel, and came up near the rudder. I groped along the deck to the transom and knelt over him, sighting him along the spear.

I jabbed at him three times successively, but failed to penetrate the tough, hidelike shell. My strength was so far gone that even this effort had me puffing. As a last resort I laid the spear aside and made an attempt to pull the turtle aboard by grabbing him.

I fitted both hands under his shell and strained to raise him to deck. I was never weaker. I couldn't even hold him from swimming away. With a few movements of his flippers he made progress abeam, nearly pulling me in.

In consternation I teetered on the railless deck edge, kicking for balance, fumbling disconnectedly. If I fell in I knew I would sink like a rock, fleshless and bony as I was. Even if I could grasp the sides I wouldn't have the strength to claw myself aboard. And the sharks! I had seen what the sharks could do.

I released my grip on him in the nick of time, and avoided falling in by throwing myself flat and backing aboard with my legs flying. I ran my knee against the fish spear. Sitting up I found that one of the rusted forks had imbedded itself an inch under my kneecap. A burning pain attended it, the kind that gave strong hint of more pain to come.

I pulled the spear point out and watched a single drop of black blood merge. I couldn't afford to lose that drop of life; I wiped it off with my finger and smeared it on my tongue, and watched for more. None came. Blood was too dense to flow. I laid back on the deck, and stayed there for over an hour, too tired to stand. Finally I got up.

When I looked for the turtle he was gone. It was strange that a sea so calm could hide anything. I heard the water slopping in the bilge, and walked back to have a look. Water was over a foot deep inside, a hopeless task of pumping.

I pumped till I was exhausted, making tiny two-inch strokes, then I waded below to bed down. My knee throbbed. The bilge water babbled like jabbering women as it flowed to and fro. I eased off to sleep.

At noon, water in my bunk awakened me and drove me out to the pump. The calm still held. Birds spiraled overhead screeching raucously. In the sea, the dolphin moved in disconsolate circles. I gave up ever seeing a wind. After pumping till my arm failed to respond to my wish to lower the depth of the bilge water, I lowered my swollen feet, and puffed knee, into the flooded cabin.

At a later hour, when ordinarily I should have gone on deck to pump out, I couldn't go. I was aware of the need, but I couldn't drive myself. My knee hurt. I lay watching the up-creeping water, knowing that each minute I languished there meant heartbreaking work later. It was easier to fall asleep.

Later, with the sun dangling over the horizon, I was startled awake by water pouring into my bunk. *Pagan* was listing badly. My first thought was that I had allowed too much water to leak in. She's tipping, I thought . . . overloaded, sinking! I expected her every moment to turn turtle, and wanted to run on deck, but could only sit up slowly. I couldn't think quickly enough to decide what to do.

I climbed out of my bunk into water past my calves. Limping to deck I was amazed to see the mast heeling before a fresh wind. It was about force five out of the south, working *Pagan* beautifully, shoving her westward — and to land!

My spirits skyrocketed. Movement! At last I was on the way to land. I felt better, my old optimism returned. Consulting the map, I estimated I was about ten days from the closest land — the pestilence-ridden New Hebrides. I refused to consider how I was going to keep my boat pumped from hour to hour on my remaining margin of strength. I would wait and tackle each problem as it came.

I pumped the bilges for as long as the muscles were willing. But because my knee was swelling and pulsating, I couldn't bend it enough to go back below. That night I slept in the cockpit.

Four times during the spanking night I arose to pump the bilges. My knee grew worse and I was at a loss what to do. I bathed it in salt water, but the pressure of my fingers made it pain. At daylight, I lay on my back in the cockpit, murmuring my morning supplications. I prayed, as every day I had prayed; I ended my prayer as always, "And Thou wills it, there will be land."

I looked across the bows, and there, not three miles distant, lay an island. I could only stare dumbly. I didn't shout and I didn't jump; too many disappointments had dulled my sense of appreciation. I just looked at the lump of land colored in around its shores with fat greenery and shaping away to its flat crest with deeply graved volcanic rock.

I had no idea what land it was and didn't care. It was land. According to my questionable calculations I should have been more than a week off land — the New Hebrides. But here it was. I didn't care if it was Timbuktu or Shangri-La: it was land, and I wasn't going to miss it.

CHAPTER XXII

Rescue

I HAULED SOUTHWARD down the coast, skirting the wide, heavily toothed open reef, at 200 yards. The small island was a bare mile and a half away, across the reef and across the lagoon. Though I had been through the New Hebrides during the war, I couldn't tag the island.

It was about seven miles long, and looked seven or eight hundred feet high. It was volcanic, capped by a craterlike summit. Along the shore the malformed lava cliffs jumped up twenty or thirty feet, deeply underwashed by the sea. Here and there a flat depression ended in a white sandy beach, grown to mangrove and coconut trees.

My plan was to locate the opening in the reef and shoot into the lagoon to anchor before a village, or beach my boat on one of the sandy shores. I was racing against time. *Pagan* hadn't been pumped in four hours; water was rising. I was saving my strength for the bout with the short, clumsy tiller, and the struggle to get ashore.

Down the full length of the coast I ran, till I neared the southeast corner, and still I found no opening in the reef. As I closed with the point I realized the danger of going around it.

I dared not pass to leeward of the protruding fist of land. Once by, I could never work back: I remembered my failure at the recent unidentified island. Nor could I turn back and reach up the long coast. My course had thrown me in hard by the reef. I hadn't room to maneuver or the strength to do it. For one thing, the bulky mast, strapped as it was angularly across the deck, was an impediment. It dragged in the sea whenever the decks sloped, and made *Pagan* difficult to maneuver. I thought of going forward to cut its lashings, but I knew I hadn't the strength to roll it off. My strength was gone; I was unable to pump out. The water in the hold was rising. The point was a hundred yards off. I had to act . . . now. A dread decision with regard to my boat was in the balance — and it had to be made.

I suddenly realized that my battered little craft was a coffin. Kim Powell in Panama had said, "She'll go as far as you can stay with her." The prophecy was true. I was finished, but my sporty little cutter was still game for the fight.

I had no alternative but to wreck her to save my life . . . what is worse, I had no time to weigh the pros and cons of the predicament.

Rather than turn that corner to sure death, rather than go about and fight hopelessly — and vainly — up the uninviting coast, I kicked the helm hard down and raced bow-on toward the exposed reef: my last official decision as *Pagan's* captain, for now she was heading into an alley from which she would never return.

I was dressed in army khaki. Earlier, when I sighted the island, I had a quick sponge bath sitting at the rail; I combed the salt from my beard and arranged my bothersome hair, now long as a woman's, into a knot and covered it with a cap. My feet were too swollen for anything but stockings. My bulbous knee I wrapped in blanket stripping.

I had grabbed a few last things and crammed them in my pockets. Hand on the tiller, I awaited the shock.

The keel passed over several coral heads, about six fathoms down. Farther on the reef began to shoal quickly, and the sea floor was only four fathoms. I can anchor in this, I suddenly realized. At a slow-motion gait I limped forward to the anchor and made to put it over.

Partly because of my boil-like knee, but mostly because I had no strength, I couldn't begin to budge the anchor. I was nearing the reef; the sea was pounding like thunder on it. I sat down, put my feet against the flukes, and pushed with all my might; but I was helpless to move it. The din was closer. I was caught in the grip of the current, and I was being swept in to the reef. I got up, took the fluke in my hands, and strained at it. It raised a foot. I lost my balance and stumbled.

Pagan caught the swell of a roller, rode in on its back, and crashed stem-to against the coral wall. She shivered as though struck by shell fire. I was sitting near the port rail. One of her planks sprung, pointing away from the stem. I could see the water gush through it. In a moment she settled by the bow, the deck was awash, the fore scuttle covered. In no time I was sitting to my pockets in water. I could only sit and watch — the decks were lurching too much to permit me to stand.

I could hear a horrible noise as *Pagan* pounded against the reef at the beam. Only the watertight stern section was buoyant. The bow was still going down. Water was up to my waist. The next two rollers lifted the stern on the reef. I could feel the dull thud of the lead-shod keel against the iron-hard coral. The next sea combed across the bows, sweeping me against the deckhouse, where I clung to the mast. Each successive sea worked her higher on the reef, turning her broadside to the destructive waves and tilting her at a crazy angle. The next impact shook me from my hold. I slipped down the abrupt incline and fell free of the boat onto the coral, only to be overwhelmed by a sea that twisted me in a somersault and threw me back onto shallower coral ground. I gathered myself up, shook free of the grasping water, and somehow moved a few feet to where it was safe.

I had backed away from my battered boat onto the dry coral and sat cursing the bullying sea. *Pagan* was thrown up to where the water was knee-deep. Each time a roller broke over her she shuddered and ground her planks on the sharp coral.

Behind me the jagged reef ran for two hundred yards. I turned and staggered in the stiff-legged way of the gaunt and hungry to the brink of the reef. There the lagoon dropped to a depth of nine fathoms, where a garden land of coral formations grew. Tiny fish were as visible in fifty feet of water as in fifty feet of clear air. I shunned the water like poison, knowing that if I should fall in, I would sink like a weight.

I lay down on the coral to rest and dropped instantly and helplessly asleep. Hours later the rising tide, marching across the reef, lapped against me. With the feel of water I jerked awake, thinking it was time to pump the bilges. Seeing myself on the crusty reef I was startled, then shocked. Then I remembered. The tide was coming in. The reef was covered. Two hundred yards away *Pagan* was taking an unmerciful pounding from the growing rollers.

I decided to struggle back to the boat and get the life raft.

I wobbled back to her, keeping in the less disturbed waters of her lee. She was thigh-deep in water, and had been bowled over several times. The little rubber life raft had been caught beneath the boat and ground into the coral spikes. After trail-

ing astern for over a thousand miles of the Pacific since the
hurricane, it ended on the coral needles.

I waded to the sloping deck and climbed uncertainly
aboard, looking for something on which to float across the
deep lagoon. *Pagan* was on her beam, teetering either way,
likely to lob over again. Knife in hand I hacked away the
stout lashings holding the thirty-five-foot mast to the deck. I
jumped off and sloshed to where water was knee-deep, and
looked back.

This rising sea was whamming *Pagan* and threatening to
bowl her over. Suddenly *Pagan* jammed her beam into the
coral and clumped over from her beam onto her decks. The
hull, pointing skyward, was ghastly with barnacles and scars
and loose planking.

I felt drowsy but there was no place to lie down. The growing waves were pushing me back away from the boat. Then
the mast worked loose and I took hold of it. I held to it as the
sea drove it slowly across the reef. When I reached the lagoon,
I climbed on its heaviest part, straddling it, floating on it.

My arms and legs were dangling in the water, my head and
chest resting on the hard curved surface. For a long time I lay
watching the island as I floated off onto the lagoon. Finally
I drifted off to a sleeplike drowse.

I awakened when the mast scraped on the soft shore. I was
in a small alcove fronted with bright sand, overtowered by a
beetling wall of volcanic rock. I plodded out of the water onto
the white sand. I slumped into the inviting warmth and fell
asleep.

The incoming tide, washing my feet sometime later, awakened me as it marched up the beach. I crawled higher on the
sloping beach to the base of the twenty-foot cliff face, where

I hoped the water wouldn't reach, and dropped off again in a slumber. In a while I was disturbed again. The rising tide. Looking on the rocks I could see a high-water mark shoulder high.

The miniature cove, soon to be filled with wind-driven water, was no place to be at high tide. I could imagine the havoc of swirling waters in the bowl pushed there by the crushing tide.

Had I not been weak or my knee tender, I could easily have scaled the cliff. There were footholds and handholds aplenty. It was only a matter of simple climbing, but my arms and legs and hands were powerless.

Looking back now, I can't explain, even to myself, how I climbed those rocks. They were twenty feet high. They were sharp — no man could say they were terribly difficult to climb, I admit. At the same time I was weak — too weak to budge a fifty-pound anchor before I wrecked — yet I managed to push and pull my eighty or ninety pounds up the twenty feet of lava formation.

The first thing I did when I got to the top was to lie down for a sleep. It was a nap that lasted the rest of the afternoon and all that night. For the first time in forty-eight days I didn't have to pull myself up at disjointed hours of the night to pump the bilges. But I awakened several times from force of habit. My ears were long tuned to the creaking of *Pagan's* timbers and the myriad sounds from her watered bilges, and from wind in her sails and rigging. The absence of those sounds was as significant as those sounds themselves, and when I couldn't hear them, I could only sleep patchily.

When day broke I labored to a sitting position, feeling fresh enough to think of food and water. I was sitting in a patch of misshapen lava surrounded by thick, recklessly grown jungle, creepers, and tight trees. A mile across the lagoon I could see the remains of my intrepid *Pagan* high and dry on the shining reef. She looked frowzy and tortured. Her standing rigging was smashed away; her deckhouse gone; she lay on her beam, halfway across the long reef, pointing her naked decks to the sky.

Below me the beach of the alcove was strewn with driftage from *Pagan* — bits of chewed planking, articles of clothing, bedding, sailcloth, water kegs, spars, and shroud wires.

I searched into the entangled jungle from my seat, looking for signs of tropical foods. I had expected to find bananas, coconuts, bird rookeries, and water easily. I saw nothing encouraging — only the dense patchwork of illimitable undergrowth topped by towering oaklike trees. From near by I selected several varieties of leaves and chewed at them. They were tasteless and more dry than otherwise.

I remembered having seen coconut palms on the shore when I was skirting the reef with *Pagan*. It was my hope now to find them and eat of them till someone came along or my strength returned to where I could manage a search inland or along the coast for a village. I decided to go south and at the same time to seek for the lee side of the isle. I wondered how far I would have to go; and I wondered how far I could go.

I figured I'd better get an early start, so I wobbled to my feet. To southward, around the beckoning point that I had nearly sailed past, appeared the shortest way to the island's leeward shores. If the island was inhabited there would be a village there.

I took a stout limb for support and started on an uncertain quest over the pocked spiny lava. I ate leaves as I trudged along, and sucked the ends of broken branches for sap. A small land crab, jumping from rock to rock, darted in front of me, and I pinioned him with my stick. Taking him up, I tore him apart and sucked his bitter-tasting insides out. I chewed his plated legs, sucked the shelly mass dry, and spit it up. It gave me fresh strength and hope.

Farther along I found another crab. He too I sucked from his shell. I had come now some fifteen or twenty yards in a couple of hours. My walking was unbearably slow. I wanted to go faster. But the rocks! They were rocks such as I had never seen before. They were like an eagle's claws inverted. The island is volcanic in origin, and evidently centuries of rain, pelting upon the wearable lava, has fined it down to innumerable stalagmite-looking points sticking up at heights from three inches to three feet. They crowd upon themselves in their formation like a close forest, making a flat space — even the width of a bare foot — something to remember. I teetered among them, placing my feet carefully on the least sharp of the points and using my hands on the higher lava spires to brace myself and push myself along.

My legs were weakening and my bad knee beginning to ache. My swollen heavy feet were too much of a load to be carried much farther. Their weight was such that often I had to lift them from behind the knees over the higher rocks. I lay down among the rocks to rest. It was easy to sleep. I could have slept forever. Sleep was as effortless as thinking to an active mind. My body cried for twenty-four hours of sleep, but my judgment complained at the little distance I had traveled. I forced myself to move on.

In an hour I wended through another ten yards of rock semi-jungle. I was so tired I trembled; I was ready to quit. I looked for a spot to lie down. From out of the rocks a coral snake glided toward me, weaving in such a way that I knew he didn't see me. My parched throat watered at the sight of him. Instantly I thought of his meat and blood — food! When he was close enough I trapped him with my stick, holding it into the center of his body, pressing hard, trying to break his back. He writhed madly. I was hoping he would soon succumb. My hunger juices, whetted by the crabs and leaves, were yearning. I wondered how one went about eating a snake. I pushed against the stick the harder.

My strength began to give out; my arms trembled so that the stick moved, losing its purchase, and the snake darted into the rocks. The exertion tired me so I sat down, napping where I sat, but not for long: I felt a compulsion driving me to round the point while I had strength to walk.

Later in the afternoon, another twenty yards along, I came upon a lone coconut tree. It was short, not reaching higher than twenty-five feet, and a dozen green nuts, most delicious for drinking, were nestled in its fronds. Slapping the tree I shouted happily, and kissed it. Here I could stay eating the nuts till I grew strong again.

In a short time my joy faded to ironic discouragement. Though the life-giving coconuts were a scant twenty feet overhead, I was powerless to reach them. I knew that I was powerless to climb the tree. I threw my hiking stick at them. The shoulder muscles were so weak that my arm came out of socket, and fell limp at my side till I pressed it in again. I gave up and slept on the mound of earth at the base of the tree.

When I arose in a few hours, I searched about and found a weazened old nut. My knife, though rusted, was suitably sharp. But not the world's sharpest knife could have availed me much then. I was too weak to use it.

Nevertheless I set to work hewing at the end of the nut. After what seemed hours I had hacked through a bare inch of the outer fibrous husk. My fingers, hands, and arms ached from the clumsy work. There was an inch to go to the inner nut. But I was so weak and tired I doddered. Even as I stared uselessly at the nut I dozed. I dropped it and fell back. I slept as I had wanted to sleep, uninhibited and without moving, the rest of the afternoon, and the whole of the night.

I awakened next morning weaker than when I had fallen asleep. Beside me lay the wrinkled nut, and near by the knife. I took them up and struck one against the other with chopping, half-strength cuts. Within minutes I was tired. My hands cramped up and refused to open or close. I had only to cut through an inch of husk to find three small depressions. By punching one of them, I could reach the inside cool milk. I picked the nut up and beat it against the sharp rocks. I pounded it till my breath came in gasps, then dropped it in despair and lay back in a heap.

The third day ashore and I had seen nothing but a tortuous floor of projecting crags and confused growth. My tongue was puffed and sticky. The bad knee was turning black. Coral poisoning, picked up out on the reef, which I had been unaware of up to this point, was festering in a dozen places on my feet and legs.

I lay about a hundred paces inland. Hard by I could hear the sea pounding into the under-washed caverns along the shore. I knew I was on my last legs — and my only chance for life lay in getting back to where I could watch the water and intercept a chance passer. I struggled to a shaky stance and trudged toilsomely in the direction of the sea, stumbling and falling, oblivious of everything, intent only on reaching the dull noise of the pounding surf.

I came out upon a small alcove making an irregular half circle around a sandspit some twenty feet below me. A strong wind — sufficient, if I had been out in it under sail, to necessitate tucking in a reef — was whirling the sand in eddies along the strand. The tide was well out, revealing a bottom heavy with rocks and ledges of coral. Out on the reef, I could see no sign of *Pagan*. The sea and coral had triumphed over her. Around the shore were indications of her presence. I lay down and slept.

Sometime later I heard sounds that weren't exactly the sea. Looking from my perch I saw three small native children racing excitedly about the beach. They were bushy haired and black skinned. They shouted and screamed in high glee over the fabulous findings they were making. They were directly below me.

I leaned over the ledge, intending to shout, "Hey Joe, come here." Instead, a weird, uncontrollable gurgle rattled forth. The boys looked around, then up. What they saw was mirrored in their faces. Their eyes grew saucerlike with terror; in one motion they dropped all they had collected and ran screaming for their lives.

I was so suddenly left alone that I was afraid I had imagined what I saw. But the footprints were there — they spoke volumes in relief and peace of mind. At least someone knew that a stranger was on the island.

I lay back and slept, waking to stare at the watery point around which they had gone, as long and as often as possible. Heavy hours dragged by. The tide worked up the beach to full. Driven by the flush wind it thundered into the worn cliff base, throwing dollops of water well back into the matted brush and vine.

Finally I heard loud shouts and watched the mouth of the alcove. An outrigger broke into view carrying six young boys. They were punting her along in the shallow water. I hailed them. They dropped on one knee, the better to see me, and stared incredulously. They were a scant thirty yards away.

I could tell that they had seen few white men before. And it was apparent that the frightened children hadn't been taken seriously in their village. The gullible teen-agers had come to investigate.

I motioned them into the cove so I could be dragged from my perch in the rocks. They tried valiantly to poke the delicate-hulled outrigger into the precarious opening, but were forced to give up. The zesty wind blowing, the tide coming in, the heavy rollers breaking into the rock-ribbed cove, baffled their seamanship. Rightfully they gave up.

They smiled gamely, indicating that it was impossible to come in. They indicated that I should move out to the ledge at the fringe of the cove mouth, about forty feet from me; from there they could possibly catch me as I jumped over. If I could but win to that point, I was safe. I tried to stand, but there wasn't enough push in my arms and legs to get me off my back, and I showed them how helpless I was.

They motioned that they were returning to their village, that they would come again. I communicated to them that I was foodless, waterless — I fell back in a fainting gesture to imply that if they didn't come for me soon, it wouldn't matter if they never came. Lying back was so peaceful. I forgot they were there and soon found myself dozing.

I was shocked awake by water splashing over me. It was dark. I thought I was aboard *Pagan* in the tight cold cabin. I was saying to myself, "It's time to pump the bilges." I felt around for the tea. Just a pinch to chew while I heaved at the pump. My hand scraped across the rocks; then I remembered and looked out onto the black lagoon.

The sea was pounding against the cliffs. The tide was coming up again. A high wind was blowing and salt water was bombarding the jungle.

I supposed the natives had come looking for me, and missed me. I was too weak to sit up for long. I propped myself on my side so that I could squint through a crevice in the rocks at the sea.

The wind and water were cold, my clothes were sticking to me. I was getting properly miserable. Then I saw lights on the water. They were well off from the shore. I knew it was the outrigger come for me. Then I made it to be two outriggers, maybe three. When they pulled up even with me they stopped, and evidently anchored to study the situation.

The torches burned fiercely in the wind as the boats huddled offshore. Occasionally, when the sea and wind were momentarily slack, I yelled gutturally. They heard me, and shouted back encouragement above the brewing storm.

It was understandable that they didn't hazard their delicate outriggers in the obstreperous surf. The surge of sea over the rocky bottom would have smashed the hulls out of them. I called to them at every favorable opportunity, and when they heard, they answered reassuringly.

Hours dragged, the torches one by one were put out, and finally only one torch shone in the water. I grew panicky, thinking I'd never be rescued. The natives were evidently waiting for daylight. I was cold, wet, and miserable. Surely they were cunning enough to devise some means of getting me out before then.

I set up such a caterwaul of despondent calls that soon the boats sprang audibly and visibly to life. Several torches flared up, voices sang out, and one of the craft detached itself and moved slowly away to the north. Something was afoot.

The other boats moved in to around fifty feet off the rocks. I could see naked shoulders and bushy heads under the fires. They called good-naturedly and pointed to the north.

I called to them in Spanish, then in French, but they gave the same friendly answers, and waved their flares to the north.

Sometime later I heard brush rustling in the jungle and the snap of limbs underfoot. I threw myself down out of sight and listened. A voice called in a strange tongue and I sat up and answered. Those on the water joined in and an excited three-way interchange cropped up.

A torch suddenly swayed in view from the dark, and stopped in the air above me. An exclamation of disbelief came from behind the sputtering light. The bearer was panting heavily from his struggle with the rocks and bramble. All I could say was, "Hello Joe." I could not sit up any longer; I could only extend a hand.

I made out massive shoulders and arms beneath the light, and a bushy head. He was a tall man. His voice, husky and full of understanding, spoke soothing words, and shouted instructions to the boats. The light disappeared, and the powerful arms closed about me, wafting me into the air.

My Good Samaritan hustled me in a jiffy over the forty feet to the overhanging ledge, where the boys earlier could have saved me. I was held in hard-muscled arms while one of the boats, heavily manned with oarsmen and punters, worked up to the battered rock face. I could hear oars slapping the water furiously and the punting poles pounding at the black, shape-

less cliff face to find the boat off. Instructions were loudly
bandied. The craft, flooded with torchlight, was directly below, heaving to the surging seas. More words passed from
mouth to mouth. This time they were desperate instructions.
The prow was scraping over the charred rock. My benefactor
twisted me upside down, and handed me down at the ankles.
Upreaching arms folded me in and exclaimed when they felt
my small girth. When I was safe aboard a yell of triumph
went up from all throats. The other boats answered.

A moment later an audible crash shook the small craft. It
was my benefactor, who had jumped aboard from his perch.
It's a wonder he hadn't broken a leg or stove the light deck in.

I was laid on the stern of the open boat. The stanch oarsmen worked the boat off the cliffy shore. My friend came to
me and covered me over with a sheet of tapa cloth. When I
clamored for food and drink he offered me a baked *kumala,* a
kind of sweet potato, which I took and nibbled a morsel from.
The long days and nights of quiet desperation were over. The
fact of food in my hands and a pot of native tea being offered
me overwhelmed me. Suddenly I lost all caution. I bit viciously into the *kumala.* I chewed it voraciously and swallowed it in great gulps, washing it down with volumes of the
hot tea.

I sighed and exclaimed over the food with pleasure, much
to the delight of my friend, who egged me on generously, gig-
gling happily as I bolted great mouthfuls. I knew I shouldn't
be gobbling as I was; but though I tried mightily, judgment
went glimmering after the first taste.

When I was gorged I lay back and fell asleep to the tune of
oar beats and punting poles and the lilt of a strange language.

CHAPTER XXIII   Tuvutha

W<small>HEN</small> I <small>CAME</small> <small>TO</small>, it was with the deep consciousness of the village around me. I was in a thatched hut, lying on my back. Above me were the rafters and ceilingless dome of a thatch dwelling. A ridgepole of coconut trunk supported a thick roofing of pandanus and coconut thatch, all lashed intricately in place with a coarse fibrous rope. This I realized was the hut of the man who had saved me.

I lay on a woven mat spread over a layer of coconut leaves stripped from the branch. My bed was a hard uncomfortable one. When I stirred, someone sitting at my side moved and looked at me closely. It was a native woman who showed relief at my stirring and whose eyes indicated she had tended me for anxious hours.

I had been in a coma a full day and night. The whole time she had sat patiently, feeding me in my delirium on a balm of coconut milk. My knee was poulticed in a soggy wrapping of native herbals; the offensive coral poisoning too was checked. My life was saved.

Itchica, as I learned, was the man who rescued me from the rocks. He carried me to his dark hut where care of me was given into the hands of his soft-spoken, efficient wife. She, with her woman's intuitiveness and native cunning, saw my condition at a glance.

She knew that the starved shouldn't eat as I had eaten, nor drink as I had drunk on the outrigger. She nodded her head gravely over my gaseous, swelling stomach, swollen to where the stretched skin burned, and my breaths that came in short gasps.

Even after I was saved from the rocks, she knew I might have died. The *kumalas* wolfed so hungrily, and the tea gulped, could have — but for her — finished me. With a long calloused finger she probed far down in my throat, turning and upsetting my stomach, freeing it of the unchewed lumps of heavy food and the flood of water. She put her hands on my stomach, pressed gently and firmly till the gases rumbled out of my throat and my breathing became normal.

After that I was pervaded with a sense of nothingness. But to return. When I awakened thirty hours later, staring into the strange rafters of the hut, she was still there, tending me. I owe her my life. And I owe my life to her husband, who scrambled over the rocks for me.

She is Una, an infinite woman; a woman of great kindness and understanding. Una rarely smiled or showed emotion. She wasn't exactly inscrutable for I know she felt deeply, and in small ways she showed it. She showed the depth of her feelings in the selfless care she gave me. She proved herself unforgettable in the numberless things I saw her do before I left the island. Anything she did, she did well. She is one of these rare women who accomplish a prodigious amount of work in a single day.

I was famished from my long coma. Una gave me a half shell of coconut milk and a hot broth of fish and breadfruit with a turtle egg to eat raw. Itchy (as I nicknamed Itchica) propped me up from behind as Una fed me a bit at a time.

It was difficult for me to chew even the small soft bread-fruit lumps. My jaw muscles grew so tired in a few motions that they refused to wag. My swallowing muscles too soon collapsed and I couldn't force anything down. I learned, before long, that the best way to eat was to have an hour's rest between tidbits. Then my jaws could munch again and my swallowing machinery was good for a few minutes' work.

When the villagers learned I had come to life they trooped in for a look. The hut was filled to overflowing. They sat around cross-legged, leaning toward me searchingly. I lay studying every face and feature for a clue to the land I was on. They weren't black so much as coffee colored. They were clean, healthy, powerfully built, tall, congenial. I couldn't identify them with any land I had seen in my travels.

I spoke to the soft-featured blacks, asking the name of their land. To a man, they spoke no English. I spoke next in French, then in Spanish; they looked blank and finally giggled at my efforts. I laughed and they laughed with me, and I knew we were pals.

Pointing to the ground, I asked, "New Hebrides?" No one moved. "New Caledonia?" No response. "Loyalty Islands?" Still silence. Though I knew I was far from the Solomons, I asked, "Solomon Islands?" This struck a responsive chord. Again I asked, "Solomon Islands?"

One of the old men came forward nodding his head: evidently in his long life he had heard of the Solomons. Indicating the surroundings he said, "Lomaloma."

"Lomaloma?"

"Lomaloma, Tuvutha."

"Lomaloma, Tuvutha?" The words meant nothing to me. I pressed him further.

"Lomaloma, Tuvutha i Lau," he said.

Lau I knew to be the easternmost part of the Fiji Islands. But I knew I couldn't be in Fiji. I had missed the Fijis and sailed on to the New Hebrides. But what the oldster said made me think. I could easily see the hale men before me were a far cry from the malarial, ulcerous, potbellied natives I had seen in the New Hebrides during the war.

I figured maybe I had misunderstood him. We haggled in blind alleys further. Eventually a crude chart was scratched on a box top. A finger was laid on a remote oblong dot in a string of dots designated as the Lau Group of Fiji. The island was Tuvutha; the village Lomaloma. The word impinged on me like a bolt — "Fiji!"

I stared long at the ludicrous map. To the south was Lakemba, to the north Vanuambalavu, to the west Nayau, and farther to west, the main islands of the group. The incredible fact that I was in eastern Fiji was hard of belief. My estimates of speed and position of *Pagan* after the hurricane had been immensely wrong. It made me wonder, had I been near Samoa or not? Where exactly had I been these last seven weeks during my blind searchings? I can never know. But I shall always wonder about it. At any rate, I still say I did what I thought best and it saved my life. That's the test.

Now I was isolated on a primitive island which I soon learned, from sign language and guesswork, was visited every four months by a native island trader. The copra schooner had just left a couple of weeks before. More than three months before it would come again. Three months out here on a lonely, unvisited tropic island.

Sitting in a semicircle about me and towering over me were twenty massively proportioned black men. Their faces, their voices, their attitudes, were friendly. I was sure they were peaceful people to be isolated with.

The average height of the bushy-haired men was a mite short of six feet, some of them running to six feet four and six feet six inches. They are what you would call "built like a brick jailhouse." They are the healthiest looking humans I have ever seen. Their teeth, which they never brush, are straight and beautifully white.

Ordinarily they dress only at the loins, men and women, wrapped around from the waist in the lavish sulu which extends to the knees. The women expose their breasts commonly — that is, all except the younger unmarried women, known as Marys, who almost never do. These islanders have a precocious, apt look, and a graceful stately carriage from balancing their food at the ends of poles across their shoulders and porting it over narrow jungle trails. They are broad at the nostril, thick at the lip, and their hair runs to a great halolike bushiness which is both ornamental and traditional. Their generous hearts, I soon learned, are the biggest part of them.

They represent the inbreeding of Melanesian with Polynesian and Tongan. A unique Negroid people are the result.

Here there is no malaria, no tropical ulcers, no dread European diseases. The "advantages" of civilization, happily, haven't invaded this remote corner of the world — and I hope they never do! Every indication of vital health is rampant. The greatest and often most unobtainable desires of so-called civilization — peace, quiet, security, health — are here the simplest commonplaces.

Now that Una had nurtured me through the first two critical days, my condition improved rapidly. The natural food of the island agreed beautifully with me. On the third day I was able to stand shakily; on the fifth I could walk to the door with the cane Itchy made me from *Pagan's* timbers and peer out at the village and call to my growing circle of friends.

Itchy also made me a rather imposing looking chair which I called my throne. I sat in it during the days that I waited for strength to come to my legs so I could walk. The natives sat around me in a deep circle, watching curiously anything I did. I was the first white man to stay on the island, though a few had visited it.

A large number of the natives gathered at Itchy's hut every night to puff at their hand-rolled jungle cigarettes and chat together over the dim lantern. On my third night at the village I was in good spirits for the first time since my rescue. I was coherent and able to sit unassisted in my chair. After a few jovialities they began asking me about the circumstances of my arrival on the island. To answer them was no easy job.

There were about fifteen words of English known to them and the same number of words of their language known to me — but luckily we had hands.

First I had to remind them that there had been a war; and that it was over. Then I explained that I had a wife, showing them Mary's pictures which I had crammed in my shirt pockets when I ate my wallet, and the white space around my finger where there had been a ring till I grew so skinny it had slipped off. I also told them that I was from the "island" of America, far away, of which they had heard. And that Mary was from the "island" of Australia. I scribbled a sprawling map on a sheet of paper, drawing in popular landmarks, including Tuvutha. They were astounded that their island was so small.

I showed them New York, Frisco, New Orleans; and explained the impossibility of obtaining transport to my bride of long absence from any of these places. I drew in Panama and indicated I had sailed from there aboard *Pagan*. I first impressed on them its great distance by pointing in a high, exaggerated arc out to and over the horizon. Then I took the approximate width of Tuvutha, one mile, and multiplied it many many times by flashing and closing my palms before them, at the same time tracing the path of my voyage on the crude map. Their credulity was strained, and yet I hadn't made the distance great enough: such a distance was incomprehensible to them.

Then one of them asked me what had happened to my shipmates aboard *Pagan*, and how many there had been. I hastened to explain there were no shipmates, that I had sailed alone. He asked the whys and wherefores of my thin bones and my being wrecked out on the reef, and again he asked where my crew mates were. I explained I was alone, that I had sailed singlehanded. He didn't understand and asked me if, in my extremity, I had eaten them. I hastened to assure them all that I had sailed from Panama entirely alone. Since they couldn't conceive of anyone attempting such a voyage singly, they couldn't accept explanations. The fellow still didn't comprehend.

Another came forward. He asked in most precise pantomime if I had eaten my crew members. He even went to the extreme of holding my arm and champing at it by way of explanation. At this point I am sure they all believed I was a cannibal. Not a breath was taken as all leaned on the next words I should utter. With the most articulate puppetry, I re-enacted the whole voyage, stressing particularly that I had started out solo; and even if I had had someone with me I would not have eaten him.

Episode after episode I related, right up to the night of rescue. Throughout, they were geared to attention; amazed and impressed in turn. The islander is strictly a seaman at heart. For the island in a sense is a ship perpetually at anchor. Things of the sea are deeply involved with his life. His respect for a seaman is unlimited; often the chieftains are such by virtue purely of their prowess at the helm.

My exploit struck them in a vital spot — though I am sure they couldn't see why I had done it for a mere woman. But since I was from "civilization" I am sure they forgave me this queerness. With childlike appreciation they demanded unanimously to hear the account again. So, not suspecting what I was getting into, I repeated the wild yarn, word for word, action for action.

They received it jubilantly; and wanted to hear it still again. To a man they shouted *talanoa* (story). Their simple, earnest appreciation threw me on my beam ends. To get out of the rut I seemed to have got into I insisted that they sing for me instead.

In their ready way they were agreeable.

They sang their ancient battle songs in booming, hypnotizing tones. They sang in a stately, ever-varying chant accompanied by solemn chords from a ringing triangular iron. The effect was gripping. The singers themselves were highly affected, seeming to be in a semi-trance. They sat hunched loosely forward, head down, eyes partly veiled with the profound emotion of their music. The dogs howled mournfully.

When the singing ended I thought the party was over. But then they insisted that I sing for them. This nearly floored me. Not only was I stricken with stagefright, but I'm not musically inclined. Truth is, I sing as most people scream. However, they insisted, so I prepared for a questionable debut.

The only thing I could think of was "Deep in the Heart of Texas," so I sang it. It went over big. It was a raving success. They crowded close, wanting more. I gave them next "The Star-Spangled Banner," which was a little slow for their taste, so I livened things up with "Roll Out the Barrel." This was right up their alley, so I led on with "Waltzing Matilda," an Aussie song, and tried to end the show with "Pistol Packin' Mamma." Once again they were laid in the aisles. I sang the rousing football song of the University of California (my alma mater) and before they could importune me further I gave the "all's finished" signal, and made ready to bed down. Una, seeing I was tired, took my part and the party dispersed.

The first week my stern dietician allowed me only soft foods like boiled fish, baked breadfruit, chicken skin, *kumala, uve* (a type of yam), turtle eggs, boiled eels, mangoes, pineapple, and papaya. I couldn't eat much at a time before my jaws tired, or my swallowing apparatus failed. Too, my shrunken stomach filled with only a few bites and before I could eat on I had to wait for digestion. I was constantly hungry. I ate as often as my complicated conditions permitted.

I took meals from a kind of table Itchy had pounded together from my faithful fore scuttle that had taken such a drubbing from head seas during the hurricane, and from which on many occasions I had stood squinting hopefully across the bows for land. Now I was eating from it!

I ate about seven meals a day, arising at least twice in the night. I had but to say "*Una, kai kai*" (food). She always stirred from her sleep uncomplainingly, elbowed Itchy, and the two of them prepared something for my middle-of-the-night snacks. Itchy lit the fire and warmed whatever Una decided I could have. Then Una would sit beside me, breaking the hot food into small bits, taking out bones, handing it to me, and speaking fast, strange words if I didn't chew well.

I always felt bad when I roused them from a deep sleep. But as it was I hadn't strength to sit, and when strength came, it was too painful to sit long because of my bony hanks. You have no idea what it is to sit or lie on fleshless bones. The Fijians don't know of inner-spring mattresses. My bed, of leaves stripped from coconut fronds, was as hard as *Pagan's* bunk boards, only harder since I had no blanket now. I felt like a ship in dry dock — shored up by my bones.

One night I attempted to climb to my feet with my cane and stagger across the room to the food shelf so as not to impose on Una and Itchy. I had a preview of what it is to be ninety. With mincing, shaking steps I got under way. Fijian children sleep where tiredness finds them. Halfway across the large room my toe touched a leg and I went reeling amidst the family of six boys. Oh the torture of being fallen on by a bony man! Judging from the squawks of the waking boys there are few things worse — like being hit by a gunny sack of wood, or worse. Una admonished me severely for not calling her. I was fed and carried back to my bed, where I slept till my intricate hunger mechanism could manipulate again.

At the end of the first week, Una and Itchy let me know that henceforth I could have any food I wanted. I promptly pointed out a small pig rooting on the common. In a short time the village boys were in wild chase, and the piglet was in the pot. Soon I was happily gnawing pork joints. Thereafter, anything I wanted was lavished on me.

From this time on Tuvutha became a shipwrecked seaman's paradise. First of all, every article of *Pagan's* gear found on the beaches or floating on the lagoon or otherwise gleaned from the reef or the sea floor was brought to me by the natives. Everything was spread out before me and what I wanted I dragged toward me, the rest I pushed back.

I kept only one of the suits of clothes and a dress shirt. My feet were too swollen for weeks to wear shoes; so I gave them to those who found them. They fitted only the small boys: the men's feet were like pillows. The remainder of my gear — several suits of khakis and an odd assortment of clothing — I handed out so that as many as possible could have an article to wear.

The pleasantest surprise came when my jewelry was returned. My silver identification wristlet, bought in England at the first of the war, and my gold wedding band from Australia, were laid before me. I was delighted. I had never expected to see them again after they dropped off my fleshless hands. The sharp-eyed divers had seen them flash at nine fathoms on the lagoon floor and retrieved them.

The *sulu,* or loincloth, wrapped about the waist and twisted under is all I wore the whole time on the island. "Going native" was fun. The Fijians got a kick out of it too.

When I was able to walk I spent my days wandering through the village, limping at half pace on my cane. At Lomaloma you don't knock, you just walk in.

I spent many of my visits in the home of the village schoolteacher. My ambition is to be a schoolteacher, so we spent a lot of time talking shop.

The village chief, Tupa, and I became great buddies also. Several times I was invited in for *kai kai* and one night I received his supreme compliment: I slept in his *koro* (house).

That night Tupa and I sat talking across the pale lantern. He prepared his native smoke, drying a greenish leaf over a smoldering coconut husk, and rolling it in dried banana stripping. Someday, he said, he was going to the island of America.

He pulled heavily on the weak cigarette with his thick lips. He had heard at Vanuambalavu, in his youth, of great hotels and their fabulous elevators that take you flying between floors in buildings higher than coconut palms. His black calloused hand rose in a quick glide; his face gleamed. He wanted to live in a hotel and take high rides.

He blew a whiff of smoke from his wide nostrils. The trains. He wanted to ride on them; he wanted to attend the theaters; eat in the great restaurants; visit the big homes — Tupa is going to do everything when he comes to America. The muscles under his black skin quivered with excitement as he told me. An infinite vision was in his eyes.

To him America will be another Tuvutha. He will go where he wants and have a good time. Americans will open their hearts to him as his island did to me.

That night before I slept, I prayed in my usual orisons

that the stately chief would never be allowed to fulfill his naïve simple dream.

Another of my friends, the grizzled old God-fearing native pastor, spent many an afternoon limping with me along the beach, talking of many things. Often we dwelt on my profound experience when I refound Va Kalou (God) out on the lonesome sea. He too had found Va Kalou in early life in stress and storm between the islands on his outrigger.

He had been crippled as a young man in a heavy offshore blow. He had foundered some five miles from land and had swum to shore only to be battered by the high seas on the coral reefs. Only Va Kalou could have saved him, so he gave his life in service to Va Kalou. He had been educated for the divinity in a Methodist school in Lakemba, capital of Lau. That was thirty years ago. Over the years he managed to hang onto ten or fifteen English words he had picked up at the trading post, with which we discussed the religion of his little wooden church and local gossip.

I asked him one day, because of my interest in sociology, what the divorce rate was among the natives. I had an idea it would be low — I knew it wouldn't be of the staggering proportions of the rate at home. He didn't understand what I meant. I was more explicit when I reasked. Still he cocked his head and squinted his eyes in perplexity.

I went to the extremes of description. I explained in my petty vocabulary and pantomime the marriage ritual. He comprehended. I indicated ten marriages, of ten men and ten women — Fijians of course. He nodded understandingly. Now, I asked very carefully, at what rate — that is, how many out of ten or a hundred — did they separate? He looked blank.

He could follow me to a point, but from there he was lost.

Then I knew the trouble. He couldn't reach me in what I sought to describe, because in his total experience no such occurrence had crossed his path. There was no such word as divorce in his vocabulary; no such custom in his island lore. He couldn't conceive of it . . . I couldn't explain it, nor could you. To his mind, marriage was marriage; and that is that. There was no divorce. People married and stayed married.

Another thing I saw in my travels about the village was the courtship ritual. There were at least three matches in the process of making that I could observe — and often the young couples were near as I hobbled about.

The young man, seeking among the village belles his choice of mate, upon finding her manages at all available moments to be somewhere within her sight. This, of course, appears quite "accidental." No matter what his preoccupation, whether it be work, play, or just loafing, most or all is done within sight of the beloved. These activities, however, are of such a nature as to impress the young lady with the young man's qualities as a possible husband.

The young Mary, by the same token, observes these advances, but of course appears not to see them. But at the same time she too turns up quite "accidentally" in his presence, rushing hurriedly about her mother's housewifely chores. This process goes on from a few short weeks to months. Then comes the final act in the affair, an ultimate test which determines whether or not the relationship shall dissolve or continue.

The young Mary, at the moment she concludes that here at last is the man in her life, in an "accidental" way allows her *sulu* to sag to her waist, or her simple cotton blouse to fall open at the front, exposing her breasts. This, the most intimate show of affection, saves the young man the strain of proposing.

The parents of the two — who all along have slyly observed developments — now, upon seeing this fullest show of affection, negotiate a marriage, which, as I learned later, soon takes place. After the marriage, the young couple separate, each returning to his respective home as formerly. On a day soon after, the whole village joins in to erect a *koro*, whereupon the newlyweds move in and set up housekeeping.

In my further travels, I met Cama, a philosopher. He too had been led to the island metropolis at Lakemba by the lure of education — to be a schoolteacher. But after two years of truck with formal knowledge and the faithless promises of civilization he returned to primitive Tuvutha. For over twenty years he had forsworn his books and his desire to bring education to his island.

Cama had a wistful face when he said the native's greatest need was to be protected from the evils of civilization. He too had a ten-word English vocabulary. But philosophers like Cama don't need an extensive word range — for they speak with ideas in the large; a universal language.

He swept his hand over the peaceful valley at the foot of the extinct volcano. What need of the outer world here? Here there is no criminality, no economic competition, no sexual perversion. The old, the infirm, never worry. Good health is unavoidable, peace has no option. If there is sickness, the jungle abounds with healing herbs. Witness my improved coral poisoning, the healing of my poisoned knee, the very fact that I was alive and not dead as all had expected.

I told him about the war, of which hints had come to the

island. He was glad to hear it was over. When I explained the devastation of the atomic bomb he was horrified. Later, the chief, schoolteacher, and pastor came to ask if this were true. I nodded gravely. They looked at me from inscrutable masks.

To impress them I explained. I used my hand to indicate an airplane, which they recognized. I whistled as I indicated a falling bomb — and then said *"Boom,"* as it supposedly struck. This too they comprehended, for they had some idea of bombs. Then I inferred that the plane was flying over the island. Raising a finger I said, "One atomic bomb," then showed it falling — explaining that it should hit at mid-island. In a motion I pantomimed that Tuvutha had been wiped out, everyone killed, the very air seared and infected. They were astonished. The old philosopher walked away shaking his head.

Another time toward the end of that first week, the five of us sat sipping the healthful coconut milk in the chief's hut. We were talking in our limited way at odds and ends. I told them of the starvation of the "islands" Europe and India. I went on to explain the shortages of England and China and Russia. I told of war shortages in food the world over.

They were in high satisfaction when I informed them that only Tuvutha, in all the world, had no shortages. They had all heard of the fabulous island of America. To their circumscribed minds all lands were islands. They couldn't believe that *kai kai* could be scarce in America. By my telling of that condition, their deformed little island became infinitely swelled with importance.

At another time, waiting to accompany a fishing trip out

on the lagoon, I described the Empire State Building, our whizzing automobiles, our skies dark with planes. I explained the movies, huge universities, and the Golden Gate Bridge. They couldn't fashion in their minds what their ears heard.

The pastor asked me if there were magnificent churches. I told him yes, but it would have been unfair not to say that the beer joints, pool halls, and night clubs were far more numerous and better patronized. Before any more embarrassing questions arose, I made adieus. They were loth to end the discussion: I was glad. Among them America's reputation by hearsay was high; I wanted the illusion to hold, so I left to go down to the lagoon beach where the outriggers were moored in readiness for the day's fishing.

A few of the village children were around to see the boats away. As yet the elders had not come from their *koros*, except for one of the Marys dressed in *sulu* and soft cotton blouse, who stood tending an outrigger, its bow resting on the beach. She helped me gain the narrow flat deck, then shoved off well onto the lagoon to tread water and await the others.

I sat facing forward, watching the activity ashore or the colorful marine world below. Suddenly something whizzed over my shoulder and plopped on the deck in a sort of receptacle near the bow — and when I saw it, I couldn't believe it: it was the Mary's soft cotton blouse!

I knew what it meant for a Mary to loosen her blouse at the front to a man — but to remove it! I gulped! And surely I must have blushed. To me there was nothing "accidental" about this: it was entirely purposive, a desperate show of intention, yet she seemed so unconcerned.

I wondered how I could say in a tactful way, to one who

didn't speak my tongue, that I was already married — happily married.

Ashore the other outriggers were pushing off to join us. Inside I stirred desperately. But as the boats glided up, I saw a startling thing. There were some seven Marys on the five craft, and all of them, after the normal manner of the married women, were undressed to the waist. Then it all came clear. The women are the chief divers, and with divers any kind of clothing above the waist is undesirable; and since fish spearing involves much underwater activity, the women — even the Marys — wear their *sulus* from waist to knees only.

The Mary on the stern was still regarding the water in a very unconcerned way. I heaved a long, peaceful breath and settled back to enjoy the trip.

CHAPTER XXIV

Going Native

I FIRST ATTENDED the native church on my seventh day on the island. Fijians attend church three times on Sunday: early morning, afternoon, and dusk. Wednesday morning too, at dawn, is a church date. The *lalo,* or native ceremonial drum, calls the hour of church. I went clad in my wrinkled blue suit wearing socks to hide my puffed, poisoned feet.

The women enter first and sing a long mournful song for about ten minutes. They seat themselves on the floor on the left side of the room at the front. When the mournful song is finished the men come in and sit on the right. Behind them in neat rows are the boys, and to the left the girls.

The natives are a beautiful sight on church day. The halo of dark frizzy hair is combed and oiled to eye-catching perfection. Sunday-best *sulus* are broken out and short-sleeved colorful shirts are worn. Where the skin shows it is oiled with *wali wali,* an aromatic coconut oil, which makes it coppery.

The proceedings, despite the Fijians' natural religious seriousness, have a dash of humor. In the back of the room sits one of the village elders, glowering over the boys. He carries a thin, twenty-foot rod. Let one of the boys scant his sabbath duty, and he is nicked sharply on the head. The little boys, in fearful fervor, bend to their songs and prayers.

My throne was placed beside the pulpit. The pastor and

his two assistants were last to enter. The pastor was wearing my pin-stripe tan coat which he had found in the wreckage. He had offered it back — but I insisted that he keep it. It was a late collegiate cut, three buttons down the front and abbreviated lapels. The sleeves struck him well above the wristbone, and across the front it was tied with a string — since it wouldn't button around his massive chest.

Services commenced with a deep-throated, fast-moving chant accompanied by the time beat on a steel triangle. A highly persuasive prayer then ensued from one of the deacons. When he finished he mopped his tear-stained cheeks with a large white handkerchief. He prayed directly to God and not with the honeyed words or through the ears of a fastidious parish.

Another weird thrilling song was voiced up. The other deacon, my philosopher friend, poured some of the salt of his wisdom into a very moving prayer. He too wept openly as he prayed. It was strange to see these towering, heavily muscled men weeping volubly on their knees. Another song ricocheted around the close walls; and my friend the pastor advanced to the pulpit.

The sermon that followed was the most convincing that I ever heard: yet I knew not a word that he spoke. He expounded the Word in no uncertain terms. In thundering tones, with his great fists beating the pulpit, he dinned his inspired message into every rapt ear.

A final song was sung and services were concluded.

I took a stroll around the barren little room. The pulpit and two crude benches were its only ornamentation. It didn't even have a kerosene lamp on the ceiling. On one wall was a colorful whisky advertisement showing a picture of a shark. The walls and floors on the inside were unpainted. Church!

The church was about twelve years old, paid for by the natives from their copra gathering and built by the Colonial British Government.

That afternoon I enjoyed one of the most delightful treats of my whole stay in Fiji. Una had caught me an *uga vule* (pronounced "oonga vooly") or giant coconut crab. It was the first I had ever seen, like something out of *King Kong* in the miniature.

Offhand he appears to be a compromise between a crab, a lobster, and a tarantula. The width of his great claws is often more than two feet, and the plier-like, heavily toothed pincers on the end can amputate a finger. On the very stern end of the *uga vule* is a fist-sized round shell, looking like a small bag. When captured he is kept alive as a future food supply by a vine tied to this bag and suspended from a limb, or the hut ceiling. Hanging thus, claws down, he is helpless. He lives by climbing palms and cutting down the nuts from which he tears away the tough fiber, somehow breaking open the tougher nut and consuming the milk and soft meat inside.

The delicious white meat of the giant crab is a meal for three men. It is tastier than lobster. I often had lobster, or *urau* as it is called, but never when I could have *uga vule*. The meat is most toothsome when boiled, though the natives prefer it roasted in the shell over hot coals. The saclike pod on the creature's back contains a rich natural sauce which seasons the soft sweet meat.

The islanders were unusually kind and generous with food. Not a meal passed but that a dozen contributions came in from the fires of the surrounding huts. When the fishermen returned at night from the coral lagoon, they always brought a delicacy or two. The men who foraged each day in the jungle invariably returned with some special fruit or vegetable. Even the children at their play ran upon odd tidbits in the jungle or along the sea front and brought them timidly forth.

Whatever was offered me, I ate. I never questioned the validity of a single bite. If I needed reassurance there was plenty of it. The natives in their buoyant health were bounteous guarantors for their food. Their beautifully muscled bodies, milky teeth, perpetually pleasant dispositions — in general, their health and verve — were a perfect testimonial to the fare they thrived on.

I ate baked eels and raw turtle eggs with perfect aplomb. Boiled octopus, fish heads, and dried sea worms — no matter what, I took them all as they came. Una prepared many odd dishes for me. Some of them looked mighty queer, but so long as my strength grew and the wrinkles filled out. I didn't care what she stewed up.

Whatever I wished to eat, I had only to suggest. I had but to say "*Kai kai uga vule*" and Una strode off into the jungle, returning in a while with one of the giant coconut crabs. If it was eels I wanted or turtle soup, or if it was lobster or clams, Una always took up her burlap sack and walked wordlessly off to the lagoon. If it was a fruit or vegetable from the jungle I wanted, Itchy or one of his six boys swung onto one of the narrow jungle trails and soon brought it in.

On Sunday night after my first week on the island I began to snap out of weakness. My body began to look like what a body should look like. A padding of flesh appeared around my thighs and I could sit down on my bones without needing to support part of my weight on my hands. The cushioning effect was better for sleep, too. Flesh was appearing throughout the body, which, because of my seemingly large hands and feet, made me look less like a clubfooted pup.

The next morning, Monday, November fourth, I felt strong enough to think in terms of getting off the island and continuing my journey to Australia. I called Itchy and gave him the lowdown. I told him I wanted to get going. He looked grave and displeased; but he called a few of his neighbors to sit in on the plans.

They were introduced, but the names turned out to be unrememberable, so I just called them Joe, Bill, and Mike. I proposed to them that we doctor up one of the outriggers and weigh anchor for Lakemba, about forty miles away. This they vetoed immediately. It was the hurricane season, a time of variable winds and unpredictable calms. Too risky; don't be in a hurry; take it easy, they said.

Itchy suggested we await the arrival of the copra boat in January. All agreed that it would be better to wait than venture out on the sea and made to adjourn the meeting. I said no, and explained I hadn't seen my wife in eighteen months, and couldn't wait any longer.

They listened as I unfolded a plan for signaling passing ships, provided there were passing ships. My sails, though chewed by the reef, were somewhat intact; so was my halyard and the copper block to heave the sail up with. I proposed we cut the top out of a prominent coconut tree and rig my gear to it, so we could raise and lower the sail as a signal if we sighted a ship.

That afternoon my ragged little mainsail was fluttering from the bald head of a conspicuous coconut palm.

In the evening the chief informed me that a ceremonial *Yangona* or native beer bust was to be held in my honor. I didn't know what he was talking about, but if it was going to be fun, I assured him I wouldn't miss it.

Shortly after, I was seated on my throne at the apex of a circle of cross-legged men on the floor of the chief's *koro*. From where I sat in my rickety varicolored chair made from *Pagan's* timbers, I looked down on the whole assemblage: a sort of king of nothing. Several weak lanterns dimly bathed the dark room. The men were in a festive mood. Elbows on knees they chatted pleasantly, waiting for the ceremonial to commence. All the village elders were present. Young boys, teen-agers, were allowed to look on from the door.

To the center of the circle walked four village girls, who sat facing me. They were to perform a *meke ta*, or dance in my honor as guest. Four more came in and sat down back to back with the others, facing away from me. Another sat just inside the doorway with the inevitable iron triangle and bar to beat time.

The faces of all were decoratively smeared with white paste. Garlands of hibiscus fiber, dyed purple and entwined with flowers, hung about their necks. Their breasts, arms, and legs glistened coppery with *wali wali*. On their wrists, ankles, and upper arms were bands of coconut frond and flowers. In their beautifully groomed bushy hair, and behind their ears, were flowers. In the right hand of each was a flower.

The time beater at the doorway started the ball rolling. The girls facing away from me sang one of the rich tribal songs and all clapped in unison. Those facing me sang with the others, at the same time waving the hands and arms gracefully in pattern. The expressive arm and hand movements were telling a story I couldn't follow, but it was beautiful and sincere. What ensued was a dance sitting down — which is the way the Fijians do it.

As the dance progressed the girls changed places several times; the singing grew to a high pitch, and more expressive and picturesque movements came into the dance. In fact, by the time they finished they had done everything possible to do sitting down, short of standing and dancing.

I arose and applauded, and insisted on shaking the hand of each performer as an appreciative gesture. Such enthusiasm prompted them to put the whole show on again. The next time I merely smiled.

Then came the *Yangona*. This comes under the title of Fijian alcoholism, without the imputation of Alcoholics Anonymous. *Yangona* is a native drink the partaking of which hasn't the distasteful results that our own similar "ceremonials" involve. The drink is evidently healthful. It is enjoyed only by the men, and then only on special occasions.

It is prepared by pounding the kava root in a hollowed log stump and mixing the pulpy root with water by hand in a large shallow wooden bowl. The pulp is strained from the water through the fibers of the hibiscus plant, leaving the water brownish and "spiked."

The leader of the singers then comes in, sitting respectfully before the kava bowl. She claps twice as a traditional expression of reverence, and a coconut shell is filled from the bowl and handed her. This she brings to me, the guest, who quaffs it off and passes the shell back. It is refilled and taken to the chief. And thence to every Tom, Dick, and Harry till the bowl is emptied. Then a new decoction is made up. While the drinks are being passed and while fresh bowls of the brew are being mixed, the men chatter and banter across the circle.

Yangona has a taste that is indescribable. But there is nothing mysterious about its effect. It is heady, inducing a giddy drowsiness. I should have quit after my second round. By the tenth, I was all for singing "Deep in the Heart of Texas," and raising general hell with the boys. Shortly after, Itchy wisely decided it was time to take me home before the party got too rough.

The next morning I had a hangover which was nothing more than a semi-diarrheic condition. It left me a bit shaky at the knees. Among the healthful qualities of *Yangona* is its action as a physic.

Una fed me lightly on breadfruit noodles cooked in coconut milk with *vasua* or clam. I washed it down with lemon-grass tea and had a papaya to finish with. She scolded Itchy for leading me astray in "that den of iniquity."

That afternoon of the fifth of November was spectacular. Shortly after lunch a cry rent the village. There was something on the horizon. A sail! Itchy and Mike came dashing in, overflowing with gibberish and pointing to seaward excitedly. I knew it was a ship from the cry of "*laca mota*" from the beach, and sought my walking stick.

Itchy was impatient with my slow gait — he picked me up in his arms and ran across the village with me as though I were a stalk of bananas. Gione, one of his sons, brought my throne. Sitting on the beach, I could see the sail and part of the cabin of a copra schooner making down the coast.

Mike and Joe were working the sail. When I said "Up," they hoisted it. When I said "Down," they hauled it in. The vessel moved along till she was abeam of us. Mike and Joe agitated the sail madly. I stood on my chair waving my cane and shouting; everybody was doing something to attract attention. We screamed, we jumped, we waved. The vessel moved serenely down the coast and out of sight. I felt empty. Everybody looked disappointed, but Una seemed pleased that the boat hadn't seen the signal, and hadn't come for me. She came up and let me know that I wasn't *bula* (strong) enough to leave the island.

I concluded that there wasn't enough diversion in the sail alone to catch attention. Possibly it couldn't be seen from so great a distance; even if it could, it might not be recognized as a danger signal. I told the chief and suggested we build some brush piles on the beach to be lit next time we sighted a sail or funnel. He agreed. At his command all the boys in sight hustled into the jungle. Soon four impressive tinder heaps graced the beach.

Itchy was dead set on giving me a shave and trimming my hair. He had been agitating to do it all week, and each day I had stalled him. I dreaded this worse than tooth pulling. Many times I had seen the men shave themselves with cold water, laundry soap, and razors honed on a chunk of grindstone. Itchy was determined to get to the bottom of my whiskers. I could delay no longer.

My beard was five inches long and blond as platinum, from the constant touch of the sun. My hair had overgrown my ears and forehead, and was well down toward my shoulders. It too had been breathed on from above and was streaked with blond. It was all this blond business behind the sun-browned face that had so startled the beachcombing children that day I had peered down on them from my aerie in the rocks.

Itchy had an old pair of dull scissors for the shearing. Bill, Joe, and Mike oversaw the job. Hair flew and whiskers scraped. After an hour of manhandling and unforgettable misery I was bald-faced and near bald-headed.

Seeing myself just after being shaved was a jolt. It was a foreview of what I may be at ninety-nine. A skeleton of my real self peered back from the glass: wrinkled at the deep-sunk eyes; enlarged at the cheekbones and shallow in the cheeks; heavily veined over the forehead: bony at the jaw and throat; wide at the ears. From cheekbones to hair line was a swath of sunburned color; below was sallow flesh long hidden by my beard.

CHAPTER XXV

A Sail!

THERE HAD BEEN SOME TALK over the last few days of an *uga vule* hunt. Una told me that one had been planned for me. It would consist of a large party — Bill, Joe, Mike, Too-kai, and Suvi and all their family. We would leave next morning, early, to be gone for three days.

I knew nothing about an *uga vule* hunt — but I was raring to go.

At daylight I wobbled down to Itchy's outrigger and climbed aboard. Six other outriggers were assembled; families and gear were aboard. Everybody was in festal mood. The village lined the strand to wave us away. My throne was lashed aboard and we shoved off. Itchy stood on the dancing bow punting the thin shallow hull along at lively speed with a long pole. Una stood on the stern helping with the same man's job.

Later, when we changed course and the wind hauled round to aft, two heavy coconut fronds were stuck in the bow and the wind pushing against them drove us along effortlessly. Una laid aside her pole and steered from the stern with a large paddle.

The purpose of an *uga vule* hunt is to mix work with pleasure and at the same time inject the quest for food. This became apparent as the hunt progressed. As we glided over the coral bottom all eyes searched the coral shelves for signs of life.

Suddenly Itchy splashed overboard, spear in hand. Leaning over the side I watched him jerk downward through six fathoms of water, overtaking a large sea turtle that had seen us and plunged. Itchy stopped in mid-water, hovering over the turtle. His muscles tensed, then rippled, and I could see he was jabbing viciously. Then he reached for the surface with long strokes, towing his kill behind.

About two miles away from the village we nosed into a flat depression on the rocky coast. It was fronted by a white beach and planted to coconut trees. The boats pulled in and threw out their stone anchors made fast to the boat by vines. Una went ashore to stew tea for my morning meal, for I still ate every three hours. Itchy carried his copra knife, burlap bags, and axe ashore.

Mike's wife brought me some "cat's eyes," on the back of which grows a sweet-meated little animal you eat raw. I had them with *kumalas*, bananas, and tea for my morning snack.

The hunt was to take us right around the island. At each coconut patch we were to stop and gather the copra, or coconut meat. When the copra work was done the women were to pitch in and comb the area in search of the *uga vule*. Then we would load the copra and the *uga vules*, if any, and proceed on along the coast to the next open shore grown to coconut palms.

The coconut palm is the basic commodity in native life. The meat and milk of the green nut are an important liquid and food of the diet. Later, when the husk has dried and the nut matured, a coconut "cream" for cooking is obtained, as well as *wali wali* or ointment for the skin. The husk is used for fires, for smoking the *koro* against mosquitoes, and making sennit or native rope. The dried meat of the mature nut is shredded and eaten or is sold or traded as copra, about the only source of income open to the native.

The plaited fronds of the palm serve as building material for house roofs and walls, mattresses for the beds, baskets and fans. The bole is used for uprights, crossbeams, and the ridgepole in the hut.

When we made our first stop the coconut harvest was on. At a bark from Itchy the boys hurried off into the palm thicket carrying coarse jute bags. Each family worked separately, and for itself. Itchy and Una had an edge with four sons in the field. The boys' job was to quest for the brown dried nuts, and when their bag was filled to bring them in to Una. She, working with the axe, split each nut in halves with a stroke and dropped them near Itchy, seated close by.

Itchy with the double-edged copra knife in hand, twisted the white meat from the shell by a magic motion. It was tossed in a pile and later sacked. Soon the area was depleted of suitable coconuts. While the men sacked the harvest and loaded it on the outriggers, the women went deftly into the jungle in search of the *uga vule*.

Searching out the *uga vule* is an extreme test of eyes and intimate knowledge of the denizen's habits. He lives in the rocks, burrows in the undergrowth, and is difficult to ferret out and subdue. Unfortunately I was still too weak to follow into the jungle, so I missed seeing how the captures were made.

In less than an hour six *uga vules* showed up among the huntresses, so we moved on.

The fronds perched in the bow caught the wind and

pushed us off onto the lagoon. One, two, four, five, seven, nine fathoms of lucent water showed under the hull. A coral tip, or a shell, or a fish at that depth is as clear as in the hand. I liked nothing better than lying on the outrigger deck searching into the constant puzzle of the lagoon bottoms.

"*Vasua!*" A piercing cry from Una. Before I could see her, she was gone. She had dived in. I wriggled around so I could watch her spiral downward through fifty feet of water, spear in hand. Her hair streamed behind. Her vivid *sulu* flashed against slanting sun rays. She pulled up short, settled in slow motion on the ocean floor. Itchy spun the boat around.

Una's objective was a giant Fiji clam. She had spied the open lip and dived on the split second. The clam blends with the coral, as rattlers in the dust. Taking them from where they nestle in the coral can be dangerous.

Itchy had lost his first wife in a tragic episode with the *vasua*. She had hunted alone on the open reef, had thrust her hand under a partly open shell, and it had snapped on her, imprisoning her at the wrist as in a vise. And there she had perished, helpless, before the rising tide.

As Una prepared to approach the clam, to spear him at a vital spot, Itchy poised himself. Spear in hand he was ready to dive down to pry her free should any commotion indicate she was trapped. I leaned more closely to the water to see what Una would do, and to see how she would do it.

She eased over her prey, and by a soft movement slipped her spear point to the shell edge. At this point a motion of water will warn the giant bivalve and he will slap his curving shell edges closed. A crucial moment. In a second she jerked. She thrust quickly, and with a joggling motion she twisted violently. The powerful, vital muscle that clamps the lids shut was severed. Then she seemed to gather herself upward with long strokes and came to the outrigger to breathe. In a moment she dived again. This time Itchy stood poised anew with his spear. Una was still in danger. A shark might be lurking in the coral heads. Una floated onto the living coral floor, spread apart the valves of the clam, and cut away its choice meats. The shell is thick and sometimes weighs hundreds of pounds. Una swam back with the chunks of fat white flesh and heaved them on deck.

Next we stopped at a larger grove farther along the north-west shore, where we lunched. We carried away eleven more *uga vules*. That night our camp was pitched on the north point of the island on the shore of a small embayment. I slept on a mattress of pandanus strippings, in an open clearing of the grove. The stars were my ceiling, while the gentle roar of the tide on the distant reef dulled my senses.

The next morning we crowded our growing copra yield onto the shallow-draft outriggers, pushed off from under bending coconut palms growing over the water, and hauled down the uninviting windward shore.

We made two stops in the morning and one in the after-noon. Itchy and Bill conferred on whether we should at-tempt to make another inlet farther along before dark. They decided yes, so we loaded up and cast off, heading southeast along the cliffy shore.

Before we reached the spot, I could see it around the point ahead. The palm fronds showed over the cruel, jagged lava, near where I had been cast up. We crept up to the point and threw our frail craft into the race that swept past it; and ran with a spurt into the open bay.

There on the exposed sand was a sight I had never dreamed

possible to see. My one-time jaunty little cutter, *Pagan*, lay washed up on the beach — keel deep in sand she was, battered and splintered by her trials. She had scraped over two hundred yards of ungodly reef, floated a mile across the lagoon, and settled on the beach straight and level, with her bow pointed out to sea. There is no logical explanation for it. Nothing I can think of can explain it. She sits there today, hopelessly denuded, wrecked beyond the wildest dream of repair. It is a heavy-hearted sight.

That night I walked over to her, and rubbed her splintered stubs. Few boats have lived her thrilling life. Though her life was short under my hand, she lived it to the full and gave a full measure of service. In our trials together I had come to know my boat as a real person, and now I saw her bones captured by the sand. I felt a welling of deeper sentiment than one should feel over the riven kindlings of a hulk. I caressed her aged timbers, looked the last time over her naked frame, and walked away.

By midmorning the following day the open shores of Pagan's Cove, as I named the miniature bay, were sufficiently hunted; we shoved off. It was from this point that Itchy had embarked the night of my rescue, and groped through the dense jungle and over the ragged rock to me. We passed the sandy nook where the sea had thrown me up; down a short way was the treacherous cove where I had lain the last day and night.

Another mile and we pulled into the last inlet before reaching the village. The spot was too close to Lomaloma to have much copra, and it yielded only three *uga vules*. Here the bags of copra were unloaded and sprinkled over the flat rocks for drying in the sun. In a few days they would be resacked, and placed in special little huts near the village till the copra boat called in January. Before we departed I noticed a new activity.

The women brought long lengths of a brown vine onto the beach. All set to and cut it into twelve-inch lengths. Then on a rock or log it was pounded into wisps and bound in small sheaves. Each outrigger took a number of the pulpy bundles and pushed off. We didn't continue down the shallow coast, but put off into the deeper lagoon.

We hovered over the coral heads, watching the grottoes beneath, where sea life teemed. Presently something was seen in one of the black recesses of a coral peak. All craft hurried to the spot and anchored in a circle over it. Several heavy steel spears were cleared for action on each boat.

The sheaves of pounded fiber were dipped for a long minute and pounded again on the outrigger prows. With these the women swam down into the limpid water, depositing them at arm's reach in the dark openings. The men stood poised on the flat prows, spear in hand, tensed to dive.

Evidently the beaten vine exudes a substance which partly paralyzes, at the same time annoying, the fish. Fish, ordinarily too quick to follow with the eye, drifted lackadaisically from the caverns. The men plunged spear first on the easy prey. In two hours there was fish enough for the village. We filled out extra space with red, blue, green, brown, white, and black fish — some of them four feet long.

At dusk we pulled back once more into the bay of Lomaloma.

In the *keteketes* or baskets were two dozen fish. Also there were two turtles, a number of *uraus*, *vasua*, oysters, eels, turtle eggs, and thirty-seven *uga vules*. The village was festive.

My buddy Tupa, the chief, told me that next day there would be a village feast in my honor.

That night I felt infinitely stronger, something like my old self. The three-day outing had done it: three days of the freshest air I ever breathed, coupled with the rich meat of the *uga vule* and the life-sustaining coconut milk. The whole time I wore only a *sulu*. I lay hours in the sun. I strolled the beaches, or I napped, or I kidded with my friends — a proper combination of activities to restore health.

I looked forward to the coming feast.

The whole morning was consumed in preparation for it. First of all, the native ovens were made ready. These are ingenious devices for baking food in the ground. Broad holes — a dozen of them — about two feet deep were dug. In the bottoms, a bed of glowing coals was built up. Over the searing bed a layer of round stones was placed. The food, well wrapped in banana leaves for preservation, was placed on the hot stones and covered with sand. In three hours it was uncovered, and presto! The meat was so tender it fell from the bones.

Two hefty pigs were slaughtered and committed to the ovens. Ten chickens were baked, a hundred pounds of fish, thirty *uga vules*, *kumalas* by the dozen as well as *jaina* (bananas), *casava* (a type of yam), *mæ* (breadfruit), *uvi* (sweet potato) — everything edible, cookable, and in season. Fruits such as eating bananas, papayas, mangoes, pineapple, passion fruit, and others I neither know nor could remember, were in abundance.

Young coconuts were stacked about to wash the feast down. On Tuvutha a feast isn't a feast unless there is plenty left over.

Palm fronds were cast side by side and end on end half the length of the grassy common in the village center. The food was uncovered from the savory ovens and crowded steaming onto the palms. Within the reach of all was a portion of everything.

We sat down cross-legged — for now I was strong enough and had flesh enough over my bones to sit comfortably — before the unbelievable abundance. My place was that of the guest — at the head of the table. Several leis of stained hibiscus fiber entwined with flowers were given me. In appreciation of the kindness and generosity of the whole village I wore them about my neck, despite their discomfort.

The chief nodded at me to begin. I dipped my fingers in the food within reach and all followed suit. The banquet was on. I ate of everything, as did every feaster. In the next hour we made classic gourmands of ourselves; for we ate to completion, then chatted awhile, and ate again. I grew sick of the sight of food; the very thought of it nearly burst me.

The Fijian loves a heavy eater. The more I ate the more they beamed.

The chief at last arose and gave a pained speech and sat down quickly. The pastor spoke; also the schoolteacher; and my philosopher friend of the wistful face. I was called upon to tell my story; which I did, to the uninhibited delight of all. The girls came forth and performed their gaudy sit-down dance. The chief stood and proclaimed a ceremonial *Yangona* to be held immediately in his hut, and the feast was over.

I was in no condition for a stag party, remembering the effects of the last. To show the boys I could take it, I went, but after my second round begged off and headed for a night of full sleep.

The next week was a hard one for me. I loved the island; I enjoyed being on it; but I longed to be on my way to Mary. At least I wanted to get some word to her and my family that I was safe. On the island I was caged and helpless.

I spent my days in quiet desperation. Hours I stood each day on the beach, searching past the thundering reef to the unbroken horizon. Every minute I hoped for a mast to appear.

To kill time and ease my mind, I strolled endlessly through the settlement, stopping in practically every hut.

I watched the women sitting in their lively social groups weaving intricate floor mats. I watched them beat out the *masi* of the mulberry tree for the decorative tapa cloth. I watched them weave baskets and fans from pandanus and palm leaves. I watched them prepare their foods, mother their children, make their homes.

The women have certain tasks about the village which they are more or less expected to do. However, in the easy life of nature, nothing is definitely the work of one sex or the other. They carry water, collect firewood, assist in preparing the native gardens and in their upkeep. They fish with throwing nets in the lagoons and dive for *vasua*, oysters, and *uraus*. They are the cooks, housekeepers, and family launderers. The Fijians are the cleanest native people I have ever seen. They bathe and wash clothes tirelessly. They keep tidy homes and grounds. Men and women are equally fastidious about their hair, keeping it combed out in a neat frizz.

The life of the Tuvutha native is essentially co-operative, though some of it is communal. The gardens, back in the jungle, are individually owned and planted. The heads of families and their sons work them mostly. When the natives dig their foods from the ground they replant shoots and roots immediately so there is an unending food supply in growth. The richness of the soil requires neither fertilizer, irrigation, nor plowing — merely weeding and simple planting. These jungle gardens yield lavishly.

Fruit groves, native trails, feasts, and the coconut thickets are communal properties. The chief is responsible for them. If they require attention he strolls through the village after dark calling off names and designating chores. And that's that.

Housebuilding and repairs are done after the fashion of the logrolling bees back in Texas — the neighbors all pitch in. The same for boatbuilding.

The old and infirm are easily provided for by the great abundance. Sickness, if any, is herbally treated. A doctor would grow rusty on the island.

An average day of life at Lomaloma is something like this: everyone hits the deck soon after daylight. Nothing much is done till about eight o'clock when the women serve up breakfast. It is a simple repast: usually *kumalas*, fish, boiled bananas, crabs, and fresh fruit.

The women clean house, wash clothes, weave mats. The men sharpen spears or knives, repair the house or boat till about eleven; then they round up their sons and head into the bush for rations. They return around two, laden with baskets of fresh jungle produce carried on the ends of a pole swung across the shoulder.

A medium-sized meal is partaken of. The rest of the afternoon is frittered away — maybe with a short fishing expedition, or a nap, or a social call, or helping the neighbors. The inevitable bath is fitted in.

The evening meal, just at dusk, is the main course of the day. This is the heavy meal, although no Fiji meal is really heavy unless it might be for occasional pork or chicken. The dinner is more elaborately prepared and offers more variety than the earlier meals of the day.

The evenings are spent sitting in doorways, watching the children at play, or chatting with neighbors. About nine o'clock everybody yawns heavily, lanterns go out, and night sounds prevail.

In this atmosphere of balanced tempo I fretted away my days, strolling the beach, eyes on the horizon. My ears were constantly on the alert for the cry that would go up if a sail should be sighted. My mind was in Sydney with Mary. I wondered what she was thinking. Had the long letter I left at Post Office Bay, nearly four months before, been picked up? If so, had she received it?

Unknown to me she had received the letter in early October, postmarked August from Guayaquil. But all she knew was that I had sailed from the Galápagos the last of July, bound westward.

I had expected to arrive in Sydney aboard *Pagan* by the end of September — and here it was half through November. Six weeks overdue! Mary's thoughts must have been very grim.

The morning of November 15 came around. Another day of anxiety was starting in its usual easy way; it was a good time for something to happen. It happened.

A sudden cry went up from the huts on the beach. In a moment it was resounding through the village. When I heard *laca moto*, I knew a sail was on the horizon. I hobbled toward the beach.

It was a sail all right — advancing down the coast. The craft was a motor schooner with an auxiliary sail, and she appeared to be footing it fast. Itchy and Mike began hauling the sail up and down while Bill and Joe lit the four fires and fanned them. Suvi and Tookai ran to and fro waving their fish nets. Una stood by implacable and still. A chorus of shouts went up. Everybody else was in motion.

Red flames broke from the stacks of tinder; blue smoke spiraled upward. Every eye was on the sail, which continued on imperturbably. Twenty minutes passed. The sail altered not a jot. I felt the same sinking feeling I had felt ten days before when we lost the other sail. More fuel was added to the fires.

The sail dropped suddenly out of sight. I knew it couldn't have disappeared over the horizon so soon — I couldn't figure it out. Then I realized that the boat had seen our signal, had dropped the auxiliary sail, and was coming to investigate. Her bow swelled into view, and suddenly I was jumping more wildly than all the rest.

A gang of us jumped on Itchy's outrigger and paddled out to pilot the newcomer through the reef. I made her out to be the *Lae*, a copra schooner of forty-five feet. When we pulled alongside, I went immediately aboard. The captain, a gnarled old Fijian who had seen many years in the island trade, spoke no English. But the mate, a young Tongan, had a speaking acquaintanceship with it.

In slowly spoken words I explained my circumstances and asked him if he could take me off the island. He conferred with the old sea dog, and turned to me saying yes. He explained that the boat was owned by Stockwell, an island trader and copra merchant, from Vanuambalavu. They were out weighing copra and had two islands to visit before returning north.

The ancient schooner rattled its ponderous anchor onto the sandy bottom off Lomaloma. In the friendly manner of the Fijis, the captain, mate, and crew came off with me to stretch their legs.

I walked promptly up to the hut, escorted by Itchy, Bill, Joe, Mike, and Tupa, all looking glum. Una had preceded us long before and had knowingly packed my few belongings in a battered chest given me by Itchy. She stood shaking her head, telling me not to go. My battered old blue suit was hanging ready for me by the door. I took it, stepped inside, unwrapped my *sulu*, and with Itchy's help slipped into the suit, my seedy white shirt, and a clean pair of socks. I walked back into the arena of drawn faces. There was nothing to do but say good-by and go quickly.

The next few minutes were the hardest of my life. How does one say good-by to the people who have saved his life and been the exemplars of kindness and generosity? What the natives saw was a simple handshake all round — but inside I was in a turmoil.

When I shook hands with Una she was still shaking her head and saying I wasn't well enough to go. Everyone who had been so good to me was there. Itchy was looking down at his feet and so was Tupa. Bill, Joe, and Mike were standing apart. The pastor, the schoolteacher, and my wistful philosopher friend looked straight into my eyes and smiled brave smiles. Tookai and Suvi were looking downcast. The families of all stood close around, silent. I felt as though I were doing wrong by leaving, so I hurried.

I waved good-by and hopped into the dinghy. At the last

minute Itchy jumped in, determined to stay to the last. An outrigger came out for him; more good-bys were said; more handshakes; and the anchor was dragged aboard. With the engine roaring and the old boat trembling, we made for the opening in the reef. Itchy's outrigger followed us to the open sea. That was the last I saw of Lomaloma.

CHAPTER XXVI

Australia

We anchored outside the reef off Nayau, a near-by island, the first of the two to be visited, at noon. I went ashore to see the copra weighed, but as soon as the local chief heard of my sea venture, I was ushered off to an impromptu *Yangona*. First a chicken was hastily boiled, a stalk of bananas was brought in, and I ate before the large circle of smiling faces.

I told my boat story by pantomime and the addition of a growing Fiji vocabulary. Once wasn't enough so I labored through it a second time. I was told that the schooner would be shoving off soon for another village down the coast. There was time for a drink of the ceremonial kava. I took it on the run. After thanking them all for their generosity I went to the boat.

The next village was a repeat performance of the first. The worst part was eating another chicken, and more bananas.

Nayau was the island from which Itchy and Una emigrated to find their happiness. I was now in the village where they had formerly lived. I met Una's worn and aged parents, a venerable old couple married forty-two years. Itchy's father was dead but I was taken to his blind old mother. She was told that Itchy had been kind to the *kai vavalage* (white man). She nodded, smiled, and sat quiet.

That night I slept in the hut of Una's parents. Before daylight, as arranged, I was awakened and hustled off to the rattling, trembling schooner. When the sun had been up little more than an hour, we were swinging to anchor off the little island of Thithia, the last step before going on to Vanuambalavu. Off to the southwest, on the horizon, I could see the gray crater top of Tuvutha.

It appears to be the bounden duty of Fijians to be hospitable. I was hardly ashore at Thithia before the "key" to the village was given me. In part payment for the food and comfortable chair that was brought me, I told my boat story twice. There wasn't time for a *Yangona*, so I shook hands with those nearest and was rowed out to the smoking schooner.

We pulled away from the reef making a course of north for the long, twisted island of Vanuambalavu.

There is a radio station there from which I intended to send an immediate message to Mary and to my mother. Also, ships often pass there bound for Suva, main city of the Fijis, I was told. It seemed incredible that in a few hours I would be in radio contact with my wife.

We nosed our way through a perplexing maze of coral reefs and coral heads. The Fiji islands abound in them. Coming up to the anchorage before the white trading post, we let go the anchor, and it rumbled down in a wide bay active with outriggers under sail. A large village, nestling among tall palms, lined the shore.

I went off with the first boat to meet the *vavalage*, Mr. Stockwell. I found him in the warehouse under a wide-brimmed hat, in island shorts and sandals. He was weighing flowing sacks of copra boated in from the outlying isles.

I stepped up and stood leaning on my cane, watching him in the midst of his dickerings with barefoot, stolid natives. He was tanned golden, had a sturdy laugh, and though grayed at the temples he hefted the great sacks to the scales. He saw me with a jolt: it was seldom he saw strange white men.

I introduced myself, clasped his hand, and tried briefly to account for my presence. He smiled quizzically as I talked. On his face was a creeping disbelief of what I was saying. The old sea dog broke in and told of what he had heard at Tuvutha. The young Tongan mate backed him strongly.

In a widening grin of appreciation, and with an occasional "blimey" whispered hoarsely forth as I recounted my siege on the sea, Stockwell listened. At the end of the part about the hurricane he said, "Stone the crows, lad!"

I could tell he was finding it difficult to believe. But he had to believe. There I stood, my bones still prominent from the rigors of my five months' cruise; and the old sea dog and the young Tongan mate pointing out that parts of *Pagan*, from her masthead to keelson, littered the beaches and the village of Tuvutha.

Stockwell sat down and bade me be comfortable. I talked on. He sat with lips apart, his eyes never leaving my face. Suddenly he stood, and taking my arm led me into the trading post and out back to his family quarters. We sat there long hours as I went on with the account of my voyage. When I finished, his first reaction was a lengthy minute of wordless appraisal. He shook his head, smiled, then launched into a series of questions covering the whole voyage. He was keen to know about the hurricane and my prolonged search for land. Finally he said, "You've probably set a record for one man under a jury rig, if it's true you sailed a crippled boat from the Suvorovs to here."

He went on to comment on my luck in slipping into Tuvu-tha past the offshore reefs. Then suddenly he said, "This wife of yours, what's she like? I want to see the woman a bloke would sail the Pacific for." Mary is always a topic of easy discussion for me; a topic of especial fluency, and one which at that moment I was able to expand upon.

At length the topic turned to Stockwell and his existence as an islander. We continued for long hours as he reminisced over over the more than thirty years he had been butting around Fiji as an island trader. He had seen the hulks of many fine craft that had met watery ends along Fiji's iron-bound coasts. I wasn't the first castaway to turn up at Vanuambalavu; and in many cases where the sea had taken a tragic toll there had been no castaways to turn up. He told of sudden hurricanes, shallow offshore coral heads, and treacherous currents. I felt fortunate to be alive, fortunate that there had been no hurricane, that somehow I had sailed past the jagged offshore reefs, and that the treacherous currents had not destroyed me.

The afternoon was wearing on to dusk, and I wanted to get word to Mary and to my people at home. Stockwell reported that the radio was broken down, that there would be no possibility of a message until I could reach Suva Bay on the main island of Viti Levu, some 180 miles to westward. But that was a problem that could wait till after dinner; he ushered me to his generous table.

Mrs. Stockwell, a charming Tongan woman, had prepared a doggoned good "Yankee" dinner for me. It was ham and eggs with real bread, coffee, and apple pie. I had eaten the native foods for so long that it was wonderful to eat the less healthful civilized concoctions again.

That night I slept on a soft mattress. I slept the more soundly because plans had been made as we talked far into the night to send me by launch to near-by Kanathea, where there lay a copra boat inbound to Suva.

After a Sunday breakfast of oatmeal, fried eggs, and pancakes, another welcome Yankee concession on the part of Mrs. Stockwell, I chatted with my genial host on his veranda. We awaited high tide so the launch could top the reef at a break in the island through which I was to pass en route to Kanathea. When the water was up sufficiently I made my adieus, and once again was on the move.

The little launch skirted a tropical coastline fringed with sleeping palms. The islets in the lagoon were misshapen, palm-grown and coral-bound; the breaking water from hidden reefs around them shot up from minute to minute like tiny explosions. Here was a harbor that in the old days had been a roadstead to tall whaling ships and pearlers. Now there were only a few petty copra schooners, and the likes of me, a broken-down twentieth-century castaway en route to his lady love. We passed over the shallow reef between two shoulders of land where the long island parted. Across an open stretch of reefy sea lay Kanathea. Suckling to it was the small copra ship.

A native conned us through the coral heads and soon we were tied alongside the copra boat. She was the *Tui Cakou* — "twee thakow." All steel, about 700 tons, well appointed, and fast. I swung aboard and found the captain.

The little ship was loaded to her Plimsolls and ready to go for Suva. She was waiting for Monday; but first she had to stop at the island of Naitamba for a passenger and small cargo. We lazed away the afternoon fishing from the sun deck.

Before daylight of Monday morning the bow and stern anchors were drawn in and we moved out of the tight coral lagoon. To the right was Vanuambalavu; to the left, Hat Island; and dead ahead the gray dome of Naitamba.

There was no break in the reef through which to make entrance into the lagoon at Naitamba. The ship had to laze back and forth outside the reef and the goods were to be lightered out in longboats under oar. I went ashore with the first boat to the fatly vegetabled island to fetch the passenger and his cargo. Naitamba slopes away from its high rugged end to a low gentle end resting on the water. The low coastal slopes are rich in coconut growth.

We steered in to a short cement jetty built to accommodate copra loading. On its seaward end, greeting us, stood old Gus Henning, a veteran islander and mariner of the Southwest Pacific. I lit as soon as the craft was secured and strode with Henning off to his tropical paradise built up and developed over the years from a desert isle.

I met Mrs. Henning, active and benign, who took us to her capacious lounge where I saw combined the grace of Europe and the cool quiet of the South Pacific. A Fiji Mary, wrapped in her *sulu* and in customary bare feet, slipped in with tea. I told the Hennings the long story of my voyage, only this time I didn't have the gnarled old sea dog to back me up when they questioned its parts.

A castaway's story wasn't a new one for the inhabitants of Naitamba. Many an adventurer down in his luck had passed through there. Yet, despite this, the Hennings were amazed with the difficulties I had encountered in my Pacific traverse;

and they took a heartfelt interest in my trials and my predicament.

Old Gus Henning, himself a veteran sailor of the Fijian group, and, in fact, a large portion of the Southwest Pacific, was sincerely disappointed that I had lost my brave little *Pagan*. Boats and the sea were an abiding love with Gus. He offered to return with me to Tuvutha to determine if *Pagan* could be salvaged. He wanted to see her alive again and before the wind. But I described *Pagan* as I had seen her last: her keel imprisoned in the sand, her lines broken and battered, her bones beginning to parch, and her few salvageable items prize possessions of the natives at Lomaloma.

Mrs. Henning was greatly concerned that Mary in all these months since my departure from the Perlas hadn't received definite word of my whereabouts. Many times she had fretted patiently when Gus's craft, overdue from a long passage, was making its way in. There were no radio facilities on the island or a message would have been readily sent to Australia.

The Hennings had come out from Europe after the First World War to take up plantationing. They reared a family and cultivated an island between the wars. The children left for the second war, and at its finish decided to stay on in England; the Hennings were left with an island full of memories.

Mrs. Henning offered to show me over the plantation. We toured the house. Nothing lacked that I could see. Comfortable ornamental bedrooms. A spacious lounge room; two porches — one glassed in, one open. A well-equipped kitchen. Soft overstuffed furniture; European rugs; radio; maid service by a bevy of Fiji belles. We stepped from the cool, five-room house onto a green sealike lawn which sprawled around it. Next to the house on the fringe of the lawn lay cultivated tropical gardens, towered over by imported shade trees and coconut palms.

Farther on the grounds were fenced and laid out in vegetable gardens. There were cows, horses, and pigs. In the fowl run I saw turkeys, geese, and chickens. A part of the warehouse was given over to a provisions store for the Hennings and the fifty natives who worked the island.

A world of men dream of such a hideaway: the Hennings told me it was very incomplete!

The *Tui Cakou,* with her markings in the water, was ready to sail in midafternoon. She headed out into the Koro Sea, making southwest for Suva. The Fijis are a lovely archipelago to sail through, blue islands to left and right. Through the night as I wakened in hunger and rose to have my customary nightly meals, I thought ahead and hoped for success in my quest for transport on to Australia.

Next morning the little ship was tied bow and stern to the copra wharf at Suva, and I was taking a last look at her. A tall decorative Fijian policeman came for me from the Immigration Department.

To one used as I was to our hard-boiled cops girt with revolvers or carrying clubs, the Fijian arm of the law is a study in contrasts. The weapon carried by the officer who came for me was a ready, jovial smile which completely disarmed me.

He wore the famous, well-groomed, bushy headdress. The navy-blue jacket was collarless and beautifully tailored, set off by polished golden buttons. It disappeared at the waist beneath a colorful crimson scarf, clasped by a thick leather belt buckled in front with a shining brass buckle. From under the bright scarf and reaching to the knees was a white *sulu* with a diamond-shaped hemline. From beneath the white skirt showed the powerful legs and customary bare feet. The result: the world's most colorfully attired police force.

At police headquarters I was accepted and politely passed through with unbelievable facility. In this world where international travel without a visa is next to armed aggression, it was strange not to sign half my life away to the authorities. From the highest commissioner to the lowest barefoot private, I was very patiently handled and cared for.

I was anxious to get a cable, announcing my safe arrival, away to Mary. The commissioner very considerately hurried my papers along.

The cable I sent read: "Am safe and well in Fiji. Taking first ship to Australia. Will cable. I love you. Johnnie."

Almost immediately, and even before Mary could possibly have received my cable, I received a cable from her. She had heard of my wrecking in a news flash, and had rushed a message whose very words showed that a heavy burden of dark uncertainty had been lifted from her mind.

Those words: I read them and reread them; they were a reprieve from doubt, a welcome home, an avenue to a whole new future.

The problem of where to stay while I was in Suva looking for transport was extremely perplexing, because I had six offers from people who earnestly wanted me to stay at their homes. I felt like a heel saying yes to one, since it meant saying no to five others.

Honestly, I don't know why seamen persist in getting wrecked in some of the outlandish places they do, when they can do it in a nice place like Fiji.

I finally decided to stay with young Ernie Hurley, from

Morris-Hedstrom Shipping. He was my age, married; we had much in common.

I was promptly taken in tow by the Fiji *Times* and escorted around town. They turned me up at the Yacht Club and introduced me to all the local helm talent. My picture was snapped with yachtsmen and members of the Fiji police force. I had a nice story in the paper; and I heard my name on the radio that night. But none of the publicity helped me get back to my wife, a project which was still as great a perplexity as it had been in New York — except that now I didn't have a thousand dollars to buy a boat.

My problem was still to find a ship bound for Australia. Nothing was expected for a month. Plane fare was exorbitant — besides, I was broke.

A British tramp had sailed for New Zealand two days before, bound to Melbourne via Hobart, Tasmania. I approached the Royal New Zealand Air Force, stationed at Suva, with the idea of hitchhiking a lift to Auckland. From there I could pick up the ship. Tough luck, I was told — there was no military traffic.

The American Consul suggested I contact the U.S. Army Air Corps, stationed across the big island of Viti Levu at Nandi. The next day I took passage over the dusty coastal, and partly inland, road aboard a rumbling native bus that rolled and pitched to outdo *Pagan*.

At the air base I gave the colonel in charge a sad account of my recent months. I appealed to his romanticism by bringing my wife into the story. Like all Americans in the face of misfortune, he grew softhearted. The Army can't carry civilians, but, as he put it, "a shipwrecked seaman is different."

At the moment he had nothing going to Australia until the

first of the year. But there was a "kite" in three days for Tontoota, New Caledonia. Plenty of traffic, he said, dropped in from the States and Honolulu to Tontoota; and plenty went back. But nothing much went on west. I might get to Tontoota and find myself stuck there. It might be better to wait at Nandi till January.

I had three days to mull the pros and cons of the prospective flight to Tontoota. In the meantime I continued to search for transport to Australia. I jaunted back across the island by bus to the head offices of the Colonial Sugar Refining Company. Could they put me on one of their sugar boats crossing the Tasman? No soap. All space was chartered by employees voyaging home for Christmas holidays.

I decided to gamble on the plane to Tontoota. There was a possibility I would get stuck there, but my wicked intuition, telling me as ever all would come out right, pressed me to take it. It was known that craft were flying out of there to the Solomons and into New Guinea. Possibly I could follow that track and connect with Australia from one of the northern points. Anything to keep moving in the right direction.

On the morning of the twenty-eighth of November I boarded a medium army bomber. I had just finished breakfast at Nandi, and when I lunched it was my Thanksgiving dinner, in the army mess at Tontoota. After having sat around helplessly for a week at Nandi, I traveled a thousand miles in a few hours.

I reported to the colonel at the field with a letter of introduction from the colonel at Nandi, and told him the sad story of my life on the sea. He listened considerately, but told me there were no flights that could assist me just then. I was billeted and told to stand by.

More days of fretful waiting were to follow. The day after my arrival a special letter came from Mary. She had written it more than a week before, and it had followed me by air mail from Suva and Nandi.

Mary's long months of patient waiting showed up between the lines. She had received my letter of July mail from Post Office Bay in the Galápagos. It had arrived in Sydney the first week in October, explaining my expected arrival before the last of September — in other words, I was always a week overdue when the letters had arrived! And here it was only a very few days from December!

At that time little or no shipping was leaving New Caledonia — nothing whatever bound for Australia. My only avenue of travel lay by air. I searched the flight schedules every day. After four days I was tempted to return to Fiji, and try from there again. The pilots dissuaded me. "Anything can happen," they said. And it did.

A great four-motored transport slithered in from the sky unexpectedly. Aboard was an inspecting officer bound for Sydney via Brisbane. Five days of nerve-worn waiting was over — the next morning at daylight I would start the final lap.

At noon of December third I landed at Brisbane on the same field that nineteen months before I had taken off from to speed south to my wedding. It was impossible to believe that in less than three hours I would be with my wife again. A lot of water had flown beneath the keel since the last time.

Reporters from Brisbane papers took pictures and asked questions about my voyage. I sent a cable to Mary telling her of my arrival time in Sydney.

The giant plane lifted easily and roared over the rugged coastal terrain that was so familiar to me. We swooped on Sydney, crossing her sinuous harbor and beloved bridge, made a wide sweep of the city, and shaped up for the approach to the runway and angled down to it.

I was the most eager passenger aboard.

My gear was first to be unloaded and I was first passenger to alight. And then I saw Mary. I remember her coming toward me — and I believe I moved to meet her. For a second I saw her unfathomable blue eyes. . . . She was in my arms . . . a thousand dreams had come true . . . my trials on the sea were far away.

I can't describe that moment any more than you could. At such a time you live too fast for description in mere words. What mattered then was that I was home from the sea . . . back again with the one person who counts in this world.